THE TRANSFORMATION OF URBAN LIBERALISM

Historical Urban Studies

Series editors: *Jean-Luc Pinol* and *Richard Rodger*

Titles in the series include:

Property, Tenancy and Urban Growth in Stockholm and Berlin, 1860–1920
Håkan Forsell

Civil Society, Associations and Urban Places
Class, Nation and Culture in Nineteenth-Century Europe
edited by Graeme Morton, Boudien de Vries and R.J. Morris

The European City and Green Space
London, Stockholm, Helsinki and St Petersburg, 1850–2000
edited by Peter Clark

Resources of the City
Contributions to an Environmental History of Modern Europe
edited by Dieter Schott, Bill Luckin and Geneviève Massard-Guilbaud

City Status in the British Isles, 1830–2002
John Beckett

European Cities, Youth and the Public Sphere in the Twentieth Century
edited by Axel Schildt and Detlef Siegfried

Culture and Class in English Public Museums, 1850-1914
Kate Hill

The Market and the City
Square, Street and Architecture in Early Modern Europe
Donatella Calabi

Young People and the European City
Age Relations in Nottingham and Saint-Etienne, 1890–1940
David M. Pomfret

Cities of Ideas: Civil Society and Urban Governance in Britain 1800–2000
Essays in Honour of David Reeder
edited by Robert Colls and Richard Rodger

The Transformation of Urban Liberalism

Party Politics and Urban Governance in Late Nineteenth-Century England

JAMES R. MOORE
University of London

LONDON AND NEW YORK

First published 2006 by Ashgate Publishing

Reissued 2018 by Routledge
2 Park Square, Milton Park, Abingdon, Oxon OX14 4RN
605 Third Avenue, New York, NY 10017

First issued in paperback 2021

Routledge is an imprint of the Taylor & Francis Group, an informa business

A Library of Congress record exists under LC control number: 2005031649

ISBN 13: 978-0-815-39829-5 (hbk)
ISBN 13: 978-1-351-12679-3 (ebk)
ISBN 13: 978-1-138-35761-7 (pbk)

DOI: 10.4324/9781351126793

Contents

General Editors' Preface *vii*

Acknowledgements *ix*

List of Abbreviations *xi*

Introduction

The Slow Death of Liberal England? 3

Part I: Reform and the Urban Radical Tradition

1 The Rise of Manchester Radicalism 25

2 Leicester Liberalism: An Uneasy Alliance 53

Part II: The Home Rule Crisis in the Towns

3 Manchester and the Home Rule Crisis 77

4 Leicester: Unionism Marginalised? 99

Part III: Municipal Government Transformed?

5 Municipal Scandals and Realignment 123

6 The 'Politicisation' of the Town Hall 147

Part IV: The Town and the Suburbs

7 Manchester's Suburban Radicalism 169

8 Incorporation – An Agent of Radicalism? 189

Part V: The Challenge of Progressivism

9 Manchester and the Rise of Progressivism 213

10 The Labour Challenge in Leicester 237

Conclusion

The Road to New Liberalism 263

Appendices *281*

Bibliography *301*

Index *317*

Historical Urban Studies General Editors' Preface

Density and proximity are two of the defining characteristics of the urban dimension. It is these that identify a place as uniquely urban, though the threshold for such pressure points varies from place to place. What is considered an important cluster in one context - may not be considered as urban elsewhere. A third defining characteristic is functionality - the commercial or strategic position of a town or city which conveys an advantage over other places. Over time, these functional advantages may diminish, or the balance of advantage may change within a hierarchy of towns. To understand how the relative importance of towns shifts over time and space is to grasp a set of relationships which is fundamental to the study of urban history.

Towns and cities are products of history, yet have themselves helped to shape history. As the proportion of urban dwellers has increased, so the urban dimension has proved a legitimate unit of analysis through which to understand the spectrum of human experience and to explore the cumulative memory of past generations. Though obscured by layers of economic, social and political change, the study of the urban milieu provides insights into the functioning of human relationships and, if urban historians themselves are not directly concerned with current policy studies, few contemporary concerns can be understood without reference to the historical development of towns and cities.

This longer historical perspective is essential to an understanding of social processes. Crime, housing conditions and property values, health and education, discrimination and deviance, and the formulation of regulations and social policies to deal with them were, and remain, amongst the perennial preoccupations of towns and cities - no historical period has a monopoly of these concerns. They recur in successive generations, albeit in varying mixtures and strengths; the details may differ

The central forces of class, power and authority in the city remain. If this was the case for different periods, so it was for different geographical entities and cultures. Both scientific knowledge and technical information were available across Europe and showed little respect for frontiers. Yet despite common concerns and access to broadly similar knowledge, different solutions to urban problems were proposed and adopted by towns and cities in different parts of Europe. This comparative dimension informs urban historians as to which were systematic factors and which were of a purely local nature: general and particular forces can be distinguished.

These analytical and comparative frameworks inform this book. Indeed, thematic, comparative and analytical approaches to the historical study of towns and cities is the hallmark of the Historical Urban Studies series which now extends to over 30 titles, either already published or currently in production. European urban historiography has been extended and enriched as a result and this book makes another important addition to an intellectual mission to which we, as General Editors, remain firmly committed.

Richard Rodger *University of Leicester*
Jean-Luc Pinol *Université de Lyon II*

Acknowledgements

The author would like to give special thanks to his research supervisor Dr. Peter Lowe for his kind assistance and support throughout his very enjoyable doctoral programme in the Department of History at the University of Manchester. He would also like to thank staff and students at Manchester, past and present, who provided advice and encouragement during his time there, especially Dr. Brendan Jones, Dr. Stuart Jones, Samantha McGhie and Dr. James Vernon, as well as his doctoral research examiners Professor Michael Rose and Professor Duncan Tanner. The author is also very grateful for the interest and support of former colleagues in the Centre for Urban History at Leicester University, especially Professor Richard Rodger, Professor Peter Clark and Dr. John Smith. All errors and omission remain the responsibility of the author.

List of Abbreviations

Personal Titles, Organisations and Collections

Ald.	*Alderman*
BLPES	*British Library of Political and Economic Science*
CPSC	*C.P. Scott Correspondence*
HLA	*Harborough Liberal Association Minutes*
ICLB	*Improvement Committee Letter Book*
ILP	*Independent Labour Party*
ILPC	*Independent Labour Party Collection*
JRULM	*John Rylands University Library of Manchester*
LA	*Liberal Association*
LCC	*London County Council*
LLA	*Leicester Liberal Association Minutes*
LTC	*Leicester Town Council Proceedings*
LTCLB	*Leicester Town Clerks' Letter Books*
LU	*Liberal Unionist*
LRO	*Leicestershire Record Office*
MCC	*Manchester City Council Proceedings*
MCL	*Manchester Central Library*
MLA	*Manchester Liberal Association Minutes*
MLU	*Manchester Liberal Union Minutes*
MMUL	*Manchester Metropolitan University Library*
NAC	*National Administrative Council*
NLC	*National Liberal Club Collection*
NLF	*National Liberal Federation*
NRU	*National Reform Union Pamphlet Collection*
NUBSO	*National Union of Boot and Shoe Operatives*
SDF	*Social Democratic Federation*
UDC	*Urban District Council*

Publications

GR	*Gorton Reporter*
HN	*Hinckley News*
LA	*Leicester Advertiser*
LC	*Leicester Chronicle*
LDE	*Leicester Daily Express*

LDM	*Leicester Daily Mercury*
LDP	*Leicester Daily Post*
LJ	*Leicester Journal*
LL	*Labour Leader*
MC	*Manchester Courier*
MCN	*Manchester City News*
ME	*Manchester Examiner*
MEN	*Manchester Evening News*
MFP	*Midland Free Press*
MG	*Manchester Guardian*
WT	*Workman's Times*

INTRODUCTION

INTRODUCTION

The Slow Death of Liberal England?

Few historical subjects attract more interest than the collapse of great political dynasties. Ancient historians have the fall of Rome, early modernists the end of the *ancien regime* and modern British historians the collapse of the Liberal Party. This fascination with the breakdown of established political orders is not difficult to explain. In the case of the Liberal Party, its fortunes seem to have almost mirrored the fate of Britain itself. The party's emergence as the dominant political force of the nineteenth century coincided with Britain's development as the world's leading industrial nation and imperial power. Its demise coincided with Britain's political and economic decline on the world stage. More fundamentally, however, the party's fortunes seemed to reflect broader social changes. Liberalism's doctrines of free trade, religious equality and political meritocracy were widely regarded as being the values of the new urban industrial middle class, expressing their desire for greater political power to reflect their growing economic status.[1] It was a movement that seemed to symbolise the urban modernisation of Britain itself. William Gladstone, Liberalism's 'high priest', came to personify the transition of Britain to mass representative democracy. His metamorphosis from 'the rising hope of those stern unbending Tories' to 'the People's William' symbolised the movement away from a Britain governed largely by a land-owning aristocracy to one governed by political parties via the secret ballot.[2] Liberalism's rise paralleled the national transition from rural semi-feudalism to urban modernity.[3] The Liberal Party was comfortably the most successful electoral force of the second half of the nineteenth century, with Gladstone alone leading four ministries of sixteen years' total duration. Yet the party's rapid decline to the status of a minor third party took little over a decade. Just five years after the party's greatest electoral success in 1906 the Liberals tasted a general election victory for the last time.

---

[1] In reality, of course, political alignments in the industrial middle class were much more complex. See H. Perkin, *The Origins of Modern English Society 1780–1880*, reprint (London, 1971), 375–80; G. Crossick (ed.), *The Lower Middle Class in Britain* (London, 1977); J. Parry, *The Rise and Fall of Liberal Government in Victorian Britain* (Yale, 1993).

[2] H.C.G. Matthew, *Gladstone 1809–1874*, paperback edition (Oxford, 1986), 1–2; S. Peaple and J. Vincent, 'Gladstone and the Working Man', in P.J. Jagger (ed.) *Gladstone* (London, 1998), 71–83.

[3] This approach can, of course, neglect the role that Conservatives played in this process of 'modernisation', particularly in the extension of the franchise and the ways they integrated working people in to their organisation. For an analysis of popular Conservatism see M. Pugh, *The Tories and the People* (Oxford, 1985).

Liberalism is a movement with a long and complex history. The party's origins can be traced back to the parliamentary and municipal reform movements of the 1830s.[4] It was during this decade that many of the key components of Liberalism emerged – including a commitment to 'open' politics and toleration of diversity in religious creeds.[5] Gladstone, who built his early career around opposition to parliamentary reform and support for 'National Religion' in the 1830s, only gradually moved from the position of moderate Peelite to that of the 'People's William'.[6] Gladstone's position in Palmerston's cabinet allowed him to develop a reputation for more progressive Liberalism – as the defender of financial prudence, Peelite free trade and peace abroad.[7] This reputation was enhanced by machinations over the 1866 Reform Bill, when Gladstone's support for franchise extension helped manoeuvre him to the premiership.[8] Little over a decade later Gladstone's Midlothian campaign was again credited with transforming the political landscape, returning him to office – and revolutionising popular political campaigning.[9] Then, in 1886, his conversion to Irish Home Rule once again redefined the mission of the Liberal Party, although on this occasion the benefits that this brought to the party were more questionable. The party split and seemingly lost significant elements of its traditional support. Thus the rise and fall of the Liberal Party's fortunes in the late Victorian period seem closely associated with one man. Such was Gladstone's impact on the party he led that he rapidly became the universal icon of British Liberalism.[10] The importance of Gladstone in understanding the ebb and flow of Liberal fortunes has naturally inspired major studies of 'high politics' and the leadership problems the party faced after the enforced retirement of the 'Grand Old Man'.[11] Yet there is a widely shared belief that these types of studies can only give a partial explanation for the rise and

---

4 The Liberal Party is often regarded as dating from the famous Willis's rooms meeting in June 1859 – although the modern party celebrated its 'centenary' as late as 1977 (the anniversary of the formation of the National Liberal Federation). However, the term Liberal was in use by the 1830s and the movement's chief ideological strands can be traced from this period.

5 Parry, *The Rise*, 4.

6 For a recent assessment of the Palmerston period and Gladstone's role in it see T.A. Jenkins, *The Liberal Ascendancy 1830–1886* (London, 1994) 90–106; E.D. Steele, *Palmerston and Liberalism, 1855–1865* (Cambridge, 1991).

7 E.J. Feuchtwanger, *Gladstone*, second edition (London, 1989) xv.

8 Matthew, *Gladstone*, 142.

9 Feuchtwanger, *Gladstone*, 185–92.

10 Quite apart from all the mugs, portraits and busts produced as a tribute to the 'Grand Old Man', Gladstone was extensively used in popular advertising, and even had a brand of cigars named in his honour. E.F. Biagini, *Liberty, Retrenchment and Reform, Popular Liberalism in the Age of Gladstone 1860–1880* (Cambridge, 1991), 405.

11 This important scholastic tradition is remarkably long, for example: J. Morley, *Life of Gladstone* (London, 1901); W.E. Williams, *The Rise of Gladstone to the Leadership of the Liberal Party 1859–1868* (Cambridge, 1934); J.L. Hammond, *Gladstone and the Irish Nation* (London, 1938); P. Magnus, *Gladstone* (London, 1954); D. Southgate, *The Passing of the Whigs 1832–1886* (London, 1962); P. Stansky, *Ambitions and Strategies: The Struggle for the Leadership of the Liberal Party in the 1890s* (Oxford, 1964).

fall of major political movements. Westminster politics cannot be taken as a general proxy of public attitudes. Indeed, in some respects the culture of St. Stephen's served to somewhat isolate members from wider public opinion.[12] Increasingly the search for the 'real' causes of decline has switched to the study of wider social and cultural trends.

The sudden demise of the Liberal Party encouraged generations of historians to investigate this rare political phenomenon – the death of an apparently indestructible political force. George Dangerfield's pioneering polemical work of the 1930s, *The Strange Death of Liberal England*, although now heavily criticised, has been so influential that its language has entered the everyday political vocabulary.[13] Dangerfield regarded the collapse of the Liberal Party as a reflection of the wider collapse of Liberal political culture. Agitation by labour unions, suffragettes, and the terrors of the Great War were regarded as highlighting the weaknesses of traditional Liberalism and the difficulties it faced in governing a modern democratic industrial society. Modern historians are generally sceptical about linking these multi-causal events and regarding them as part of a broader phenomenon. Moreover it is unclear why the Liberal Party should find it harder to respond to the challenges of democratisation than the Conservatives, or indeed the Labour Party who, until 1918, owed much of their political thought to the Liberal Party. Its significance, however, lay in the debate that it helped foster.

Interest in the Liberal Party's decline was heightened, rather than diminished, by the rise of social history in the post-war period. Marxist historians became extraordinarily influential in debates about the rise of class and class-consciousness in the nineteenth century and many began to see the decline of the Liberal Party as a by-product of the increasing division of society between worker and capitalist. Yet by making narratives on the 'rise of class' a central component of our understanding of nineteenth-century history, the detailed complexity of social and political relationships could sometimes be neglected. Moreover the failure of the working class in the first industrial nation to form an effective independent political movement was potentially very embarrassing for Marxist historiography. As time passed it became increasingly important for Marxists to find examples of successful independent working-class action destroying the existing political infrastructure. The decline of the Liberal Party seemed to offer these historians a powerful example of the eclipse of the middle class. Once E.P. Thompson's legendary study of early industrial society had placed the formation of the working class in the period 1780–1832, there was a desperate need for Marxists to explain the failure of working-class political movements during the rest of the century.[14] Various strategies were adopted. Some, including Thompson, argued that Britain had actually come close

[12] W.C. Lubenow, *Parliamentary Politics and the Home Rule Question* (Oxford, 1988), 327–8, 332.

[13] G. Dangerfield, *The Strange Death of Liberal England* (London, 1935).

[14] E.P. Thompson, *The Making of the English Working Class*, revised 1980 edition reprinted (London, 1991), see esp. 8–12, 213–18.

to a working-class revolution.[15] Others looked to explain the failure in terms of Britain's mid-century economic success or the formation of a 'labour aristocracy' who lost a sense of their 'true' class interests.[16] These debates produced, and still produce, valuable scholarship on nineteenth-century politics and society. Increasingly explanations have moved away from a focus on economic factors to political and cultural developments – including the role of elites in limiting the opportunities for reform.[17] Vernon, highly critical of much Marxist historiography, has demonstrated how constitutional and cultural constraints led to a reduction in the opportunities for popular political participation from the mid-nineteenth century.[18] Hewitt's case study of Manchester, while demonstrating the continuities of working-class consciousness, highlighted the ways in which restrictions on the press and the decline of the public meeting helped limit working-class politicisation.[19] The 'rise of Labour' narrative was attractive, however, because it was ultimately a story of triumph – the triumph of the working class over middle-class attempts to deny them political citizenship.[20]

The decline of the Liberal Party has become an important part of this narrative, with the Home Rule crisis being seen, famously, as 'the geological shift in the structure of British politics'.[21] The crisis was regarded as a key watershed in the rise of class-based politics. Long before the Home Rule controversy, it was argued, the Nonconformist middle classes that were the backbone of Liberal support were moving away from the party. As Liberals began to accede to working-class demands, corporate business began to drift towards the Conservatives and the Nonconformist middle class gradually moved towards the Church of England. As an increasingly self-confident middle class aspired to be seen as the equal of the aristocracy, the barriers between the two classes gradually came down, reinforcing the bifurcation of society between capitalist and worker.[22] This placed the Liberal Party, with its

15 Thompson, *The Making*, 898–9.

16 For a brief discussion of these issues see D. Cannadine, *Class in Britain* (London, 1998), 1–6.

17 N. Kirk, *The Growth of Working Class Reformism in Mid-Victorian Britain* (London, 1985), see especially 349–52; P. Joyce, *Work, Society and Politics: The Culture of the Factory in Later Victorian Britain* (Brighton, 1980); J. Forster, *Class Struggle and the Industrial Revolution: Early Industrial Capitalism in three English Towns* (London, 1974).

18 J. Vernon, *Politics and the People: a study in English Political Culture, c.1815–1867* (Cambridge, 1993).

19 M. Hewitt, *The Emergence of Stability in the Industrial City: Manchester 1832–1867* (Aldershot, 1996), see esp. 193–229 and 262–93.

20 For a short summary of the debate on 'class politics' and the Liberal Party see G. Searle, *The Liberal Party, Triumph and Disintegration 1886–1929* (London, 1992), esp. 55–9. For an important defence of class-based interpretations of the period see N. Kirk, 'In Defence of Class: A critique of recent revisionist writings upon the nineteenth-century English working class', *International Review of Social History*, 32 (1987), 2–47.

21 Perkin, *The Origins*, 434.

22 Perkin, *The Origins*, 431–5.

professed aversion to 'class politics', in an anomalous position. Indeed some have implied that with a wider franchise its decline would have been even more rapid.[23]

The Home Rule crisis became widely regarded as a watershed in both the development of class politics and as the beginning of the end for the Liberal Party. Even sympathetic biographers of Gladstone came to regard the defection of Hartington's Whigs as a key stage in the development of class-based political parties, with the 1892 general election as the first to be fought 'to a great extent upon class'.[24] Yet in recent years many social historians have begun to move away from seeing class as the primary category of social analysis, as the empirical and theoretical basis of earlier work has been re-examined.[25] Even those who still regard class as an important category of analysis have conceded that class is a complex phenomenon that may bind together relatively diverse cultural groupings.[26] Moreover the experience of class consciousness and collective injustice can, of course, be mitigated by strategies of governance that seek to include rather than alienate.[27] Other work has demonstrated that old narratives that emphasise the bifurcation of society into two classes – workers and capitalists – can conceal continuing important differences between the professional–commercial interests and the aristocracy. Although the 1832 Reform Act is often depicted as the emergence of the middle class, few members of the middle class actually gained prominent positions in national government until the latter part of the nineteenth century. Indeed barriers to middle-class political success at national level continued to be much greater than for their aristocratic counterparts.[28] Historical geography has also played a part in questioning class formation by undermining notions that urban industrial communities were becoming increasingly segregated on class lines. On forensic examination, the new suburban communities of the mid-nineteenth century were not seen generally to reflect homogenous social groups – and there was surprisingly little

---

23 H. Matthew, R. McKibbin and J.A. Kay, 'The Franchise Factor and the Rise of Labour Party', *English Historical Review*, 91 (1976), 723–52. Some, however, have pointed to Labour's success in the 1919 municipal elections, on a more limited franchise, as an indication that there was not a straightforward causal relationship between the extension of the franchise and the growth of the Labour Party. See D. Tanner, 'Elections, Statistics and the Rise of the Labour Party, 1906–1931', *Historical Journal*, 34 (1991), 906.

24 Magnus, *Gladstone*, 394.

25 For brief discussion see Cannadine, *Class*, 8–12; J. Lawrence, 'Popular Radicalism and the Socialist Revival in Britain', *Journal of British Studies*, 31 (1992), 163–86.

26 J. Thompson, 'After the Fall: Class and Political Language in Britain, 1780–1900', *Historical Journal*, 39 (1996), 785–806; M. Steinburg, '"A Way of Struggle": Reformations and affirmations of E.P. Thompson's class analysis in the light of postmodern theories of language', *British Journal of Sociology*, 48 (1997), 471–92.

27 R. McKibbin, 'Why was there no Marxism in Great Britain?', *English Historical Review*, 99 (1984), 297–331.

28 For example see J. Garrard, 'The Middle Classes and Nineteenth Century National and Local Politics', in J. Garrard, D. Jary, M. Goldsmith and A. Oldfield (eds), *The Middle Class in Politics* (Farnborough, 1978), 36–66.

evidence of social segregation increasing across time.[29] Moreover where a degree of social segregation was observed, empirical research tended to locate it as much in ethnic and religious cleavages as those purely of class.[30]

Some, of course, have argued that the apparent obsession with class has resulted in a neglect of other social identities. The rise of feminist writing and the so-called 'linguistic turn' have brought into question the primacy of class as an explanatory tool and consequently revolutionised much social history.[31] Stedman-Jones's writings on the languages of class in the mid-Victorian period have helped stimulate a greater awareness of how language shapes social identities and the subjectivities of class identity.[32] Joyce's work, in particular, seems to suggest the need to develop a much more multi-faceted view of urban popular culture if we are really to understand the way in which nineteenth-century workers viewed their political universe.[33] Similarly, recent work on the relationship between class and Radical politics has illustrated both the extent of working-class engagement in cross-class movements and the role of ethical populism as an alternative form of political mobilisation.[34] Marxian interpretations of class formation and consciousness, which for so long had such a powerful influence on Liberal historiography, no longer seem quite so convincing.

These changes in the intellectual climate have impacted on the way the changing fortunes of the Liberal Party have been viewed. The structural and class-based views of Liberal decline, so popular in the 1960s and 1970s, have faced critical examination. Although it is easy to see how class politics *could* threaten a party that relied largely on cross-class appeals and declining religious Nonconformity, empirical research is far from conclusive. Firstly, forensic scrutiny of the Liberal Home Rule split at Westminster seems to uncover only a very weak correlation between high social

---

29 R. Dennis, *English Industrial Cities in the Nineteenth Century – A Social Geography*, reprint (Cambridge 1986), 238–49.

30 C. Pooley and R. Lawton, 'The Social Geography of nineteenth century British cities: a review', in D. Denecke and G. Shaw (eds), *Urban Historical Geography – Recent Progress in Britain and Germany*, (Cambridge, 1988).

31 Cannadine, *Class*, 11–17. Important contributions to the debate about postmodernism and social history include D. Mayfield and S. Thorne, 'Social History and its Discontents: Gareth Stedman Jones and the Politics of Language', *Social History*, 17 (1992), 165–88; J. Vernon, 'Who's afraid of the linguistic turn? The politics of social history and its discontents', *Social History*, 19 (1994), 81–97; P. Joyce, 'The Return of History: Postmodernism and the Politics of Academic History in Britain', *Past and Present*, 158 (1998), 207–35.

32 G. Stedman Jones, *Languages of Class* (Cambridge, 1983).

33 P. Joyce, *Visions of the People, Industrial England and the Question of Class, 1848–1914* (Cambridge, 1991); P. Joyce, *Democratic Subjects: the self and the social in nineteenth-century England* (Cambridge, 1994).

34 E. Biagini and A. Reid (eds), *Currents of Radicalism: popular radicalism, organised labour and party politics in Britain, 1850–1914* (Cambridge, 1991); E. Biagini (ed.), *Citizenship and Community:Liberals, Radicals and collective identities in the British Isles, 1865–1931* (Cambridge, 1996); Biagini, *Liberty*; J. Lawrence, *Speaking for the People: party, language, and popular politics in England, 1867–1914* (Cambridge, 1998); M. Winstanley, 'Oldham Radicalism and the Origins of Popular Liberalism, 1830–1852', *Historical Journal*, 36 (1993), 619–43.

status and rejection of the Gladstonian leadership, finally demolishing the idea that the party divided primarily on class lines.[35] Secondly, supposedly declining traditional loyalties continued to be important in many areas well into the 1930s. Doyle's work on Norwich, for example, illustrates how the Edwardian middle classes continued to cling on to their Liberal and Nonconformist allegiances well into the 1930s.[36] Indeed they continue to be a significant political force in parts of Western England, Wales and Scotland over a century after Gladstone's death. Thirdly, the Liberal Party went into sharp decline after it had begun to develop into a modern social democratic party. Moreover, the Labour Party rarely offered more radical solutions to working-class grievances than the party it 'replaced'. It was Lloyd George's People's Budget of 1909 which heralded the beginnings of a welfare state, while much of the new political thinking of the period came from figures within the Liberal Party, such as Hobhouse, Hobson and Masterman. The first Labour government, in contrast, was considerably less radical than the pre-war Liberal government, presenting little in the way of socialist programme. During the depression of the 1920s it was the Liberal Party, not Labour, who sponsored the most radical solution to mass unemployment – Keynes's inspired 'Liberal Yellow Book' on *Britain's Industrial Future*.[37] Even when the Labour Party did introduce a radical programme in 1945, much of its inspiration came from the work of a Liberal – William Beveridge.[38] Thus those who are sceptical about the structuralist approach tend to look to how the party was a victim of historical accidents – particularly the party's internal divisions and the political upheaval of the First World War. This debate has naturally led to much interest in the Edwardian period with attempts to assess just how much the party was in decline and how the social democratic 'New Liberalism' had transformed Liberalism as a political movement.[39]

Yet more recently historians have again begun to look back to the 1880s as the 'real' source of the Liberal collapse. Although there is now a greater reluctance to blame simply the rise of class tensions for the split, the period is still widely regarded as a key stage in Liberal decline. Here there does seem to be a role for traditional so-called 'high history', as it is difficult to escape the conclusion that personal conflicts amongst Liberal leaders played a significant role in the Home Rule crisis.[40] Thus for some the Home Rule split was all the more tragic because it was an 'accident' that

---

35 Lubenow, *Parliamentary Politics*, 335–6.

36 B. Doyle, 'Urban Liberalism and the "Lost Generation": Politics and Middle Class Culture in Norwich 1900–1935', *Historical Journal*, 38 (1995), 617–34.

37 R. Skidelsky, *Politicians and the Slump* (London, 1967), 51–6.

38 For an assessment of the impact of Beveridge's ideas see J. Harris, *William Beveridge – A Biography*, revised edition (Oxford, 1997) especially 466–9, 495–6.

39 See, for example, H.V. Emy, *Liberals, Radicals and Social Politics*, 1892–1914 (Cambridge, 1973); M. Freeden, *The New Liberalism: An Ideology of Social Reform* (Oxford, 1978); M. Freeden, *Liberalism Divided: A Study in British Political Thought* (Oxford, 1986); J.R. Hay, *The Origins of the Liberal Welfare Reforms* (London, 1975); A.J.A. Morris (ed.), *Edwardian Radicalism 1900–1914* (London 1974).

40 Magnus, *Gladstone*, 343–66.

possibly could have been avoided. Hartington, the party's leader in the Commons between 1875–80, was by no means keen to leave the Liberal Party and was the only serious contender as Gladstone's permanent successor. Gladstone's refusal to compromise drove Hartington out of the party, depriving the Liberal movement of one of its most widely respected figures.[41] Similarly had Gladstone treated Joseph Chamberlain more sympathetically, then Chamberlain too may have stayed within the party. Even after the split the Round Table Conference on Liberal Reunion offered the possibility of reconciliation – yet personal differences and ambitions marred any hopes of progress.[42] Consequently the party's most well-known Radical politician, Chamberlain, and Gladstone's heir apparent, Hartington, were forever lost to the party. Many contemporaries confidently predicted that the crisis would mark the destruction of the Liberal Party. It is a view that continues to be influential. Parry, one of today's most influential historians of the Liberal Party, has seen the crisis as marking the 'fall' of Liberal government in the Victorian period.[43] Yet six years later after the apparently cataclysmic division Gladstone returned to office for a fourth time, albeit in alliance with the Irish Nationalists. After Gladstone's resignation in 1894 the party again entered troubled waters with heavy general election defeats in 1895 and 1900 – but in 1906 the party was back in power, this time with its largest ever majority. The Liberal Party's ability to bounce back from major crises makes its rapid decline after 1918 even more perplexing. Moreover for those who see the 1886 general election as marking the fall of Liberalism, its revivals in 1892 and 1906 are not easy to explain. Indeed the decade following 1886 seems to illustrate the ability of the party to renew itself in the face of crises.

There is little doubt that the Liberal Party underwent significant change in the 1880s and 1890s, not least in its intellectual outlook. Gladstone has been frequently seen as coming to dominate – even personify – the party to such an extent that he is often charged with turning it into a single-issue pressure group for Irish Home Rule. This was also a period, however, in which the national party organisation became more influential in decisions taken at Westminster. Even Gladstone was not immune to this trend, being forced to accept the National Liberal Federation's Radical Newcastle Programme of 1891 as 'official' party policy.[44] This move acknowledged the key role party associations were beginning to play in giving popular legitimacy to policy-making and the selection of candidates. This trend had great significance

41 Indeed there is even the suggestion that Gladstone deliberately drove Hartington out of the party in response to Hartington's attempt to assume the Liberal leadership in January 1885. Gladstone's sudden recovery from ill health and the Soudan crisis precluded the move and, arguably, left Gladstone determined to bring the party back under his control. See A.B. Cooke and J. Vincent, *The Governing Passion: Cabinet Government and Party Politics in Britain 1885–1886* (Brighton, 1974), 27–34, 55–7.

42 M. Hurst, *Joseph Chamberlain and Liberal Reunion* (London, 1967). See especially 351–66.

43 Parry, *The Rise*, 20.

44 For details of the Newcastle Programme see 'Fourteenth Annual Meeting of the National Liberal Federation', in *Pamphlets and Leaflets 1888–1892*, Bristol University Library, NLC, JN 1129.L4.P2; Emy, *Liberals*, 38–44.

for the future political direction of the party. The growth of party organisations at national level was part of a wider process by which 'representative' political associations were taking a more central role in local political life. With the extension of the franchise and the redrawing of parliamentary constituencies in the mid-1880s, many new Liberal Associations were established around the country, while many larger city associations were divided into smaller constituency associations. This had the tendency to undermine the role of elite political clubs in the local political process, with decision-making devolved to grass-roots organisations, often with a more Radical leadership. The formalisation of party machinery combined with more localised representative organisations naturally made it more difficult for local Liberal oligarchies to maintain exclusive control.

The growth and development of local party organisations naturally had significant implications for the development of Liberal policy and the party's electoral revival. The health of local Liberalism is clearly a crucial factor in contextualising debates on Liberal decline. It certainly cannot be assumed that local and regional politics followed the political trends of Westminster. Yet surprisingly local politics have attracted few historians, especially in the period 1886–1900. Clarke's *Lancashire and the New Liberalism* stands out as the classic study of local Liberal revival – the emergence of New Liberalism in the former Conservative heartland of Lancashire.[45] Other works have focused on the limitations of the Liberal revival. Bernstein's study of Norwich, Leicester and Leeds demonstrates the difficulties the Liberal Party had in trying to retain Labour within the Liberal Progressive coalition.[46] Thompson's work on London has also been influential, although Liberal and Labour politics in London are generally regarded as being highly atypical of urban Britain as a whole.[47] Indeed the capital is often considered to be the place in which many Radical and labour movements of the nineteenth century foundered. Therefore if one is to study local politics and make meaningful statements about how subsequent conclusions may be applied more generally, one needs to find areas that can be regarded as 'typical'. Here lies the main difficulty. Liberalism in Britain was an astonishingly diverse political force with very wide geographical appeal. The Liberal Party was the party of the Cornish tin miners, the Highland crofters and, at its height, was practically the national party of Wales.[48] Yet the English urban boroughs can provide the most fruitful area of research for local studies for a number of reasons. Despite the breadth and diversity of Liberal support it is not too fanciful to suggest that the Liberal Party was primarily an urban party. At the party's two most successful general elections

45 P.F. Clarke, *Lancashire and the New Liberalism* (Cambridge, 1971).

46 G. Bernstein, 'Liberalism and the Progressive Alliance in the Constituencies 1900–1914: Three Case studies', *Historical Journal*, 26 (1983) 617–40.

47 P. Thompson, *Socialists, Liberals and Labour – The Struggle For London, 1885–1914* (London, 1967). In contrast to Clarke, Thompson identifies a sharp decline in the fortunes of the party after 1892, and considers the lack of a viable electoral standpoint, working-class electoral base and financial backing as major reasons for this pattern. These are all viewed as the product of a rise in class-based voting patterns.

48 In 1885 Liberal candidates won all but four Welsh parliamentary seats.

of the late nineteenth century, 1868 and 1880, Liberals took twice as many urban borough and university seats than the Conservatives, while Conservatives took twice as many county seats than the Liberals.[49] Thus English urban boroughs represented the backbone of Liberal general election victories and were the constituencies which, in general, were among the first to go when the general electoral decline of the party set in after 1918. In contrast the constituencies of the 'Celtic fringe' were numerically less important and Liberal support in these areas declined much more slowly. Indeed the 'Celtic fringe' remained remarkably loyal to the Liberal cause and to a large degree still does. The study of urban constituencies is also often a more practical proposition than the study of their rural counterparts. In rural areas without long established archive services detailed local party records and minutes rarely exist – and many rural areas lacked formal constituency Liberal associations even after 1885. Few rural areas had a substantial local press reporting political activities in any detail and, before the advent of district councils, few local government elections were conducted on partisan lines. Moreover, innovation in local government policy usually came in those authorities with the power and resources to turn vision into practical results – such as in the Birmingham City Council of the 1870s and the London County Council after 1889. Research into the Liberal politics of English urban boroughs is, therefore, not only an intellectual priority, but is also an attractive and potentially very fruitful exercise.

Clarke's work on New Liberalism has highlighted the importance of the party's emerging social democratic ideology for attracting the support of working men.[50] It is clear that New Liberalism, although not carried into practical effect until the advent of the 1906 Liberal government, was actually a product of the last two decades of the nineteenth century. Joseph Chamberlain's housing policy in Birmingham, Rosebery's Progressivism at the LCC and C.P. Scott's Radicalism in Manchester clearly had great significance in pointing the way to a new agenda in Liberal politics. By the time of Gladstone's fourth ministry the Local Government Board were already calling for local authorities to initiate collectivist public works programmes to combat seasonal unemployment, while Asquith called upon local Liberal leaders to construct local municipal programmes to address labour grievances.[51] Despite these national directives, municipalities were responsible for initiating policy and therefore the changing attitudes of Liberal municipal elites towards the New Liberal agenda is particularly important. Few urban municipalities had a reputation for Radicalism before the 1880s – indeed some had a reputation for corruption and mismanagement.[52] Yet by the mid-1890s the situation appears to have changed with

---

[49] Although the figures are slightly misleading as by this time many county constituencies had adopted some urban characteristics and some included towns of significant size. *Constitutional Year Book* (London, 1886), 294.

[50] Clarke, *Lancashire and the New Liberalism.*

[51] As early as 1886 the Local Government Board, under Joseph Chamberlain, had issued a circular encouraging sanitary authorities to employ the seasonally unemployed on public works programmes. See Emy, *Liberals*, 312.

[52] See the accounts in the *City Ledger*, February 1888.

several towns adopting Progressive municipal programmes. For a party that had for so long been characterised as being hostile to government intervention and increased taxation, the collectivist nature of Liberal local government at the turn of the century was remarkable.

The growth in the collectivist nature of local government was not, of course, monocausal, but rather the product of legislators attempting to address the many problems and challenges of urban social organisation. The collectivisation of gas and water services was rarely, if ever, done for purely ideological reasons, but rather in response to the 'practical' needs of public health and to generate profits that could subsidise the rates.[53] By adopting the position of monopoly capitalists in the key service industries, local authorities could meet the demands of the electorate for increased public service without the need for politically sensitive rate increases. As cities grew and industry multiplied, so did the demands for gas and water, thus creating substantial municipal trading empires. These empires, which began in the mid-nineteenth century as small-scale enterprises, required increasing investment. Commercial municipal projects developed hand-in-hand with municipal pride. Great infrastructure projects, such as the piping of water from the Lake District to Manchester took on great symbolic significance for the cities that sponsored them. Notions of municipal pride and prestige encouraged local government into new areas of economic interventionism. When the private companies associated with the pioneering Manchester Ship Canal encountered difficulties, city pride dictated the Manchester City Council should rescue the scheme. This municipal interventionism made it difficult for moderate and classical Liberals to resist moves towards the establishment of Progressive programmes. Socialists were later to use the precedents established by municipal trading to advocate the further expansion of municipal activity for the provision of municipal workshops, retail outlets, factories and lodging houses.[54]

The period 1886 to 1895 saw an unprecedented growth in socialist politics. Assisted by the expansion of new trades unions in the formerly largely unorganised unskilled trades, groups of the Socialist League and the Social Democratic Federation sprang up in many English urban communities. By the mid-1890s the Independent Labour Party seemed to many to represent a fundamental challenge to urban Liberalism, threatening to deprive the party of a substantial part of its working-class support. The response of the Liberal Party to the ILP's development was important both for the development of New Liberal ideology and for the party's ability to hold on to both middle- and working-class support. The loss of middle-class London suburbia to the Conservatives has been suggested as an important trend in the growth of class politics and in the fragmentation of Liberalism on class lines.[55] However

---

53 This is not to deny that municipal collectivism reflected important attitudes towards the role of the local state. See P.J. Waller, *Town, City and Nation: England 1850–1914* (Oxford, 1983), 298–316.

54 H. Russell Smart, *Municipal Socialism* (Manchester, 1895).

55 Thompson, *Socialists*, 295–6.

it is altogether unclear that the Metropolitan area, with its very substantial areas of middle-class suburbia, was typical of other British cities. Although the growth of suburbia was a phenomenon experienced by most industrial towns, it is unclear whether the new suburbs were predominantly middle class. Moreover it is also unclear whether residents of such areas were voting overwhelmingly in defence of narrow class interests. Ethnic, cultural and denominational loyalties continued to be of importance to many citizens – particularly at times when issues that stirred the 'Nonconformist conscience' appeared on the political agenda, such as Home Rule and religious education.[56]

Local political culture and local controversies could modify, and sometimes undermine, class-consciousness.[57] While the growth of the political press gave electors increasing access to the views and speeches of the great political personalities of the era, much of urban politics revolved around local issues. Even when national and international issues emerged which had particular resonance to local communities – such as Home Rule to the Irish community – local leaders often shaped the way in which issues were discussed and decisions made. Although the visits of national political leaders brought out massive crowds at public demonstrations, the everyday experience of politics was through the medium of the political clubs, trade unions and debating societies which dominated the public culture of Victorian urban society. Local organisations proved to be key tools, not only in social integration, but also in giving meaning to the lives of many middle-class citizens, giving them an involvement and a sense of self-worth in the increasingly corporatist urban community. Crucially, too, they provided a means by which working men could participate in politics and a social hierarchy through which they could climb. Local ward and community Liberal organisations were sufficiently small and their functions sufficiently wide for men from a relatively humble background to develop significant local influence. With elections organised like military campaigns, there was always the possibility that men could 'rise through the ranks' from local canvasser to street captain or area superintendent. Municipal elections every November allowed for the regular renewal of party conflict, with all the excitement and colour of a theatrical melodrama and the tension of a sporting event. However, unlike a performance at the 'Palace of Varieties' or a local cup-tie, the audience at the political show were participants whose activities could directly determine the outcome. Indeed careers could depend on the results. The politically active were, of course, a minority – but they were a minority who sustained the life of local political parties and shaped

[56] Those who stress the decline of Nonconformist influence after 1880, however, suggest that its influence could only be maintained in smaller towns and more isolated communities. See H. Pelling, *Social Geography of British Elections, 1885–1910* (London, 1967), 430–33.

[57] Works such as D. Howell's *British Workers and the Independent Labour Party* (Manchester, 1983); D. Tanner's *Political Change and the Labour Party, 1900–1918* (Cambridge, 1990) and J. Lawrence's *Speaking for the People* illustrate the importance of regional and local factors on the development of class identity and the Labour movement.

the popular interpretation of political events. For many, participation in a political association was not merely a hobby but a way of life.[58]

Manchester and Leicester offer an exciting opportunity to study the vitality of local Liberalism and emergence of new Liberalism in the final decades of the nineteenth century. Both communities had strong and distinctive Liberal political traditions. Manchester came to personify the Free Trade Movement of the mid-century and gave its name to the 'Manchester School' of economic and social theorists. Indeed in many respects Manchester led the anti-corn law agitation with the Manchester Anti-Corn Law Association becoming the model for the national organisation.[59] Just as the Anti-Corn Law movement came to exemplify the success of an emerging industrial middle class over a landed aristocracy, Manchester became a symbol of middle-class triumph and of the success of the 'self-made man.' Yet in reality relatively few of the city's most successful cotton barons came from working-class backgrounds. Many already had commercial interests in the proto-industrial mercantile economy of the eighteenth century and a number were from landed families from the surrounding counties.[60] Nor were the industrialists of the early nineteenth century exclusively Liberal and Nonconformist, with groups like the John Shaw's Club testimony to a continuing 'Church and King' tradition.[61]

The Manchester Liberal movement was never an exclusively middle-class tradition. Earlier in the century Manchester had become synonymous with the movement for parliamentary reform, with the Peterloo massacre forever providing the city with a place in Radical propaganda and iconography. This movement for parliamentary reform did not die with the enfranchisement of the urban middle class in 1832, but rather, in the form of Chartism, contributed to a national movement for democratic reform. Chartism, although a failure, became a proud component of the Manchester Liberal tradition. Fifty years later Chartist veterans still talked proudly of their movement and mere mention of a Chartist background would ensure any speaker of an audience at any Liberal meeting. Thus both of the major popular movements of the early nineteenth century could claim Manchester as their intellectual home. Such was the intellectual influence of Manchester on British politics that the term 'what Manchester thinks today, London thinks tomorrow' soon became part of the universal vocabulary. Much of Manchester's political influence was no doubt linked to its economic prosperity brought about primarily by cotton and associated industries. Many regarded the cotton industry as the single most important component of the British economy and vital to international trade and prosperity. The Cotton Famine of the 1860s demonstrated that this was something of a myth, but the Manchester region's prosperity continued to grow.[62] By the end of the century Manchester was no longer simply 'Cottonopolis,' but had a very

58 See the example of William Roche of Manchester, *Pioneer*, 21 July 1886.

59 A. Kidd, *Manchester*, second edition (Keele, 1996), 69–70.

60 J. Walton, *Lancashire: A Social History 1558–1939*, reprint (Manchester, 1994) 129.

61 F.S. Stancliffe, *John Shaw's 1738–1938* (Manchester, 1938).

62 Kidd, *Manchester*, 105.

diverse economic base and had become a major distribution and financial centre. Manchester's Liberal leaders, therefore, could no longer be characterised as cotton barons, but were an equally diverse occupational group. Professional men like Edwin Guthrie and C.P. Scott were as well represented in the city's elite as cotton merchants and industrialists.[63]

The fact that Manchester came to symbolise the popular Liberal movements of the early nineteenth century has led to some misunderstanding of Manchester's own political history. Just as the Liberalism of the Manchester school did not reflect the views of all the city's entrepreneurs, Manchester was not always as Radical in its Liberalism as other cities. Palmerston's 'gunboat' foreign policy was popular in Manchester, and led to the rejection of the city's Radical MPs, including, remarkably, John Bright, the government's leading critic and an icon of the free trade movement.[64] Liberalism also benefited little from the electoral reforms of 1867–68. Although the party attracted the support of a number of leading trade unionists and secured the ex-Chartist Ernest Jones as a candidate, it struggled to cope with the expanded electorate. Jones polled 3,000 votes fewer than his Liberal colleague and the city's first Conservative MP was elected.[65] Manchester's three-member constituency, in which each elector had just two votes, prevented the Liberals from dominating and ensured that the substantial Conservative minority had a parliamentary foothold. Much of the next 17 years was spent trying, often unsuccessfully, to cope with the changed electoral conditions. The problems of the Liberal Party in mid-century are important in placing debates about the late nineteenth-century Liberal Party in perspective. By exaggerating the party's mid-century unity and strength, it is easy to carelessly assume that the late nineteenth century was simply a period of decline following a 'golden age'. Manchester Liberalism had great influence on the national political stage, but never exercised complete dominance over its own city.

Manchester was, of course, not the only new industrial community to have a major impact on national politics. Until 1886 Birmingham probably had an equal claim to be the Liberal capital of provincial England. Its leader, Joseph Chamberlain, was regarded by many of his supporters as the natural successor to Gladstone. At municipal level Birmingham Liberalism was known for its innovative interventionist policies in housing and public health – policies which seemed to point the way for future Liberal policies at national level. The Home Rule crisis, however, split the Birmingham Liberal Party and left Leicester as the main spiritual centre of Liberalism in the Midlands. Leicester, too, had a strong Radical Liberal

63 For detailed analysis of early twentieth-century Liberalism in Manchester see B. Jones, 'Manchester Liberalism 1918–1929: the electoral, ideological and organisational experience of the Liberal Party in Manchester, with particular reference to the career of Ernest Simon', Unpublished PhD thesis, University of Manchester, 1997 and S. McGhie, 'Liberal Politics in Manchester, Oldham and Stoke-on-Trent, 1906–1922', Unpublished PhD thesis, Manchester Metropolitan University (forthcoming).

64 Kidd, *Manchester*, 72.

65 P. Whitaker, 'The Growth of Liberal Organisation in Manchester from the Eighteen Sixties to 1903', Unpublished PhD thesis, University of Manchester, 1956, 64–5.

tradition. During the early part of the century it became a major organising centre for parliamentary reform and Chartism. Formidable public speakers such as Thomas Cooper were able to build substantial support and the movement continued to be influential throughout the 1840s.[66] The strength of Chartism in Leicester no doubt contributed to subsequent Radical progress in the town. During much of the period to 1865 the party effectively had a three party system, with at times Radicals and Whigs operating as two separate parties.[67] Although the Liberal Party largely operated as a united movement from 1868 onwards, the divisions between Radicals and Whigs were institutionalised by Leicester's two-member parliamentary system – typically a Radical took one seat and a Whig the other. Again this is important in placing the Liberal Party's later difficulties into context. The Liberal Party may have dominated Leicester's local politics since the mid-century, but it was rarely a united force.

Leicester Liberalism drew much of its traditional strength from local religious Nonconformity. By the late nineteenth century it had firmly established its reputation as being the 'capital of dissent' – the leading Nonconformist town in England. This Nonconformist influence had a major impact on the character of local Liberalism. Even as late as the 1880s the town's leading Radical thinker, the Rev. J. Page Hopps, was a Nonconformist minister. Much of Leicester's Liberalism took on a moralistic, absolutist tone. The movement of civil disobedience to resist the compulsory vaccination legislation was led largely by Nonconformist ministers of the town – who even led mass demonstrations outside prisons where protestors were incarcerated.[68] The evils of gambling took on great significance in Liberal and Nonconformist campaigns. The Radical *Midland Free Press* refused to print any horse racing columns in its pages and the Liberal-controlled city council controversially 'blacked-out' the racing and gambling pages of other papers in public libraries for fear they would encourage immorality.[69] These campaigns did not always attract public support. The practice of censoring newspapers caused such an outcry that the council was eventually forced to reverse its decision. Debates over excessive drinking were also a prominent feature of local politics, and were a special concern of the local Liberal leadership. One town mayor provoked substantial popular criticism after he condemned working men's drinking habits. Moves to limit drinking were, however, popular with some. Liberal property developer Arthur Wakerley was sufficiently confident in the attractions of temperance that he banned the public houses from his newly constructed housing estates.[70]

The intensity of Nonconformist influence in Leicester was partly a product of the relative size and insularity of the town compared to the larger urban centres of

66 Alan Little, 'Chartism and Liberalism: Popular Politics in Leicestershire 1842–1874', Unpublished PhD thesis, University of Manchester, 1991, 40–88.

67 Little, 'Chartism and Liberalism', 252–93.

68 *LDM*, 16 March 1886.

69 *MFP*, 30 January 1892.

70 J. Simmons, *Leicester Past and Present Volume II: The Modern City* (London, 1974), 122.

Manchester and Birmingham.[71] Economically Leicester was much less diverse. It had two main industries – hosiery and boot and shoe – and was relatively late in developing large-scale factory production. There were few other large industries in the area and Leicester's economic base still depended to some degree on its role as a county town, serving the largely agricultural community in its immediate environs. Leicester's market, which dated back to the Middle Ages, continued to be the hub of the county's economic life and maintained that role well into the twentieth century. The relatively insular economic character of Leicester naturally influenced patterns of immigration to the town. In the latter half of the nineteenth century Leicester had a claim to be the most prosperous town in the Midlands, and arguably one of the most prosperous in England. This naturally attracted a large number of immigrants from the surrounding countryside and other nearby towns. However, this trend seems to have had little influence on the ethnic and cultural structure of the working population. Leicester, unlike Manchester, developed little in the way of large Irish and Jewish communities. No doubt the relative isolation and small size of the town was a deterrent to international migrants of the nineteenth century. It was not until the twentieth century that Leicester developed into a genuinely multi-cultural city.

Superficially Liberalism appeared to be the dominant political creed in both Leicester and Manchester. This is significant in as far as it seems to demonstrate that Liberalism could still appeal in both large cosmopolitan industrial cities and smaller insular county towns, which underwent much later industrialisation. However, in truth, Liberalism faced significant challenges in both boroughs. Both Manchester and Leicester were something of Liberal islands in otherwise largely Conservative counties. By the late nineteenth century the Lancashire working class had become synonymous with Conservatism. The cotton unions were associated with political moderation – an association reinforced with the defection of union leader James Mawdsley from the Liberals in 1886. The presence of a large Irish Catholic population in Lancashire is often cited as a primary reason for English working-class support for Tory and Orange organisations. In Manchester Orange organisations were far less prominent in city politics than in Liverpool and the violent sectarianism associated with Liverpool politics was largely absent from Manchester in the final quarter of the nineteenth century.[72] Yet local politics did have a sectarian dimension, particularly as many Irish nationalist organisations worked closely with the Liberals. The revival of Conservatism in Manchester, however, was not primarily the product of growing sectarianism. Rather it was the result of a new populist style of Conservative politics that combined Primrose League-style activities with community organisation based around the alehouse. Stephen Chesters Thompson, a brewer with a chain of public houses in East Manchester, became very adroit at using his watering holes as an

[71] Although it is questionable whether Nonconformist influence in Leicester was as strong as that in other comparable small industrial towns. See B. Lancaster, *Radicalism, Co-operation, Socialism* (Leicester, 1987), 65–7.

[72] S. Fielding, 'The Irish Catholics of Manchester and Salford: Aspects of their Religious and Political History, 1890–1939', Unpublished PhD thesis, University of Warwick, 1988, 141–5.

organisational platform for local Conservatism. It was with Chesters Thompson's help that Balfour established his political ascendancy in Manchester and thus the ascendancy of the Conservative Party in the eastern party of the city.[73] Such was the success of his campaigns in that part of the city that Chesters Thompson began being dubbed in the press as the 'King of Ardwick'. Populist leaders like Chesters Thompson soon became very adroit at exploiting the Liberal Party's failings at municipal level. When, in 1884, the city's citizens' auditor discovered widespread municipal mismanagement by the Liberal ruling group, it was Chesters Thompson who led the barrage of criticism and by doing so helped the Conservative Party re-emerge as a significant municipal force. With the middle-class commercial elites in central Manchester also apparently drifting away from the Liberal Party, Manchester Liberalism seemed to be facing a crisis. When a by-election in 1883 saw the Liberal Party split with its Radical section, the crisis intensified.[74] When, a year later, the Liberal Party won just one of Manchester's six new parliamentary seats, many began to entertain the belief that Manchester Liberalism was a thing of the past.

Leicester Liberalism also faced formidable problems. For over 30 years an uneasy peace had existed between the 'moderate' and Radical sections of the local Liberal Association and Club. In 1884 relations broke down completely over the selection of a replacement Liberal candidate. Although the dispute did not lead to the collapse of the Liberal Association, many Radicals felt isolated from the official party machinery.[75] The incident emphasised just how much the Liberal Party in Leicester represented a marriage of convenience between the old Whig and Radical traditions who, at times, seemed to have little in common. The fragmented nature of Leicester Liberalism naturally did much to encourage pioneering socialist groups, and later the ILP, who could see the fault lines in local Liberalism all too clearly. Moreover, despite the Liberal Party's domination of Leicester's municipal and parliamentary politics, the party had done little to spread its influence to the county constituencies. Land-owning families, such as the Manners, continued to have a semi-feudal grip on the rural electorate with Leicester representing something of a red island in a sea of blue. Even the city's Liberal municipal elite, apparently so secure in their control of local administration, were not in quite such a strong position as appeared. Firstly, the packing of the aldermanic bench exaggerated the real electoral strength of the party. Secondly, they were increasingly coming under renewed public scrutiny as the cost of local government mounted.[76] The party that had prided itself in keeping down the rates was finding it difficult to cope with the increasing demands on the municipal coffers after 1880. The extension of the city's boundaries in 1891 was to bring the

---

73 G. Suess Law, 'Manchester's Politics 1885–1906', Unpublished PhD thesis, University of Pennsylvania, 1975, 157–61.

74 *MG*, 5 October, 1883.

75 *LDM*, 26 March 1884.

76 *MFP*, 2 April 1892.

city's growing financial crisis to a head, threatening to undermine over half a century of Liberal control.[77]

Yet this is not an account of the death of Liberal England, but rather its revival and renewal. The decade after 1885 was a period of rapid transformation in both local and national Liberal politics. Although one cannot identify a single cause for the emergence of what became known as the ideology of 'New Liberalism', it is clear that its roots lie in the final two decades of the nineteenth century. It was the era in which party interests finally replaced personal loyalties in determining most municipal voting behaviour. It was the era of Home Rule crisis, but also a time when parties began to develop comprehensive programmes for government rather than relying on single-issue campaigns. Crucially, too, it was an era in which Liberals were forced to rethink their political priorities in the wake of Gladstone's resignation from the leadership and competition from the ILP.

Those who study the development of new political ideologies often look to the theorists and political leaders who develop and codify political programmes in order to understand how and why they were developed. Figures like Hobhouse, Masterman and Hobson are naturally given a starring role in the history of New Liberal ideas.[78] It is important to be aware, however, that many of the ideas and approaches promoted by these thinkers were pioneered in the late nineteenth century and popularised at local level by the action of local politicians. Often this was partly as a response to the challenges that the party faced in fighting a more confident Conservative Party and resolving internal differences. The Home Rule crisis saw Chamberlain leave the Liberal Party – but he did not take the Liberal Party's Radicalism with him. Gladstone had embarked on a Home Rule campaign that dominated the domestic political agenda for a time – but the campaign did not eliminate the other political issues of the day. Instead it was left to local parties and the National Liberal Federation to address domestic grievances and find answers to the problems of industrial society.

Examination of local politics can therefore give many clues as to how urban Liberalism responded to the challenges it faced, how it transformed, and why it continued to be a significant political force well into the twentieth century.[79] Although the experiences of Leicester and Manchester may not reflect the experiences of other industrial communities, they can illustrate ways in which major Liberal groups came to renew themselves in the face of major political difficulties. Such research, however, is unlikely to provide much support for those who see the strange death of Liberal England beginning in 1886, or those who see political history solely in

77 See 'Stray Notes', *MFP*, 29 October 1892.

78 See, for example, P. Weiler, 'The New Liberalism of L.T. Hobhouse', *Victorian Studies*, 16 (1972) 135–61; L. Masterman, *C.F G. Masterman*, second edition (London, 1968).

79 Back in 1972 Hamer remarked that much work remained to be done on grass-roots Liberalism – and, to a large degree, this still holds true. D.A. Hamer, *Liberal Politics in the Age of Gladstone and Rosebery* (Oxford, 1972), x. Fortunately, recent years have seen a growing interest in the way localities shape political culture and partisan preference. See Lawrence, *Speaking for the People*, esp. 6, 228–33.

deterministic class terms. Indeed the ability of the Liberal Party to redefine its agenda and recover from the Home Rule crisis, Gladstone's resignation and many minor crises suggests a movement with anything but a death wish. The Liberal Party's popularity in the wealthier mixed suburbs implies that even if the upper middle class had fled to Conservatism, the party retained significant support amongst the 'shopocracy'. Similarly the characterisation of the Liberal Party as one obsessed by laissez-faire is dramatically undermined by an examination of the party's record in municipal government. Rarely a dogmatic movement, sometimes its openness to outside influences could be a weakness. The enthusiasm of Radicals, such as C.P. Scott, in standing aside for ILP candidates could be interpreted by opponents as an example of fear rather than generosity. Much hostility between the parties arose not because the Liberal Party refused to endorse working-class candidates, but rather because the ILP refused to accept any compromise short of complete Liberal surrender. If the problems the party faced in the decade after 1886 were formidable, the success it achieved was remarkable.

PART I
Reform and the Urban Radical Tradition

CHAPTER ONE

The Rise of Manchester Radicalism

For many historians the Irish Home Rule crisis was *the* defining moment in the history of late nineteenth-century Liberalism. It has been seen as marking the point at which Gladstone redefined the purpose of the party, producing a lasting and fundamental realignment in British politics.[1] In Manchester, however, Liberal political realignment was as much the product of events between 1883–85 as those in 1886. For much of the period from 1883 to the reorganisation of the party following redistribution of parliamentary seats in 1885, the Radical wing of the Manchester Liberal Association seemed to be in retreat.[2] Its attempts to secure official Liberal sanction for a Radical candidate in 1883 had failed and its efforts to organise itself separately were equally unsuccessful. By the general election of 1885, however, the Radicals had strengthened their position in the new smaller Liberal Associations established following the creation of single member constituencies. Once very hostile to the machinery of 'official' Liberalism, many began to use it to persuade the party to adopt more Radical candidates and deprive the old party managers, usually from the centre-right of the party, of their traditional role. Consequently the organisation of the party became a battleground for the future direction of Manchester Liberalism.

Before the general election of 1885, the city of Manchester constituted a three-member parliamentary borough. As with other three-member boroughs the nature of the franchise, providing each elector with two votes, placed a premium on effective disciplined party organisation to discourage vote splitting.[3] Manchester Liberalism, however, had a history of internal conflict, not only between 'official' and Radical Liberalism, but also between the supporters of different Radical factions. In 1868, the first election on anything resembling a mass franchise, the Liberal leadership made an explicit attempt to recruit candidates with working-class appeal and a committee of working men was established to assess trade union opinion. However, divisions between those who favoured veteran Radical printer Abel Heywood and the ex-

---

1 For a recent summary of the debate on the consequences of the division see G.R. Searle, *The Liberal Party: Triumph and Disintegration 1886–1929* (London, 1992), 29–76.

2 The term 'Radical' is used here as a generic term to describe adherents of what is sometimes referred to as 'new Radicalism' and 'advanced' Liberalism. It does not imply formal affiliation with any specific Radical association or organisation.

3 For a classic critical description of the mechanisms of disciplined party organisation see M. Ostrogorski, *Democracy and the Organisation of Political Parties*, volume one (London, 1902), especially 371–493. See also J. Dunbabin, 'Some Implications of the 1885 British shift towards Single-Member Constituencies: A Note', *English Historical Review*, 108 (1994), 89–100.

Chartist Ernest Jones soon became apparent. Heywood's supporters felt that he had been snubbed by the Liberal leadership and a rift between Heywood's Radicals and 'official' Liberalism continued for over a decade. Dr. Richard Pankhurst, husband of Emmeline, and the *de facto* leader of Manchester Radicalism in the early 1880s, was an avid supporter of Heywood. In 1879 Pankhurst used his position on the council of the Manchester Liberal Association in an unsuccessful attempt to secure for Heywood the second Liberal nomination in Manchester ahead of the eventually successful centre-right John Slagg.[4] During the 1883 Manchester by-election, in which Pankhurst was an independent Liberal candidate, Abel Heywood's son endorsed Pankhurst and later took a leading role in the formation of the Manchester Radical Association.[5]

Despite the continuing divisions within Liberal ranks, general Liberal Party organisation in Manchester did become more cohesive in the 15 years between 1868 and 1883. The party's defeat in the 1874 general election brought about a thorough overhaul of party organisation and the creation of a Manchester Liberal Association loosely based on the Birmingham model, with a paid secretary and a representative committee structure. Most of the important business of the Association was conducted by its executive committee made up of the chairmen and secretaries of the ward organisations, together with other specially elected ward representatives. This executive selected a general purposes committee, which was responsible for the day-to-day running of the party machinery.[6] The new structure was seen by Whitaker as representing the centralisation of ward power in more efficient executive bodies, with the practical value of this arrangement being demonstrated with the return of the Liberal candidate, Jacob Bright, in the 1876 Manchester by-election. New centralised organisation seemed to foster party cohesion.[7]

The growth of centralised party control, however, can be overstated. Certainly Jacob Bright's candidature was supported by an apparently united Liberal Party, but this probably had more to do with the fact that he was able to attract support from opposing wings of the party, than any intrinsic value benefits brought about by the new more centralised party structures. As a brother of John Bright, Jacob was identified with an icon that all Liberals respected and, like his brother, was closely identified with the Radical wing of the party. The battles over the second Liberal nominee in 1880 and the refusal of many Radicals to accept the organisation's decision not to contest the by-election of 1883 would seem to indicate that even if the body had a formally centralised decision-making structure, it lacked the legitimacy and respect necessary for genuinely cohesive and politically binding decision-making. Even the party's official ward committees had their roles contested by local

---

4 P. Whitaker, 'The Growth of Liberal Organisation in Manchester from the Eighteen Sixties to 1903', Unpublished PhD thesis, University of Manchester 1956, 60–66. Whitaker offers a valuable descriptive organisational history, but rarely analyses the important ideological shifts in local politics that underlie these changes.

5 *MG*, 5 October 1883.

6 Whitaker, 'The Growth of Liberal Organisation', 67–8.

7 Whitaker, 'The Growth of Liberal Organisation', 69–70.

semi-independent Liberal clubs.[8] These powerful local groups made a substantial contribution to registration and organisational activity in many districts and had to be given a voice in local affairs.[9] Similarly the Manchester Reform Club, the Manchester Junior Reform Club and the independently minded Liberal group on the city council ensured that the executive committee of the Liberal Association never had complete control of city-wide politics. The Manchester Reform Club, founded in 1867, had a membership of over 1,000 and traditionally played such a major part in election campaigns in East and South-East Lancashire that even its critics were forced to acknowledge its importance.[10] The chief influence of the Reform Club was through its assistance in the organisation of Liberal registration work in Manchester and the surrounding district.[11] The Manchester Liberal Association only gradually assumed this function – the Association still did not have a permanent registration committee as late as 1880.[12] In years of little party competition, and when ward organisations worked effectively, the central Manchester Liberal Association funds were able to help bear the cost of the operation without too much pain.[13] However when the Conservative Association went on the offensive in a vigorous registration campaign in 1882–83, the funds required by the Liberal Association to compete exceeded their own resources and they were forced to ask the committee of the Reform Club to make a grant from their own funds to finance the project.[14] Clearly the days of Reform Club involvement in organisational work had not completely passed.

The central committees of the Liberal Association, although apparently exercising substantial influence over at least the formal procedure for selecting parliamentary candidates, had little or no influence over the Liberal majority on the Manchester City Council. A powerful localist tradition remained. Individual wards were responsible for selecting candidates and the ward representatives who made up the executive committee showed considerable resistance to the idea of that body taking any part in directing their local contests or influencing local decision-making.[15] The rejection of more interventionist measures was not the result of indifference towards local politics, as the Association had a record of assisting wards where specific problems existed. The executive frequently made grants to local wards for local elections.[16]

---

8 MLA, General Purposes Committee, 26 November 1880, MCL, M283/1/1/1. MLA, General Purposes Committee, 2 December 1880, MCL, M283/1/1/1.

9 MLA, General Purposes Committee, 2 June 1881, MCL, M283/1/1/1.

10 J.L. Hammond, *C.P. Scott, 1848–1932, The Making of the Manchester Guardian* (Manchester, 1932), 39; cited in Whitaker, 'The Growth of Liberal Organisation', 137.

11 Whitaker, 'The Growth of Liberal Organisation', 136.

12 MLA, Executive Committee, 2 October 1880, MCL, M283/1/1/1; MLA, Executive Committee, 5 August 1880, MCL, M283/1/1/1.

13 MLA, General Purposes Committee, 2 June 1881, MCL, M283/1/1/1.

14 MLA, General Purposes Committee, 9 January 1883, MCL, M283/1/1/1.

15 MLA, Executive Committee, 12 December 1882, MCL, M283/1/1/1,

16 MLA, Executive Committee, 16 September 1884, MCL, M283/1/1/1. MLA, General Purposes Committee, 8 May 1883, MCL, M283/1/1/1. MLA, General Purposes Committee,

Ward representatives on these bodies, however, were reluctant to surrender control of local politics to a central body. Although some wards were financially dependent on outside assistance there is no evidence to suggest that, before 1885 at least, this assistance was conditional or led to the selection of a different type of candidate than would have otherwise been the case.

To talk, therefore, of a centralised and more cohesive Liberal Association structure in the 1880s can be a little misleading. The party still encompassed a wide range of separate traditions – from the 'new' Radicalism of the Pankhursts to the 'moderate' Liberalism characterised by the city's second Liberal MP John Slagg. It was socially very diverse, attracting support from the middle-class professionals and merchants of the Reform Club to the industrial workmen of New Cross. The diversity of Liberalism's followers and the need to secure the co-operation of the many Liberal clubs and Radical groups meant that the authority the central committees of the party could actually exercise was limited. The central committees were themselves substantially made up of representatives from local groups with different ward, as well as city-wide, political priorities. The disputes over parliamentary representation in 1880 and the conflicts between Liberal Association branches and clubs illustrated that the position of the Liberal Association as the sole legitimate body for managing Liberal politics was still questioned. It was a question brought under sharp focus following the death of local Conservative MP, Hugh Birley, in 1883, and by the decision of the Liberal Association's central governing committees not to engage in the subsequent contest.

Dr. Richard Pankhurst, the Radical nominee for the by-election, was no stranger to political controversy, having been a supporter of Abel Heywood's nomination for the Liberal candidature in 1880, and an influential member of the Manchester Republican movement in the 1870s. Active in the Women's Suffrage Society, he was a close associate of Jacob Bright and had drafted Bright's amendment to the Municipal Corporations Bill of 1869, giving women once again the right to vote in municipal elections.[17] It was on the issue of women's suffrage that Pankhurst was said to have resigned from the Liberal Party, in protest at Gladstone's refusal to include the parliamentary suffrage for women in the 1884 Franchise Bill.[18] However, as Whitaker has observed, this seems unlikely unless Pankhurst had seen an early draft of the Bill as he tendered his resignation on 2 August 1883 – well before the details of the 1884 Bill became public.[19] The precise reason for his resignation and the timing of it are therefore open to speculation – Pankhurst offered no public explanation and his resignation letter was received without recorded comment by the Liberal Association executive committee on which he had served since the 1870s.[20] It

11 November 1884, MCL, M283/1/1/1.

[17] A. Kelly, *Lydia Becker and the Cause* (Lancaster, 1992).

[18] R. Stracey article in the *Dictionary of National Biography* on Emmeline Pankhurst (suppt. 1922–30, 652–4) cited in Whitaker, 'The Growth of Liberal Organisation', 70.

[19] Whitaker, 'The Growth of Liberal Organisation', 70 (see footnote).

[20] MLA, General Purposes Committee, 2 August 1883, MCL, M283/1/1/1; *MG*, 29 September 1883.

was clear, however, that Pankhurst had been estranged from the mainstream Liberal ranks for some time. An anonymous *Manchester Examiner* correspondent accused Pankhurst of turning his back on the party after failing in his attempt to win the Liberal nomination for Abel Heywood in 1880.[21] A member of the Liberal executive also criticised Pankhurst's recent record for the party, his failure to publicly support Gladstone's Irish policy and general 'contempt of party obligations.'[22]

By the time the executive committee of the Liberal Association were considering possible courses of action in relation to the parliamentary vacancy, there were already strong rumours circulating in the city that Pankhurst would contest the seat regardless of any decision the Association might take.[23] Both major Liberal committees came down heavily against contesting the vacancy. Only three of the 19 members voting on the general purposes committee, and six members voting on the much larger executive committee, supported engaging a Liberal candidate. The main advocates of a contest were Radicals Percy Glass and George Mason who hoped to persuade the party to adopt Pankhurst.[24]

The Liberal executive knew that given the operation of the minority clause – each elector having two votes in a three-member constituency – it would be very difficult for the party to carry all three seats at the forthcoming general election. Indeed, to field three candidates at a general election would probably only serve to spread the Liberal vote more thinly and result in the return of two Conservatives. Consequently even if the Liberal Party won the third seat at the by-election, it would be forced at the subsequent general election to ask one of its local MPs to retire in order to assist the success of the other two. As the member asked to retire was most likely to be the 'junior' member, it would have been very difficult to find a candidate willing to spend large amounts of money in order to serve in the Commons for what could turn out to be just a few months. [25] Pankhurst was available but given his recent behaviour he was unlikely to be willing to obey the Liberal Association and willingly surrender his seat whenever the general election took place.[26] Other reasons also weighed heavily. Many Liberals supported the minority clause on principle in that it guaranteed minority parties at least some representation in large boroughs, mitigating some of the unfairness of an otherwise majoritarian electoral system.[27] Perhaps of most significance, however, was the financial cost of a possible by-election, considering the very short-term benefit a by-election win would bring for

21 *ME*, 1 October 1883.

22 *MG*, 26 September 1883.

23 *MG*, 14 September 1883.

24 MLA, General Purposes and Executive Committees, 15 September 1883, MCL, M283/1/1/1.

25 *MG*, 17 September 1883.

26 Indeed there was a rumour that Pankhurst had already stated his intention to contest the forthcoming general election – as an independent – in any case, threatening the position of the sitting Liberal members Bright and Slagg. *MG*, 17 September 1883.

27 Had the Liberals won the by-election they would have all three seats in the borough, breaking the spirit of minority clause representation.

the party. The size of the borough meant that a by-election contest for a single seat in Manchester was much more costly than for smaller one or two member boroughs. Although fighting for just a solitary seat, a campaign had to be run across the whole city as if all three members were up for election. In the event the returning officers' expenses alone cost the two candidates £972.10.7. This compared with little over £100 per candidate for some of the single member divisions of the city in 1885.[28] Moreover the by-election came at a time when the Liberal Association was having one of its periodic shortages of funds after a costly registration campaign.[29] With this in mind it is, perhaps, little surprising that there was a reluctance to support a candidate who had resigned from their ranks and who, if successful, might insist on standing at the following general election, resulting in the loss of either John Slagg or Jacob Bright, the sitting MPs.[30]

The decision of the Liberal executive committee to remain aloof from the contest had to be ratified by the Liberal council for Manchester – a larger committee of around 600 activists, partly elected from wards and partly co-opted. This body did not have a history of rebelling against the executive and rarely did more than 'rubber stamp' executive committee decisions.[31] The executive and council were elected at the same time with the party's leading opinion formers sitting on both bodies, preventing a situation arising where one faction controlled the council and one the executive.[32] On the question of the by-election, however, several amendments challenging the executive's decision were received. The problem was that not all council members who wanted to see the Conservatives challenged at the polls were enthusiastic about Pankhurst's candidature and the executive fended off the opposition. After the council chairman, Robert Leake MP, appealed for unity only about 20 Radicals refused to endorse the executive's position.[33]

By this time Pankhurst had decided to stand with or without official endorsement. An election committee had been formed with Abel Heywood Jnr., the son of the defeated candidate for the 1880 Liberal parliamentary nomination, at its head.[34]

---

28 Parliamentary Election Expense Returns, MCL, MISC 268, 39–43, 44–7. The returning officer's expenses in 1885 were £104.0.2 per candidate for the South-West division (the lowest) and £138.11.5 for North West (the highest).

29 MLA, General Purposes Committee, 9 January 1883, MCL, M283/1/1/1; MLA, Executive Committee, 12 June 1883, MCL, M283/1/1/1.

30 In the event, of course, redistribution of seats made this calculation irrelevant, although in the Autumn of 1883 most assumed that the general election would take place under the existing conditions.

31 Whitaker, 'The Growth of Liberal Organisation', 67.

32 Each year the contests were comprehensively reported in the *Manchester Guardian* and *Manchester Examiner* and usually took place annually in the last two weeks of January.

33 MLA, Council Meeting, 17 September 1883, MCL, M283/1/1/1; *MG*, 18 September 1883.

34 When the Liberal council meeting was held it was already clear that Pankhurst intended to pursue his candidature. It may have been this fact that finally dissuaded many Liberals in the council from pushing for a contest, feeling that Pankhurst was forcing their hand. *MG*, 18 September 1883.

Despite being deprived of official party machinery, Pankhurst's campaign soon picked up momentum and prominent Radical support. Abel Heywood Jnr.'s presence at the head of the Pankhurst campaign probably did much to rally those Radicals who had supported his father. On the platform of one of Pankhurst's first election meetings was R.D. Darbishire, a wealthy South Manchester Liberal, from one of the city's most influential Liberal families. He was accompanied by two of the city's leading party organisers, George Mason and A.F. Winks.[35] Later additions to Pankhurst's committee included leading social reformer and philanthropist Cllr Charles Rowley and Percy Glass, the principal opponent of the Liberal Party's abstentionist policy on the party executive. The Pankhurst campaign was not, however, entirely dominated by traditional middle-class Radicals and party insiders. Robert Austin, the secretary of the influential Amalgamated Society of Engineers, joined the election committee, whilst J.S. Murchie, of the Amalgamated Society of Joiners, also declared publicly for Pankhurst.[36]

Although Pankhurst was unashamedly from the Radical wing of the party, the Pankhurst campaign stressed not his differences with traditional Liberal doctrines, but rather his loyalty to them. At a meeting early in the campaign Pankhurst's advocacy of land reform, condemning the system of landholding in England and Ireland, hinted at his Radicalism. However after having won the support of C.S. Parnell, Michael Davitt and local Irish nationalist groups, his campaign followed traditional Liberal themes.[37] Pankhurst was continually at pains to point out his loyalty to the Liberal cause adopting the traditional Cobdenite slogan of 'peace, retrenchment and reform' and referring to Gladstone as 'the greatest Prime Minister of modern times'.[38] His Radical supporters tried to depict the caucus bosses of the Liberal Association as the principal threat to party unity – by failing to listen to the party's membership it was the caucus bosses who had precipitated the division.[39] Percy Glass declared that in supporting Pankhurst he was acting as a loyal member of the Liberal Association executive and council, acting in support of a candidate standing on a Cobdenite platform. Similarly, Pankhurst, at a meeting in the Manchester Athenaeum went to the lengths of quoting a speech of Cobden to the city's chamber of commerce in 1862 to illustrate Radical adherence to and reverence for Liberal principles and traditions.[40]

Not all Liberal and Radicals were convinced. Pankhurst had been actively involved in the formation of the current Liberal Association and initially approved of its decision-making structure. For three years, however, after he had failed to secure the nomination of his own favoured candidate in 1880, he had taken no part in the

35 *MG*, 21 September 1883.

36 *MG*, 22 September 1883.

37 Irish Nationalists initially tried to secure their own candidate, but following advice from Parnell and Davitt endorsed Pankhurst. *MG*, 21 September 1883; *MG*, 29 September 1883; *ME*, 1 October 1883.

38 *MG*, 21 September 1883.

39 *ME*, 1 October 1883.

40 *ME*, 3 October 1883.

association and then resigned from the party.[41] This invariably seemed to mark him out as a rather erratic supporter of the Liberal cause. The Manchester Liberal press had little enthusiasm for his candidature. The *Manchester Guardian*, yet to emerge as a distinctively Radical organ, was initially conciliatory and felt Pankhurst's candidature should be judged by the likelihood of its success.[42] As the campaign progressed, however, the *Guardian* became increasingly critical. Pankhurst was seen as essentially an opportunist attempting to hi-jack Liberal principles and rhetoric for his own ends – 'to make vigorous play with the current political catch words and to seek support in the name of the great party leader whom all Liberals alike acknowledge and revere'.[43] It feared that if Pankhurst was successful others would follow his example and the unity of the party would be permanently undermined.[44] The *Manchester Examiner* – traditionally seen as the leading Radical paper in Manchester – took up broadly the same position. If Pankhurst succeeded the Liberal Association would lose all legitimacy and 'be dead to all interests and purposes, and might as well be buried.'[45] The history of Manchester Liberalism seemed to show that when the party was divided, it was defeated. If a section of the party were to receive electoral reward for breaking away it would be even more difficult in future to contain Liberal differences as the route of independence appeared increasingly attractive.[46]

The attitude of Pankhurst towards the Manchester Liberal Association was somewhat ambivalent. The rumours of his independent candidature before the Association had made a decision and his resignation from that body two months before the by-election suggest that he regarded the organisation as seriously defective and unrepresentative of Radical Liberalism. However, his action in attempting to woo the organisation during the course of the election campaign seems to suggest that he still regarded it as being of considerable political importance for the Radicals to win it over to his side. Of course, as Pankhurst's committee had no party organisation themselves, other than that they had scrambled together during the course of the campaign, they would have greatly benefited from having the 'official' party machine supporting their candidate. Moreover the Manchester Liberal Association had considerable prestige nationwide and if it had adopted Pankhurst as an official candidate this would probably have been seen as a considerable coup for the Radical wing of the party – particularly after the success of Jacob Bright in the 1876 by-election – and have re-established Manchester as a rival to Birmingham as Britain's Radical capital. Pankhurst, in a move to soothe fears that his candidature threatened the future of the existing Liberal members, declared that if he was a candidate at

41 Letter, E.C. Richards, *MG*, 26 September 1883.

42 *MG*, 17 September 1883. It is unclear who actually wrote the leader. There is no apparent evidence that C.P. Scott, so well known for his support of Radicalism in the 1890s, played any public part in the election.

43 *MG*, 5 October 1883.

44 *MG*, 4 October 1883.

45 *ME*, 3 October 1883.

46 *MEN*, 2 October 1883.

the next election he would be prepared to submit his candidature to a representative council of the Liberal Association for decision. Meanwhile his supporters petitioned the leaders of the Liberal Association to call a meeting to reassess the Radical candidature.[47]

The presidents and vice-presidents of the Association obliged but also issued a circular urging members to attend and support the original decision.[48] At a special meeting of the executive many members took the view that it would be unconstitutional for them to give a particular intention of meaning to the wish of the supposed sovereign body – the council – with the result that of the 80 or so members present only 12 voted to re-open the issue. Pankhurst's supporters were no more successful at the subsequent council meeting.[49] The Association had decided that whatever the short term benefit of electing another Liberal MP, victory for Pankhurst could only increase divisions, threatening the Association and the political future of the sitting members. Radicals were enraged. A handbill distributed at the council meeting called the Association 'an organised hypocrisy' run by 'Money-Bags'. Many had completely lost faith in the Association to represent their views and felt that the existing decision-making structures were frustrating Radical influence.[50]

Radicals had to accept a division in Liberal ranks, with all its inherent dangers to the electoral position of the party, in order to try to gain more influence in the management of Liberal politics in the city. In the event, however, this approach failed, with the result of the by-election demonstrating the continuing authority of the Association and the somewhat weak Radical position. Pankhurst's crushing defeat was seen as a vindication of the decision of the Liberal executive not to take part in the election and a demonstration of the power of the caucus in Manchester politics. [51] Pankhurst's actions had put the caucus on trial, not just in Manchester, but countrywide, in the eyes of the national press and the Liberal journals.[52] *The Pall Mall Gazette* saw the defeat of Pankhurst as not merely a matter for relief, but for considerable satisfaction:

> Manchester has done well. A great danger has been averted and a great moral victory has been gained. One of the largest English constituencies has pronounced a decisive condemnation upon a candidate that struck at the root of party discipline – that is to say, of party success.[53]

---

47 *MG*, 2 October 1883.

48 MLA, Executive Committee 3 October 1883; printed circular 2 October 1883, MCL, M283/1/1/1.

49 *MG*, 4 October 1883; MLA, Executive Committee, 3 October 1883, MCL, M283/1/1/1.

50 *MG*, 4 October 1883.

51 *MG*, 5 October 1883; *ME*, 5 October 1883.

52 See quotation from *The World*, in the *Pall Mall Gazette*, 25 September 1883.

53 *Pall Mall Gazette*, 5 October 1883.

The London correspondent of the *Manchester Evening News* reported similar sentiments from the capital seeing the demise of Pankhurst as 'a great triumph for the party machinery'.[54] Fear of permanent party division had destroyed the Radical candidature.

Pankhurst's response to the news of his defeat drove a further wedge between his loyalists and the leaders of the Liberal Association. He publicly railed at the 'Whig oligarchy, a Liberal Association that was not representative and a press which was not Liberal, though it called itself so' while the leaders of the Manchester Liberal Association were dismissed as 'a handful of invisible plutocrats'.[55] The leadership of the Association had rendered it impossible, he claimed, for Radicals to participate in the Association without fear of censure. For this reason he advocated, for the first time, the creation of a separate Radical organisation and press distinct from the Liberal caucus – a suggestion immediately picked up on by his colleagues George Mason and Abel Heywood Jnr, who offered to assist in the organisation of just such a body.[56] A crushing defeat for Pankhurst had re-established the legitimacy and status of the Liberal Association in the eyes of the press, but it had done so at the cost of alienating many Radicals who set up an organisation that would prolong Liberal divisions and institutionalise opposition to the 'official' party machinery.

Within days of defeat around 100 Radicals met to hear George Payne propose plans for 'the organisation of the Radical party' in the city, although from the start it was clear that there was no clear consensus as to the form Radical organisation should take. Some objected to the very phrase 'Radical party' – a phrase that seemed to suggest the future for the Radicals might lie outside the Liberal Party.[57] Although the Radicals eventually accepted the title of a 'party', there was reluctance amongst many to be seen as setting themselves up in opposition to the official party organisation. Payne was keen to stress that the majority of Radicals at the meeting were in favour of working with rather than against the 'official' Liberal organisation.[58]

The Manchester Radical Association never quite proved the challenge to 'official' Liberalism that some of its early sponsors hoped. It acted as a rallying point for discontented Liberals into the late 1880s, with some of its branches – particularly that in Hulme – surviving into the period of Gladstone's fourth ministry. It was unable, however, to retain the active support of many of those influential Radicals who had supported Pankhurst's candidature in the by-election, such as H.J. Roby and R.D. Darbishire. George Payne, the president of the Association, led it into

---

[54] *MEN*, 5 October 1883.

[55] *MG*, 5 October 1883.

[56] *MG*, 5 October 1883.

[57] *ME*, 9 October 1883.

[58] The Radicals were particularly concerned not to be seen as a one-man organisation and Payne emphasised that only when he was satisfied that the newly formed Radical Association would be free of any automatic pledge to support Pankhurst or any other Radical candidate, did he agree to support its formation. It was probably for similar reasons that Pankhurst declined to serve on the Association's provisional organising committee, although he did promise the Association his support. *ME*, 10 October 1883; *ME*, 9 October 1883.

the role of an internal party pressure group, acting as the Radical conscience of Manchester Liberalism and ensuring that 'official' Liberalism had at least to listen to the Radical wing of the party. However, in the first year of its existence few major issues of principle divided Radicals from mainstream Manchester Liberalism. The Association criticised the proposed grant of £4,000 per annum as an allowance to the retiring Speaker of the House of Commons.[59] It condemned Lords amendments to contagious diseases legislation and gave public support to Chamberlain's Merchant Shipping Bill.[60] These were, however, scarcely issues that would rouse mass public support behind the Radical Association. The issue of the age was the Lords' rejection of Gladstonian franchise reform. On this issue the Liberal Party had discovered an enemy that would serve to unite all but the most Whiggish factions behind the party leadership. Faced with a common foe, the Radical Association had little stomach for further factionalism, still less separatism, and the organisation quickly began to look like just another propaganda arm of the Liberal Party. The Radicals did have a distinctive policy on the issue – calling for the complete abolition of the hereditary chamber – although this was a view shared by many Liberals outside the Radical Association, and was hardly controversial enough to divide Liberal ranks at a time of widespread anger at the Lords' action.[61] At a special council meeting of the Liberal Association at the beginning of October 1884 a resolution calling for the abolition of the House of Lords was carried almost unanimously.[62]

There were few apologists for the Lords in the ranks of local Liberal leaders. In July the council had called for 'speedy reform' of the Lords and the abolition of the veto, before organising a massive demonstration in Pomona Gardens, in support of the Franchise Bill, attended by Lord Hartington and John Bright.[63] Having attracted Hartington to speak, some local Liberal leaders were anxious not to risk offending Lancashire's leading Liberal peer, who disapproved of the Franchise issue being turned into one about the future of the second chamber.[64] The Pomona Demonstration Committee therefore decided not to allow any resolution to be put forward on the issue of the Lords' veto. Unsurprisingly the Radicals were outraged and condemned the proposed Pomona rally as 'worthless and misleading' unless it accepted motions on the future of the second chamber.[65] On this occasion the weight of Liberal opinion and sentiment was with the Radicals. Despite Hartington's presence, Radicals were allowed to move an additional resolution at the meeting calling for the complete abolition of the Lords – a resolution that only about 20 of the press's estimated 'scores of thousands' present, opposed.[66]

---

59 *MG*, 29 February 1884.

60 *MG*, 9 April 1884.

61 *MG*, 14 July 1884; *MG*, 19 July 1884.

62 MLA, Council Meeting, 1 October 1884, MCL, M283/1/1/1.

63 MLA, Council Meeting, 11 July 1884, MCL, M283/1/1/1.

64 *MG*, 28 July 1884.

65 *MG*, 24 July 1884.

66 *MG*, 28 July 1884

Lancashire Liberalism seemed almost unanimous in its opposition to the action of the Lords. Although Radicals had played a major part in the Liberal campaign against the Lords, there was no real internal party battle to be fought on the issue. The episode had merely brought into question the need for a separate Radical Association, as on the main issue of the day 'official' Liberalism seemed open to Radical views. Moreover, 'official' Liberalism seemed to have learnt something from the disputes that arose during the 1883 by-election. In the face of public opinion the Liberal demonstration committee compromised and allowed Radicals to bring forward their resolution, despite the offence that it could have caused to one of their most influential patrons. There were also signs that the Liberal Association's central committees were increasingly worried by their inability to incorporate all elements of the party within their own organisation. Despite the claims that the by-election had been a victory for party discipline, many were worried that Liberal supporters were somewhat suspicious of their party's governing committees, unaware of how the Association was constituted and did not understand how they could become involved. The general purposes committee was commissioned to bring forward proposals to increase general understanding of the representative character of Liberal organisation.[67] This led to a wide-ranging discussion that frankly recognised the widespread ignorance of how the party machinery worked. It was clear to party leaders that not only did the organisation have to be representative of active Liberals in order to have legitimacy, it also had to be seen to be representative. Various remedies were proposed aimed at increasing attendance, including improved advertisements and new meeting locations.[68] The suggestions were later embodied in a circular from the Association headquarters to all ward secretaries, emphasising that ward branch committees should be 'large and thoroughly representative'.[69]

Although it is difficult to calculate the precise changes this brought to the overall political orientation of the committees, its most significant effect was to make the Liberal Association appear more democratic in its composition and transparent in its operation than had appeared during the October by-election. By showing Liberal electors that they wished actively to encourage their party's supporters to stand for election to party bodies, and by making it clear how they could do so, Radical criticism of the organisation could be blunted. As it was unlikely that completely new members would gain sufficient support to progress directly onto the executive committee or council, any new influx of members probably had more influence at ward level, leading to an expansion of local committees, rather than changing the fundamental balance at the centre. Moreover, Manchester's Liberal Association was not as formally democratic as the original 'Birmingham model', as it allowed for the selection of co-optative members onto its central committees.[70] Of an executive committee of around 80 active members, up to 30 could be co-optative members.

67 MLA, Executive Committee, 17 November 1883, MCL, M283/1/1/1.

68 MLA, General Purposes Committee, 10 December 1883, MCL, M283/1/1/1.

69 MLA, Circular to Ward Secretaries, 1 January 1884, MCL, M283/1/1/1.

70 Whitaker, 'The Growth of Liberal Organisation', 94.

The active membership of the council was usually around 300, which could have included 100 co-optative members.[71] One should not assume, however, that co-option was necessarily used by the right wing of the party to overwhelm Radicals democratically chosen through the ward branches. Indeed some Radicals benefited from the co-optative system. The co-optative members of the executive committee in 1884 included prominent Radicals J.H. Crosfield, Percy Glass, H.J. Roby and S. Norbury-Williams.[72] Yet, in general, the system favoured the re-nomination of incumbents. In 1884 the first 50 names of the retiring council from the previous year were re-elected *en bloc*, leaving the other 66 candidates to fight for the remaining 50 places. However, most of these 50 incumbents who were automatically elected were some of the most well-known Liberals in Manchester who would have easily succeeded in a direct election by ward branches, had this been necessary. In 1884 these incumbents included MPs Jacob Bright and John Slagg, veteran Liberal Sir Thomas Bazley, and senior alderman Joseph Thompson. The problem was that many upper-middle-class Liberals active in the city's politics no longer lived within the city's municipal or parliamentary boundaries and consequently were not in a position to be elected by the ward committees to the Liberal Association's central representative bodies. Of the 50 incumbents re-elected *en bloc* to the 1884 Liberal council, Jacob Bright lived in Alderley Edge, Ald. Schofield in Old Trafford, Ald. Thompson in Wilmslow, James Worthington in Sale and Sir Thomas Bazley in Stow-on-the-Wold![73] Although some of these individuals could have stood for direct election, on account of their business qualifications in the central wards, the only way to ensure that all those who had an interest in Manchester Liberalism could take part in local organisation was to adopt some form of co-optative system.[74] Manchester's parliamentary boundaries included little of the newly developing suburbia that would be included in the municipality from 1885 onwards. After the redistribution of parliamentary seats in 1884, Manchester was given just six parliamentary divisions, emphasising just how small the parliamentary borough was compared with other large cities, leaving large tracts of Manchester's suburbia isolated from the city in county constituencies. As Manchester's party organisation largely serviced the area within the parliamentary boundaries, ways were clearly needed to involve those who saw Manchester as their political base but did not make it their home.

71 MLA, Executive Committee and Council Meeting, 29 February 1884, MCL, M283/1/1/1. Precise figures for attendance were rarely recorded in the minute books, particularly for the Council, and it seems likely that the numbers attending varied markedly depending on the nature of the business being discussed. It is impossible, therefore, to say whether co-optative members had better attendance records than elected members, although it is clear if they could all have been persuaded to attend they would have clearly made up a substantial proportion of voting members.

72 MLA, Executive Committee, 29 February 1884, MCL, M283/1/1/1.

73 MLA, Council Meeting, 29 February 1884, MCL, M283/1/1/1.

74 By the mid-1880s it seems that most urban Liberal Associations used co-option as a way of increasing subscribers and activists. See M. Ostrogorski, *Democracy*, 335.

The need to make Liberal Party organisation 'representative' of the Liberal electorate had to be balanced with the need to involve large numbers of largely middle-class activists resident outside the city who brought much needed money and labour to assist the party cause. Yet it is significant that few who sought positions on the party's central committees were excluded from participation by the process of co-option – it was rather a way of involving anyone who could bring physical or material assistance to the party. In 1884 only 14 Liberals who sought membership of the executive committee by co-option were excluded, and just 16 of the 116 candidates for co-option for the council failed to secure election.[75] Therefore although co-optative mechanisms did undermine the notion that central committees were directly and proportionately representative of local opinion, the co-option process was relatively open and few activists who sought membership of these decision-making bodies were excluded. They allowed Radical as well as 'moderate' sections of the party to obtain positions on the executive and council, giving the elected members a form of patronage which could be dispensed to encourage dissentient members to remain within the ranks of the party, securing for them a position which some of the more controversial figures may have struggled to obtain if they had been forced to rely on direct election.

With the Liberal Party united in opposition to the House of Lords and the Manchester Liberal Association seemingly anxious to appear, at least, more democratic and representative in its operations, the prospects for an independent Radical challenge at future elections was much diminished. Any lingering prospects of a permanent party split ended with the decision of Richard Pankhurst to move his family to London and accept the Liberal candidature for Rotherhithe in 1885.[76] With the removal of Manchester's most prominent Radical to London, there was no obvious alternative independent Radical candidate, even if the Radical Association had been inclined to support such a candidature. Significantly none of Pankhurst's supporters seemed to have considered following his example, permanently leaving the Manchester Liberal Association. Leading figures in the Pankhurst campaign, such as H.J. Roby and Percy Glass, continued to serve on the Association's executive committee and George Payne, the president of the Radical Association, was among those placed on the 1884 general purposes committee which managed day-to-day local party business.[77] George Mason, a key organiser of the Pankhurst campaign, was placed on the registration committee, which oversaw the local party's crucial pre-election campaign.[78] Leading Radicals seemed largely reconciled to a future within the organs of 'official' Liberalism.

Following the election of the Liberal Association's committees in 1884, something of an equilibrium had been restored within the party's ranks. A three-

---

75 MLA, Council Meeting, 29 February 1884, MCL, M283/1/1/1.

76 R. Butler, *As They Saw Her...Emmeline Pankhurst* (London, 1970), 18–20.

77 MLA, Executive Committee, 29 February 1884 and 11 March 1884, MCL, M283/1/1/1.

78 MLA, Executive Committee, 11 March 1884, MCL, M283/1/1/1.

member borough had given the Liberals two seats, with John Slagg representing an older Liberal tradition and Jacob Bright the more Radical wing of the party.[79] In the absence of another Radical candidate, future conflict over parliamentary candidates seemed a distant prospect. However, redistribution of seats and the division of the borough into six separate parliamentary constituencies soon disturbed the apparent equilibrium. The issues of party organisation, committee reform and the selection of parliamentary candidates were again opened by the necessity of a complete reorganisation of the Manchester Liberal Association in response to these changes. The changes were certainly dramatic. The three men who were to represent Manchester Liberalism in parliament after 1886, Charles Schwann (MP North Manchester 1886–1918), Sir Henry Roscoe (MP South Manchester 1885–95) and Jacob Bright (MP South-West Manchester 1886–95) all professed Radical views, seemingly indicating a triumph for Radicalism – and yet several of Manchester's leading Radical politicians and organisers of the early 1880s had left the party by 1886. This remarkable turnaround can only be understood by a close examination of the fundamental changes brought about by the reorganisation of Manchester Liberalism in the wake of the Redistribution Bill.

The Manchester Liberal Association did not develop a policy towards the details of the Redistribution Bill until late in December 1884. Special sub-committees gradually assembled a plan for the division of the city.[80] The plans would have created constituencies almost all of which included both middle-class commercial areas and working-class industrial districts – avoiding class-based constituencies. Yet the boundary commissioner rejected them on precisely this ground, pointing out that he was instructed to keep together areas of similar economic characteristics 'and so far as possible to have the artisan population grouped together'.[81] Liberal Party managers immediately saw problems for the future party in a city divided on economic lines. Some felt there was a danger that poorer divisions would be neglected whilst wealthier divisions prospered. There were also fears that indirect bribery, through private patronage of localities, would be much easier and that local sectional interests would be able to dictate terms to candidates.[82] Even if these prophecies proved to be overstated, it was clear that single-member constituencies were about to revolutionise the way in which city politics was managed and organised.

Manchester Liberal Association's boundary sub-committee was acutely aware of the need to rapidly reorganise the party to meet the new conditions. It recommended immediate steps be taken to initiate party organisation in the new divisions and the Association agreed to establish a provisional consultative committee made up of the chairmen and secretaries of the branch committees and the officers of the central

[79] See language used in a speech of T. Wright at Homer St Schools, *ME*, 4 October 1883.

[80] MLA, Executive Committee, 9 December 1884, MCL, M283/1/1/1.

[81] MLA, Executive Committee, 8 January 1885, MCL, M283/1/1/1.

[82] Letter, C.J. Hurst, *MG*, 1 January 1885.

Liberal Association to oversee this work.[83] There was never, it seems, any question of the central committees or council formally exercising control over matters of divisional policy or the selection of divisional candidates. The special committee recommended that divisional councils should be responsible for candidates, and there were no reported objections to this suggestion.[84] There was a strong feeling, however, that a city like Manchester needed some organisation to represent Liberalism across the city and co-ordinate important functions. It was thus agreed that the various divisional councils should come together in a 'United Liberal Council of Manchester' when required and that a consultative committee be formed made up of the officers of the United Council and of each divisional council.[85]

Not all Liberals, however, were willing to wait for the Manchester Liberal Association to sanction a new form of organisation. South-West Manchester divisional Liberal Association was the only new divisional association to be formed from two existing ward branches, without any re-drawing of boundaries, and was the first to assert its authority.[86] The division was generally regarded as the strongest new constituency of the Liberal Party, as well as being an important centre of Radical influence, being home to the Hulme Radical Club.[87] It was not surprising, therefore, that Liberals in this division were anxious to secure the services of existing Radical Liberal MP Jacob Bright as their standard bearer. A special meeting was called of the ward committees for the St. George's and Medlock Street wards on the initiative of Robert Gibson, the chairman of the St. George's ward branch. Concerned that other divisions would soon call upon Bright, he urged that they should be the first to approach him. Gibson knew that the course he had taken would be controversial and that some would argue that an open meeting of Liberal ratepayers should be called to select any future candidate, but urged local Liberals to remember that 'in the first instance the ward committees always fulfilled that duty.'[88]

Despite widespread respect for Bright, not all Radicals were prepared to allow ward committees elected 12 months previously to choose their candidate. L.D. Prince, a publicly-declared supporter of Bright, accused the meeting of being unrepresentative and recalled the controversial way in which the previous year's committee elections had taken place, excluding many from the Radical wing of the party. Prince's attempt to delay selection until the new committee elections failed.[89] His action, however again brought into question what the legitimate functions of a local Liberal association were and how local leaders were to be selected. Some openly charged the South-West Liberal leaders with dictating the selection of a

83 MLA, Executive Committee, 8 January 1885, MCL, M283/1/1/1.

84 MLA, Executive Committee, 20 January 1885, MCL, M283/1/1/1.

85 MLA, Executive Committee, 20 January 1885, MCL, M283/1/1/1; *ME*, 21 January 1885.

86 Whitaker, 'The Growth of Liberal Organisation', 76–7.

87 *MG*, 27 November 1885; *ME*, 13 January 1885.

88 *ME*, 8 January 1885.

89 *ME*, 8 January 1885.

parliamentary candidate.[90] Others emphasised the need for rapid action to start up new Liberal associations to prevent the sort of divisions that were already opening up at Hulme.[91]

Radicals, once the enemy of the caucus, began to see an opportunity to make party machinery more 'representative' and to increase Radical influence over the selection of candidates. New local party bodies could be used to check the power of individuals and small party cliques. Just as L.D. Prince opposed the action of an unrepresentative Liberal committee in attempting to select fellow Radical Jacob Bright for South-West Manchester, George Mason cautioned those who were attempting to push forward the claims of his old ally Richard Pankhurst in North-East Manchester before Liberal electors had properly been consulted through new representative party organisation.[92] In an ironic change of circumstance from 1883, Manchester's two leading Radical parliamentary prospects were being warned by their own Radical party managers not to accept candidatures unless they were offered by the legitimate new divisional associations. The muscles of grass-roots Radicalism were being flexed. Previously party committees had used the caucus to legitimise their own decisions. Now Radicals were using party machinery to limit committee power.[93]

The situation in Hulme was calmed somewhat by Jacob Bright's response to the invitation to stand for South-West Manchester. In order not to disappoint local Radicals, he announced that when the South-West divisional association was officially formed he would consent to stand – but only if it could be shown that he was the desired choice of the constituency.[94] Bright made the democratisation of local associations a precondition of his acceptance of the candidature – a move that would have great significance for the rest of Manchester.[95] Unfortunately, the divisions in South-West Manchester were not quick to heal. When the official meetings were called for St. George's and Medlock Street wards there was a significant demonstration of Radical force against the former party leaders in the districts. L.D. Prince replaced W.P. Wainwright, an ally of Robert Gibson who had initiated the unconstitutional meeting of the old committees in early January,[96] as the honorary secretary of the Medlock

90 Letter, W. Rothwell, *ME*, 9 January 1885.

91 Letter, 'WW, Mcr', *ME*, 10 January 1885.

92 Letter, G. Mason, *MG*, 9 January 1885.

93 Some on the left of the party continued to be suspicious of Liberal Party organisation, even in its revised form. In Hulme there were calls for a working-men's candidate to be selected by the engineers and joiners of the area with a view to being adopted thereafter as a labour candidate by both parties. There were also calls for the Liberal Party to allow Irishmen to select their own parliamentary representative in North-East Manchester, with Charles Russell being suggested as a possible Irish candidate. In general, however, it seemed that Radicals had learned the lessons of 1883 – that without party machinery electoral prospects were poor. Letter, J. Daryshire, *MG*, 13 January 1885; Letter T.F. Kelly, *ME*, 10 January 1885.

94 *Manchester Weekly Times*, 17 January 1885.

95 *MG*, 13 January 1885.

96 *ME*, 16 January 1885.

Street branch. Tension between rival factions continued – with Radicals accused of 'packing' Liberal ward meetings.[97]

The Radical successes in South-West Manchester may have been the inspiration for the next Radical campaign – the attempt to remove co-optative members from the constitution of local Liberal Associations. Although there is no direct evidence that the co-optative system necessarily disproportionately favoured the centre-right of the party, many Radicals objected on principle to non-elected representatives. One old Chartist characterised co-optative selection as 'essentially vicious, a "House of Lords" created in the very heart of the governing body, who are responsible to nobody and who have no constituents to face'.[98] It was not just that co-optative members were unaccountable, some believed they were positively harmful to the vitality of local Liberal politics. Conservative advances in recent municipal elections in Ardwick, New Cross and St. Michael's were blamed on the failure of aldermen and co-optative members of the Liberal council to keep in close contact with ward organisations and train the activists of the future. By using co-option as a political honour to be conferred on the worthy, the activity of the party suffered, especially in working-class wards.[99]

The first major challenge to the co-optative system was in the largely working-class North-East Manchester division. In order to limit outside influence, it was suggested that only local voters should be eligible for nomination to the divisional council.[100] The problem with such a restriction was that it would have excluded senior Liberals who made a significant contribution to local politics. Ald. Walton Smith, a leading sanitary reformer from the centre-left of the party, opposed the move on the grounds that it would deprive the division of C.P. Scott and H.C. Pingstone, both identified with the Radical wing of the party, and the proposal was defeated. Ultimately North-East Manchester Liberals voted to retain co-optative membership, although on a much reduced basis. The proportion of co-optative members to elected members – one to ten – was much smaller than had formerly existed on the old Manchester Liberal Association council and executive, suggesting a desire to retain co-option for only a very limited number of senior sponsors and subscribers.[101]

In the largely working-class district of South-West Manchester, the scene of recent Radical election successes, further attempts were made to exclude co-optative members from the main ward management bodies. The proposals were defeated by a majority of just three and although calls to hold a public meeting on the subject

---

97 Letter, 'An Old Worker In The Ward', *MG*, 3 February 1885.

98 Letter, 'An Old Chartist...', *MG*, 17 February 1885.

99 Letter, 'An Old Chartist...', *MG*, 17 February 1885.

100 Statement at meeting, *MG*, 18 February 1885.

101 *MG*, 18 February 1885; 100 additional members could be co-opted onto the old Manchester Liberal Association Council and 30 onto the old Manchester Liberal Association Executive Committee – nominal membership is unclear but attendance at these committees averaged around 300 and 80 respectively – see above (footnote 71); MLA, Executive Committee and Council Meeting, 18 December 1884, MCL, M283/1/1/1.

failed, the matter was not left there.[102] At the first meeting of the Liberal council for Medlock Street ward, Radicals succeeded in passing a resolution to ensure that only ward residents were chosen as co-optative members.[103] Similar rules were later adopted in nearby Oxford ward.[104] Outside these Radical strongholds, however, efforts to restrict co-option failed. In Cheetham ward, part of the Northern division, moves to delete co-optative membership from the constitution were defeated 26-13, whilst in the middle-class Exchange ward, a move to end co-optative membership secured just two votes.[105] Although there is little doubt that in some wards there was a resentment to co-optative membership being given to largely middle-class Liberals from the suburbs as a political honour, reasons of local prestige and patronage, as well as practical politics, meant that trying to exclude those from outside the district from local caucuses was going to be difficult. Had New Cross Ward decided to exclude co-optative members both the ward president and vice president, both Radicals, would have been removed. Other large working-class wards may also have worried that to end co-option meant running the risk of losing middle-class patrons, including Radicals such as Edwin Guthrie, S. Norbury Williams and even Richard Pankhurst. However much Liberals on the left of the party valued the principles of local democracy and accountability, they had to be balanced by the practical requirements of local ward politics.

Devolution of power to local divisional associations created other problems. By May 1885 the residual Liberal Association executive committee were becoming aware of the need to co-ordinate the efforts of individual divisional associations in key aspects of campaign work. It had been decided as early as January to recommend that the various divisional councils of Manchester should meet together in a United Liberal Council of Manchester and that a joint consultative committee be formed to co-ordinate the work of the divisions.[106] By mid-May the central Liberal executive was faced with the issue of how to ensure that the cornerstone of their work – the annual registration campaign – was conducted effectively. The new divisional associations had only just been elected so unsurprisingly the executive recommended that the six divisional executives appoint members to a Joint Consultative Committee to consider the registration question with members of the old central executive.[107] When this recommendation reached the South-West divisional association, it seemed to the Radical section led by L.D. Prince that the old centralised methods of party management were reasserting themselves. The resolution put forward for adoption by the executive of the South-West division not only agreed to the establishment of a JCC, but also allowed for apparently unlimited co-option of other Liberals unconnected with the new divisional associations. Many Radicals saw this as an

102 *MG*, 23 March 1885.

103 *MG*, 11 April 1885.

104 *MG*, 8 April 1885.

105 *MG*, 11 April 1885; *MG*, 12 March 1885.

106 MLA, Executive Committee, 20 January 1885, MCL, M283/1/1/1.

107 MLA, Executive Committee, 18 May 1885, MCL, M283/1/1/1.

attack on the representative characteristics and independence of their new association. It seemed that the benefits single-member constituencies had conferred were being taken away. A Radical attempt to force the South-West division to reconsider the central executive committee's proposals was defeated. Prince resigned in disgust from the association, claiming it had lost all its independence, taking with him several disillusioned colleagues.[108] Most Radicals, however, reluctantly accepted a compromise with at least one going on to serve on the distrusted JCC.[109]

The degree of conflict over organisation varied partly because not all that many well-known Liberals were willing to offer themselves as candidates for the less winnable parliamentary seats. The supposedly 'safe' seat of South-West Manchester had been reserved for Bright by local Radicals, whilst the other Liberal incumbent John Slagg accepted the most prestigious division which contained most of Manchester's commercial and business community, North-West.[110] Unless they were able to attract wealthy outsiders, local figures, often with limited resources, had to be relied upon. Charles Rowley, a well-known Radical social reformer, would have made a formidable opponent to the incumbent William Houldsworth in North-East Manchester, but was unable to finance a campaign.[111] His position left the way open for the selection of controversial Irish MP, R.P. Blennerhasset.[112]

Blennerhasset was perceived by many English Liberals as being an ideal choice in an English urban constituency with a large Irish electorate. He had represented County Kerry as a Liberal since 1872 when he was elected at the age of just 22. Although he had sat unopposed for Kerry since then, the creation of single member constituencies and the growing nationalist sentiment in Ireland found him looking for a safer seat.[113] Although elected as a supporter of Home Rule, his commitment to the issue had become more ambiguous with time and by 1885 he was declaring himself in favour of merely 'the largest measure of local self-government consistent with maintenance of the full authority of the Imperial Parliament'.[114] The North-East Manchester Liberal council elected Blennerhasset as their candidate by a large majority, apparently assuming that his views would still satisfy Irish electors. At Blennerhasset's first meeting in support of his candidature, it soon became clear that the Irish were far from unanimous in support of the newly selected Liberal candidate. Amidst considerable protest and disorder a hostile amendment rejecting Blennerhasset's candidature attracted considerable support from the many Irishmen present.[115] It was the beginning of some uncomfortable months for North-East Manchester's Liberals. With few Irishmen formally involved in party councils, Liberals misjudged just how much Blennerhasset's vacillating views on Home Rule

---

108 *MG*, 9 July 1885.

109 *MG*, 23 April 1885; *MG*, 9 July 1885.

110 Whitaker, 'The Growth of Liberal Organisation', 77–8.

111 *ME*, 23 January 1885.

112 *MG*, 5 June 1885.

113 *MG*, 5 June 1885.

114 *MG*, 5 June 1885.

115 *MG*, 18 June 1885.

had marked him down as a traitor in Irish eyes. Howling mobs and death threats greeted the Liberal candidate.[116]

The Liberal council's decision to select and promote Blennerhasset's candidature in the face of so much opposition again brought into question just how 'representative' Liberal organisation was. In South-West Manchester a key component of Liberal support was the Radical group and yet a number, despite getting their own parliamentary candidate chosen, left in disgust after finding they were permanently left in a minority on key bodies. In North-East Manchester a large proportion of Liberal voters were Irish and yet few Irishmen had been actively drawn into Liberal organisations – with the result that perhaps the most unsuitable candidate possible was chosen by the party's council.

In the remaining Manchester city constituencies local candidates were chosen amid much less controversy as it became clear that the new constituency associations were determined to select candidates with more 'advanced' views. Grass-roots Radicalism was in the ascendancy and few 'moderate' Liberals attempted to pursue seats. In North Manchester Radical Charles E. Schwann was a strong candidate with powerful local connections.[117] Schwann had earlier withdrawn from the nomination in South Manchester in favour of Sir Henry Roscoe, also from the 'advanced' wing of the party.[118] Local connections were important here too. Roscoe was probably in a stronger position in the south of the city, and was well known through his work at Owen's College.[119] The Liberal nomination for East Manchester was less fiercely fought over and was the last constituency to select a candidate. It was regarded as 'safe' Conservative territory and it is significant that this was the only constituency – other than the commercial dominated North-West – where a centre-right Liberal candidate was chosen.[120] Sir Alfred Hopkinson, professor of law at Owen's College and a principal and vice chancellor of Victoria University, eventually agreed, somewhat reluctantly, to the solicitations of the East Manchester Liberal Association, whilst privately acknowledging that his prospects for success were poor.[121] Hopkinson was opposed to most of the 'advanced' issues taken up by the party. At the Pomona Gardens rally in the summer of 1884 against the action of the House of Lords, Hopkinson was one of the few who voted against the abolition of the Lords' veto. Despite the Nonconformist background of his family, he was a

116 *MG*, 10 November 1885.

117 Whitaker, 'The Growth of Liberal Organisation', 79; *MG*, 10 June 1885.

118 Schwann was also courted by other constituency parties, notably Accrington. Letter, C. Schwann to J.P. Hartley, 9 June 1886, Bristol University Library, NLC, DM1134.

119 For details of Roscoe's career in Manchester see his autobiography: Sir H.E. Roscoe, *The Life and Experiences of Sir Henry E. Roscoe* (London, 1906). At the time of withdrawing from the South, C.E. Schwann probably knew he was a front runner in the race for the Liberal nomination in North Manchester, as little over a month later after the South Manchester nomination, he was elected without opposition as the Liberal candidate for North. *MG*, 10 June 1885.

120 *MG*, 5 June 1885.

121 Whitaker, 'The Growth of Liberal Organisation', 78; Sir Alfred Hopkinson, *Penultima* (London, 1930), 144–5.

staunch Anglican and had opposed disestablishment ever since his days as an Oxford undergraduate.[122] His final break with the party came soon after the 1885 general election on the Home Rule issue, but he had long been out of step with some in his own local East Manchester Association.[123] Local Liberals adopted Hopkinson despite rather than because of his 'moderate' views.[124]

In the old three-member days Manchester Liberals had traditionally fielded the balanced ticket of two candidates – one from the right and one from the left of the party. Single-member constituencies and the devolution of power to local divisional associations meant that this type of compromise was no longer possible. Candidates were now to be chosen by a simple majority of the divisional councils. This produced mixed results for the various party factions in Manchester. In the event the only Liberal candidate returned in what turned out to be a disastrous election for the party in Manchester, was Sir Henry Roscoe, the least experienced Liberal candidate, but one with clear associations with the Radical wing of the party.[125] There was little surprise about the defeat of Hopkinson in East Manchester at the hands of Arthur Balfour, who had been adopted long before his Liberal rival, in a division which included what was perhaps Manchester's safest Conservative municipal ward, Ardwick.[126] John Slagg, the incumbent Whiggish Liberal MP, chose to fight the middle-class commercial North-West division and in doing so had to face William Houldsworth, an incumbent Conservative. He had chosen unwisely and after being defeated by over 700 votes, left Manchester politics in search of safer territory.[127] In contrast the two most unequivocally Radical candidates – Jacob Bright and Charles Schwann – although both going down to defeat continued in Manchester Liberal politics and were returned to Westminster little over six months later at the scene of their earlier defeats.

For the Radical wing of the party there were considerable reasons for optimism. Despite divisions and the alienation of some grass-roots support in South-West and North-East Manchester, candidates with 'advanced' views had been selected for three of Manchester's six constituencies. Local party managers in the new constituencies were aware of the electoral importance of Radicalism. The new divisional organisations were more open to grass-roots Radical influence and, in the wake of the 1883 by-election, the central Liberal committees were keen to be seen as more inclusive and democratic. The failure of the party's centre-right candidates at the polls reinforced the Radical position. Blennerhassett was humiliated. Slagg

122 Hopkinson, *Penultima*, 51–3.

123 Hopkinson, *Penultima*, 152–4.

124 Even the chairman of one of his election meetings alluded to this fact, expressing the hope that the candidate's views would 'stiffen' during the course of the contest. Hopkinson, *Penultima*, 148, 152–4.

125 See chapter eight.

126 *MG*, 27 November 1885.

127 F.W.S. Craig (ed.), *British Parliamentary Election Results 1885–1918*, second edition (Aldershot, 1989), 150. Slagg later served as MP for Burnley 1887–89 after the death of Peter Rylands.

moved on to Burnley and Hopkinson moved out to the Liberal Unionists. With its leaders gone the centre-right had no obvious future champion in Manchester.

'Moderate' Liberalism had not, however, been completely eclipsed. Ostrogorski argued that growing Radical influence following the division of major urban boroughs was partly due to wealthy middle-class Liberals being reluctant to become involved in more parochial divisional politics.[128] In Manchester, however, organisations such as the Liberal Union committee and the Reform Club allowed wealthier Liberals to remain closely involved in the more prestigious city-wide Liberal politics. Thus the influence of more conservative Liberal business magnates in central party bodies ensured that 'advanced' sections of the party could still be outmanoeuvred, even where Radicals seemed able to dominate in the new local party machinery. The battle for the Liberal parliamentary nomination in the newly created Gorton division of Lancashire illustrated the limits of the authority of the new constituency associations when faced with the opposition of powerful local figures and the party's traditional leadership.

The constituency of Gorton was probably one of the most urban county divisions in the country. By the 1880s it had effectively become an industrial suburb of East Manchester, dominated by the engineering, railway and mining industries. Although separated from Manchester in both municipal and parliamentary terms, it had many political connections with the city, not least because two of the area's most prominent local politicians, George Clay and J.H. Crosfield, also served on the Manchester City Council.[129] The great expansion of the electorate and the creation of a single-member constituency meant that the political composition of the area had yet to be tested by a mass poll, although South-East Lancashire as a whole had a history of returning Liberals under the pre-1885 county franchise.[130] The township of Openshaw was the main centre of Radical activity and had played an important role in the Franchise Bill agitation the previous year. It had a reform club active in local politics and there were close connections between the party and the Nonconformist churches.

The new Liberal Committee for Openshaw developed out of the committee established for franchise agitation in 1884. It was chosen in three parts, unlike most other new Liberal groups who were selected from a public meeting. In all 59 people were selected to represent local workshops and factories, 41 elected from places of worship and 29 'to represent the Reform Club and local and influential gentlemen not included in the above'.[131] Radical J.H. Crosfield was elected chair and quickly became a leading contender for the parliamentary nomination.[132] In opposition to these moves rumours began spreading about a possible entente between some local Liberals and the Conservatives in order to nominate Richard Peacock, a local engineering and

[128] Unfortunately this is not an issue that has been explored widely by historians. Ostrogorski, *Democracy*, 361–2.

[129] *GR*, 18 April 1885; *GR*, 20 March 1886.

[130] *GR*, 17 January 1885; *GR*, 28 February 1885.

[131] *GR*, 24 January 1885.

[132] *GR*, 7 February 1885.

railway magnate, as an independent candidate. Peacock was a 'self-made' man who had begun his career as an apprentice in an engineering firm and went on to establish the world-renowned Beyer Peacock engineering company in Gorton. His decision, as the then locomotive superintendent of the Manchester, Sheffield and Lincolnshire Railway, to remove the company's major railway works to Gorton had established the township as one of Britain's leading railway engineering centres. Peacock was well known for his philanthropic work in the area and had been an important patron of local Nonconformist institutions, particularly the Unitarian church. He also had a long association with the Liberal Party in the old South Lancashire constituency.[133]

Although Peacock had strong local credentials, Radicals regarded him with suspicion, particularly as he had not played an active part in the agitation for the extension of the county franchise. Consequently, rumours of a Whig–Tory entente to promote Peacock's parliamentary nomination was met with Radical contempt and ended any hope there was of Peacock being accepted by the Radicals as a Liberal candidate.[134] Peacock attracted little support in the Liberal council, coming sixth of seven potential candidates in an indicative poll of council members. All three candidates who led the straw poll were clearly identified with the Radical wing of the party, including J.H. Crosfield who led with 86 votes. [135]

Peacock's rejection by the Liberal council failed to deter his supporters, who continued campaigning on his behalf, reminding voters of the philanthropic and financial contribution their champion had made to the district. To Radicals this smacked all too clearly of old-style electioneering based on political patronage and wealth.[136] At the formal Liberal selection meeting Crosfield defeated fellow Radical George Clay by 88 votes to 46.[137] Peacock's supporters, however, refused to accept the decision and pushed for an adjournment. The adjournment motion was defeated, but only narrowly by 59 to 48 – perhaps the worst possible result for party unity. Crosfield had been officially adopted but the large number of votes for the adjournment gave weight to those in Peacock's camp who believed he had been unfairly treated.[138] Some interpreted it as a sign of a gradual change of opinion in the Liberal council and clearly believed that if continued pressure was applied the issue would be reopened.[139] Within days of the official selection meeting a committee of Peacock's supporters had been formed with the intention of overturning the council's decision. Many were clearly suspicious of the new 'caucus'-style associations, hinting at the possibility of an independent candidature, while G.H. Underwood, who had tried

---

[133] Peacock had served as chairman of Gladstone's Committee for South Lancashire in the 1865 election and had been actively involved in the 1880 general election campaign. Manchester Cutting Collection, vol II 1880–92, 56–7, MCL, F942.7389 M119; *MCN*, 9 March 1889.

[134] Letter, T.D. Sykes, *GR*, 28 February 1885.

[135] *GR*, 14 March 1885; *GR*, 18 April 1885.

[136] Letter, 'An Elector', *GR*, 25 April 1885.

[137] *MG*, 18 May 1885, *GR*, 18 April 1885.

[138] *MG*, 18 May 1885.

[139] *MG*, 18 May 1885.

to foster Liberal–Conservative co-operation in the local board election, defended Peacock's action in receiving a Conservative deputation by arguing that this simply demonstrated his suitability and 'the breadth of [his]... Liberalism'.[140]

As Crosfield's campaign developed, his brand of working-class Radicalism became more vocal and pronounced. He made a great virtue of his humble wealth relative to the plutocrat Peacock and Radical supporters responded with more explicit class-based appeals, and attacks on Peacock's 'money bags'.[141] Unsurprisingly the Radical labour position that was being adopted further alienated the right wing of the Liberal Party. One 'moderate' went as far as accusing Crosfield of attempting to imitate the revolutionary Socialists of Paris in his 'hysterical ravings about capital, capitalists and labour'.[142] Others merely saw him as an irresponsible and offensive agitator.[143] Peacock attempted to rally 'moderate' Liberals and Conservatives behind his candidature by exploiting these concerns. However, in order to convince Liberals that he continued to be a supporter of the party, Peacock was forced to produce a detailed statement of his views on contemporary issues. In it he declared himself in favour of the Affirmation Bill, reform of the Land Laws, the House of Lords, disestablishment and county boards.[144] Peacock's views clearly surprised many Conservatives who were totally unprepared for the announcement. It was clear that the policy difference between even 'moderate' Liberals and the Conservative mainstream was much greater than Peacock had appreciated. Conservative opinion quickly turned against Peacock and by mid-July the party had found an alternative candidate in D.I. Flattely. Significantly, his principal platform was the defence of the House of Lords and the Established church.[145]

Liberals from outside Gorton were alarmed at the conflict between Crosfield and Peacock and external pressure was soon applied for a settlement. External arbitration seemed to be the only answer. Peacock believed external Liberal arbitrators would rule in favour of the candidate strongest placed to win the seat – and the one, no doubt, who could demonstrate that he could finance an effective campaign. Radicals simply assumed arbitration would assess whether or not the correct selection procedures had been followed and whether Crosfield had been selected fairly.[146] After private negotiations it was agreed to refer the whole matter to a jointly selected arbitration committee without restriction or reservation on the issues that would be assessed.[147] By not giving the arbitrators a clear remit, however, it was soon clear that Radicals had surrendered a significant hostage to fortune. The battle lines had been drawn in largely ideological terms – between a Chamberlainite Radical Liberal, J.H. Crosfield, and a candidate of the 'Gladstonian, Hartingtonian and Goschenite

140 *GR*, 13 March 1885, *MG*, 20 May 1885.

141 *MG*, 17 June 1885.

142 Letter, J. Murray, *GR*, 11 July 1885.

143 Letter, 'In Tenebris', *GR*, 13 June 1885.

144 *MG*, 16 May 1885.

145 *GR*, 25 July 1885.

146 J.H. Crosfield at Denton, after accepting arbitration, *MG*, 6 November 1885.

147 *MG*, 5 November 1885; *GR*, 7 November 1885.

section' in the shape of Richard Peacock.[148] Both candidates were allowed to choose two arbitrators, although convention dictated that they would have to be very senior Liberal figures in the city. Peacock's nominees were the sitting local MPs William Agnew and John Slagg, while Crosfield opted for Ald. John Harwood and Thomas Ashton, president of the newly formed United Liberal Councils of Manchester.[149] Ideologically all four were associated with the centre-right of the party, and if made on this ground alone, Crosfield's choices would seem hard to explain. It can only be assumed that Crosfield had nominated his arbitrators largely through personal considerations of their integrity and judgement. Ald. John Harwood was a colleague of Crosfield on the Manchester City Council and one may have expected Thomas Ashton, as president of the city's Liberal 'caucus' to be a staunch defender of the rights of the newly formed Liberal Associations to select their own candidates. Unfortunately this confidence was misplaced.

The whole attitude of 'official Liberalism' to Peacock was very different to that afforded to Pankhurst, the last 'independent' Liberal candidate in the Manchester area. Pankhurst, although he had resigned from the party organisation, had never worked with an opposing party or opposed an officially adopted Liberal candidate. Peacock had done both and cheerfully admitted to the same. Yet the result of the Gorton arbitration was unanimously in favour of the rebel. Whether the arbitration committee found any serious maladministration or misconduct in the Gorton, Openshaw and Denton Liberal councils is not known for just as they declined to give any reasons for their decision, they also made no recommendations for the Gorton Liberal Association in the future. This may have been a sensible attempt to close the matter and curtail harmful future discussion, but if it was it was not entirely successful. Crosfield himself, having agreed to submit to arbitration, had little choice but to accept the decision – to do otherwise would only have led to certain defeat and probably jeopardised his career as a councillor in East Manchester. Crosfield sympathisers were less circumspect and organised a protest meeting where 'the money bags and the Whigs, who at present control the Liberal Party', were roundly condemned.[150] There were clear signs that some Radicals felt they had been sadly misled by the arbitration process and the leaders of the Manchester Liberal organisations who had in effect denied the legitimacy of their own local Liberal councils.[151]

In 1883 Radicals had been accused of threatening the Liberal Party organisation by running a candidate in defiance of the official movement. Now it was the Radicals who were charging the party leaders in Manchester with conspiring to foist an

---

148 *GR*, 14 November 1885.

149 *MG*, 10 November 1885.

150 *MG*, 23 November 1885.

151 'The Radical electors of that division had been hoodwinked... Mr Peacock had attempted to override the constituency, and had to a large extent extinguished Liberal organisation in that division. If any man was allowed to foist himself on that constituency independent of any Liberal organisation, then all he could say was good-bye to Liberal organisation in the future.– (Cheers)', T.H. Dillow, a supporter of Crosfield, *MG*, 27 November 1885.

independent candidate on a constituency that had already freely elected an 'official' Liberal candidate through its own representative machinery. However, as in 1883, the Radicals lost the argument at the polls. Many Radicals would not support a Conservative at any price and with an election imminent there was an acute sense of potential costs of rebellion. Radical support was not to be given without conditions, however, and Peacock was made 'well aware that any future backsliding will inevitably terminate his Parliamentary career'.[152]

Crosfield saw the futility of trying to oust a sitting MP and left Gorton politics.[153] With the removal of Crosfield from the division, the new MP seemed keen to do all he could to build bridges with the Radical wing of the Liberal Party. He was soon sharing platforms with Richard Pankhurst, professing his commitment to Home Rule and even suggesting the abolition of the House of Lords.[154] This was enough to convince Radical leader Thomas Woolfenden, a long time supporter of Crosfield, that Peacock was indeed 'a good Liberal' despite what had gone before.[155] The change that had come over Peacock may have, ironically, had much to do with the election of the new divisional Liberal council, which, like its predecessor, had a strong Radical presence. Woolfenden was elected as the president of the new council, while Peacock's leading election aides either did not come forward or were heavily defeated.[156] A well-organised Radical group had again demonstrated their grass-roots popularity and secured leading positions on the Liberal council. The sitting MP could ignore them, fight them, or come to an accommodation with them by adopting at least some Radical policies. In the midst of the confusion and uncertainties of the Home Rule crisis, the desire for political self-preservation, above all else, dictated the latter course.

Manchester's Radicals, once highly suspicious of the apparently closed world of Liberal Association caucuses, and particularly so after the 1883 by-election, saw the reorganisation of the party in 1884–85 as an opportunity. Independent Radical Associations had proved vocal but had limited success in reforming the existing Liberal Association. Only when much more localised – and at least nominally – autonomous divisional Liberal Associations were created could Radicals have a significant say in local decision-making. The level of their influence largely depended on the character of individual divisions. In divisions with a Radical tradition such as South and South-West Manchester, a largely Radical Association could select a Radical candidate. In the largely business and commercial North-West division, they could obtain little say on issues like co-optative membership and were forced to acquiesce in acceptance of a centre-right candidate. In Gorton representative institutions were novel, and the centre-right of the party were unwilling to accept Radical domination of the Association, resorting to old-style appeals of personality,

152 Letter, G. Payne, *MG*, 25 November 1885.

153 *GR*, 6 March 1886.

154 *GR*, 8 May 1886.

155 *GR*, 8 May 1886.

156 *GR*, 22 May 1886; *GR*, 5 June 1886.

status and independence to override elected local Liberal Associations. Gorton may have simply represented the death throes of the old system of party management, but the fact that senior Manchester Liberals were prepared to override the 'official' local Association during arbitration suggests that their commitment to more decentralised and representative local politics was not always as strong as they professed. In 1883 Manchester Liberal leaders declared that support of the local Association's collectively agreed position was essential if the whole party organisation was not to break down. In 1885 they overruled the local Association in Gorton in favour of an independent who had previously received a Conservative nomination and, for a time at least, the local party organisation did break down.

The general election of 1886 saw the election of three Liberal MPs for Manchester – C.E. Schwann, Sir Henry Roscoe and Jacob Bright – all of whom were associated with the Radical wing of the party, suggesting that the reorganisation of 1885 brought fundamental change in placing Radical-leaning MPs in the city's three most winnable constituencies. The defeats in 1885 for all three centre-right candidates, John Slagg, R.P. Blennerhassett and Alfred Hopkinson, encouraged all three to move on – Slagg to Burnley, Hopkinson to the Liberal Unionists and Blennerhassett out of English parliamentary politics altogether. Bright and Schwann returned in victory six months later, whilst both East and North-East Manchester selected Radicals to replace former centre-right candidates. Only Henry Lee was left to fight the 'Whig' corner, predictably standing, and predictably losing, in North-West Manchester. Home Rule may have transformed the Liberal Party nationally but locally, in Manchester at least, the increase in the city's parliamentary representation, and consequent overhaul of the party's organisation seemed to open up Liberal politics to Radical influence more than conflicts over Home Rule.

An increase in Radical influence, however, did not amount to a Radical take-over of the party. Indeed it is remarkable how many of those who played a key role in the Radical movements of the 1880s became frustrated and either left the party completely or became peripheral figures. Following his defeat in East Manchester at the 1886 general election, J.H. Crosfield continued his municipal career but never stood for parliament again. George Clay followed his Radical hero Joseph Chamberlain into the political cul-de-sac of Liberal Unionism. L.D. Prince, the influential Radical organiser in Hulme, left the party and eventually joined the ILP. Richard Pankhurst, following a failed candidature in Rotherhithe, returned to haunt Manchester Radicals by becoming active in the Manchester ILP and standing for Gorton as an Independent Labour candidate in 1895. He was again unsuccessful and this former Radical bastion fell to the Conservatives, never again to return to the Liberal Party. By the late 1880s Radicalism had established itself as a strong influence in the new Liberal Party councils, but too slowly and insufficiently for some leaders of the Radical movement. In the short term the loss of figures like Pankhurst and Prince relieved some internal Liberal Party strife but at the cost of losing men who in the future would lead independent political forces against the party to which they once belonged.

CHAPTER TWO

Leicester Liberalism: An Uneasy Alliance

Liberalism in Leicester had faced two major problems since the mid-nineteenth century – one political and one structural. The first problem was the difficulty of reconciling its Radical, Chartist and Secularist elements with the more 'moderate' Nonconformist mainstream. The second was how to spread the influence of 'Red Leicester' to the surrounding county constituencies, for so long Conservative strongholds. The two issues were not unrelated. Indeed the continuing concern over county politics exhibited by Leicester Liberals had significant implications for the nature of Liberal politics in the borough. These twin concerns were brought into sharpest focus during the mid-1880s when corrupt practices legislation, franchise reform and redistribution of parliamentary seats seemingly gave Liberals the opportunity to break out of their Leicester stronghold and challenge Conservative domination of the county. The challenge of county politics was to serve as something of a safety valve for urban Liberalism, with Radicals attracted to rural campaigning by the potential brought about by electoral reforms. As with Manchester, the reforms were to change the structure of local politics and, ultimately, the ideological nature of local Liberalism.

Leicester Liberals were able to assist the county divisions only because of the near hegemonic position they had obtained in the borough. However this position had not been long established and had been bought at the cost of institutionalising the 'moderate' and Radical divisions in Liberal Party ranks. Modern divisions dated back to the Leicester by-election of 1856 when the death of MP Richard Gardner prompted Radical John Biggs to resign the borough mayoralty and come forward as a candidate against moderate Thomas Tertius Paget.[1] In response the moderate Liberals formed an unstable coalition with the Conservatives and it was not until 1865 that the two branches of the Liberal Party were reunited.[2] Only by agreeing to what was in effect a permanent division of the borough's parliamentary representation between the moderate and Radical sections of the party could a semblance of unity be effected. This compromise did not demand that both elements of the party adopted common policies or imply an acceptance of collective party discipline. As late as 1882 Radical MP Peter Taylor continued to make outspoken

---

1 A. Little, 'Chartism and Liberalism, Popular Politics in Leicestershire 1842 to 1847', Unpublished PhD thesis, University of Manchester, 1991, 281.

2 Little, 'Chartism and Liberalism', 282–4.

attacks on Liberal government policy, particularly on Irish issues and imperial policy in Egypt. He also joined with Radical Nonconformist leaders, such as the Rev. J. Page Hopps, in condemning the 'gagging' of parliament – Gladstone's use of the closure motion on Ireland.[3]

Despite these divisions, Liberalism continued to be the dominant force in borough politics – indeed until the 1880s it seemed that, as in Manchester, its diversity was part of its strength. Middle-class Liberalism expressed itself through a highly successful Liberal Club in Gallowtree Gate with 1,000 members – many of whom were actively involved in canvassing at election times and ward organisation.[4] In 1876 Liberal leaders scrapped the old registration society and replaced it with a broader Liberal Association based on the 'Birmingham model', supposedly with the aim of developing a more inclusive and participatory system of party organisation.[5] Meanwhile Taylor continued to represent the largely working-class ex-Chartist tradition in Leicester.[6] Religious Nonconformity also provided Liberalism with an important political constituency. Although the position of Leicester as the 'capital of dissent' has been exaggerated, Nonconformity continued to be an important force in Liberal politics.[7] The staple trade of Leicester – the boot and shoe – was highly unionised and also provided an important plank of Liberal strength. Thomas Smith – the Liberal borough agent for much of the 1880s and 1890s – was the first general secretary of the National Union of Boot and Shoe Operatives. His union successors, George Sedgewick and William Inskip, were also active in the party and became Liberal town councillors.[8]

The Conservatives, in contrast, struggled to make any impact on Leicester politics. In 1881 their major club was said to have barely 100 members – even though reports for public consumption claimed over 1,000.[9] Until the mid-1880s the party lacked any formal representative association for the town or county. In the borough the Conservative Club was the major decision-making body, while in the county the party was more informally organised, generally around prominent local gentry. Up to 1885 this informal county organisation had not proved too much of a weakness. In North Leicestershire the Conservative Party – supported by the powerful Duke of Rutland – had held both seats since 1837. In the Southern division only one Liberal

---

3 M. Elliott, *Victorian Leicester* (London, 1979), 165–6.

4 R. Read, *Modern Leicester* (London, 1881), 259–62.

5 R.A. McKinley and C.T. Smith, 'Parliamentary History since 1835', in R.H. Evans (ed.) *The Victoria History of the County of Leicester*, IV (1958), 224–51.

6 Little, 'Chartism and Liberalism', 284.

7 Figures from the 1851 religious census suggest Leicester actually had less religious accommodation than comparable towns. Moreover some statistics indicate that Anglicanism enjoyed faster growth than Nonconformity in Leicester during the second half of the nineteenth century. See B. Lancaster, *Radicalism, Co-operation, Socialism* (Leicester, 1987), 65–7.

8 B. Lancaster, 'Breaking Moulds: The Leicester ILP and popular politics', in D. James, T. Jowitt and K. Laybourn (eds), *The Centenary History of the Independent Labour Party* (London, 1993), 78–9.

9 Read, *Modern Leicester*, 261–2; Leicester and Leicestershire Conservative Club, First Annual Meeting, 26 March 1881, LRO, DE 1574.

had broken Conservative hegemony between 1832 and 1880.[10] After the reforms of 1884–85 this long-established pattern of borough county politics was broken – the Liberals extending their influence in the county, whilst finding that their internal differences were more and more acute, and their nature as a socially and politically diverse force as much a weakness as a strength.

The resignation or retirement of a sitting MP was often the signal for the renewal of factional rivalries. That had been the case in 1856 and despite the institutionalised division of borough representation between the two major wings of Leicester Liberalism, difficulties were not completely eliminated by this compromise. By February 1884 Liberals were coming to realise they would again soon face the hard choice of selecting new parliamentary candidates – since the 1880 general election Taylor had suffered almost continual poor health.[11] With Alexander McArthur, the representative of 'moderate' Leicester Liberals also incapacitated, after an accident, it became clear that at least one new candidate would have to be found for the forthcoming general election.[12] The Liberal Association – and it seems, the Radical press – were acutely sensitive to the problems that might be experienced if the selection process was not carefully managed. Within a week of Taylor announcing his retirement rumours began circulating that the Liberal Association had appointed a committee to bring forward a list of suggestions for Taylor's replacement. The *Leicester Daily Mercury* – a mainstream Liberal organ – strongly denied the rumours and emphasised that the elected Liberal council – 'the 300' – would 'have the subject entirely in their own hands'.[13] The Radical *Midland Free Press* also moved swiftly to quash rumours that the Liberal executive committee had met privately to discuss a potential short-list.[14] Yet there was a clear attempt, on the part of the senior officials of the Liberal Association, to 'introduce' a favoured candidate, J. Allanson Picton, to Leicester's Liberal electors. Picton was invited as principal speaker and one prominent Liberal was bold enough to publicly suggest that Picton was 'the coming man for Leicester'.[15] Association president E. Clephan, apparently fearful that the cat was to be let out of the bag, quickly assured voters that the executive committee had not yet met to discuss the issue and that the final decision would, in any case, be taken by an open meeting, where several possible candidates could be invited.[16]

Any moves made by the Association leadership to 'manage' the selection of a parliamentary candidate had to be made very carefully and balanced against demands for popular participation in the decision and the need to ensure the decisions gained legitimacy. Even some groups allied to the Liberal Party shared this desire to tread carefully and avoid a damaging split. The Anti-Compulsory Vaccination League,

10 Read, *Modern Leicester*, 261–2.

11 *LDM*, 16 March 1884.

12 *LDM*, 26 January 1884.

13 *LDM*, 20 February 1884.

14 *MFP*, 23 February 1884.

15 *LDM*, 27 February 1884.

16 *MFP*, 1 March 1884.

in bringing forward a motion urging the party to adopt a candidate committed to repealing the 'compulsory' clauses of the Vaccination Acts, made it clear that their stance was in no way designed to foster a party split.[17] The trades council engaged in lengthy discussion about the possibility of bringing forward a labour candidate, but eventually ruled out the suggestion as impractical and decided instead to urge the Liberal Association to adopt Richard Chamberlain as candidate.[18] As time passed it became clear that the Liberal leadership's preferred choice, Picton, lacked universal approval, and as other candidates dropped out of the running, Chamberlain emerged as the major challenger. The Radical and secularist lecturer George Holyoake was rumoured to be a potential alternative, but by making abolition of the parliamentary oath and the blasphemy laws central to his platform, did little to recommend himself to the 'moderate' wing of the party.[19]

Despite assurances from the Liberal Association president that the decision over a candidate would be taken at an open meeting, a preliminary Liberal executive meeting was held in early March narrowed the options available to members by drawing up a short list. The executive justified their action by arguing they were merely simplifying the selection process, but it did mean that between 50 and 60 senior Liberals ruled out the candidature of, among others, Joseph Arch, George J. Holyoake and Francis Schnadhorst.[20] Only Richard Chamberlain, J.A. Picton, Passemore Edwards, C.B. McLaren and Frederick Harrison were permitted to go through to the next stage of the selection. When existing MPs McLaren and Harrison withdrew, the choice was further reduced. This process of elimination, however, did not greatly benefit Picton, who at the subsequent meeting of the Liberal Association general committee was only narrowly successful, taking 99 votes to Chamberlain's 74. With such a large minority supporting Chamberlain, the final decision clearly had to be delayed and the committee adjourned to a further week of deliberations.[21]

The delay was almost fatal to Picton's chances and demonstrated the difficulties Leicester party leaders had in managing their diverse constituency. Picton had been before the Leicester electors, had the apparent support of senior Liberal figures in the town, and by the end of March, the support of Leicester's most influential pressure group, the Anti-Compulsory Vaccination League.[22] In contrast Richard Chamberlain was in Australia as the result of a family bereavement, was almost certainly unaware of his nomination, yet was quickly gathering the support of much of the rank and file and influential trade union organisations. Supporters of Picton urged the party leadership not to wait on Chamberlain's return from Australia and questioned his Radical credentials.[23] This only seemed to galvanise the Leicester Trades Council

17 *LDM*, 7 March 1884; *MFP*, 8 March 1884.
18 *LDM*, 4 March 1884.
19 *MFP*, 15 March 1884
20 *LDM*, 8 March 1884.
21 *LDM*, 19 March 1884.
22 *MFP*, 24 March 1884.
23 See letters, *LDM*, 25 March 1884.

into yet more active support of Chamberlain's candidature, issuing circulars with endorsements of Chamberlain from the Birmingham Trades Council, stressing his suitability for 'a Radical and working class constituency',[24] The Textile and Building Trades Council also responded to attacks on Chamberlain with a pledge of their support.[25]

At the subsequent meeting of the Liberal Association's general council it soon became clear that Chamberlain's campaign had gathered significant momentum. A straw poll was taken giving Chamberlain a majority for the first time taking 116 votes to Picton's 112. Deadlock had been reached. Then, in what may have been a calculated move to undermine Chamberlain's candidature, the Association president, Clephan, proposed that senior representatives contact both nominees to ascertain whether they would be prepared to come to Leicester and address the Association with a view to becoming a candidate.[26] This was an unusual move for two reasons. Firstly, most associations waited until a final poll had been taken before inviting a single potential candidate to address them. Secondly, as Chamberlain was in Australia he was unlikely to be able to respond to such a request. However, given the deadlock, there was probably little alternative.

While the Association waited on the candidates' response, open warfare broke out in the local party. An article in the *Christian World* accused Richard's brother, Joseph Chamberlain, of putting the 'screw' on the Leicester Association – an allegation that was fiercely denied in the mainstream Liberal press.[27] J.H. Woolley, from the trades council, quickly leapt to the defence of Chamberlain, accusing Picton's supporters of class prejudice and making it clear who he thought was guilty of wirepulling:

> I can quite understand the offended dignity of some of our pastors and masters on being asked to support the nominee of a lot of stockingers and shoemakers, the residuum you know, and they seem to forget that they have built their comfortable mansions at Stoneygate out of the sweat of them.[28]

For others, however, bitter memories of past Liberal divisions and their consequences were a powerful incentive not to push their favoured candidate to the point of splitting the party. In terms of personal political beliefs, Picton seemed little different to Chamberlain, as far as any differences could be ascertained, and some were clearly frustrated at Radicals 'squabbling upon side issues'.[29] This may have been part of Joseph Chamberlain's reasoning in expressing his reluctance to call his brother back from Australia – after all Chamberlain's 'Birmingham model' Liberal Association was designed to prevent just these types of split. Understandably too, Joseph Chamberlain was unwilling to call his brother back to what could have easily

24 *LDM*, 25 March 1884.

25 *MFP*, 29 March 1884.

26 *LDM*, 26 March 1884.

27 *LDM*, 29 March 1884.

28 *MFP*, 5 April 1884.

29 See 'Stray Notes', *MFP*, 5 April 1884.

turned into an unpleasant selection contest 'a mere competition, which would be undignified alike to Mr. Picton and Mr. R. Chamberlain'.[30]

Even this move, however, did not end the dispute. At the subsequent meeting of the Liberal general committee, opposition to Picton continued – although without an alternative candidate, the battle was lost.[31] Picton's opponents no longer had a focus for their opposition and had little choice but to acquiesce in the decision. The only real danger to Liberal hegemony in Leicester was a split in the party organisation provoked by an alternative Liberal candidate. Once that had been averted the danger of smaller pressure groups rebelling was limited, given the weak state of Conservatism in the borough. Working-class organisations, such as the trades councils, could have presented a danger if allied to a significant dissident Liberal faction – but alone, with no candidate or independent resources, there was little prospect of a challenge to Liberal authority.

Despite their historical weakness in Leicester, the early 1880s did see some attempts by the Conservatives to widen their appeal to Leicester's working-class electorate. The first election held under conditions of household borough suffrage saw Lord John Manners help organise a Conservative working-men's organisation and this was followed by similar attempts in subsequent elections to build urban working-class support.[32] By May 1884, the Conservatives had secured a candidate from London, Captain Cruikshank, and were preparing to try to exploit the rather lukewarm enthusiasm for Picton's candidature.[33] Thomas Canner, chairman of the Working-Men's Conservative Club, took a prominent part in Cruikshank's lecturing tours, with the club being used as a platform for promoting a 'classless' popular imperialism.[34] The club, only established in the summer of 1883, claimed to have over 500 members and quickly became a model for others in the district.[35] Despite these preparations, the Conservatives still seemed a little caught out by Taylor's resignation in June 1884, and organisational weaknesses were soon exposed. Cruikshank raised expectations of a contest by announcing to the Conservative Working-Men's Club that he was prepared to stand if called upon to do so.[36] This caused considerable problems when the main, largely middle-class, Conservative Club began to consider the implications – and costs – of a contest. While the main club was fairly evenly divided on the question, the Conservative working men felt that Picton must be opposed.[37] Cruikshank seemed to be genuinely undecided, but a financial scandal undermined his candidature when he was fined for failing to pay

30 *LDM*, 3 April 1884.

31 *LDM*, 9 April 1884; *LDM*, 19 April 1884.

32 Evans, *Victoria History*, IV, 224–31.

33 *LJ*, 2 May 1884.

34 *LJ*, 9 May 1884.

35 *LJ*, 4 April 1884.

36 *LDM*, 20 June 1884.

37 *LDM*, 23 June 1884.

certain excise duties on his Brentwood home.[38] The Leicester Radical press did not allow the story to go unnoticed.[39]

Cruikshank was absent from Leicester for some time and when a number of leading Conservatives went to meet their candidate off a London train, Cruikshank failed to materialise.[40] Efforts to secure an alternative candidate through the Carlton Club were equally unsuccessful and on the Carlton's advice the Conservatives decided not to contest Picton's return.[41] Thus the most significant opposition to Picton's return had proved to be from members of his own party during the nomination process. The experience of the by-election confirmed Conservative weakness in the borough, but also revealed just how precarious Liberal unity was. Picton helped the healing process by issuing a manifesto that few Radicals could disapprove with support for manhood suffrage, the abolition of the House of Lords, local option and church disendowment.[42] Picton, like Taylor, was a Radical. Unlike Taylor he had been tamed by local Liberal officials – 'he is also a supporter of the present government – not a thick-and-thin Ministerialist, but at the same time one who will not ride hobbies to the danger of the Liberal Cabinet, or "desert" at dangerous crises...'.[43]

Fear of a party split was not the only reason why Radicals and trade unionists did not press their opposition to Liberal Association decisions. Many Liberals and Radicals were simply not focused on the problems of borough organisation. Conservative strength in the county meant that the Leicester Liberal Association spent much of the 1880s engaged in organising county associations, rather than tackling any deficiencies in their own representative bodies. The county divisions preoccupied urban party managers. The Corrupt Practices Act, the extension of the franchise in the counties and general redistribution of seats brought both a clamour for improved voluntary electoral organisation and bitter partisan battles over electoral 'gerrymandering'. Conservatives, as the dominant political force in the counties, had most to lose from the changes and quickly moved to shore up their position. The Leicester and Leicestershire Conservative Club – as its name suggests – saw itself as responsible for organising the whole of the county. Local organisers warned the club that the passage of the Corrupt Practices Act meant there would be a need for fundamental changes in rural organisation in order to secure the voluntary labour necessary to run successful campaigns. Clubs, rather than associations based on a specific geographical area, became the principal tools of organisation.[44] This was significant for two reasons. Firstly it indicated a reluctance to move to the type of caucus favoured by the Liberals and secondly it allowed the Conservatives to organise their political machinery well before the outcome of the 1885 boundary review had

38 *LJ*, 6 June 1884.

39 *MFP*, 7 June 1884.

40 *LDM*, 25 June 1884.

41 *MFP*, 28 June 1884; *MFP*, 5 July 1884.

42 *LDM*, 21 June 1884.

43 *LDM*, 27 June 1884.

44 *LJ*, 2 May 1884.

become known. Smaller units like clubs did not have to concern themselves with precisely where constituency boundaries would be placed, concentrating instead on working the main population centres.

The Leicester and Leicestershire Conservative Club was itself a major force in creating these new clubs. By 1884 new Conservative clubs had been established in all the major towns in the county – including Hinckley, Melton and Loughborough. Leicester county suburbs Aylestone and Belgrave were similarly provided for, as were major villages such as Syston, Castle Donnington, Kibworth, Syston and Shepshed.[45] The Conservatives were particularly concerned about their prospects in South Leicestershire after surprisingly losing one of their seats in 1880. Hinckley was seen as the principal Liberal centre in the district and steps were taken to try to neutralise this influence. The population of Hinckley was at this time 'chiefly of artisans employed in the lower classes of hosiery manufacture' – an industry with unsettled employment that seemingly encouraged Liberal and Radical politics.[46] The Conservatives, however, also had influential members in the district, and the first meeting of the new town group attracted Col. R.W. Worswick, former high sheriff of Leicestershire, Thomas Cope, a leading local landowner, and Rev. R. Titley, a well-known district clergyman.[47] The Conservatives followed their success in Hinckley by establishing a similar organisation in nearby Market Bosworth. Central to this rural Conservatism was a concern for the 'traditional' aspects of country life – the Anglican church and the agricultural economy. Local clergymen joined together and made an explicit appeal for their colleagues to come forward and help the Conservative effort. Rev R. Watts warned that those clergy not actively assisting the Conservatives were failing to do their duty to themselves, their church and their parishioners. Albert Pell, the local Conservative MP for South Leicestershire darkly pointed to how agricultural interests could become lost in a redistribution favouring the towns and how rural interests could become 'swamped'.[48]

In their drives to reorganise, North Leicestershire was not forgotten. Liberals regarded many of the industrialised villages and suburbs to the north of Leicester as centres of Liberal strength – areas such as Belgrave, Thurmaston, Sileby, Humberstone and Evington.[49] Belgrave had its own local board of health and school board, for which the Liberal Party already had a rudimentary local organisation. Conflict between Nonconformists and Anglicans had rarely arisen in the school board, so it was more difficult here to mobilise the Anglican clergy in defence of educational interests. Until the mid-1880s the Conservatives had enjoyed almost a monopoly of power on the board of health, but by 1885 this had been undermined by renewed Liberal efforts.[50] Partly as a response to this expansion of Liberal activity

[45] *LJ*, 4 April 1884.

[46] *LJ*, 25 April 1884.

[47] *LJ*, 25 April 1884.

[48] *LJ*, 13 June 1884.

[49] *LDM*, 2 December 1885.

[50] *MFP*, 8 March 1884.

in local politics, local MP Lord John Manners supported the formation of a Belgrave Conservative Club in June 1884. Manners, like many county Conservatives, had, however, a rather ambivalent attitude towards formalised party organisation. He reluctantly recognised the need for such organisations after the changes brought by the Corrupt Practices Act, but warned clubs against attempting to exercise too much control over the freedom of elected representatives, there being a danger that 'the freedom of the member will be lost in the obedience of the delegate'.[51] Moreover not only were Conservatives ambivalent about the new organisations, some still seemed sceptical about the benefits of household suffrage in the counties. E.J. Holyoake, speaking at the Belgrave Conservative Club, shortly after the House of Lords had demanded a new redistribution alongside any franchise extension, doubted that the franchise would bring any significant advantages to the agricultural labourer.[52] Despite this rather reluctant acceptance of the new electoral conditions the Belgrave Conservative Club prospered, with a membership of over 250.[53] Liberals soon responded and by March 1884 were making plans for a district club of their own.[54]

Throughout their organisational work the Conservatives made strenuous efforts to appeal to the new 'unknown' electorate of the agricultural and county labourer by adopting a more populist style. In the Northern division they recruited the newly formed Leicester Working-Men's Conservative Club to assist organisation work. Typical of these efforts was a combined picnic and lecture tour of the Northern division organised in mid-summer 1884.[55] The priority was not just to create a body of Conservative voters, but also to create a body of willing Conservative workers. The sheer uncertainty of the forthcoming election drove the party into frantic action. By August 1884 Loughborough Conservative Association had 292 members – in what was supposedly a Liberal town. Still the local Conservative MP was little impressed and urged members to recruit more voluntary activists.[56] This sort of effort did not go unrewarded. By 1888 even villages like Ashby – in the mining area of South Leicestershire – had a Conservative Club which could boast over 200 members. Supported by the local gentry and offering a centre for both politics and entertainment, these types of clubs helped the Conservatives move from being a party reliant on informal organisation and paid workers to one utilising formal organisational machinery and bands of voluntary activists.[57]

It is difficult to assess just how much a parliamentary election cost before 1884 in Leicestershire's county divisions. Even if one assumes that the more colourful stories of bribery, corruption and treating were largely fictitious, the new limitations on electoral expenditure and the numbers parties could employ undoubtedly had more

---

51 *LJ*, 15 June 1884.
52 *LJ*, 1 August 1884.
53 *LJ*, 15 June 1884.
54 *LDM*, 8 March 1884.
55 *LJ*, 4 July 1884.
56 *LJ*, 15 August 1884.
57 *HN*, 24 November 1888.

effect on county organisation, given the sheer geographical size of constituencies and the widely scattered population. The new division of Harborough, created from part of the old Southern division was perhaps the most rural, consisting of 95 parishes and hamlets. Voters were serviced by 60 polling stations in the county and a further 12 in the borough (for borough freeholders). The largest settlements consisted of the suburbanised villages of Wigston and Aylestone with 868 and 704 voters respectively. Outside Leicester's immediate suburban area there were few settlements of any size – the largest being the small town of Market Harborough itself with 557 voters on the new register.[58] The most urban county division was the new Bosworth division, created from the other half of the old South Leicestershire constituency, but even here the more urban towns and villages had many smaller agricultural villages located between. The new constituency consisted of 65 parishes but, aside from the hosiery district of Hinckley and the quarrying and mining areas of Ashby and Coalville, most of the remaining areas were primarily engaged in agriculture.[59] Yet the Conservatives demonstrated an ability to respond to the changing circumstances and it needed a formidable effort from Leicestershire's Liberals to meet this challenge, with the borough's Liberal Association being forced into a missionary role to try to take advantage of the county franchise.

It was not, however, the franchise issue which caused most controversy in Leicestershire. It was the scheme for redistribution that was most contentious, with both parties scrambling to obtain a division of the county and borough that would be most favourable to their own prospects of future success. The issue was controversial not just because of the implications it had for the parliamentary elections, but also for the possible implications it had for future local government of the county. It was known that the largely Liberal town council was likely to bring forward proposals to incorporate the urban and suburban districts immediately around Leicester, currently governed largely by Conservatives and independents through local boards.[60] By December 1884 it had become clear that the redistribution scheme might not simply divide the two county divisions, but instead actually take out some of the more urban districts and incorporate them into the borough, without increasing the representation of the borough from two to three members. Part of Belgrave – where the Liberals had recently done well in local board elections – was thus scheduled for incorporation into the parliamentary borough of Leicester.

The Leicester Liberal Association moved quickly to organise opposition to this proposal arguing that the borough already had sufficient population to justify its two MPs.[61] A specially formed redistribution subcommittee was given the task of investigating the issue further.[62] The transfer of Belgrave into the parliamentary

58 *LDM*, 3 December 1885.

59 *LDM*, 8 December 1885.

60 See reported discussion at town council meeting, *LDM*, 28 January 1885.

61 LLA, Finance and General Purposes Committee, 8 December 1884, LRO, 11 D 57/2.

62 LLA, Redistribution Sub-Committee, 30 December 1884, LRO, 11 D 57/2.

borough suited neither Liberals in Leicester or Belgrave. Clephan, president of the Leicester Liberal Association, argued that the incorporation would be the worst of all worlds – making Leicester too large for two members and not large enough for three. As the redistribution Bill set an ideal figure of 55,000 people per member and Leicester had a population of 130,000, this was a strong argument, although Clephan's main concern was that the proposal would place additional costs on the Association in organising the new area on Leicester lines.[63] J.G. Ward, the Liberal chairman of the Belgrave Local Board, was equally hostile to the proposal, and accused the Conservatives of attempted 'gerrymandering'. Arguing that Belgravians were overwhelmingly opposed to the proposal, he suggested that the district was being pushed out of the county to secure a seat for a particular member in the Eastern (Melton) division – an obvious reference to Lord John Manners.[64] Despite what looked like a form of gerrymandering there was a shared confidence that if Leicester and Belgrave Liberals organised opposition, then the proposal could be changed at the public inquiry. Thus the Liberal Association petitioned the boundary commission expressing their opposition.[65]

Unfortunately for the Liberals the boundary commission's guidelines meant that the numerical population of each division was only one consideration in drawing up new constituencies. When the boundary commission opened its inquiry for Leicester, the assistant commissioner stressed that the geography and economic character of areas were at least equally significant and that his aim was to devise a scheme that would separate the manufacturing population and place it in a separate division.[66] However the proceedings of the inquiry gradually began to reveal just how problematic defining the difference between rural, urban and suburban actually was and the impossibility of obtaining universal agreement. Moreover new community names had to be invented in an attempt to describe divisions that had little justification in terms of geography. There was, for example, no existing community name that could be applied to the new Bosworth constituency, highlighting just how 'artificial' the new divisional boundaries were. The Rev. A.J. Spencer, the vicar of Hinckley, protested that 'Ashby' could not be used, as it was not the largest settlement in the area and that 'Hinckley' should be used instead. Pell suggested 'Market Bosworth' as this was the central place – although this was hardly acceptable as Market Bosworth was little more than a small agricultural village. The only general district name that anyone could recall was 'Sparkenhoe' – from the old Sparkenhoe Hundred – but in practice the term had long fallen into disuse. 'Bosworth' was eventually settled on as an uneasy compromise – but if constituency names could not be agreed upon for these newly invented communities, what prospect was there that agreement could

63 *LDM*, 6 January 1885. Leicester would have expanded to 137,000 under the proposal.

64 *MFP*, 10 January 1885. Ward probably also shared the widely held belief that if Belgrave was incorporated into the parliamentary borough, incorporation into the municipal borough would become more likely.

65 LLA, General Committee, 5 January 1885, LRO, 11 D 57/2.

66 *LDM*, 9 January 1885; *MFP*, 17 January 1885.

be secured on the details?[67] Even the Conservatives were unable to come to produce a unified policy they could all agree upon. Lord Manners eventually came out in support of Belgrave actually being retained in the county division of Melton, perhaps because he feared being accused of malpractice in trying to procure the removal of Belgrave in order to secure his own electoral position.[68] Amid much bad feeling both sides accused the other of seeking to gain party advantage and the inquiry quickly degenerated into a partisan squabble – which was perhaps to be expected given the difficulty of the task and what was at stake for each party.[69]

Leading Liberals decided to give the debate a further partisan flavour by organising a mass demonstration in the Floral Hall against the incorporation of Belgrave and attracted among others the mayor, Israel Hart, and the borough's two MPs, Picton and McArthur. By now any attempt at objective arguments based on local identity were neglected in favour of accusations about boundary fixing. For Picton bringing 'Radical Belgrave' into 'Radical Leicester' was 'like carrying coals to Newcastle' – directly implying that Liberal votes would be put to more effective use in the counties rather than stacking up further huge majorities in the borough.[70] The seriousness of the situation is evinced by the fact that both Picton and McArthur attended the final hearings of the commission in the town hall. After close examination of the criteria for the incorporation of suburban districts into the town, it became clear that the commissioner was unlikely to recommend expansion of the borough to three members. Liberal efforts therefore concentrated on attempting to prove that Belgrave had independent 'urban' rather than 'suburban' characteristics, which according to the boundary commission's guidelines would allow it to be retained in the county.[71]

These efforts were initially unsuccessful. When the report of the boundary commission was laid on the table of the House of Commons the original proposal to move the eastern portion of Belgrave from the county to the borough was retained. The battle was not, however, over. After further negotiations and lobbying, Sir Charles Dilke agreed to overturn the commission's recommendation – but only after Leicester Liberals had spent some three months campaigning for these changes.[72] Such a reverse for the Conservatives only seemed to press them into yet more determined organisational activity in the county divisions – and particularly Belgrave. The Belgrave Local Board election of that year was, for the first time, fought overtly on party lines, generating an unusually large turnout, with a Conservative gaining a seat from a well-known local Liberal shoe manufacturer.[73] The Conservatives were clearly fired up by this victory, and continuing Liberal foreign policy embarrassments.

---

67 *LDM*, 9 January 1885.
68 *LDM*, 9 January 1885.
69 *MFP*, 7 February 1885.
70 *LDM*, 31 January 1885.
71 *LDM*, 31 January 1885.
72 *LDM*, 28 March 1885.
73 *HN*, 11 April 1885.

In Bosworth a new Hinckley and District Conservative Association was formed organising large rallies against Gladstonian foreign policy in the Soudan.[74] Nearby in Earl Shilton a Working-Men's Conservative Association soon followed.[75] Loughborough Conservatives responded quickly to their leader's call for more members and activists. Formed in September 1884, by the end of October 1885 group membership had expanded from around 300 to 639 and new premises had to be acquired. The minimum subscription was set low in a deliberate attempt to attract working men, with the cost of premises being covered by a founders' fund rather than by member subscribers.[76]

Leicester Liberals were acutely aware of the need to expand their county organisation in response to this challenge and inevitably, Leicester, as the Liberal 'heart' of the county, took on much of the burden of organising local rural politics. In all cases the new county divisional associations mimicked those in Leicester, formed with elected councils from across the various districts. For example, the new association for the Southern division had a general council elected from meetings of Liberals in each parish or district, with a ratio of one representative for every 500 of the population, and 25 members representing the freeholders of Leicester. The executive committee similarly consisted of 28 members, 14 each from the Bosworth and Harborough Divisions.[77] Almost immediately an agent was obtained and registration work commenced.[78] Across the country Liberals tried to export models of urban party organisation into rural areas. It was soon discovered, however, that registration and campaigning work in the counties provided unique difficulties that were unfamiliar to urban activists.[79]

Leicester's often poorly educated electors were familiar with the conduct of parliamentary elections because of the intensive nature of urban political life. Each week the local newspapers were filled with details of mass demonstrations, lectures and ongoing political campaigns in the town. Urban Liberals were concerned that the new rural electorate, many with little experience of intensive political activity, would take little or no interest in the franchise, or simply vote as their Conservative employers or Anglican church leaders directed. In rural districts outside the main village centres the 1885 election brought many examples of alleged 'territorial influence'. In Melton there were several reported cases of farmers standing outside

74 *HN*, 22 August 1885.

75 *HN*, 17 October 1885.

76 *HN*, 31 October 1885.

77 Liberal Association for the Harbough and Bosworth Divisions' Minutes, Committee, 28 March 1885, LRO, DE 1637/3. The Association was divided into two separate divisional associations after the 1885 election, but the basic structures remained.

78 Liberal Association for the Harbough and Bosworth Divisions' Minutes, Registration Committee, 11 April 1885, LRO, DE 1637/3.

79 In some counties it seems that the new divisional Liberal Associations were little more than small committees based in the county town. In Leicestershire, however, each county division had at least one small town that could be used as the focus for party organisation. M. Ostrogorski, *Democracy and the Organisation of Political Parties*, volume one (London, 1902), 364–6.

polling stations instructing labourers how to vote. Liberals could only respond by stressing the benefits of Liberal government and the absolute secrecy of the ballot.[80] Nationally produced literature emphasised how the agricultural labourer had suffered through lack of voting rights, by robbing him of traditional grazing rights and common land. Reform of land ownership, the Game Laws and the county magistracy were policies aimed specifically to politicise the newly enfranchised.[81] Other leaflets reassured electors that the ballot was indeed secret – despite Conservative suggestions to the contrary – and that no farmer, employer or clergyman could discover the way a vote had been cast.[82] Mere assertions were not enough – it was thought necessary by some pamphleteers to explain in great detail the significance of numbered ballot papers and how they were sealed and later destroyed away from public gaze, such was the suspicion of many new electors.[83]

The squire and landowner represented the great enemy of rural Liberalism. It is difficult to assess just how much influence employers exercised over the votes of agricultural workers, but it is clear that Liberal organisers believed they continued to exercise considerable influence, and consequently they quickly became the demons of Liberal propaganda. Liberal literature emphasised the importance of the free conscience.[84] In some areas of Leicestershire employer influence prevented any effective organisation in the more rural districts. Although Harborough Liberals had had much such success in organising the major centres of their constituency by 1888 they had abandoned attempts to organise several of the smaller villages, after many local residents had declined to take part in political activity for fear of attracting the 'displeasure' of their employers.[85] The only way around the problem seemed to be to persuade an enthusiastic local labourer to organise a more informal political discussion – which was less likely to attract the suspicion of employers than if a stranger were to come into the area. Although working agricultural labourers were less scared of discussing politics with 'one of their own number' even these efforts were not completely successful.[86] Liberal difficulties were compounded by the reluctance of some candidates to visit unknown villages for fear of the reception they might receive. James Ellis, Liberal candidate in Bosworth, was reluctant to visit the 'unexplored' village of Ashby, only to find when he got there no Conservative presence whatsoever.[87] There were, however, very real problems of rural organisation when Liberals faced the concerted efforts of rural employers. Harborough Conservatives

---

80 *LDM*, 2 December 1885.

81 'What is the Good of a Vote?', NRU 60, 15, MCL, 306 N6.

82 'The Absolute Secrecy of the Ballot', National Liberal Federation Leaflet No11, NRU 60, 6, MCL, 306 N6.

83 'A Question and an Answer', National Press Agency Leaflet, NRU 60, 14, MCL, 306 N6.

84 'Are Pledges to Vote Binding?', R.M., National Press Agency Leaflet, NRU 60, 8, MCL, 306 N6.

85 HLA, Annual Meeting, 11 February 1888, LRO DE 1637/1.

86 HLA, Annual Meeting, 11 February 1888, LRO DE 1637/1.

87 *LDM*, 2 December 1885.

were better financed than their Liberal counterparts and could afford to employ three agents – each of whom exercised considerable influence over the local overseers and electoral officials.[88] In rural districts returning officers, their staff and local magistrates tended to be more sympathetic to traditional – that is Conservative – rural leaders than their often urban Liberal opponents.[89] Some had little interest in helping the newly enfranchised onto the register. One remote village of Harborough was left out of the rate book and off the electoral register allegedly because 'they were only labourers and never had been on'.[90] Local help ensured that the village in question was eventually included, but Liberal agents continued to be greeted with hostility from the local revising barrister. These problems were compounded, of course, by the relative financial weakness of the Liberal Association. Harborough Liberals calculated that by 1890 their opponents had five times the amount of money available for registration purposes than themselves.[91]

There was great difficulty in delivering the Liberal message to small rural communities and county associations were highly reliant on lecturers sent from Leicester. The Harborough Liberal Association used Leicester lecturers to good effect in stimulating new political activity in their villages.[92] Similar efforts were made in Bosworth, but not always with great success. When Liberal Thomas Slater, a Leicester lecturer, failed to get a hearing at a Conservative meeting in Stoke Golding, near Hinckley, he resolved to set up a rival meeting in the parish school. Unfortunately when he got there he was met with what he described as a group of 'Tory roughs' – including some in military uniform – who proceeded to break up the meeting.[93] Interestingly, however, these experiences did not seem to dishearten Leicester Liberal activists, but rather encourage them into further pioneering activity. Fighting for success in these conditions offered the possibility of a romantic triumph against the odds – reinforcing old prejudices, appealing to a crusading spirit and offering a great contrast to easy victories in Leicester. The difficulties thus became part of the attraction:

> The true type of a Tory is a brute. He believes in force and force only. You might as well try to reason with a hungry tiger as with him. These survivals from the barbarous past prevented our meeting, but they did not prevent our victory at the polling booths the following day.[94]

Another great barrier to Liberal success in the county was the Anglican church. In Melton complaints were heard that local Anglican churches had been turned into

---

88 HLA, Annual Meeting, 18 May 1889, LRO DE 1637/1.

89 A.W. Marks, 'Suggestions for the Establishment of a Voters' Protection Guild', National Liberal Club Leaflet, NRU 10, 5, MCL, 306 N6.

90 HLA, Annual Meeting, 12 April 1890, LRO DE 1637/1.

91 HLA, Annual Meeting, 12 April 1890, LRO DE 1637/1.

92 HLA, Annual Meeting, 7 May 1887, LRO DE 1637/1.

93 Letter, T. Slater, *LDM*, 11 December 1885.

94 *LDM*, 11 December 1885.

'Tory lecture halls' with Liberal speakers darkly warning that if the Established church decided to align itself with one party, it must expect to fall with it.[95] In the Harborough constituency Liberal lecturers were frequently refused access to Anglican schoolrooms where they wished to hold meetings. Eventually the Liberal Association became so frustrated with the situation that parliamentary candidate J.W. Logan built himself a portable meeting room which he took from village to village. This mobile contraption – dubbed the 'Free Speech Hall' – obviously worked and following its introduction the local clergy were less reluctant to hire out school halls to Liberal candidates.[96] However even when the clergy were more co-operative in granting the use of rooms they could still be seen disrupting Liberal meetings.[97] Even in areas such as Loughborough, where rural Nonconformity was by no means unknown, the influence of the clergy was still in evidence, with Liberal shopkeepers allegedly being threatened with boycotting if they displayed their political loyalties.[98] The clergy's attacks on rural Liberals were, of course partly based around their opposition to disestablishment and fears that the Liberal government may take up the issue. This was a nation-wide occurrence and even in industrial county divisions, such as Leigh in Lancashire, the clergy were mobilised in opposition to the Liberal Party.[99] However in Leicestershire, with its more scattered rural population, the Anglican clergy may have exercised greater influence than was generally the case. Although there was historically much antagonism between rural Anglicans and Radical leaders, it is not at all clear that Liberal discussion of the disestablishment question was the main cause of the renewed hostility. In Bosworth, at least, there is evidence that the Conservatives were trying to use the church as an organisational vehicle by attributing policies to the Liberal candidate that would upset Anglican leaders. In this constituency supporters of the Conservative candidate produced an inflammatory pamphlet accusing the Liberals of wanting to drive the clergy out of the villages and destroy their charitable giving to local communities.[100] In fact, the Liberal candidate, James Ellis, took a relatively moderate view of the Church question and made a point of paying tribute to his Anglican colleagues on the Leicester School Board, leaving it to others to comment on disestablishment.[101] In Harborough Liberal Anglican H. Simpson Gee criticised Liberals who were considering abstaining from voting because of the church question, pointing out that it was simply not an issue at the election.[102] Liberals, despite their obvious antagonism to many figures in the local Anglican church, were wary of the disestablishment issue. Conservatives, in contrast,

95 An obvious reference to disestablishment. *LDM*, 30 November 1885.

96 HLA, Annual Meeting, 12 April 1890, LRO DE 1637/1.

97 Letter, J. Smallman (a Liberal Party organiser), *LDM*, 11 December 1885.

98 See speech of J.J. Ferguson, *LDM*, 7 December 1885.

99 J. Howes, 'The Church in Danger', NRU 4, unnumbered, MCL, 306 N6.

100 *LP*, 27 November 1885.

101 *LP*, 2 December 1885.

102 *LP*, 27 November 1885.

often made it the central plank of their campaign, such as in Harborough, where Conservatives issued crude placards depicting Liberals pulling down churches.[103]

Leicester Liberal Party organisers made strenuous efforts to counter Conservative campaigns in the counties. Just days after the 1885 borough election the Leicester Liberal Association organised a mass meeting at the Liberal Club to secure volunteers to assist in the county divisions, an action which prompted large numbers to come forward.[104] The borough also provided legal assistance with Leicester organiser F.J.F. Kirby acting as not only a lecturer, but also as an agent for the Melton and Bosworth divisions.[105] The Leicester Liberal Association could not, however, provide the knowledge of local communities necessary for efficient organisation, or large sums of money, especially as it was forced to fund two borough elections in less than one year. By the summer of 1885 the Association was already predicting an annual shortfall of around £120 and making a somewhat desperate appeal for local councillors and aldermen to subscribe more to funds.[106] However while county organisation underwent a revolution, largely as a result of efforts by Leicester Liberals, the problems of the Leicester Liberal Association were neglected. Despite the controversy over Picton's selection as parliamentary candidate, there were few attempts to make urban party organisation more inclusive. The finance and general purposes committee of the Leicester Association did agree to extend the general committee from 350 to 500 members, but this move coincided with the mid-1885 financial crisis and was principally an attempt to attract new subscribers to the Association, rather than to broaden its decision-making processes.[107] Not all were impressed. Radical and secularist G.J. Holyoake called for a much greater widening of membership, whilst others suggested an association explicitly aimed at both voters and non-voters, combined with the construction of new Liberal assembly rooms to allow larger deliberative meetings.[108] As in Manchester the most controversial aspect of the Association's constitution was the system which allowed co-optative membership of the major committees. In January 1886 the influential East St. Margaret's Ward Liberal Association passed a resolution calling for the complete abolition of the co-optative system and for party organisation to be placed 'on a directly representative basis'.[109] Yet with the Association short of funds and with many of its wealthier supporters living outside the parliamentary borough it is not surprising that the borough Association showed little interest in removing co-option from its constitution.

Radicals were also frustrated by the refusal of the Association to discuss several of their pressing concerns. Many were very unhappy with aspects of the Redistribution

---

103 *LP*, 4 December 1885.

104 *LDM*, 30 November 1885.

105 *LDM*, 2 December 1885; *LDM*, 9 December 1885.

106 LLA, Finance and General Purposes Committee, 13 July 1885, LRO, 11 D 57/2.

107 LLA, Finance and General Purposes Committee, 13 July 1885, LRO, 11 D 57/2.

108 Letter, J. Atkins, *LDM*, 9 March 1885.

109 East St. Margaret's Ward LA, Ward Representatives' Meeting, 8 January 1885, LRO 11 D 57/5.

Bill and the failure of party leaders to consider either a second ballot or proportional representation in the national package of electoral reform. At a Liberal Association debate in January 1885 the new 'Radical' member for Leicester, Picton, did little to appease those who had favoured Chamberlain, when dismissing proportional representation as impractical and sectionalist.[110] This caused considerable anger amongst some Radicals, including leading Nonconformist minister Rev. J. Page Hopps.[111] In response to the charge that proportional representation was impractical, several members of the Liberal Club organised a mock ballot to demonstrate its simplicity. When only nine of the 839 ballot papers were returned spoiled, even the mayor had to acknowledge that the scheme had proven itself 'simple and workable'.[112] Faced with the 'Belgrave question' and difficulties of party organisation, Leicester Liberal leaders wanted to avoid potentially divisive debates on proportional representation and eventually, after several weeks of informal consideration, passed a compromise resolution in favour of the introduction of the second ballot system – although by then the matter had practically been settled.[113]

More differences emerged over the government's conduct of foreign policy. At the end of February 1885 the town's leading Radical newspaper issued a hard hitting editorial criticising imperial policy toward Egypt and the Soudan. The *Midland Free Press*, although warning Liberals against taking action that would bring down the government, called for 'a loud and strong protest against this outrageous war from all parts of the country'.[114] When the Liberal Association met and passed a strange compromise resolution on the subject – assuring Gladstone of their support and 'welcoming' the government's commitment to withdrawing at the earliest opportunity – Radicals became increasingly indignant, pointing out that the government had made no such 'commitment'. Although acknowledging that excessive criticism could endanger the government, many wanted a more critical response to what they regarded as 'one of the most unjustifiable, cruel and wicked wars which a nation ever entered upon'.[115] The Leicester Liberal Association was again exposed as critically divided, with an amendment calling for the march on Khartoum be abandoned falling by just a few votes.[116] Radicals responded by organising a massive demonstration at the Floral Hall calling for an honourable withdrawal. The demonstration attracted around 3,000 people and was supported by senior aldermen, councillors, Nonconformist ministers and James Ellis, the future MP for Bosworth.[117] These divisions continued throughout the summer. J.A. Picton, considerably embarrassed by the affair and the consequent division in his Association, realised that differences

---

110 *MFP*, 24 January 1885.

111 *MFP*, 31 January 1885.

112 *LDM*, 3 February 1885.

113 LLA, General Committee 5 January 1885, LRO, 11 D 57/2; LLA, General Committee, 24 March 1885, LRO, 11 D 57/2.

114 *MFP*, 28 February 1885.

115 See 'Stray Notes', *MFP*, 28 February 1885.

116 *MFP*, 28 February 1885.

117 *MFP*, 5 April 1885.

would not be healed quickly and attempted, somewhat perversely, to turn them into a virtue. At the first 'Liberal 500' election – the new general committee of the Liberal Association – Picton acknowledged the differences and argued that the plurality of opinion and political breadth of the Association was a source of strength.[118] Divisions in the Liberal Association were nothing new, of course, but now there were signs that a significant number of Radicals were not only unhappy with the Liberal Association, but also with the very Radical MP who was supposed to be the voice for their section of the party.

The borough's Conservatives based their strategy around trying to exploit these difficulties. By putting up only one candidate at the 1885 general election they hoped to absorb votes from those dissatisfied with the one or other of the Liberal nominees.[119] Unfortunately, however, Conservatives in London were again unwilling to find either a candidate or funding for such a contest, leaving local Leicester councillor and magistrate Colonel William Millican as the only possible Conservative nominee.[120] Millican's campaign was, however, more successful than generally anticipated, with the single Conservative candidate taking 23 per cent of the total vote.[121] Although the reduced Liberal majority may have been in part a consequence of protests by Catholics against Liberal Irish policy, the relatively poor result brought added criticism of party organisation and Leicester's Liberal leadership, with one activist complaining bitterly of the lack of support given by wealthier members of the party in the campaign.[122] The result seemed to offer a warning about the consequences of continuing to neglect borough organisation and failing to resolve political differences within the Association.

The reduced majority in Leicester was, of course, a small price to pay for the success of the party in the county divisions. All but Melton – for so long dominated by the aristocratic Manners family – fell to the Liberal Party, a tribute to the organisational work of Leicester Liberals in the county. However, just as Leicester Liberals exported some of their methods of political organisation to the county, they also exported some of their divisions, as Radicals exploited the opportunities presented by the creation of single-member constituencies. As in Manchester, grass-roots Radicals used the decentralisation of party management to their advantage. In South Leicestershire, the decision of sitting MP Thomas Paget to contest Harborough rather than the better Liberal prospect of Bosworth left the way for Radical James Ellis to contest the more urban Bosworth without any apparent internal party opposition. In Loughborough, however, the creation of a new Liberal Association on Leicester lines, helped bring into focus a significant division in local Liberalism. Hussey Packe, who had twice contested the old Northern division was nominated alongside J. Johnson Ferguson, who had previously been invited to contest a by-election in

118 *LDM*, 14 October 1885.

119 *LDM*, 26 November 1885.

120 *MFP*, 21 November 1885; *MFP*, 28 November 1885.

121 *LDM*, 27 November 1885; *MFP*, 28 November 1885.

122 Letter, G.W. Bruce, *LDM*, 28 November 1885.

the constituency. Packe was a local squire and not known for 'advanced' views. Radicals favoured Johnson Ferguson, a merchant manufacturer from Lancashire. A vote by ballot of the Loughborough Liberal Council gave Johnson Ferguson a 65 to 21 majority.[123] Although policy differences between the two candidates existed, these were little referred to in public, as the battle became increasingly personal. Packe's supporters had little time for the decision-making structures of the new association. Packe's agent attacked Radical supporters of Johnson Ferguson for packing the Liberal Association council, amid rumours that Packe intended to come forward as an independent Liberal candidate.[124] Strenuous efforts were made to placate Packe with Melton Liberal leaders immediately approaching him to stand in their division, even though several of their members expressed a preference for a more 'advanced' candidate.[125] Perhaps not surprisingly, in view of the strongly Conservative nature of the constituency, Packe declined.[126] In the event Packe decided not to come out as an independent Liberal, but there were persistent rumours that he was in acting in support of Johnson Ferguson's Conservative opponent, Hon Montague Curzon, and even actually canvassing on his behalf.[127] In contrast to Packe, Johnson Ferguson's campaign for representative county government and land reform delighted Radicals, and when Johnson Ferguson's new constituency strongly endorsed a particular policy, he was flexible enough to respond to their demands. After considerable pressure from the Anti-Compulsory Vaccination League, Johnson Ferguson became a convert to the cause just days before the election.[128] Johnson Ferguson and Packe did not just have different backgrounds and ideologies, they had very contrasting views on the role of representative party organisation and the influence they were entitled to exercise over a parliamentary representative. Johnson Ferguson stressed the importance of reflecting the views of his electorate. Packe, like Conservative Lord John Manners, was wary of the influence the new party organisations were seeking to exercise and was determined to assert his independence as a parliamentary candidate.[129] The demise of Packe demonstrated how Radicals could use the new organisations to secure not only a new candidate with more advanced views, but also a new type of local representative.

The expansion of the county electorate represented a great test for Leicester Liberalism. Despite Conservative attempts to consolidate their position with a mixture of organisational zeal, employer influence and 'church defence' campaigns, Leicester Liberals succeeded in reshaping county politics. 'Red Leicester' had become 'Red Leicestershire'. County campaigns offered the Liberal leadership an escape from the difficulties of internal differences and provided opponents against which all Liberals

---

123 *LDM*, 9 March 1885.

124 *HN*, 21 March 1885.

125 *LDM*, 20 March 1885.

126 *LDM*, 20 March 1885; *LDM*, 30 March 1885.

127 *LDM*, 26 November 1885. Packe later joined the Liberal Unionists and stood in Loughborough at the general election of 1900.

128 *LDM*, 28 November 1885.

129 *HN*, 7 March 1885.

could rally – the Anglican church – the traditional enemy of Nonconformists – and the agricultural landowning interest – the old enemy in the struggle for free trade. County work provided a psychologically attractive and politically worthwhile alternative to the internal bickering and bloodless victories in the borough. Leicester Liberals rendered great service to their county colleagues and the successful rural campaigns has distracted attention from internal divisions. However because Leicester remained a two-member borough, Radicals had not been able to take advantage of any decentralisation of borough politics in the way they had in Manchester. Safe in the knowledge that the Conservatives would not be able to launch an effective assault on the borough, the Leicester Liberal Association launched itself into reform of county organisation, yet left its own structures largely unmodified. Over a period of 30 years the divisions between Radical and 'moderate' Liberalism had become institutionalised in separate parliamentary representatives serving each major strand within the party, yet by 1885 Radicals no longer saw Radical MP J.A. Picton as representative of their particular political concerns and demanded greater attention to what they saw as grass-roots views. Aggressive Conservative tactics in the county elections, particularly the 'church defence' campaign, had tended to polarise opinion and strengthen the position of local campaigners on the left of the Liberal Party. The Radical wing, buoyed by the success of the county campaign, were soon to adopt a more assertive approach in the borough of Leicester itself.

PART II
The Home Rule Crisis in the Towns

CHAPTER THREE

Manchester and the Home Rule Crisis

The large crowd that gathered under the drizzly Manchester skies on 26 July 1884 in Pomona Gardens witnessed an important milestone in Liberal politics.[1] It was to be the last time that Lord Hartington, widely regarded as a future Liberal leader, and John Bright, the embodiment of the Manchester School, would appear on a public platform with the leaders of Manchester Liberal Association. Within two years Hartington and Bright were launched in hostile opposition to their former colleagues over the Home Rule question. At national level the party split and fell from office as life-long colleagues became bitter enemies.[2] This division of the Liberal Party into rival Gladstonian and Unionist groups has dominated discussions of late nineteenth-century Liberalism, with some suggesting that the crisis effectively marked the end of the Victorian Liberal Party.[3] In Manchester, however, the consequences of Liberal Home Rule divisions were mixed, but by no means disastrous. While the party did suffer from a loss of activists and supporters, the presence of a large Irish community in Manchester meant it was able to reach out to other areas of the city for support. Despite the Liberal Unionist secession, the 1886 general election saw the Liberal Association recover from the Irish electoral boycott of 1885, making two gains and taking three of Manchester's six parliamentary seats. The most damaging effects of the split were seen at municipal level where the party lost its overall majority on the council for the first time since incorporation, despite successful attempts by the Liberal group to broaden its appeal by recruiting trades council and Irish nationalist leaders into its ranks.[4]

Manchester Liberals did face significant organisational problems in the 1880s, but few of these problems were directly attributable to the withdrawal of Liberal Unionists from the party. The Manchester by-election of 1883 and the subsequent reorganisation of the Liberal Party brought debates about the role and structure of local political organisation into sharp focus. For many, the growth of party machines

---

1 W. Haslam Mills, *The Manchester Reform Club 1871–1921* (Manchester, 1921), 41.

2 W. Lubenow, *Parliamentary Politics and the Home Rule Crisis* (Oxford, 1988); A. Cooke and J. Vincent, *The Governing Passion: Cabinet Government and Party Politics in Britain, 1885–1886* (Brighton, 1974).

3 J. Parry, *The Rise and Fall of Liberal Government in Victorian Britain*, (Cambridge, 1993), especially 304–6; 'Gladstone's behaviour in 1886 turned the Liberal party from a great party of government into a gaggle of outsiders', 306. See also T. Jenkins, *Gladstone, Whiggery and the Liberal Party, 1874–1886* (Oxford, 1988); D. Southgate, *The Passing of the Whigs 1832–1886* (London, 1962).

4 S.D. Simon, *A Century of City Government* (Manchester, 1938), 400.

was a trend to be deprecated, with many Liberals worried that politics had developed from a battle of ideas to a battle of party machines.[5] However the experience of 1883 demonstrated that only by constructing a party machine that was seen to incorporate all sections of the party would that machine be able to command the loyalty of Liberal activists. Thus the crushing defeat Manchester Liberals suffered in 1885 did little to quell the criticism of those who regarded the central party organisation as neither representative of the party's wider support nor politically effective. These criticisms were not new, with one Liberal veteran, George Meulor, arguing that the problems of party organisation went back at least a decade.[6] In particular there was scathing criticism of party leaders who took up positions of authority but were perceived as doing little to actively promote the interest of the party:

> Is it not pertinent to ask for what purpose, is all the rank, pomp and circumstance of direction kept up when there is nothing to direct. An army of generals, colonels and captains is absurd. That apathy exists none can deny. The proof of it can be found in the smallness of the number of members of the Liberal Executive who can be found at election times with book and lamp doing the work that needs to be done. In spite of the apathy, there is never an election but we get considerable help from working men who have no connection whatever with the associations or clubs, and who cheerfully work for the principles they love.[7]

Criticism of the party for failing to involve party workers in decision-making developed into a general critique of the new associations. Although formally 'representative' and elected by public meeting, party organisation was often very carefully managed. For example, although chairmen of ward meetings were nominally chosen by the meeting, in practice they were chosen beforehand by the local association's retiring officials.[8] Leading officials, particularly the presidents of associations, were in office for long periods of time. The representative committees that were elected were often so large that they had to be divided into subcommittees and it was in these committees that real power lay – small fragmented committees heavily influenced by 'a few wirepullers of the Reform Club'.[9] Members with controversial opinions were often weeded out and meetings were arranged at times when it was impossible to expect working-class representatives to attend.[10]

The meetings of some of the local Liberal Associations in the first two months of 1886 gave added weight to these criticisms. At a public meeting in New Cross ward, held to elect representatives to the divisional association, only 60 people attended, despite New Cross being an area of substantial Liberal strength.[11] The annual

---

[5] The classic statement of this position can be found M. Ostrogorski, *Democracy and the Organisation of Political Parties*, volume one (London, 1902).

[6] Letter, G. Meulor, *MG*, 26 February 1886.

[7] Letter, G. Meulor, *MG*, 26 February 1886.

[8] *MG*, 26 January 1886.

[9] *MG*, 27 February 1886.

[10] *MG*, 10 January 1886.

[11] *MG*, 30 January 1886.

meeting of Oxford ward Liberals was described as 'a farce' when only 19 Liberals turned up to elect 22 representatives to the divisional association.[12] The problems of organisation preoccupied most ward organisations in the early months of that year. Responses to the crisis varied. St. Anne's Liberals, together with colleagues in St. James and New Cross, passed resolutions for improved political education measures. In Moss Side there was reluctance to adopt this model, with some arguing political education was the responsibility of groups like the National Reform Union, not local political associations.[13] Rusholme Liberals discussed the possibility of founding a Liberal club. St. Luke's ward Liberals favoured the creation of a broader based 'voluntary Liberal Association'.[14]

These organisational problems, however, can be overstated. All divisional associations ran municipal election campaigns in November with little sign of disagreement. Finance was not a significant problem. All Liberal candidates in Manchester spent very close to the legal limit and, on average, were asked to fund a smaller proportion of their campaign expenditure than their Conservative counterparts.[15] Yet some local associations were heavily dependent on central funds for their running costs. Figures for 1885–86 show that only the commercial North-West division was able to raise even half its running costs locally, while the largely working-class North-East division apparently failed to collect any subscriptions at all.[16] A total of £400 had to be paid out in grants to divisional associations in the first year. This may not simply have been a reflection of the political weakness of local associations, however, but rather a reflection of the historic unitary structure of Manchester Liberal organisation, with its focus on the commercial centre of the city and the Manchester Reform Club. Large subscribers to the old Manchester Liberal Association, particularly those living in the suburbs outside the city, continued to give to central party funds rather than adopting a particular division.[17] This arrangement continued to offer the possibility of a redistribution of funds to poorer areas, but also meant the central party continuing to exercise significant influence over the management of local politics beyond the transitional stage.[18]

The executive committee of the Manchester Liberal Union responded to criticism by taking an active role in the consolidation of local party organisation. After the 1885 debacle it pressed for the local divisional associations to appoint registration

12 Although this occurrence was unusual and a reflection of the fact that a large number of voters in this city centre ward lived outside the city.

13 *MG*, 2 January 1886.

14 *MG*, 28 January 1886.

15 Official returns published in *Manchester Weekly Post*, 2 January 1886.

16 MLU, Joint Consultative Committee, 3 February 1886, MCL, M283/1/1/2.

17 MLU, Memorandum of subscriptions and donations, 1886–91, M283/1/1/2.

18 Of course, because party membership did not imply the payment of a subscription, subscribers only made up a small part of total party membership. To become a member all one had to do was signify allegiance to the objects and rules of the association, and be an elector in the division concerned. See MLU, *Rules of the North West Manchester Liberal Association 1885*, MCL, M283/1/1/2.

secretaries and, within three months, all but one divisional association had a secretary in place – before even the Union committee itself had appointed a registration sub-committee and secretary.[19] Despite these efforts the Union committee continued to come in for considerable criticism and there was a reluctance to give it any credit for the 1886 parliamentary election gains. The *Manchester Guardian* did not attempt to hide its disappointment that the Liberal achievement had not been greater and blamed the party's organisational failure rather than the Home Rule crisis for the result. Similar sentiments were expressed at a victorious post-election reception in the Manchester Liberal Club.[20] Manchester Liberals clearly suffered from uneasiness about their party organisation and leaders well before the Home Rule crisis. Ironically the crisis helped foster organisational improvements by forcing Liberal leaders to face up to internal problems and, in particular, to address the party's financial difficulties.

It is also crucial to place the Home Rule crisis in its full electoral context. Although the loss of Liberal Unionist support was significant, the crisis did produce some electoral benefits. The support of Manchester's large Irish population must have compensated, at least in part, for the loss of Liberal Unionists. However, one regional study of voting behaviour suggests that the Irish electoral dividend to the Liberal Party in North-West England has been overstated. It suggests for the region as a whole that there was an inverse relationship between the size of local Roman Catholic populations and the size of the Liberal vote.[21] Regional studies, however, ignore the important differences between the major urban centres of the North-West. In Manchester sectarian feeling between Catholics and Protestants was much more limited than in nearby Liverpool. Although some Manchester neighbourhoods had a very high proportion of Irish Catholic residents, Protestants and Catholics did not live in separate, segregated estates. The Orange movement in Manchester was historically weak and the only sectarian disturbance of note in the late nineteenth century occurred in 1888 when a relatively small Orange march attempted to pass through an Irish Catholic area.[22] Consequently the Liberal Party in Manchester inherited strong Irish Catholic support, without provoking strong organised working-class opposition through the Orange movement. In 1885 the Irish Nationalists opposed the Liberal Party and Liberals took just one of Manchester's six parliamentary seats. In 1886 they were allied to the party and Manchester Liberals won three seats, against the national trend, and held them until 1895. In two of the constituencies held by the Liberal Party between 1886 and 1895, North and South-West Manchester, Irishmen made up over 10 per cent of the electorate. The Irish made up a similar proportion of North-East Manchester's electorate and although never won by the party in this period, the

[19] MLU, Joint Consultative Committee, 21 December 1885, M283/1/1/2; MLU, Union Committee, 31 March 1886, M283/1/1/2.

[20] *MG*, 3 July 1886.

[21] J. Hill, 'Working Class Politics in Lancashire 1885–1906: A Regional Study in the Origins of the Labour Party', Unpublished PhD thesis, University of Keele, 1969, xxii.

[22] S. Fielding, 'The Irish Catholics of Manchester and Salford: Aspects of their Religious and Political History, 1890–1939', Unpublished PhD thesis, University of Warwick, 1988, 141–5.

division was regarded as the most marginal in Manchester. Irish support also brought substantial dividends to the party at municipal level, with the Irish-dominated St. Michael's and New Cross wards regularly returning Liberal representatives to the town hall. Two councillors from these areas, Dan Boyle and Dan McCabe became the first Irish Catholics on the city council and went on to develop successful careers as Liberal representatives.[23]

Precise calculations of the Liberal electoral dividend from Home Rule are clearly impossible. An organisational crisis for the Liberal Party prior to the 1885 election may have damaged the party more than loss of Irish support. While it is clear that the Irish vote was a key component of Liberal Party support after 1886, Irish and Catholic leaders were reluctant to lose their independence and continued to operate outside the auspices of the Liberal Party. The Manchester branches of the Irish National League had their own electoral organisation, which they were not prepared to subsume into that of the Liberals. Thus at the Gorton by-election of 1889 the Irish organisations formed their own election committee and took responsibility for their own part of the constituency. Although the relationship between the Irish organisations and the Liberals was harmonious, they remained distinctly separate.[24] At the North-East Manchester by-election of 1891 the local Liberal Association attempted to take responsibility for both English and Irish areas of the division. The Irish, however, acted on their own and there was unnecessary duplication of effort. From that point Liberal organisers came under pressure to leave Irish groups to mobilise voters in predominantly Irish areas.[25] Irish reluctance to merge their political organisations with that of the Liberals was not simply an expression of a separate cultural identity. Important political differences remained. The local Catholic press called for the creation of a separate Catholic party to look after specifically Catholic interests after the granting of Home Rule.[26] Editorials called upon Irishmen to resist Liberal attempts to bind them 'hard and fast to the Liberal Party for all purposes' and reminded them of Liberal hostility to public funding for separate Catholic education.[27] The Catholic Bishop of Salford similarly warned his followers about becoming too closely bound to the major parties whilst the *Catholic Herald*, even during the 1895 election campaign, stressed the importance of Irish independence from the British parties.[28] Of course, not all Manchester's nationalists even voted Liberal after the Parnell crisis, with a small number even opposing C.P. Scott, a passionate Home Ruler, during the 1891 North-East Manchester by-election.[29] Loyalty to the principle of Home Rule kept most of Manchester's Irish Catholic community within the Liberal

---

[23] Fielding, 'The Irish Catholics of Manchester and Salford', 191–2, 223–4. Local Liberal Associations also lobbied for Irish representation on other public bodies including the local bench, see: Letter, C. Walls to C.P. Scott, 9 January 1893, JRULM, CPSC 119/148.

[24] *Weekly Herald*, 29 March 1889.

[25] Letter, C.P. Allen to C.P Scott, 9 October 1891, JRULM, CPSC 119/93.

[26] *Weekly Herald*, 22 November 1889.

[27] *Weekly Herald*, 29 November 1889.

[28] *Catholic Herald*, 12 July 1895.

[29] Letter, J.E. Taylor to C.P. Scott, 6 October 1891, JRULM, CPSC 129/208.

coalition, but Irish leaders made it clear their support was conditional and limited. The Liberal Party's electoral base became broader, but it could not consolidate its position organisationally because Irish Catholic leaders had their own priorities and wanted to limit their own integration into the party. This makes study of the changes in Liberal and Liberal Unionist organisation and strategy even more important. Most Irish Catholics did not become Liberals or 'replace' Liberal Unionists in the party organisation – rather they merely allied themselves with the Liberal Party. Thus if the Liberal Unionist secession in Manchester was indeed so great, how did the Liberals survive organisationally as a party?

There have been few attempts to analyse the Unionist split from a local perspective and paucity of Liberal Unionist records for Manchester makes detailed assessment difficult. The principal problem is that, unlike the Liberal split at Westminster, at local level divisions were often much more blurred, with dissident Liberals only gradually dropping out of the 'official' Liberal Association and forming rival Unionist groups. Initially, however, leaders of the Manchester Liberal Union were clearly taken aback by the scale of the dissatisfaction believing that 'divisions throughout the Liberal ranks resulting from the introduction of this measure [the Irish Home Rule Bill] have been acutely felt in Manchester, more so, perhaps than in any other place excepting Birmingham'.[30] There was particular concern at the loss of party income consequent on the withdrawal of some subscriptions. Financial worries meant that the treasurer could only promise to pay a £50 subsidy to each of the divisional associations in the following financial year.[31] Efforts to find new subscribers were not overwhelmingly successful, and attempts to persuade Liberal Unionists to continue with their party subscriptions were abandoned by mid-1887.[32] However, the party struggled through and actually made grants of £320 to the divisional associations that year.[33]

It is also important to place these financial difficulties in the context of the political cycle and the problems experienced by other Liberal Associations. With two general elections in nine months it would be surprising if local parties did not suffer some short-term financial problems.[34] What is remarkable in the case of Manchester is just how quickly the party recovered. By the end of 1887 the party had attracted five major new subscribers who contributed a total of £90, while six other existing subscribers increased their contributions.[35] Total subscriptions and donations fell from just over £680 in 1887 to just under £360 in 1888. Yet close

---

30 MLU, Secretary's Report, 22 April 1887, MCL, M283/1/1/2.

31 MLU, Union Committee, 28 March 1887, MCL, M283/1/1/2.

32 MLU, Union Committee, 27 June 1887, MCL, M283/1/1/2.

33 MLU, Annual Meeting, 2 May 1888, MCL, M283/1/1/2.

34 The financial difficulties the party faced following the Home Rule crisis pale into insignificance when compared to the chronic financial problems Manchester Liberals faced after 1918. See B. Jones, 'Manchester Liberalism 1918–1929: the electoral, ideological and organisation experience of the Liberal Party in Manchester, with particular reference to the career of Ernest Simon', Unpublished PhD thesis, University of Manchester, 1997, 13, 119–22.

35 MLU, Memorandum of Subscriptions and Donations, 1886–91, MCL, M283/1/1/2.

examination of the balance sheets indicates that around two-thirds of this decrease can be accounted for by Home Rulers, such as C.E. Schwann MP and H.J. Roby MP, reducing their subscriptions to the central funds, rather than by a withdrawal of funds by the Liberal Unionists. Indeed figures like Schwann and Roby may well have been contributing the same amounts to the party as a whole, but funding the divisional associations directly, rather than through the central committees. Any problems the Manchester Liberal Union had were only of a short-term nature. After an appeal to members, donations and subscriptions leapt to £830 in 1889, allowing the Liberal Union to increase its grants to divisional associations from £240 to £600 – a figure which increased further in the run-up to the 1892 general election. This recovery looks even more impressive when compared to the problems Rochdale Liberal Association faced when confronted with the problem of Liberal Unionist secession, where the influence of local Liberal Unionist MP John Bright was clearly significant. In 1888 the Rochdale association's ordinary subscriptions fell by two-thirds, despite strenuous efforts by local party activists.[36] This difficulty in funding party activities helped the Liberal Party's opponents record their first net registration gains in Rochdale for several years when the local electoral register was revised.[37] Manchester Liberal Union did suffer a short-term loss of subscriptions after 1886, but they were relatively trivial and were quickly reversed, helping the central committees to establish party organisation on a much firmer footing and provide substantial assistance to local divisional associations.

The Liberal Unionist rebellion in Manchester was limited by the cautious and measured response of senior party officials to the 'Hawarden Kite' – the announcement of Gladstone's conversion to Home Rule. Initially declining to support a proposal endorsing the Home Rule measures, the officers of the Liberal Union instead called upon officers of the divisional associations to call meetings to consult and pass resolutions giving their views.[38] Within a fortnight all six divisional councils had held meetings endorsing the Gladstonian proposals, although the North and North-West Liberal divisional councils stressed the importance of compromise, where possible, to retain Liberal unity.[39] During two key council meetings in May, several Liberal Unionists attempted to overturn Home Rule policy, but in both cases were overwhelmingly defeated. Percy Glass, a senior party organiser, unsuccessfully tabled a Unionist amendment, whilst at a mass meeting in the Free Trade Hall just '8 or 10' Unionist dissidents recorded votes against Home Rule.[40]

---

[36] Rochdale Reform Association Minutes, 19 November 1888, Rochdale Record Office. The Rochdale Reform Association was the official local Liberal Association but had retained its old Reform Association title in recognition of its heritage as a parliamentary reform association.

[37] Rochdale Reform Association Minutes, 4 October 1888, Rochdale Record Office.

[38] MLU, Union Committee, 15 April 1886, MCL, M283/1/1/2.

[39] MLU, Union Committee 29 April 1886, MCL, M283/1/1/2.

[40] MLU, Union Committee 4 May 1886, MCL, M283/1/1/2; MLU, General Meeting, 7 May 1886, MCL, M283/1/1/2.

Almost from the outset Liberal Unionists struggled with their ambivalent and sometimes ambiguous position. To try to fight the battle through the party caucuses was clearly a lost cause and to argue the Unionist case within them could be seen as imposing on them an obligation to accept the majority view. The majoritarian decision-making process of the party institutions left them with no role in the official party organisation, but the alternatives were unclear. By the July general election some Liberal Unionists had formed a branch of the Hartingtonite Liberal Committee of the Maintenance of the Legislative Union between Great Britain and Ireland. The branch organised an open-air public meeting in the city centre to coincide with the general election, but it was a very curious election meeting. Sir Henry James, the main speaker, thanked Liberal Unionists in Manchester for their support, but gave little indication as to what Liberal Unionists were actually supposed to do during the course of the general election.[41] The answer was, of course, nothing. It soon becomes very difficult to maintain the interest of political activists if the only direction they are given by their political leaders is to stay at home. The logic of their position demanded that specific activities be organised to retain loyalty and interest.

With Liberal reunion talks on the agenda at national level, some Liberal Unionists began to drift back to the party and engage in local political activity. Many Gladstonian Liberals welcomed this trend and put aside the enmities of the 1886 general election. The South-West divisional association issued a special circular to woo Liberal Unionists back into the fold. St. Luke's Ward Liberals continued to elect Liberal Unionists to the divisional council.[42] Elsewhere, however, the failure of Liberal Unionists to support the party at the 1886 general election was not quickly forgotten. In South Manchester, one of the first areas where an independent Liberal Unionist organisation was formed, the election of members to the divisional council produced acrimonious exchanges between the two factions of the party. In East Manchester the election of Liberal Unionists back on to party committees brought fears that the move would make divisions in the party worse. Although most leading Gladstonian Liberals expressed the general desire for reconciliation, there was little public discussion on the forms it might take or on areas of potential compromise. Moreover some important opinion-formers were losing patience with those who they charged with deserting the party at the time of its greatest need. The Liberal *Manchester Weekly Post* was particularly uncompromising, describing attempts at reunion as a 'well-meant waste of time and labour'.[43]

The Liberal Union executive committee seemed little troubled by moves by Liberal Unionists to organise separately. Their only real concern was how to treat Liberal Unionist voters when organising registration campaigns. Should the Liberals register Liberal Unionists on the grounds that the division was merely temporary, or would this action only help their opponents? Annual municipal elections meant this was an issue that had to be addressed immediately. The Liberal Union executive

41 *MG*, 2 July 1886.

42 *MG*, 19 January 1887.

43 *MWP*, 11 December 1886.

committee declined to offer guidance to local divisions, leaving the matter to local discretion.[44] Decisions not to include Liberal Unionists in registration work had important implications. Liberal Unionists were put beyond the pale as far as Liberal representative institutions were concerned, effectively barring them from party activities. Consequently Liberal Unionists were given a focus for their political activism – the registration of their voters – which did not necessary imply 'disloyalty' or force them to associate with the Conservatives. It was, however, an important step in the transition of Liberal Unionists from being a casually organised committee to developing into a separate political party. Despite Gladstonian concerns that the Manchester Liberal Party had suffered much damage at the hands of the Unionists, the lack of electoral confrontation, the relatively peaceful relations on the city council, and the limited activities of the Liberal Unionist association, led Gladstonians to become increasingly dismissive of their former members. The loss of erstwhile colleagues had been surprising, but few believed that the Liberal Unionists could operate as a fully functioning political party.[45]

Sir Henry James aptly illustrated the difficulties faced by Liberal Unionists, in attempting to define their own role as an independent political force, in a speech to the Manchester Reform Club. As many in his audience did not share his Unionist sympathies, he sought common ground with his hosts by launching a strongly worded attack on the Conservatives' Primrose League. This, however, enraged the leading Conservative newspaper in Manchester and, no doubt, many Conservative activists, with whom the Liberal Unionists had made common cause.[46] Speaking at the Reform Club allowed Sir Henry James to retain his symbolic associations with the Liberal tradition; however only by offending his new allies, the Conservatives, could he find shared ground with his former Liberal colleagues. If controversy could not be avoided even in the genteel atmosphere of an after-dinner speech at the Reform Club, the chances of Liberal Unionists maintaining their connections with the Liberal tradition at election time, whilst preserving a harmonious alliance with the Conservatives, were clearly limited. With Liberal Unionists institutionalising their position by attempting to create their own registration machinery and organisation, the potential for conflict was certain to grow.

The decision to launch a Liberal Unionist Association proper for Manchester was taken at a conference in February 1887 – although the precise role the organisation planned for itself was unclear.[47] One senior conference delegate believed the

44 MLU, Union Committee, 17 May 1887, MCL, M283/1/1/2.

45 '…there are no signs either that they [the Liberal Unionists] have increased or that they are in a position to do any of the ordinary work undertaken by a party organisation. There has not been, to the knowledge of your committee, a single instance of desertion from the Liberal ranks. But if the survey be extended and consideration be given to recent by-elections in various parts of the country, it will be seen that there has been a return to their allegiance to Liberal principles on the part of many doubters or dissidents…'. MLU, Annual Report (for 1888–89) to Annual General Meeting, 2 May 1889, MCL, M283/1/1/2.

46 *MC*, 8 February 1887.

47 *MG*, 7 February 1887.

association should act as a pressure group to influence the views of parliamentary candidates. Similarly, another felt that the primary aim should be to re-establish Unionist influence in Liberal Associations. At this stage there was no widespread wish to organise a separate political party, rather the aim was to establish organisational machinery to force the Liberal Party to address Liberal Unionist concerns about proposed Irish legislation. However in adopting this position it seemed they underestimated the commitment of the party to Gladstone and Gladstone's Home Rule scheme. Having largely opted out of Liberal Party activity for almost a year, it was difficult for them to influence the local associations to reverse their commitments to Home Rule, dominated as they then were by Home Rule enthusiasts.

Unlike some other areas, Liberal Unionists in Manchester seemed to have been very cautious about actively supporting Conservatives at the 1886 general election, or even co-operating with them to return Liberal Unionist candidates. After the 1886 election the Conservative press criticised the Liberal Unionists for failing to bring forward possible candidates for joint nomination.[48] Although Withington Conservatives boasted that 'a large number of Liberal Unionists voted for the Conservative candidate', there was no reference to Liberal Unionists actually taking an active part in the campaign.[49] North-West Manchester Conservatives rejoiced that some of their Liberal opponents had been taken 'out of the field', but regretted that they had not received the active help from Liberal Unionists that Conservatives in other parts of the country had enjoyed.[50] Liberal Unionist abstention characterised the election.

Liberal Unionist reluctance to withdraw fully from the Liberal Party and cooperate with the Conservatives made planning the future role of Liberal Unionism in Manchester very difficult. Manchester's Liberal Unionists looked largely to Hartington rather than Chamberlain for leadership, but Hartington showed only limited interest in developing Manchester as a political base, despite his connections with the area. When invited to a meeting at the Free Trade Hall, he declined to attend on the grounds that it was likely to be broken up by opponents, damaging the party's reputation. He was eventually persuaded to speak in Manchester, but the hostile reception he received on leaving the Free Trade Hall must have done little to persuade him that Manchester could be strong Liberal Unionist territory.[51] Without strong leadership, it was difficult to unite dissident Liberals behind a common strategy. No sooner had the Manchester Liberal Unionist Association been launched than the frustrations of party activists began to show. One conference delegate openly warned that if Liberal Unionists leaders did not adopt a more positive approach, many dissidents would return to the Liberal Party. Some believed that offering alternative proposals for land reform and Irish local self-government could provide a basis for

48 *MC*, 14 February 1887.

49 *MC*, 8 March 1887.

50 *MG*, 10 February 1887.

51 Sir Alfred Hopkinson, *Penultima* (London, 1930) 152–5.

reuniting the party.[52] Although Gladstonians encouraged Liberal Unionists to debate the possibility of reunion, they also made it clear that any compromise would have to involve the acceptance of some form of Home Rule.[53] Liberal Unionists remained in a dilemma – should they try to convert or conquer Home Rulers?

The death of Peter Rylands, the Liberal Unionist MP for Burnley, marked an important turning point for Manchester Liberal Unionism in two respects. Firstly the party lost a formidable supporter and organiser in the north-west. Secondly it forced local Liberal Unionists into an open and active alliance with the Conservatives for the first time. The failure of the Liberal Unionists nationally to find a candidate meant that Manchester Liberal Unionists, as one of the largest groups in the region, were called upon to support the Conservatives. Other than issue an election address full of embarrassing grammatical errors, it is unclear just what material assistance they rendered, but their involvement was sufficient to antagonise Arthur Symonds, secretary of the Manchester-based National Reform Union and, no doubt, many other Manchester Liberals.[54]

Whatever decisions the national Round Table Conference on Liberal Reunion reached, local Liberal activists were being forced into direct conflict by electoral events.[55] In an era when loyalty to a political tradition was only second to loyalty to religion, the emotional significance of former colleagues working with historic enemies cannot be understated. The language of moral absolutes that governed much of Gladstonain rhetoric left little room for compromise. Liberalism in Manchester was not simply a label, but a historic mission, with a rich history. It could fire up the most powerful emotions and motivate the committed to devote extraordinary amounts of energy and time to political activity. Memories were long. When one Conservative canvasser enquired of one Liberal's voting intention, he had a boiling bottle thrown at him; the elector concerned making it clear he declined to vote for 'the Peterloo butchers'.[56] On approaching a Catholic church in North Manchester the same canvasser was 'assailed with all manner of refuse, and covered with filth from an excited mob', whilst others had almost physically to fight their way out of Liberal districts.[57] In such circumstances co-operating with opposing political parties was regarded as little short of treachery.

The strength of feeling generated was little surprising when one considers the political longevity and experience of many senior activists. Ancoats Liberal organiser William Roche, who died in 1886, had been involved in the party since his

---

52 *MG*, 9–10 February 1887.

53 *MG*, 7 February 1887.

54 *MG*, 26 February 1887.

55 For background on the conference see M. Hurst, *Joseph Chamberlain and Liberal Reunion* (London, 1967).

56 Odds and Ends Magazine of the St. Paul's Literary Society, Volume XXXV (1889), 418–19, MCL, M38/4/2/35. No specific dates are given for the instances reported in this essay, but the implication seems to be that they took place within the author's recent memory.

57 Odds and Ends Magazine of the St. Paul's Literary Society, Volume XXXV (1889), 418–19, MCL, M38/4/2/35.

childhood. He had been actively involved in the temperance movement, in Chartism, and later was an active member of the Reform League. Locally he was a founder of the influential Piercey Street Liberal Club and was a long time activist in the local Liberal Association.[58] Youthful experiences and the political traditions of their families often shaped even those activists who did not take an active role in politics in their early life. Liberal Unionist Nathaniel Bradley's father was a radical activist at Peterloo and as a young man was also much influenced by the Chartists.[59] With traditions and histories as strong as these it is unsurprising that Liberal Unionists clung to their Liberal identity and were very cautious about embracing their old enemy.

At national level Liberal Unionists were gradually beginning to accept the logic that, with Britain's majoritarian electoral system, isolation from the Liberal mainstream necessitated co-operation with the Conservatives. By the time of the Bradford Conference of 1888, the prospects for agreement at national level between the two Liberal groups seemed hopeless – the differences between Home Rulers and Unionists seemed to become more intractable as time went on.[60] The Conservatives and Liberal Unionists were co-operating at Westminster and many felt similar relations should be fostered locally. Joseph Chamberlain, argued that some distinction should be retained between the two Unionist parties, yet also called for the creation of 'a party which is greater than all parties – a party for the nation; a party which shall have national interests, national security and national faith as the only watchwords to which it owes its existence'.[61] Although his use of the term 'party' may not necessarily have implied a single integrated organisation, it was a clear statement of an intention to maintain the Unionist alliance at parliamentary level.

Closer links fostered at national level naturally influenced Manchester Liberal Unionists to investigate a closer alliance locally. However, to a large extent, the Manchester Liberal Unionists were forced into a closer relationship with the Conservatives more by necessity than by choice. Two years after its creation, the Manchester Liberal Unionist Association still had no ward organisations or representative institutions on the Liberal model. Only three of the six parliamentary divisions had local committees. The Association claimed to have 'many Liberals of great influence' as members, but few held significant public office, and it is unclear how heavily involved they were in the work of the Association.[62] The limited reporting of Liberal Unionist activity in the Liberal and Conservative-dominated press makes an evaluation of their organisational work difficult, but it is clear that the resources of the Manchester Liberal Unionist Association were stretched very

58 *Pioneer*, 24 July 1886.
59 *Faces and Places*, 7 (1895–96), 117.
60 *MG*, 21 September 1888.
61 *MG*, 21 September 1888.
62 *MG*, 23 January 1889.

thinly.[63] The Manchester Association was active in organising Liberal Unionist activities across large parts of South-East Lancashire, but their regular rounds of anti-Home Rule public meetings were not overwhelmingly successful, often attracting more Home Rulers than Unionists. When speaking at a meeting in Littleborough, one Manchester Liberal Unionist saw his anti-Home Rule resolution defeated by 'at least ten to one'.[64] Even in John Bright's Rochdale often at least half of those attending the Unionist meetings were Home Rulers.[65] The party's failure to obtain a majority at its own poorly attended meetings can have done little for party morale and may partly explain the move to closer co-operation with the Conservatives. A joint Unionist demonstration at the Free Trade Hall, at which Liberal Unionists agreed to participate, was much more successful and on a scale that the Liberal Unionists alone could not have contemplated.[66]

The South Manchester Liberal Unionist Association was the strongest divisional association in Manchester, with several senior members determined to challenge the sitting Liberal MP at a future general election. They were not, however, an especially active branch. Their annual report for 1888 admitted that the 'past year had not furnished any scope for political activity' and there was no evidence of registration work being undertaken – a core activity for a nineteenth-century political association.[67] A year later the party did undertake a complete canvass of the district, from which they identified 772 members, 371 individuals who declared themselves to be supporters and 107 who declared general sympathy for Unionism. In all they claimed to have an estimated 1,500 Liberal Unionists in the constituency. However, in South-West Manchester, where Alfred Hopkinson was put forward as a Liberal Unionist parliamentary candidate in 1892, party strength was put at just 500. Many believed even these figures were exaggerations but it was thought that if the party could draw just 10 per cent of the Liberal vote in any Manchester constituency, then Home Rule candidates could be defeated. Liberal Unionists had come to accept that outright victory was unlikely and limited their ambitions to preventing Home Rule candidates from gaining election. Although this limited strategy was almost inevitable given their small size, the adoption of this negative approach put paid to any local hopes of reunion and increased the mutual hostility between the two wings of the Liberal Party.[68]

A number of leading Liberal Unionists in Manchester had differences with the Liberal Party well before the Home Rule crisis. Some Anglican Liberals,

63 Paradoxically, the only detailed coverage of Liberal Unionist activities is to be found in the pages of the Gladstonian *Manchester Guardian*. To the alarm of some Gladstonians, a consortium of Liberal Unionists took over the struggling *Manchester Examiner* at the end of 1888 but were unable to prevent that paper's demise. See Letter, W. Mather to C.P. Scott, 28 December 1888, JRULM, CPSC 118/120.

64 *MG*, 6 March 1889.

65 *MG*, 31 January 1889.

66 *MG*, 4 March 1889; *MC*, 4 March 1889.

67 *MG*, 19 March 1889.

68 *MG*, 28 March 1890.

such as George Milner, were known to be unhappy with the party's flirtation with disestablishment and had voted against their party in 1885 as a protest.[69] Others were estranged for more prosaic reasons. Henry C. Pingstone, a long-serving councillor in New Cross Ward, was always a controversial figure and in 1885 he was bitterly attacked by a ratepayers' association in connection with alleged irregularities in council business.[70] These allegations remained with him throughout his council career and given this was a time of increased scrutiny of council activity during gas scandals in Salford, mayoral corruption in Stockport and police scandals in Manchester, the allegations naturally inhibited the development of his municipal career in the Liberal Party.[71] George Clay, Liberal Unionist councillor for Oxford Ward, had long been at odds with his Liberal ward committee and was the first Liberal Unionist councillor to face a Gladstonian opponent.[72] Clay, however, played little active role in Liberal Unionist politics.[73] Other Liberal Unionist members of the city council similarly seem to have played only a limited role in party work. Alderman Schofield, a council veteran, although nominally becoming a Liberal Unionist, never regarded himself as a 'party' politician, although years previously 'he was regarded as a Whig'.[74] Older Liberals who opposed Gladstone's Home Rule plans were often very reluctant to come out in public opposition to their party. Both Oliver Heywood and R.N. Philips only declared themselves after much persuasion by local leaders.[75] As time passed, many were very uncomfortable with the growing alliance with the Conservatives at national level. Sir Thomas Bazley severed his connection with the Liberal Unionists in protest at the parliamentary leaders seemingly acting in outright opposition to all Gladstonian Liberal proposals, whatever their merits, and condemned 'a Liberal Unionism which is fast becoming a synonym for Toryism'.[76] The loss of such a senior figure from Liberal Unionist ranks prompted the national Liberal Publications Department to issue a pamphlet containing his resignation letter. It was an embarrassing blow for Manchester Liberal Unionism.[77]

Not all Liberal Unionist members were elderly veterans moving to the ends of their careers. Nathaniel Bradley, a Medlock Street councillor, did not become actively involved in Liberal politics until after the Liberal Unionist secession.[78] He was, however, the only genuine new recruit to the Liberal Unionist city council group in the decade after 1886. The major problem for the Liberal Unionists in bringing forward new figures for election to public office was the danger of provoking a

[69] See correspondence in the *ME*, 2–6 July 1886.

[70] *Faces and Places*, 8 (1896–97), 86.

[71] A. Redford, *The History of Local Government in Manchester*, volume three (London, 1940), 8–15.

[72] *MG*, 27 October 1891.

[73] *Faces and Places*, 8 (1896–97), 75.

[74] *Faces and Places*, 2 (1890–91), 101.

[75] Hopkinson, *Penultima*, 154–5.

[76] LPD Leaflet No 1668, NRU, 37, 20, MCL, 306 N6.

[77] LPD Leaflet No 1668, NRU, 37, 20, MCL, 306 N6.

[78] *Faces and Places*, 7 (1895–96), 150–51.

contest with Gladstonian Liberals. There was little desire, until the 1890s, to provoke contests on purely partisan lines – if a sitting councillor was thought to have served the public well there was often a reluctance to bring forward an opposing candidate. Moreover up until the 1890s, the Liberal Unionists were widely regarded as allies of the Liberals at municipal level. The Liberal assault on George Clay marked a new period in municipal conflict, with Gladstonians beginning to challenge sitting Liberal Unionist councillors.[79]

The 1892 general election, however, probably did more to harden attitudes on both sides than the harsh words exchanged in the Clay contest or in the council chamber. The impossibility of a Liberal alliance at municipal level and a Unionist alliance at parliamentary level soon became clear and by 1892 the Liberal Unionists were regarded as having moved into alliance with the Conservatives at municipal level, too.[80] This move to closer relations on the city council had, perhaps, wider ramifications than any other single Liberal Unionist action. Liberal Unionists only ever consisted of around a fifth of the total Liberal representation on the council. With the enlargement of the city council in 1890, they were reduced to less than a sixth of the total Liberal force. However, with ten Liberal Unionists allying themselves with the Conservatives, the Liberals lost their nominal majority on the council for the first time since incorporation. A combination of convention, continuing hopes for reunification and a fear of importing 'Imperial' politics into the council chamber meant that Gladstonian Liberals failed to oppose the re-election of no less than eight Liberal Unionists between 1887 and 1891. Many of these unopposed Liberal Unionist returns were in wards which Gladstonian Liberals would probably otherwise have won. New Cross, H.C Pingstone's ward, returned Liberals in every contested election between 1886 and 1895. Exchange Ward, in which a Liberal Unionist had an unopposed return in 1888, also returned a Gladstonian Liberal in every contested election during the same period. Even in newly created wards such as Rusholme, Liberal Unionist victories were often largely due to Liberal reluctance to engage in a fight with former colleagues. On the two occasions the Liberal Party fought a contested election in the ward between 1891 and 1895 they won. Once ground had been relinquished, however, it could not always be regained easily. After 1892, with a Liberal government in office struggling first with Home Rule and then over its own leadership, unseating established Liberal Unionist figures at local level was an unenviable task.

It would be a mistake, however, to believe that Liberal Unionist councillors were in an intrinsically strong position or that they were supported by a strong independent party organisation. Desperate appeals for subscribers fell largely on deaf ears and the central district association became heavily indebted.[81] The largely suburban South

---

79 See the election summary sections in the *Official Handbook of Manchester and Salford* (Manchester, 1891–95).

80 Simon, *A Century of City Government*, 400.

81 Manchester and District Liberal Unionist Association circular, 19 June 1891, MCL, Local Studies Box 517, 329.942.

Manchester division was organisationally the strongest for the party, but by 1892 the party had just one councillor in this division. In South-West Manchester the Conservatives allowed the Liberal Unionists to put forward their own nominee for the local parliamentary seat, safe in the knowledge they were unlikely to win, as the Liberal Unionists did not have as much as a single councillor in the district. North-West Manchester was the strongest municipal district for the Liberal Unionists – the party having councillors in Exchange, Oxford, St. Anne's and St. James's wards – yet it was organisationally the weakest division for the party. In 1890 it was the only division in Manchester that had neither an official Liberal Unionist association or even a 'good nucleus' of activists.[82] This apparent paradox is not as puzzling as it might first appear. The North-West division incorporated the whole of the central and the commercial quarter of the city, and with its large number of non-resident ratepayers was notoriously difficult to organise.[83] Although Liberal Unionist strength was greatest in middle-class and commercial communities, the geographical dispersion of Liberal Unionists, many living outside the city, made it very difficult for them to be mobilised effectively. Had Liberal Unionist support been concentrated in one suburb of Manchester, they could have possibly built a powerful political base in that area. However, the majoritarian electoral system was not designed to reward third parties with geographically dispersed strength and consequently the physical distribution of Liberal Unionist support further forced the party to rely on a Conservative alliance. Without a physically concentrated organisation of its own, the bipolar tendencies of the electoral system were irresistible.

The growth of separate Liberal Unionist organisations caused the Conservatives, as well as the Liberals, some alarm. The 1886 general election had demonstrated that in areas of Liberal Unionist strength, such as South Manchester, Liberal Unionist leaders were unwilling merely to be junior partners in a Unionist alliance.[84] Most Liberal Unionist organisers, however, were aware of Conservative concerns and were careful not to antagonise their Unionist partners unnecessarily. In North Manchester, for example, special care was taken to ensure those voters identified as Liberal Unionists were indeed former Liberals and not 'stolen' Conservatives.[85] Yet although the Liberal Unionists were completing some form of canvass in their most active divisions, it was not on the scale of the major parties who took their registrations claims to the revising barrister and fought out registration battles through the courts. This, after all, was an expensive and time-consuming process which required the attention of a professional registration agent on a full-time basis and massive voluntary assistance – something which the Liberal Unionists clearly lacked. By 1890 the Liberal Unionists were regularly holding joint public events

[82] *MG*, 6 February 1890.

[83] It was this division that was famously termed the Exchange Division by Winston Churchill during his short tenure of the seat between 1906 to 1908.

[84] See chapter one for details of the South Manchester Unionist nomination dispute.

[85] *MG*, 1 April 1890.

with the Conservatives and co-operation in registration work was the next logical step if the parties were not to duplicate work.[86]

Intelligent Conservative tactics and the lack of a viable alternative drove Liberal Unionists into a closer alliance with their former adversaries. By 1890 Liberal Unionists still had only three divisional associations and had only recently obtained a registration agent.[87] Although Liberal Unionist grandee Sir Joseph Lee boasted of a collective membership of 1,500 to 2,000, there was, in the words of the *Manchester Guardian*, 'a fine generality about that statement which is suggestive'.[88] Although the notion of 'membership' was a loosely defined one in relation to late nineteenth-century political parties, the level of activism and attendance at meetings would indicate an active membership of little more than a tenth of that figure.[89] To put these statistics into context, the Manchester Reform Club with a system of election for membership and a large annual subscription rate had at least 1,200 members during this period and a long waiting list of those keen to join.[90] With Liberal Unionists lacking an organisational framework of any sort in half of Manchester and over-stretched in the remainder, Conservative overtures and offers of co-operation could not be spurned cheaply. The Conservatives offered the Liberal Unionists generous terms – including a Joint Conference Committee, with an equal number of representatives from each party, to co-ordinate registration work.[91] The first action of the Conservatives on the JCC was to offer the Liberal Unionist Executive the joint parliamentary candidature of the South-West Manchester division. This was an intelligent move by the Conservative representatives. When the local Liberal Unionist chairman, Alfred Hopkinson, accepted the candidature, it gave the leader of the Liberal Unionists a vested interest in bonding the two parties together, while not threatening the Conservatives' existing electoral position. Furthermore there was great significance in whom Hopkinson was being invited to challenge – Jacob Bright – a Radical icon, brother of John Bright and president of the Manchester Reform Club – the spiritual and historic home of Manchester Liberalism. Hopkinson was later to claim that he accepted the candidature against Bright with much reluctance, implying that he foresaw the crisis that was soon to break out at the Club.[92]

The Manchester Reform Club had been, hitherto, a passive player in the Home Rule debate. Standing at the head of one of Manchester's finest streets, it was a powerful symbol of the triumph of Manchester Liberalism and there was a desire on

86 *MG*, 31 January 1890.

87 *MG*, 6 June 1890.

88 *MG*, 6 June 1890.

89 The largest recorded membership total for a Liberal Unionist organisation in the period is 204 for the South Manchester Liberal Unionist Association in 1890 (*MG*, 28 March 1890). This was regarded as the strongest parliamentary division of the party in Manchester. Regular attendances at Liberal Unionist Council meetings were usually substantially smaller.

90 See the minute books of the Manchester Reform Club, 1885–95, JRULM (Deansgate).

91 *MG*, 6 February 1890.

92 Hopkinson, *Penultima*, 161–3.

all sides not to bring conflicts over Home Rule beyond its portals. When the Liberal Unionists organised their first major conference in Manchester, they were thus granted the use of the Reform Club for their evening entertainment.[93] Respect for the past services of leading Liberal Unionists inhibited Gladstonian Liberals from taking action against the minority of Liberal Unionist members.[94] The first president of the club, R.N. Phillips, had gone over to the Liberal Unionist side, as had the club's vice-president, Benjamin Armitage.[95] It was also feared that attempts to remove Liberal Unionists could alienate those who were genuinely undecided on Home Rule.[96]

By continuing to accommodate Liberal Unionists, the Manchester Reform Club managed to avoid the damaging split that engulfed the National Liberal Club and which saw 300 Liberal Unionists follow Hartington's example and resign their membership.[97] In Manchester, personal sentiment towards former colleagues had much to do with the accommodation. John Bright, in many respects the father of the 'Manchester School' and an inspirational figure for North-West Liberals, continued to use the club intermittently right up to his death and Gladstonians clearly had little desire to provoke a conflict with this frail icon of past glories. Thus it is very significant that no action was taken against Liberal Unionist members of the club until after the death of Bright in 1889. The nomination of Hopkinson against club president Jacob Bright in South-West Manchester, however, 'was held by the majority of the members to be a breach of club etiquette' and the truce was broken.[98] Gladstonians protested to the club's officers and a special general meeting passed a resolution condemning Hopkinson by 'little short of three to one'.[99] Having established their numerical preponderance and expressed their disgust at Hopkinson's action, the Gladstonians took their opposition no further. It was, however, a sign of a gathering storm.

Despite the powerful bonds of club life, electoral competition provoked more conflict. A by-election, held in North-East Manchester in 1891, drew the two Liberal parties into open conflict. C.P. Scott, editor of the *Manchester Guardian*, and a leading figure in the Reform Club, faced Sir James Ferguson, a Conservative Unionist. This represented an important test for the Government in a marginal seat and came immediately after a series of promising by-election results for the Liberals. Leading Liberal Unionists in the Reform Club actively supported Ferguson and Scott

---

93 By this time the Reform Club itself played no formal role in local party politics other than providing a meeting place for Liberals on major social and political occasions. Mills, *The Manchester Reform Club*, 81.

94 *MG*, 7 February 1887.

95 *MG*, 6 February 1890; *MG*, 23 February 1887. There were two senior Manchester Liberals called Benjamin Armitage. The one referred to here was a resident of Sorrel Bank, Salford and was usually referred to in printed contemporary sources as 'Benjamin Armitage (Sorrel Bank)' to distinguish him from his namesake.

96 Letter, J.A. Beith to C.P Scott, 23 July 1889, JRULM, CPSC 118/126.

97 *MG*, 25 January 1889.

98 Mills, *The Manchester Reform Club*, 78.

99 Mills, *The Manchester Reform Club*, 78.

went down to a narrow defeat.[100] Gladstonians were appalled at the action of Liberal Unionists in assisting the Conservatives. H.J. Roby condemned 'the presence of traitors in the camp' and accurately predicted that the current state of affairs, with Liberal Unionists actively involved in Liberal organisations while fighting official Liberal candidates, could not survive a general election.[101] There was a suspicion that Liberal Unionists had used their position as members of the Club to pass on information from private discussions held within its walls. The club committee came under pressure to take decisive action and issued a circular making it clear that active support for a Conservative candidate was inconsistent with membership of the Club.

Gladstonians struggled to deal with their Unionist dissidents partly because they had such mixed feelings about them. The correspondence of a 'Twenty Year Member' illustrates their confusion.[102] He divided Liberal Unionists into three categories – those who were really Tories at heart and were using Home Rule as an excuse to leave, those who simply wished to draw attention to themselves and those who remained genuinely Liberals but had conscientious doubts about Home Rule. Thus Manchester Liberals found it difficult to condemn the whole body of Liberal Unionists outright – the bonds of fellowship were too great – and this helps explain why some were still discussing the possibility of Liberal Reunion after 1892. Liberal Unionists, while angry with what seemed tantamount to a dismissal notice, began to recognise that their position in the Reform Club was somewhat anomalous. A least one Liberal Unionist resigned before the internal conflict started, accepting that his own views were moving further and further away from those of the Gladstonian majority and recognising that 'it is no longer the home rule question pure and simple which divides the two sections, and the sooner this fact is realised the better'.[103] With political differences already institutionalised with the creation of formal Liberal Unionist associations, some Liberal Unionists began to suggest a complete withdrawal from the Reform Club, to avoid further irritation.[104]

After several years of trying to reconcile differences the only solution seemed to be separation, at least during times of major electoral conflict. The truce did not survive the 1892 general election, when the Liberal Unionists reneged on their gentleman's agreement to withdraw from partisan actions within the bounds of the club. Benjamin Armitage chose the occasion of the election to invite Arthur Balfour, and the controversial Conservative brewery owner, Stephen Chesters Thompson, to lunch at the Club.[105] Armitage was still a member of the club's general committee and must have known the reaction the move was likely to provoke. Inevitably, a protest meeting was called. It was to be the last major clash between Gladstonians

100 Sir J. Ferguson (Conservative) 4058, C.P Scott (L) 3908.
101 *MG*, 16 October 1891.
102 *MG*, 15 October 1891.
103 *MG*, 15 October 1891.
104 *MG*, 21 October 1891.
105 Mills, *The Manchester Reform Club*, 79.

and Unionists in the Reform Club. After 1892, with the ever-closer relationship between Liberal Unionists and their Conservative allies, Unionist activity in the club declined. Although few would now regard the Liberal split of 1886 as simply a 'revolt of the Whigs', it is clear that the elite Reform Club suffered more than most Manchester Liberal institutions from divisions over Home Rule. Up to a quarter of its active membership resisted moves to exclude Liberal Unionist parliamentary candidates. To understand why this was so, it is important to look beyond issues and personalities to the culture of the organisation. In attempting to be a catholic institution, it was always more likely to suffer during times of ideological division. The majoritarianism of the caucus gave little hope to those in minorities – they had little choice but to leave and start afresh. In the Reform Club differences of opinion seemed to be actively encouraged as a reflection of a healthy Liberal environment.[106] Thus it would be wrong to infer that divisions in the Reform Club were more intense because it was an upper-middle-class organisation and Liberal Unionists were disproportionately upper middle class. The general atmosphere of tolerance and fellowship in the Reform Club meant that Liberals and Liberal Unionist continued to work together in this forum long after they had been divided into separate political associations. Thus when conflicts did arise they arose later and were of much greater intensity.

Liberal Unionists did not slide easily into a Conservative alliance, despite welcoming Conservative tactics and the lack of a viable alternative. South Manchester Liberal Unionists possessed the strongest association in the city and had the confidence to assert an independent line when required, particularly when local Conservative leaders acted without consulting their allies. The most potentially damaging dispute came when Sir Thomas Sowler retired as the jointly agreed Unionist parliamentary nominee for the division. Liberal Unionists were kept largely in the dark about Sowler's resignation and only heard the decision through the local press or a few moments before it was publicly announced at a meeting in a local Conservative Club.[107] The Conservatives then compounded Liberal Unionist anger by bringing forward an alternative candidate, J.W. Hamilton, without consultation, and then simply asked the Liberal Unionists to confirm the decision that they had already taken. This flew in the face of an earlier decision by both parties to set up a joint committee to discuss key decisions and take collective action.[108] The complete bypassing of this committee by the Conservatives caused much anger amongst Liberal Unionist leaders who made it clear they would not accept the decision.[109]

[106] 'One may be permitted to point out that the club is not a political organisation, but it provides a home for Liberals in which they can discuss questions of public interest in a liberal spirit. Agreement is not expected on every question of public policy, and the main thing is the Liberal atmosphere.' Mills, *The Manchester Reform Club*, 81.

[107] *MG*, 12 January 1891.

[108] *MG*, 24 March 1891.

[109] It is unclear whether this joint committee ever actually met. There were no discussions of its proceedings at the Liberal Unionist annual meeting of 1891, or any reference to its activities in the party's annual report.

Deadlock continued for several months until a joint meeting of the Conservative and Liberal Unionist divisional associations agreed to submit a new candidate, Viscount Emlyn, to each association separately, before formal adoption proceeded.[110]

Emlyn was adopted as the joint Unionist candidate later that year. The battle had not been so much over which party should be empowered to select candidates, rather the level of recognition the Liberal Unionists should have in the alliance. Emlyn, was after all, a prominent Unionist, son of the Earl of Cawdor, and Conservative MP for Carmarthenshire between 1874 and 1885.[111] Nor is it at all clear that the divisional Conservative association were in any way committed to a particular personality. Conservative insensitivity rather than a desire to marginalise Liberal Unionists seems to have been the major cause of the problems. The Liberal Unionists were angry but could not afford to press their claims too hard. Despite South Manchester's Liberal Unionist chairman asserting that the Manchester group were 'probably the strongest in England outside Birmingham', they were not strong enough to assert any real degree of independence in strategy, candidate selection or organisation without damaging their own cause.[112]

Following the 1892 general election the Liberal Unionists gradually merged their every-day political activities into joint endeavours with the Conservatives. Thus when a Liberal Unionist candidate won the South Manchester parliamentary seat in 1895, it was a victory for the Conservatives in all but name. Although the Manchester and District Liberal Unionist Association continued, its politics and outlook were little different to those of the Conservatives. Indeed in terms of its policy towards Home Rule, some of its members became even more uncompromising on the issue than their Conservative colleagues. At the Liberal Unionists' annual meeting in 1893, the mover of the principal motion, W. Hughes, declared that Liberal Unionists should have supported Randolph Churchill's call to defend Ulster by force of arms.[113] Faced with statements like this, Manchester Liberals increasingly regarded their former colleagues as having simply become Conservatives, and worthy of no special consideration. Rumours about negotiations between Liberal Unionists and Gladstone at Westminster just before the 1892 general election attracted little interest in Manchester and even less public discussion. The Liberal *South Manchester Chronicle* spoke for many when it felt there was 'small chance of an agreement or even preliminary negotiations'.[114] It was also clear that many senior Liberals no longer regarded the return of the Liberal Unionists as being at all desirable. Sir Henry Roscoe MP, harassed by Liberal Unionists in his South Manchester constituency, made it clear that he neither regretted the Unionist secession or believed there was any way in which they could ever return to the Liberal Party.[115]

110 *MG*, 28 June 1891.
111 *MG*, 26 March 1891.
112 *MG*, 26 March 1891.
113 *MG*, 13 April 1893.
114 *SMC*, 17 June 1892.
115 *MG*, 4 November 1891.

Liberalism had more pressing concerns. By 1890 organised labour was becoming discontented with its marginal position in the Liberal coalition, and in particular its exclusion from the city council.[116] Veiled threats from the trades council produced the desired results and its two leading figures , George Kelley and Matthew Arrandale, were successful in obtaining Liberal nominations for the town council. Both had been active Liberals for some time, but their determination to promote labour-related issues both within the party and the council chamber, meant that the issue of Home Rule no longer dominated the local political agenda as it had done in the late 1880s.[117] From 1892 the Independent Labour Party became a significant influence in local political life, forcing Liberals to re-examine their priorities. When Manchester Liberals produced their first formal political programme, the Progressive Municipal Programme, it was clear that local labour issues, not Irish government reforms, had become central to local political debate. The Liberal Unionist secession could be dismissed as an inevitable consequence of the march of democracy toward 'New Liberalism'.

Contemporaries in both wings of the Liberal Party regarded Liberal Unionist strength in Manchester to be greater than that of any other part of the country outside Birmingham. However, the culture and framework of local political institutions limited the prospects of an independent third party. The divisions of 1886 did not significantly damage Manchester Liberalism because Liberal Unionists, desperately clinging to the claim that they were true to Liberal traditions, were very reluctant to assist their historical enemies. The Liberal Party had never had a particularly strong local organisation and the reorganisations provoked by the 1885 electoral reforms produced much internal dissent and confusion. By June 1886 most structural and organisational questions had been settled, and the rout of 1885 was partially reversed. The withdrawal of Liberal Unionist subscriptions produced only short-term inconvenience for the party that did not have a measurable impact on party activity. In the November municipal elections the party made two net gains in both 1886 and 1887, and took two-thirds of the seats in the new wards created in 1890. In contrast the Liberal Unionists failed to develop significant party organisation in four of the six parliamentary divisions of Manchester, and none at all in the one which furnished most of their town council representatives. Their only significant political success was in depriving the Liberal Party of an overall majority on the city council for the first time. This change was not as serious as might have appeared partly because both members and voters did not see the city council merely in party terms and partly because the change made it more difficult for the Independent Labour Party to blame Liberals for existing council policies on labour issues. Indeed with the Liberal Party in a minority it could now freely criticise council management and develop an ambitious Progressive Municipal Programme, knowing that it would not be called upon immediately to redeem the pledges within it.

---

[116] J. Hill, 'Manchester and Salford Politics and the Early Development of the Independent Labour Party', *International Review of Social History*, 26 (1981), 171–201.

[117] *Faces and Places*, 7 (1895–6), 145; *Faces and Places*, 2 (1890–91), 92.

CHAPTER FOUR

Leicester: Unionism Marginalised?

The enduring strength of Manchester Liberalism during the Home Rule crisis illustrates just how local parties could survive disagreements that rocked the parties at Westminster. Regional and local circumstances were often very important in determining the effect political conflicts had on individual Liberal Associations. Indeed, national issues sometimes played only a limited part in local political debate. When the Home Rule crisis broke at Westminster, Leicester Liberals were preoccupied by a political battle of a very different sort and initially seemed to take little interest in the Irish debate. Without a substantial Irish population in the town, the issue had far less resonance and immediacy than was the case in Manchester. Although a significant number of senior Liberals left the party over the issue, the Home Rule campaign brought back into the Liberal fold many who were dissatisfied both with Leicester's new Radical MP and the Liberal Association's leadership. The issue gave all Gladstonian Liberals an issue to campaign around and even when the Liberal leadership brushed aside democratic convention and effectively chose a new parliamentary candidate themselves in 1890 the outcry was far less than might have been expected because the candidate was a staunch Home Ruler.

Had Radicals had their way in 1884, and selected Richard Chamberlain, brother of Joe, as their parliamentary candidate, the local party may have ended up much more divided and the Liberal Unionists may have obtained an important foothold in the East Midlands.[1] During the early 1880s many Radicals undoubtedly looked to Joseph Chamberlain as a major political inspiration. Leicester, surrounded by a largely agricultural county, was a natural constituency for his 'Unauthorised Programme'.[2] Chamberlain's failure to capture Leicester suggests that there were profound limitations to the influence of Birmingham's former first citizen on nearby towns. Despite the growth of a national media and national campaign tours, the urban politics of Leicester demonstrated that ever smaller boroughs could retain an autonomous political culture, sometimes resisting the influence of national debates in favour of more specific local issues. Leicester stayed largely with Gladstone and, as a consequence of Birmingham's defection to the Unionist cause, could thereafter lay claim to being the leading centre of Liberalism in the Midlands.

Leicester's own dynamic local political agenda diluted the immediate impact of the Home Rule controversy. Leicester Liberals had their own particular

---

1 See chapter two.

2 For an evaluation of the Programme see C. Howard, 'Joseph Chamberlain and the "Unauthorized Programme"', *English Historical Review*, 65 (1950), 477–91.

preoccupations in the spring of 1886 and were involved in a major campaign on the 'Vaccination question'.[3] Leicester had a strong tradition of libertarian opposition to the national legislation for the compulsory vaccination of children, with Leicester Liberals taking a leading role in the Anti-Compulsory Vaccination League. Their campaigns achieved considerable success. In 1878 of the 4,446 children born in Leicester, 3,730 were vaccinated. By 1884, although the number of births had increased to 4,849, the number vaccinated had dropped to 1,700.[4] Parents of children not vaccinated were liable to fines and imprisonment, but until the early 1880s the local enforcement authority, the board of guardians, had taken a non-confrontational approach.[5] On the Leicester Board, those in favour of compulsory vaccination – and prosecution of 'offenders' – were almost exclusively Conservatives, giving this extremely controversial issue a strong partisan dimension. When, in October 1883, 1,000 prosecutions were authorised on the casting vote of the board chairman, a substantial campaign of resistance and civil disobedience followed.[6] At the triennial board elections in 1886, the local Radical press backed a campaign to unseat Conservative supporters of compulsory vaccination and the contest rapidly developed into a straight partisan battle between the two parties.[7] The strength of feeling against the guardians was little surprising given the numbers opposed to compulsory vaccination. The prosecutions did little to deter the opposition and each prosecution was met with a wave of civil disobedience. By March 1886, 25 people had been sent to prison, 101 parents had had their homes broken up under distress for unpaid fines and over 2,500 people had been brought before the magistrates, according to Liberal calculations.[8] Each imprisonment became an opportunity to publicise the anti-compulsory vaccination cause and each release from prison a celebration of defiance against the Conservative guardians. Release from prison turned figures of modest social standing, such as Charles Paling, a shoe worker from Aylestone Park, into popular celebrities embraced by local Nonconformist ministers and senior public figures.[9]

There are several reasons for the Liberal Party breaking with tradition and campaigning as a party in the guardians election. The very intensity of feeling on the issue within the party was clearly a major factor. The Liberal Association's network of extensive ward organisations could clearly play a successful part in

[3] R. Lambert, 'A Victorian National Health Service: State Vaccination 1855–71', *Historical Journal* 5 (1962), 1–18; N. Durbach, 'Class, Gender and the Conscientious Objector to Vaccination 1898–1907', *Journal of British Studies*, 42 (2002), 58–83.

[4] *LDM*, 7 April 1886.

[5] A ruling by the Local Government Board, in response to a request from the Dewsbury Board of Guardians, meant that vaccination officers were expected to obtain the consent of the guardians before proceeding with prosecutions – effectively giving the guardians the choice of whether to prosecute. *LDM*, 16 March 1886.

[6] *LDM*, 5 May 1886.

[7] *MFP*, 27 March 1886.

[8] *LDM*, 31 March 1886.

[9] *LDM*, 16 March 1886.

the campaign. All the Conservative guardians had, with just two exceptions, voted in favour of prosecutions. They had, however, only succeeded because a number of supposed Liberals had also supported prosecutions. Moves to stand 'official' Liberal candidates were thus designed to ensure that in future the party would have more control over nominees claiming to carry the Liberal ticket for important and controversial public bodies.[10] Moreover the Anti-Compulsory Vaccination League was inexperienced in fighting local elections.[11] The only way Liberal demands for a more vigorous prosecution of the campaign could be met were if Liberal ward organisations themselves took up the challenge of organising nominations. Hence while the Conservatives were organising a large loyalist demonstration at the Temperance Hall in opposition to the first Home Rule Bill, Leicester Liberals seem to have hardly noticed events at Westminster, embroiled as they were in a bitter and bruising board of guardians' election.[12]

The guardians' contest was useful to the Liberal Association in giving the party a common goal to fight for after almost two years of internal dissension. Radicals not only numbered amongst the strongest opponents of compulsory vaccination, but they also saw the board elections as an opportunity to highlight other issues of local government reform. North St. Margaret's ward Liberal Association passed a resolution calling for the abolition of the £30 rental qualification for guardian candidates and in favour of 'one man, one vote' for guardian elections.[13] All Saints' Ward Liberals took similar steps.[14] Even the 'moderate' Liberal *Leicester Daily Mercury* spoke out in criticism of the electoral procedures of the Sturges Bourne system as being detrimental to Liberal prospects of success.[15] Indignation at an electoral system that allowed the dead to 'vote' and voting papers to be filled in without the knowledge or consent of the elector was tapped to rouse Liberal voters in support of the work of local ward organisations.[16] Elsewhere the elections offered the opportunity to mobilise dormant associations, such as that in St. Leonard's parish, which reportedly 'had been asleep for some time'.[17]

The election brought the Liberal Party an impressive victory under very difficult conditions. Some of the electoral divisions of the board, such as Castle View and Newarke where two Conservatives were returned unopposed, were very small, making opposition to entrenched representatives almost impossible. However the old regime, with its compulsory vaccination majority, was turned into a Liberal majority of 23 to 13. In all, 26 members of the new board opposed the 'compulsory clauses' of the Vaccination Acts.[18] The election was a complete success for the

10 Letter, John Atkins, *LDM*, 6 April 1886.
11 See comments of G. Collins, *MFP*, 27 March 1886.
12 *MFP*, 10 April 1886.
13 *LDM*, 24 March 1886.
14 *MFP*, 27 March 1886.
15 *LDM*, 20 March 1886.
16 See comments of A. Both, *LDM*, 6 April 1886.
17 *LDM*, 1 April 1886.
18 *MFP*, 17 April 1886.

Liberals, justifying their opposition to the vaccination prosecutions and giving weight to calls for reform of the electoral system for board contests.[19] Following the Liberal triumph the Board passed a resolution rescinding authority to prosecute by 26 votes to 8, as Conservative opposition collapsed.[20] Even in mid-May however, as the Home Rule debate gradually squeezed into the columns of the local press as the most prominent issue, the vaccination question was not quite dead. A major anti-compulsory vaccination demonstration was organised to coincide with the seizure of goods for non-payment of outstanding fines. The home of one anti-vaccinator was completely barricaded to resist the bailiffs and it took a squad of police officers, assisted by the chief constable, to break in and seize property from the house. The local Highfields brass band and a large body of hostile demonstrators completed this particular piece of street theatre with the secretary of the Anti-Compulsory Vaccination League buying back the property at the subsequent sale.[21] The issue was also kept alive by the Conservatives who ordered an inquiry into their electoral defeat. Several Conservative opponents of compulsory vaccination were alleged to have voted for Liberal candidates and, as the system of voting allowed party officers to identify the 'guilty' men, action was deemed necessary to deter future disloyalty. Perhaps somewhat unwisely, the committee of the Conservative Club summoned the alleged offenders to explain themselves. After two members of the club resigned in anger and others refused to discuss the matter, the issue was allowed to drop, but not until considerable ill-feeling had been generated.[22]

The anti-compulsory vaccination agitation was valuable not only in bringing Liberals together in a successful campaign and in rebuilding ward organisation, but also in diverting attention from the potentially divisive Home Rule issue. The representative of the 'moderate' section of Leicester Liberalism in parliament, Alexander McArthur, had severe doubts about Gladstone's first Home Rule proposals and for a time seemed destined to vote against the government. Although a supporter of a limited form of Irish self-government, he was extremely wary of the more extreme brands of Irish Nationalism. McArthur remarked that if the Irish were to suffer under a future Conservative government 'the verdict of the people would be that it served them right' for forcing the Liberal government out.[23] Perhaps believing McArthur would be prepared to be guided by the views of his Liberal Association, Leicester's Liberal leaders moved quickly to pass a policy resolution in support of Home Rule. As early as 12 April 1886, the Association's finance and general purposes committee met and called a meeting of the wider general committee to discuss the proposals.[24] From the point of view of fostering party unity, the meeting was not an unqualified success. McArthur failed to attend, supposedly through

19 Of the 17,034 voting papers that had been sent out, 4,414 were not filled in and 937 were declared spoilt or otherwise disallowed. *LDM*, 14 April 1886.

20 *MFP*, 8 May 1886.

21 *LDM*, 13 May 1886.

22 *LDM*, 5 June 1886.

23 *MFP*, 30 January 1886.

24 LLA, Finance and General Purposes Committee, 12 April 1886, LRO, 11 D 57/2.

illness, and his absence only helped to increase speculation about his own intentions toward the Home Rule proposals. Picton gave the proposals only a guarded welcome and took exception to the exclusion of Irish MPs from Westminster. Only Paget, representing Harborough, exhibited any enthusiasm, urging members to sink minor differences.[25] Indeed, the grass roots of the party seemed, in general, much more enthusiastic about the proposals than their parliamentary representatives. On the initiative of Nonconformist leader Rev. J. Page Hopps, the general committee passed a resolution in favour of the Government of Ireland and Land Purchase Bills without any recorded opposition.[26]

Leicester's Liberal leaders were clearly concerned at the danger of a breach with their MPs over the Irish question and there was soon speculation that if they did threaten to vote against the Gladstonian proposals the Association would be ready to apply considerable pressure to persuade them to reconsider. This threat was not altogether welcomed by some parts of the Radical press, some of whom felt a more subtle approach would be more beneficial.[27] In early May representatives from the finance and general purposes committee met with the borough MPs to discuss the possibility of holding a demonstration in favour of the Home Rule Bill – a clear attempt to get Picton and McArthur to commit themselves in general support of the Home Rule proposals. This move was clearly unsuccessful, with the Leicester committee deciding it to be 'inexpedient' to pursue plans for such a rally.[28] This was clearly an unsatisfactory situation, but Leicester Liberals probably had little option other than to pursue a 'wait and see' policy, for the consequences of trying to force the issue could have created a permanent gulf between the local party and its MPs. While the Liberal Association was forced to follow a policy of inaction, the Conservatives rallied opposition with large demonstrations in the Temperance Hall and with the formation of a local Primrose League Habitation.[29]

Wavering MPs came under intense lobbying in the May of 1886 to commit themselves on the crucial Home Rule issue. The action of the Press Association in publishing McArthur's name in a list of MPs supposedly pledged to Home Rule may have been another covert attempt to persuade McArthur to commit himself. If it was, it was unsuccessful. McArthur immediately issued a statement making it clear that he would not support the Bill as it originally stood, although he was prepared to support the 'principle' of Home Rule at second reading, if the Bill was substantially modified.[30] This was hardly a ringing endorsement although equally McArthur showed no sign of allying himself with the Liberal Unionists. Like Johnson Ferguson in Loughborough, he may have merely been taking up a tactical

25 *MFP*, 24 April 1886.

26 *MFP*, 24 April 1886; LLA, General Committee, 20 April 1886, LRO, 11 D 57/2.

27 *MFP*, 28 April 1886.

28 LLA, Finance and General Purposes Committee, 10 and 14 May 1886, LRO, 11 D 57/2.

29 *LJ*, 9 April 1886; *LJ*, 21 May 1886.

30 *LDM*, 11 May 1886.

position to force the government to modify the measure.[31] After all, by this time the government had already begun to make major concessions to backbench concerns – such as suggesting a joint commission of the Westminster and Dublin parliaments for financial and foreign affairs.[32] Yet many Leicester Liberals were uncomfortable with the uncertain position of their MPs and the inaction of the Liberal Association. Indeed the whole issue was largely ignored by the official Liberal organisations, with no public demonstrations being held or official public meetings organised to debate the issue. Perhaps this was wise party management, in view of the uncertainty of McArthur's position, and perhaps partly a reflection of limited local interest in the issue, but it meant that enthusiastic local advocates of Home Rule were left frustrated.[33]

Picton eventually relieved some Gladstonian worries by making it clear that despite his concerns he would support the Bill, as the consequence of its defeat would be too damaging to risk.[34] After much lobbying McArthur followed Picton's example, although in doing so made it clear that his support was conditional on major modification to the Home Rule proposals being accepted at committee stage.[35] Both MPs conditionally supported the Bill, but the long delay in reaching that conclusion meant that Leicester's Liberal electors had received little guidance from their parliamentary representatives on the issue. Although the general committee of the Liberal Association was strongly in favour of the Home Rule Bill, they had been given little opportunity by their leaders to campaign for the cause. Consequently the wider public demonstrated only limited interest in the issue. At the Liberal Temperance Hall meeting called to give McArthur the chance to explain his views on Home Rule, the first question asked of the speakers by the floor was not about Home Rule at all, but rather the compulsory vaccination question.[36]

Although McArthur's stance did little to satisfy the Home Rule enthusiasts and limited the ability of the Liberal Association to campaign actively for Home Rule, his caution may have helped reassure other 'moderate' Liberals that the problem of Ireland was being considered in a careful and restrained way. An Irishman by birth, McArthur remained critical of the Irish Nationalist Party throughout the election campaign and hit out at Irish MPs for not using their influence 'to prevent the tyranny of boycotting, and repress the diabolical outrages against property, man and beast that have disgraced the country and the civilisation of the age in which we live'.[37] As one who still had interests in Ireland, McArthur's condemnation of the more extreme activities of Irish nationalism no doubt struck a chord with Leicester's business community who had commercial links with the country. At the parliamentary

31 Letter, J.E. Johnson Ferguson, *LDM*, 17 May 1886.

32 *LDM*, 22 May 1886.

33 Letter, 'Old Judge', *LDM*, 25 May 1886.

34 *LDM*, 22 May 1886.

35 *MFP*, 5 June 1886.

36 *MFP*, 26 June 1886.

37 *LDM*, 4 June 1886.

adoption meeting for the Liberal nominees, little opposition was heard either to their adoption or to a resolution acknowledging Gladstone's efforts to secure a parliament for Ireland. It is unclear just how many of the 'Liberal 500' – the general committee of the Liberal Association – attended, but only five representatives actually recorded their votes against Home Rule.[38] Moreover, public demonstrations seemed to suggest that the wider Liberal electorate were equally supportive of Gladstone. When the Liberal leader passed through Leicester's Midland railway station on his way to Scotland and made a 'whistle-stop' address, around 10,000 people crammed into the station yard in the hope of hearing him. Few heard much in the massive crush but the size of the turnout was a vivid demonstration that Gladstone remained a powerful influence on Liberal supporters in Leicester.[39]

The major problem for Leicester's small band of Liberal Unionists was a lack of local organisation and a lack of time to prepare for a general election contest. There is no evidence Liberal Unionists made any formal preparations for a contest until the Liberal Association readopted Picton and McArthur as official Liberal candidates. This may have been because they believed there was a strong prospect of McArthur voting against the second reading and in consequence losing official Liberal backing. If this was the case it was a bad miscalculation. By the end of June rumours began circulating that the Liberal Unionists were actively seeking a candidate, although no official statement was made. The Conservatives were not anxious to find a candidate, probably believing that a Liberal Unionist would do more damage to Liberal unity than a Conservative nominee.[40] Liberal Unionists finally announced their choice of candidate at a meeting in early July, and for the first time it became clear that a number of significant figures and substantial subscribers to the Liberal Association were prepared to come out in open rebellion against the 'official' candidates. Among the dissidents were no less than four members of the Faire family, from Knighton, and Harry Simpson Gee. These individuals headed the most famous boot manufacturing companies in the town – Smith, Faire and Company and Stead and Simpson Limited.[41] Both the Faires and Simpson Gee represented the wealthiest and most strongly Anglican element in the local Liberal Party – as did another leading dissident, Thomas Fielding Johnson, the well-known philanthropist. Therefore it is tempting to believe that Leicester Liberal Unionism fits closely the 'traditional' historiographical framework by representing a revolt of Liberal Anglican Whigs – albeit Whig manufacturers – worried about Gladstonian policies towards the church and rights of property. However this analysis needs to be treated with some caution. The Faires and Simpson Gee were all active in the 1885 campaign when disestablishment was much more of a central issue – indeed during

---

38 *LDM*, 12 June 1886.

39 *LC*, 19 June 1886.

40 *MFP*, 25 June 1886.

41 W. Pike and W. Scarfe, *Leicestershire and Rutland at the Opening of the Twentieth Century* (Brighton, 1902), reprint (Edinburgh, 1985), 170.

that campaign Simpson Gee even gave disestablishment a cautious welcome.[42] Moreover, reports suggest that only around a dozen 'gentlemen of position' became actively involved in the Leicester Liberal Unionist group, with the vast majority of Liberal manufacturers remaining loyal to Gladstone.[43] It is, however, the case that few Radicals were associated with Leicester Liberal Unionism. Leicester's leading Chamberlainite Radical, Rev. J. Page Hopps, remained in the Gladstonian camp and became an enthusiastic advocate of Home Rule.

After consultation with the central Unionist Committee in London, Liberal Unionists agreed to invite Robert Bickersteth to stand against the 'official' Liberal candidates. Bickersteth was an Anglican too, educated at Corpus Christi, Oxford, and the eldest son of a Bishop of Ripon. He also had significant local connections, being the grandson of a former vicar of Sapcote, a village in South Leicestershire. Formerly MP for North Staffordshire, he was rejected by his constituency association after rebelling over Home Rule, and was thus forced to look elsewhere for a seat.[44] Despite Bickersteth's Anglican background, it is again unclear that the disestablishment question was a major reason for his defection. Indeed, in his former constituency he was believed by some to be an advocate of disestablishment and had a reputation for advocating 'advanced' Liberal positions, including the reform of the land laws and the abolition of the House of Lords.[45] In Leicester, however, he achieved a reputation for much more conservative politics.

It did of course suit many Liberals to characterise Liberal Unionists as simply wealthy manufacturers defending old privileges. One characterised them as merely 'a small knot of Stoneygate Liberals' – a reference to the wealthy suburbs of Clarendon Park, Stoneygate and Knighton where several leading Liberal Unionists resided.[46] Another attacked 'Liberal manufacturers and Liberal goslings ... being made the tools of Tory and Whig lords'.[47] Although this depiction of Liberal Unionists was attractive to Liberal propagandists it represented only a half-truth at best. Liberal Unionist leaders may have been mainly from the wealthier manufacturing elements of Leicester society, but this was also true of Gladstonian Liberal leaders. Nor could it be said that Stoneygate and Knighton, the largely middle-class suburbs, had overwhelmingly gone over to the Liberal Unionists. Knighton, Stoneygate and Clarendon Park remained important Liberal centres and 1886 saw the formation of a new Liberal Club and Association to serve the area, with a lecture in support of Home Rule inaugurating the club's formal proceedings.[48]

Despite Liberal attacks on the allegedly 'elitist' nature of Liberal Unionism, the dissidents' campaign was boosted by two significant developments. Firstly Peter

42 *LP*, 27 November 1885.
43 *MFP*, 3 July 1886.
44 *MFP*, 3 July 1886.
45 Letter, 'Reformer', *LDM*, 1 July 1886.
46 Letter, 'Reformer', *LDM*, 1 July 1886.
47 Letter, 'An Old Liberal', *LDM*, 1 July 1886.
48 *LDM*, 1 May 1886.

Taylor, the former Radical MP for Leicester, came out in support of the Unionist cause. Had the Unionists been able to persuade Taylor to come out as a Liberal Unionist candidate – or even come to Leicester to speak for Bickersteth – Liberal Unionists may have enjoyed significant success. However, all they obtained was a telegram indicating Taylor's general opposition to the Irish proposals.[49] Of more long-term significance was the decision of Cllr. Thomas Wright, one of the town's most high profile Liberal councillors, to support the Liberal Unionist campaign. Wright quickly became the popular public face of Leicester Liberal Unionism, presiding at major public meetings and lecturing in favour of the Unionist cause.[50] These advantages, however, could not disguise the fundamental difficulties the Liberal Unionists faced in trying to promote candidates and policies which would appeal both to Leicester's Radicals and be acceptable to the Conservative Association with whom they were co-operating.

From the outset Conservatives and Liberal Unionists worked together in order to secure a candidate from London.[51] Although there were rumours that Thomas Fielding Johnson or Stephen Faire were possible candidates, the selection of an outsider obviated any difficulties that might arise from the Conservatives being forced to work and vote for a local Liberal who for so long had been closely identified as an opponent.[52] The selection of Bickersteth, however, did little to persuade any dissatisfied Radicals to support Liberal Unionism. In the town that had been clamorous for Joseph Chamberlain's brother to become its Radical representative, just two years earlier, the selection of a Radical Unionist could have met with considerable success. The Radical press admitted that the selection of 'an out-and-out radical of the Chamberlain type' was what the Liberal Association feared most.[53] Instead, Bickersteth's candidature was seen simply as one inspired by Whigs, reflecting Whig values. It was one which repelled Radicals and stimulated little interest from Conservatives, who, despite Bickersteth's 'moderate' platform, feared that he would simply return to the Liberal fold when the Home Rule crisis was over.[54] Not only were Bickersteth's views not regarded as sufficiently 'advanced' by Radicals, the Radical credentials he did have were quickly disavowed. Despite pleadings from Cllr. Wright, Bickersteth refused to support the repeal of the 'compulsory clauses' of the Vaccination Acts – an issue that had become the litmus test of a Leicester Radical.[55] Bickersteth came under much pressure to restate his support for disestablishment of the Church and the abolition of the House of Lords. Liberal activists knew that if they could force the Liberal Unionist to go on record in favour of these measures the Conservative–Liberal entente would be significantly

49 *MFP*, 3 July 1886.
50 *MFP*, 10 July 1886.
51 *LDM*, 29 June 1886.
52 *LDM*, 1 July 1886.
53 See 'Stray Notes', *MFP*, 10 July 1886.
54 See 'Stray Notes', *MFP*, 10 July 1886.
55 *LDM*, 3 July 1886.

undermined. Instead Bickersteth declared his opposition to both measures, ensuring that the Conservative–Liberal Unionist alliance held, but at the same time ending any real prospect of a significant Radical defection to Liberal Unionist ranks.[56]

The Liberal Unionist cause was not helped by poor organisation and several disastrously managed public meetings. Newly formed and with little chance to establish electoral machinery, they appeared more as an informal, transitory committee than a political party. Even at successful meetings, such as the Temperance Hall meeting in early July, the Liberal Unionists present were comfortably outnumbered by the Conservatives, giving the impression that they were little more than an appendage of the Conservative Party.[57] At least this was an improvement on the image portrayed at an earlier meeting that broke up in disorder with Fielding Johnson having to leave under the safety of a police escort.[58] Worse still the Liberal Unionists' most ambitious meeting – a large rally in Victoria Park – had to be cancelled at very short notice when it was discovered that a local by-law prohibited the use of the park for public demonstrations. A hastily rearranged alternative meeting was continually interrupted by Gladstonian supporters and abandoned before the Liberal Unionist candidate had the opportunity to speak.[59] It is impossible to say whether the disruption was organised by Leicester's Gladstonian leaders, but it left the clear impression that Liberal Unionists were merely generals without an army.

Although the Liberal Unionists were poorly organised they did have access to the central and branch organisation of the Conservative Club.[60] Indeed the overall Unionist campaign was more vigorous than that of the Liberal Party . The Liberal Association provided no conveyances to take electors to the poll and conducted no systematic, organised canvass.[61] This may have been a reflection of their overwhelming confidence in the prospects of success, but it was also in part a rejection of the 'Birmingham model' of electioneering, following Joseph Chamberlain's fall from grace in the eyes of Gladstonian leaders. Leicester Liberals sought to distance themselves from their competitors in Birmingham and go in search of a 'purer' form of party organisation. Picton contrasted Leicester's 'free organisation, depending on the willing consent of thoughtful voters', with the Birmingham model dependent on 'personal dictation'.[62] The renewed hostility to political organisations pressurising electors to support particular candidates may also have been partly a reaction to Leicester Liberals' experiences in the county elections of 1885, where reports of alleged organised coercion by Conservative farmers, churchmen and employers were commonplace.[63] While Leicester remained a 'safe' Liberal constituency these attitudes were a luxury the party could afford, but they left Leicester Liberalism

56 *MFP*, 10 July 1886.
57 *MFP*, 10 July 1886.
58 *MFP*, 3 July 1886.
59 *MFP*, 10 July 1886.
60 *LDM*, 6 July 1886.
61 *MFP*, 10 July 1886.
62 *LDM*, 7 July 1886.
63 See chapter two.

poorly prepared for the formation of the Independent Labour Party and a renewed Conservative challenge in the 1890s.

The 1886 borough election, however, represented a high point in local Liberalism and an overwhelming victory for the official Liberal Party candidates in Leicester. The main hope for the Liberal Unionists was that a sufficient number of 'moderate' Liberals would 'split their ticket' between the Unionist Bickersteth and the Gladstonian 'moderate' McArthur – who was, of course, only conditionally pledged to Home Rule. This hope was not realised. Only 85 voters supported Bickersteth and McArthur, with surprisingly more, 230, supporting the combination of Bickersteth and Picton, who had the most divergent views on Home Rule.[64] This anomaly could be partly explained by Radicals preferring to vote for Bickersteth – or indeed anyone – rather than the 'whiggish' McArthur. It further lends weight to the view that Liberal Unionists would have been much better bringing forward a Chamberlainite Radical to oppose the official Liberal candidate, if they could only have persuaded the Conservatives to agree to such a candidature. In the event, Bickersteth polled fewer votes than the Conservative candidate in 1885 – given the changed circumstances a disastrous result for the Liberal Unionists, destroying their claim to be a serious threat to the Gladstonian party. The scale of the victory left the Gladstonians in little mood to compromise with their former colleagues. When, during post-election celebrations, Ald. Barfoot suggested that the Association should try to attract back the Liberal Unionists, others made it clear they were happy to let the Liberal Unionists go off on their own.[65] Some grass-roots opinion continued to regard Liberal Unionists as 'traitors' and only a large police presence deterred some over-enthusiastic Gladstonians from doing serious damage to the Leicester Conservative Club.[66] As feelings ran high the prospects for Liberal reunion diminished.

Despite the loss of the Liberal Unionists from the Leicester Liberal Association, the organisation of the party in Leicester remained healthy. Outgoing Association president, E. Clephan, looked with great optimism to the future observing that 'those who conscientiously differed from us were not of the class to whom the party looked for support during the course of an election'.[67] The Liberal press similarly regarded the loss as being of little consequence, claiming that most Unionists regarded themselves as 'too "respectable" for politics'.[68] Elsewhere they were dismissed as 'a few crotcheteers [who] have allowed their fads to run away with their Liberalism' and were Liberals 'whom it has always been difficult to distinguish from Tories'.[69] Although Simpson Gee and the Faire family had taken an active role in Liberal organisation, other Liberal Unionists had been on the fringes of the Liberal Party for some time. This relative political inexperience may go some way to explain the

64 *MFP*, 10 July 1886.

65 *LDM*, 7 July 1886.

66 *MFP*, 10 July 1886.

67 LLA, Finance and General Purposes Committee, 8 November 1886, LRO, 11 D 57/2.

68 *LDM*, 1 July 1886.

69 *LDM*, 7 July 1886.

rather blundering public meetings and the somewhat unwise choice of candidates. Nor did the withdrawal of wealthy subscribers from the Liberal Association have any significant impact on the organisation's ability to fund its political activities. The finance and general purposes committee had made renewed attempts to attract subscription after a minor financial crisis in mid-1885.[70] However there is no evidence that the Association was struggling for funds in the wake of the Home Rule crisis and, although the Association set up a subcommittee in 1889 to look at ways of raising further subscriptions, this funding review was in the context of a general consideration of registration and organisational improvements.[71] Indeed the summer of 1886 saw a considerable expansion of Liberal organisation. As well as the new Liberal Club for Clarendon Park – the supposed middle-class and Unionist 'heart' of Leicester – a new working-men's Liberal Club was formed in the town centre. The Gladstone Club and Institute, as it was known, naturally took up a Gladstonian position on Home Rule and acted in concord with the Liberal Association.[72] Its constitution, by freeing itself from wealthy patrons and middle-class leadership, signalled the determination of working-class Liberals to establish a political organisation that remained unequivocally loyal to Gladstone, and one that could not be thrown off course by a minority of rebellious middle-class Liberals.[73]

Harborough Liberals suffered from the Liberal Unionist secession to a much greater extent than their borough counterparts – although even here the problems were mainly of a short-term nature. The largest Liberal Unionist centre – the Knighton area – was located on the fringe of the borough inside the Harborough constituency and a narrow Liberal success in the 1885 general election was turned into a heavy defeat just over six months later.[74] The magnitude of the turnaround – a drop of over 1,000 in the Liberal vote – can in part be explained by the retirement of the sitting member T.T. Paget, the popular Liberal MP for South Leicestershire since 1880. The Harborough Liberal executive, however, were in little doubt that the 'result [was] largely due to the abstention of Liberal voters who disapproved of Mr. Gladstone's proposals for the Government of Ireland'.[75] Moreover as the Liberal Association had acquired most of the debt of the old South Leicestershire branch, a withdrawal of subscriptions was a significant problem for the Association – although not so significant that they could not afford to employ a new registration agent in May 1887.[76] Fortunately, although organisation in Knighton had suffered as a result of the Home Rule crisis, elsewhere new Liberal Associations were developing after the zealous reorganisation in the counties in connection with the extension of the county franchise. Even in small villages like Blaby, Liberal Associations sprung up, such that

70 LLA, Finance and General Purposes Committee, 13 July 1885, LRO, 11 D 57/2.

71 LLA, Finance and General Purposes Committee, 7 January 1889, LRO, 11 D 57/2.

72 *MFP*, 28 August 1886; *MFP*, 25 September 1886.

73 *MFP*, 25 September 1886.

74 F.W.S. Craig (ed.), *British Parliamentary Election Results 1885–1918*, second edition (Aldershot, 1989) 334.

75 HLA, Annual Meeting, 7 May 1887, LRO, DE 1637/1.

76 HLA, Annual Meeting, 7 May 1887, LRO, DE 1637/1.

by June 1886, this small settlement had 100 members and could attract 500 people to an inaugural tea.[77] Financial problems continued but were largely containable. By 1888 the constituency association had a deficit of over £189 and expected to continue to run up deficits of £116 per year. Although a considerable sum, the executive committee did not believe there would be any difficulty in attracting an additional £100 per year in subscriptions.[78] This prediction proved to be a little too optimistic and the problems of the Association were not really completely resolved until they recruited a parliamentary candidate, J.W. Logan, who was able to make considerable contributions to the Association. Even then the executive committee feared they might have to reduce their activities unless extra funds for organisational work were obtained – although at Knighton, the supposed centre of Liberal Unionism, enough wealthy Liberals remained not only to fund the operation of the local Liberal club, but also to arrange the registration campaign in the district.[79] It is important to put these difficulties into context, as rural organisation was necessarily more expensive than that in the towns and the new county associations were far less well established than that of the borough.[80] In fact, despite the withdrawal of some subscribers in 1886–87, the Liberal Association in Harborough continued to be a powerful force in local politics. When T.K. Tapling, the sitting Conservative MP, died in 1891, the resultant by-election saw a Liberal, J.W. Logan, take the seat with a majority of more than three times that of Paget in 1885. The constituency continued to send Liberals to Westminster continuously right up to the end of the First World War.[81] Whatever the short-term problems created by the Unionist divisions in Harborough, the Liberal Party was still able to turn this marginal constituency into a 'safe' Liberal seat – and at a time when the growth of Leicester's southern suburbia was bringing about social changes in the area which one might think would be of benefit to the Conservatives.

In Leicester it was the Conservatives rather than the Liberals who were suffering most from internal dissension and organisational collapse. Although Liberals suffered some internal difficulties at the 1886 municipal elections, these differences arose over personalities and local matters rather than Home Rule.[82] When Arthur Wakerley, one of the town's foremost young Conservative politicians, came out as a Liberal candidate for Middle St. Margaret's ward, it was a major blow for the Conservatives and illustrative of the problems the Conservatives faced in retaining ambitious and influential local men in their ranks, when it was so difficult for Conservatives to gain election to the council and difficult for them to make any impression when they got there.[83] Conservative humiliation continued when the Conservative Working-Men's

77 *LDM*, 16 June 1886.

78 HLA, Annual Meeting, 11 February 1888, LRO, DE 1637/1.

79 HLA, Annual Meeting, 12 April 1890, LRO, DE 1637/1.

80 See chapter two.

81 Craig, *British Parliamentary Election Results*, 332.

82 See 'Stray Notes', *MFP*, 16 October 1886.

83 *MFP*, 23 October 1886.

Club had its fittings seized in distress for unpaid rent and the East St. Margaret's Conservative Club decided to reopen as a 'non-political' club.[84] The organisation of the Liberal Unionists' allies seemed almost as weak as that of the Liberal Unionists themselves.

The relative weakness of Unionist organisation may have been a significant factor in bringing the two parties together in closer co-operation. However, the Conservatives were divided as to how the issue of party organisation should be approached. Many supported the establishment of a habitation of the Primrose League in Leicester, a move that obtained official endorsement with J.F.L. Rolleston becoming chairman of the first habitation.[85] Despite this move, and the gain of two council seats in 1886, there was still much dissatisfaction with Conservative organisation and especially the role of the Conservative Club. Lacking both a Conservative daily newspaper and formal organisation in several wards, it was perhaps inevitable that Primrose Leaguers would come into conflict with the traditional leaders of the Conservative Party in the borough and county – the Conservative Club.[86] In order to try to preserve its position as the leading force in local politics, in March 1888 the club organised a round table conference with representatives from around the county to discuss party reorganisation.[87] On the initiative of Sir Henry Halford a resolution was passed for the appointment of a new full-time party agent and in discussions it was agreed that the new county franchise meant that new methods of party organisation were required. These moves were insufficient to repel critics of the club and at the annual meeting divisions opened up. Several members attacked the 'stand-still policy' of the club's leadership and called for the club to engage in 'a more popular political and social policy' with lectures, smoking concerts and Primrose League-style activities.[88] The club's leadership narrowly won what amounted to a confidence vote, but only at the cost of revealing deep tensions between 'traditional' Conservatives and those calling for a more democratic party organisation and campaigning style – between 'the old and new schools of Conservatism'.[89] The club committee may have retained nominal leadership of the Conservative party in Leicester, but if the Conservative Party were to be successful in the town major changes would have to be made. The Conservative Club, despite being a major social centre for the area, was even criticised by one of its guest speakers, Sydney Gedge MP, for having so few members.[90] Between 1888 and 1895 there was no long term increase, with membership remaining at around 1,400, even though the club was turned into a constitutional club in 1893 to attract the subscriptions of Liberal Unionists.[91]

---

84 *MFP*, 25 December 1886.

85 *LJ*, 21 May 1886.

86 *LJ*, 5 March 1886.

87 *HN*, 10 March 1888.

88 *LJ*, 6 April 1888.

89 *LJ*, 6 April 1888.

90 *LJ*, 37 April 1888.

91 Leicester Constitutional Club Minutes, Annual Report, December 1895, LRO, DE 1574.

The formation of the Leicester Conservative Registration Association in May 1888 marked the beginning of the end of the Conservative Club's pre-eminence in town and county politics. Having attracted a large number of promised subscriptions, the association was formed with the intention of developing branches in each ward of the town.[92] These efforts were not only supported by the efforts of the rank and file, but also leading municipal figures such as Cllr. Thomas Canner who hoped that the new structures would of greater assistance in local elections than the Conservative Club had hitherto been.[93] As a number of dissident committee men from the Conservative Club had been involved in the formation of the new registration association, the club had little choice but to recognise and work with the new body, even though subscriptions to the new association were disappointing and limited the sphere of its initial activities.[94] Strangely the Conservative Club, despite competition from the new more representative association, made constitutional changes that rendered itself less representative of the ordinary rank and file. Apparently concerned at the gradual loss of the country gentry from the club committee, the rules were changed, more than doubling the number of ex-officio vice-presidents allowed on its ruling body. Faced with the perennial problem of how to finance club activities and the knowledge that the registration association was struggling for funds, the club needed to retain the involvement of its most affluent rural supporters.[95]

Although the relationship between Conservatives and Liberal Unionists had been cordial during the 1886 general election, Liberal Unionists played little role in the debates about the reorganisation of Unionist forces – many Conservatives initially believing that the Liberal Unionists would eventually return to the Liberal fold. For 12 months after the 1886 election no significant efforts were made by Liberal Unionists to establish either a permanent association or engage in registration work. Finally, in July 1887, a conference of Liberal Unionists met to discuss future strategy, perhaps prompted by the Liberal Unionist Central Association. A majority of those present favoured formally instituting an association and affiliating to the national party, although, not, it was stressed, to provoke further divisions, but to prevent Liberal Unionists drifting into the Conservative Party.[96] Some warned against establishing separate organisation, believing their only prospect of influence was within the existing Liberal Associations, and felt that if they did try to form a separate party 'they would form a small party and only make themselves ridiculous'.[97] T.H. Downing, one of the Liberal Unionists' major financial supporters, feared that any new association would drift into Conservatism – unthinkable to those like Downing who continued to profess their loyalty to Gladstone. Despite the failure of the Round Table Conference on Liberal Reunion, Liberal Unionists had still not abandoned

[92] *LJ*, 11 May 1888.
[93] *LJ*, 15 May 1888.
[94] *LJ*, 5 April 1888.
[95] *LJ*, 4 April 1890.
[96] *LDP*, 16 July 1887.
[97] *LDP*, 16 July 1887.

hopes of reconciliation, with W.H. Walker suggesting a policy of 'Home Rule all round' as a way of bringing the party back together.[98] This reluctance to establish a separate party organisation suggests that most continued to view divisions as temporary and that no fundamental difficulties – other than the Home Rule issue – stood between the parties and reunification in Leicester. It was eventually agreed to establish a separate association and affiliate to the national Liberal Unionist party, but the widespread reluctance to do so compromised their ability to construct a party machine that could rival the Leicester Liberal Association.

Many Liberals, although unhappy with Gladstone's proposals for Home Rule, were not prepared to withdraw from the Liberal Association over the issue, join the Liberal Unionists or do anything to assist Liberal Unionist candidates. During the 1886 election the local Conservative press observed with mild disgust that Liberals who opposed Home Rule continued to feel bound by their Liberal allegiance.[99] Even figures who publicly declared against Home Rule often declined to associate themselves with moves to establish a formal Liberal Unionist organisation. When Liberal Unionists published a list of prominent local opponents of Home Rule, at least one town councillor demanded to have his name withdrawn, whilst others wrote to the Leicester Liberal Association assuring officials of their continuing support for the Association.[100] Significantly, too, the Liberal Association made no distinction between Liberal and Liberal Unionists in its registration work, therefore continuing to count Liberal Unionist officially as still supporters of the party.[101] Many Liberal Unionists remained subscribers to the Liberal Association and the Liberal Club and there were no recorded moves to try to remove Liberal Unionists from the ranks of the Liberal Association. Indeed many Gladstonians felt the threat from the Liberal Unionists to be so insignificant as to be unworthy of serious consideration. Claims that the Liberal Unionists had 2,500 supporters in Leicester were scoffed at in the Liberal press with the observation that Liberal Unionists 'have just as much chance of returning either a Hartingtonian or Conservative for Leicester as they have of discovering the philosopher's stone'.[102]

Had the late 1880s seen intensive political conflict at municipal level the Liberal Unionist Association may have been forced to make difficult choices about potential candidates and future alliances. However the relative weakness of the Conservative party meant that, in general, Conservative municipal leaders were happy to enter into electoral agreements with Liberals and Liberal Unionists to avoid contests. The Liberals having, by 1889, 42 representatives to 14 for their opponents, had little incentive to chase the remaining seats. Hence in 1887, 1888 and 1889 there were no contests when councillors' usual terms of office ended in

98 *LDP*, 16 July 1887.

99 *LJ*, 16 July 1886.

100 See 'Local Notes', *LDP*, 13 July 1887.

101 LLA, Finance and General Purposes Committee, 12 July 1887, LRO, 11 D 57/2.

102 *LDP*, 11 July 1887.

November.[103] Issues of Home Rule played little part in local politics and indeed the willingness of local ward organisations to allow those with Unionist sympathies to stay active in local Liberal politics probably did much to undermine efforts to establish independent Liberal Unionist ward organisations. Despite complaints from the East St. Margaret's Ward Liberal Association, the party's municipal leaders still nominated Liberal Unionist Thomas Wright for the borough mayoralty, and Wright continued to participate in local Liberal Association meetings.[104]

The most significant impact of the Home Rule crisis in Leicester may have been on the attitudes of Liberal Association leaders in attempting to 'manage' the decisions of ward organisations and the general council in an attempt to avoid further damaging splits. Division over selection of candidates in 1884 had demonstrated just how difficult it was to manage representative machinery and many felt new methods were required to avoid repeated difficulties. In 1887, in order to regularise the membership of ward committees and prevent their packing by individual factions, the Liberal Association approved new guidelines to give local officers and committees more power to manage public ward meetings. The new rules meant that ward officers and committees were required to meet before the annual ward meeting, recommend a list of candidates for election, carefully deleting beforehand 'the names of those who do not attend, or who from any other cause it is deemed undesirable to re-elect'.[105] Ward chairmen were also provided with detailed rules on how to conduct the election of committee representatives. The recommended list of nominees, provided in advance by the committee, had to be taken *en bloc* and only after those names were adopted could additional names be proposed for the remaining places. Only registered voters were allowed to vote for nominees, propose or second candidates or stand for election. Despite all the protestations that Liberal organisation was the democratic expression of public ward meetings, it was clear Liberal leaders were becoming increasingly anxious to control the nomination process.[106] Moreover, although ward organisations were supposed to exhibit a high degree of autonomy, in practice the secretary of the Liberal Association had significant influence over matters of local organisation. Indeed, the reorganisation of the party in preparation for the general election was largely conducted by the secretary in small meetings with leading ward officials.[107]

The most obvious example of increased central management of party decisions came with the retirement of McArthur from the Commons in March 1890. Rumours of McArthur's impending resignation had been circulating for some time and when the announcement finally came many senior Liberals feared 'a rush of gentlemen

---

[103] *LDP* 28 October 1887; *LDP*, 27 October 1888; *LDP*, 1 November 1889. There were also, of course, isolated municipal by-elections, but these were of little consequence for inter-party relations.

[104] *LDP*, 22 October 1887.

[105] LLA, General Committee, 22 September 1887, LRO, 11 D 57/2.

[106] LLA, General Committee, 22 September 1887, LRO, 11 D 57/2.

[107] LLA, Finance and General Purposes Committee, 11 February 1890, LRO, 11 D 57/2; LLA, Executive Committee, 10 March 1890, LRO, 11 D 57/2.

willing to step into a safe seat, and don the "blue ribbon" of Liberal borough representation'.[108] The Liberal Association executive committee, prepared for the eventuality, came out unanimously in favour of firmly selecting a candidate before referring the matter to the supposedly sovereign body, the general committee. This move was designed to obviate the kind of problems experienced in 1884.[109] Sir James Whitehead, a former Lord Mayor of London, was recommended as one; although from a 'Whiggish' background, he had a reputation for 'advanced' views, supporting the National Liberal Federation's latest programme, and being involved in the arbitration surrounding the London Dock Strike in 1889.[110] Whitehead was a long-time advocate of Home Rule and Church disestablishment, views that indicated the Leicester Liberal Association's determination to provide a candidate to satisfy the Radical wing of the party and head off dissension.[111] The general committee meeting to select Whitehead was carefully managed, with circulars being issued to all recognised representatives and entrance to the meeting carefully contained. Whitehead alone was proposed by the Executive who tried to push the business through rapidly, much to the chagrin of some Radicals, including Page Hopps, whose attempts to persuade the meeting to consider at least one alternative name were unsuccessful. By making a quick decision, opposition could be headed off, before it gathered momentum.[112] Not surprisingly, some were unhappy with this decision and questioned how being offered just one candidate constituted any kind of free choice.[113] However within two weeks Whitehead visited Leicester to address the '500' and, with no Radical alternative on offer, he was selected with just half a dozen hands held in opposition.[114] The Leicester Liberal Association had successfully avoided a split but at the price of diminishing internal party democracy and again leaving some Radicals dissatisfied with the local party leadership.

While many Liberal Unionists had maintained close connections with the Liberal Association and Club, and continued to co-operate with the party at municipal level, the prospect of another parliamentary election meant these connections would soon come under renewed strain. Moreover by 1887 the Leicester Liberal Association was at last beginning to place Irish issues at the forefront of their campaigning platform. This was partly in response to the revulsion at the consequences of the Crimes Act and in September 1887 went as far as sending representatives to Ireland in order to express 'practical sympathy' with the victims of coercion.[115] By adopting Whitehead as a parliamentary candidate, a man who placed Home Rule at the centre of his platform, the Association made it clear they were no longer prepared to 'hedge' the

---

108 *LDM*, 15 March 1890.

109 LLA, Executive Committee, 18 March 1890, LRO, 11 D 57/2.

110 *LDM*, 19 March 1890.

111 *MFP*, 29 March 1890.

112 LLA, General Committee, 20 March 1890, LRO, 11 D 57/2; *LDM*, 21 March 1890.

113 Letter, JWB, *LDM*, 1 April 1890.

114 LLA, General Committee – the 'Five Hundred', 1 April 1890, LRO, 11 D 57/2; *LDM*, 2 April 1890, LRO, 11 D 57/2.

115 LLA, General Committee, 22 September 1887, LRO, 11 D 57/2.

issue as they were forced to do in the early days of 1886. The Liberal Unionists were not in a position to proffer a challenge and further lost credibility when one of their visiting speakers J. Caldwell, the MP for Glasgow St. Rollox, rejoined the Liberal Party shortly after speaking in Leicester.[116] Co-operation with the Conservatives continued to be problematic, and although the Conservatives participated in a joint lecture programme in the spring of 1890, even one of the Conservative promoters, J.H. Marshall, recognised the difficulties inherent in such a venture, with many not wanting to identify themselves with the Liberal Unionist party.[117] While Irish Home Rule dominated the national political agenda, Liberal Unionists and Conservatives became reluctant allies. Even Leicester's municipal leaders could not escape the controversy, particularly when an Irish Nationalist MP was arrested in Leicester during February 1889. The arrest sparked massive controversy – municipal leaders and the former president of the Liberal Association had been entertaining their Irish guest at the Liberal Club only minutes before his apprehension.[118] With the arrest becoming such a major public event – highlighting repressive legislation – even those Liberals who had hitherto taken only a limited interest in Ireland were increasingly forced to take sides as the two strands of Liberalism became more polarised.

The failure of both Unionist parties to find a candidate to oppose Whitehead, a staunch Home Ruler, only highlighted the continuing weakness of the Unionist camp in Leicester. Partly as a response to these difficulties the Liberal Unionist and Conservative Associations agreed to form a joint committee to make arrangements for registration work and to find a candidate.[119] Without an effective local organisation it was impossible to attract candidates from outside Leicester. The arrangements were not, however, uncontroversial. Although Rolleston, the president of the Conservative Association, felt that the new arrangements were beneficial, others, including Cllr. Thomas Canner, felt that the organisation of the party and enthusiasm of party workers still left much to be desired.[120] The Unionists did not have to wait long to put their new joint arrangements to the test. With the expansion of the borough's municipal boundaries in 1891, the town wards were rearranged, ensuring an all-out election for the town council in November of that year. In the event, however, the election again only served to highlight Conservative weakness and Liberal Unionist irrelevance. The Conservatives were reduced from 11 seats in the old council to just seven in the new – and three of these seats represented success in just one ward – De Montfort.[121] The Liberal Unionists mustered just one candidate, Samuel Faire, who topped the poll in their Knighton 'stronghold'.[122] Yet Liberal Unionists could take

116 *LDM*, 16 March 1890.

117 *LJ*, 28 March 1890.

118 It seems unlikely that the arrest was staged by the Liberals for propaganda purposes as it seemed to take the Liberal leadership by surprise. *LDM*, 5 February 1889.

119 *LJ*, 27 March 1891.

120 *LJ*, 27 March 1891.

121 *LDM*, 4 November 1891.

122 *LDP*, 4 November 1891.

little comfort from Faire's success, gained as it was largely through the assistance of the local Conservatives.[123]

Faire was not, however, the only Liberal Unionist on the new council. Ald. Thomas Wright, by virtue of his continued membership of the aldermanic bench, continued to support the Liberal Unionist Association on the council, although his municipal ambitions deterred him from taking a strongly partisan position. With a council dominated by Gladstonian Liberals, Wright could only maintain a pre-eminent position by adopting a curious bipartisan approach. During a bad tempered council debate on the redrawing of ward boundaries, Wright claimed to be a member of 'both parties', before attacking the Liberal Association for allegedly coercing councillors to vote according to party whip.[124] By placing himself 'above' the partisan struggle, he retained his status in the council and was appointed the first mayor of the expanded borough in 1891.[125] Liberal Unionists also got another minor boost with success in a Knighton ward by-election in the same month, but hopes that Wright would become a high profile figure advancing Liberal Unionist views soon disappeared as he donned the mayoral robes.[126] Indeed the Liberal Party 's decision to elect Wright as mayor may have been a calculated move to push Wright out of active Liberal Unionist politics. With the onset of the 1892 general election, both the Liberal Unionist and Conservative Associations made substantial efforts to persuade Wright to come out as a Liberal Unionist candidate. Wright did not reject the proposal out of hand. The Liberal Association responded by making it clear that Wright's position of municipal influence depended on him remaining outside active Liberal Unionist politics.[127] Not surprisingly, given that the prospects of Unionist success were small, Wright eventually issued a statement indicating that he felt it would be wrong to abandon the mayoralty for a partisan appointment. The Conservative press, anticipating a more positive response from Wright, made their annoyance at his decision very clear, claiming that the borough mayor had originally expressed no reluctance to accept the Unionist candidature.[128] Wright's decision left the Unionist camp with very little time to find an alternative candidate and generated considerable ill feeling between the Unionist allies. It also marked the beginning of the end of Liberal Unionism as a separate force in Leicester politics. Wright's position depended on the Gladstonian party and, after annoying Conservatives by declining the Unionist candidature, he returned to the Gladstonian ranks in December 1892. Wright repudiated the Liberal Unionists, declaring that he had never regarded himself as permanently separated from the Liberal Party , believing Chamberlain's opposition had gone too far and criticising Salisbury's government for failing to

123 *MFP*, 7 November 1891.

124 *LDM*, 1 July 1891.

125 *LDM*, 9 November 1991.

126 *LDM,* 23 November 1891.

127 *LDE*, 20 June 1892.

128 *LDE*, 21 June 1892.

redeem their pledges on Irish local self-government.[129] Others followed Wright's departure back to the Liberal Party , while several who remained, particularly local business leaders, were increasingly uncomfortable with the protectionist language of some local Conservatives. By this time, however, the Liberal Unionist group in Leicester had little influence in either municipal and parliamentary life – the Liberal *Leicester Chronicle* observing that Liberal Unionism's 'disappearance will hardly cause a ripple on the surface of local politics'.[130] With the withdrawal of leading figures from the Liberal Unionist Association, and the loss of major subscribers, the decision to dissolve the Association was probably inevitable. Several members of the Faire family subsequently became active in the Conservative Party, with Arthur Faire joining the executives of the Leicester and Melton Conservative Associations, while Samuel Faire was actively involved in the formation of the new Leicester Constitutional Club.[131] Leicester Liberal Unionism as a distinct and separate force, however, had ceased to exist.[132]

The Leicester Liberal Association had not initially embraced Home Rule with any great enthusiasm. Activists seemed more interested in the anti-compulsory vaccination movement and one of their MPs was, at best, a very reluctant Home Ruler. Once, however, McArthur had committed himself to the Gladstonian side, Liberal Unionism in Leicester faced major difficulties. Although its leaders were significant local businessmen, support for Liberal Unionism was socially and geographically limited. In only one area of the town was it strong enough to win a contested election – the wealthy suburb of Knighton. The party's ally, the Conservative Association, was organisationally weak and many Liberal Unionists were both suspicious of co-operating with it and reluctant to set up a rival association to that of the Liberals for fear of institutionalising 'temporary' differences. When Liberal Unionism's leading public figure quit the party, taking others away with him, Liberal Unionism collapsed. Its lasting significance lies chiefly in the changes it brought about in the management of local Liberal politics. Concerned to avoid future splits, the Liberal Association's leadership made determined efforts to carefully manage the election of members on to its committees and exert greater central control over the activities of ward organisations. Electorally the Leicester Liberal Association survived the Home Rule crisis almost unscathed. Organisationally, however, the structure of the party was rendered less open and less democratic. Unanimity over the selection of parliamentary candidates could only be secured by careful manipulation of the party caucus and by denying activists any real alternatives. It was a strategy that worked in the short term, but in the long term had the potential to leave some sections of the party disillusioned and excluded from the Liberal Party 's decision-making processes. Leicester had become the new 'capital' of Midlands' Liberalism but its

[129] *LC*, 31 December 1892.

[130] *LC*, 31 December 1892.

[131] Pike and Scarfe, *Leicestershire and Rutland*, 169–70.

[132] A new Leicester Liberal Unionist Association was established at end of the century but it was little more than an adjunct of the local Conservative Association.

party structures had obtained the same reputation as those in Birmingham, whose position it had inherited.

The failure of Liberal Unionists to make a major impact on Leicester politics illustrates the rather patchy nature of Liberal Unionist support and the limitations of Chamberlain's regional influence. Before the Home Rule crisis many Leicester Radicals clearly looked to Chamberlain for new radical social policies – but very few followed him into Liberal Unionism. This contrasts sharply with the situation in Birmingham where his personal influence was much stronger and where he persuaded many to leave the party on the issue of Home Rule.[133] Although personal loyalties could still be important on a local basis, both Hartington and Chamberlain found that their influence on nearby towns was very limited. Chamberlain's influence on Leicester was ultimately no stronger than that of Hartington in Manchester. In general Liberals in both Manchester and Leicester saw their loyalties to Gladstone and Liberal unity as more important – just as the majority of Liberal MPs and constituencies had done. The failure of the round table talks on Liberal reunion left Liberal Unionists in something of a wilderness and ensured that Chamberlain would be forced into ever-closer cooperation with the Conservatives. At national level the Liberal Unionist many have contributed to Liberal general election defeats in 1886 and 1895, but they could not prevent Gladstone returning for a historic fourth term in 1892. The departure of Chamberlain did not result in the departure of Radicalism. In both Manchester and Leicester, the majority of Radicals remained in the Gladstonian Liberal ranks. The majority of Liberal Unionist defectors came from the centre-right of the party, reinforcing the traditional view that the Home Rule served to strengthen the position of Radicals in urban party organisation.

[133] See M. Hurst, *Joseph Chamberlain and West Midlands Politics, 1885–1895* (Oxford 1962).

PART III
Municipal Government Transformed?

CHAPTER FIVE

Municipal Scandals and Realignment

For Manchester's Liberal municipal leadership the achievements of their party in promoting schemes of public health and social improvement were a matter of considerable pride. Liberals had been in a numerical majority on the council since incorporation of the city in 1839. After the failure of Manchester Tory anti-incorporationists to invalidate the borough's charter, the local Tory Party boycotted the proceedings of the council for 15 years, leaving the Liberals to dominate the city's new official organs of local government.[1] Even in the early 1880s the legacy of one party government was still being felt and it was a legacy not without public policy achievements. In the 25 years from 1861 to 1886, the corporation doubled its acreage of public parks, doubled the average daily volume of water supplied and trebled the number of books in public libraries while managing to reduce the city's total rate from 4s 6d in 1861 to just 4s in 1886.[2] Nor were the city's Liberal elite reluctant to make long-term investments for the public good, having committed themselves by the mid-1880s to a massive new water supply scheme to pipe water direct from Thirlmere in the Lake District and to support the ambitious ship canal scheme, which the corporation was eventually forced to rescue through substantial public loans.[3] However by the early 1890s it was becoming increasingly clear that the corporation was struggling to deal with the many new demands being made upon it. Poverty, poor housing, unhealthy sanitation and atmospheric pollution made for death rates which, in some parts at least, reflected only shame on the city. One local physician estimated that approximately 3–4,000 people died annually in the city from preventable causes.[4] A social investigator for the Manchester Statistical Society estimated that as many as 40 per cent of the city's 'wage-earning' classes were found to rely on poor relief at some point during the year.[5] This type of research, inspired

1 P. Whitaker, 'The Growth of Liberal Organisation in Manchester from the Eighteen-Sixties to 1903', Unpublished PhD thesis, University of Manchester, 1956, 211–12.

2 *MG*, 10 November 1886.

3 G. Seuss Law, 'Manchester's Politics 1885–1906', Unpublished PhD thesis, University of Pennsylvania, 1975, 50–52. Seuss Law provides an interesting survey of council politics in the period with useful statistical appendices. His account, however, is gravely let down by his failure to mention the series of scandals of the late 1880s which are regarded here as being of considerable significance for the working of city politics.

4 See J.R. Galloway, 'The Evidence of Statistics in Relation to our Social Conditions', *Transactions of the Manchester Statistical Society, 1889–90* (18 December 1889), 49.

5 G. Rooke, 'On the Report of the Royal Commission on the Aged Poor, 26th February 1895', *Transactions of the Manchester Statistical Society*, 1895–96 (11 December 1895), 29–55. Rooke was vice-president of the Manchester Board of Guardians.

by Charles Booth's papers to the Royal Statistical Society in 1887 and 1888, helped stimulate public concern and bring new demands for far greater public intervention from the city's authorities.[6] In common with other industrial cities the agenda of social and sanitary reform quickly grew from the provision of municipal parks and piped water to demands for the municipality to take responsibility for all living and working conditions in the city.

The emergence of a more interventionist social reform or 'Progressive' agenda took longer to materialise in Manchester than in some other cities. Progressivism as a collectivist social reform ideology is traditionally associated with the success of the Progressives on London County Council in 1889, although by the early 1890s the language of municipal Progressivism and its associated policies was being moulded into a new official Liberal Party approach to local government.[7] During a speech at Leeds in October 1893, Herbert Asquith spoke of council housing and slum clearance being part of the 'Liberal Municipal Programme' and emphasised the importance of local authorities acting as model employers of labour.[8] Manchester Liberals did not formally adopt a 'Progressive Municipal Programme' until 1894, and even then pressure to adopt such a programme seemingly came as much from the party managers, concerned at the challenge of the ILP, rather than from a council group genuinely trying to find solutions to pressing social problems.[9] Although some Liberals, such as Alderman Walton Smith, chairman of the corporation's unhealthy dwellings committee proposed an active Progressive programme on slum clearance well before the success even of the Progressives on the London County Council, the city's Liberal leadership as a whole failed to produce a co-ordinated, programmatic response to the city's social problems until after they had lost their numerical majority on the council. Parliamentary restrictions on municipal initiative, the growing costs of capital projects, the lack of co-ordination between policy-making bodies and a series of financial scandals involving senior members of the council frustrated the efforts of Radical and Progressive council members in trying to establish new priorities. When the Independent Labour Party published their municipal programme for the first time in 1893, veteran Liberal Councillor James Southern remarked that he and his fellow 'advanced' Liberals had supported many of its elements for 20 years.[10] Their failure to persuade the Liberal majority to carry the principal policies of the 'advanced' wing into effect and to overcome the substantial difficulties in their way was to have significant implications for the credibility of the Liberal espousal of their Progressive Programme at the end of the century.

---

6 E.P. Hennock, 'The Measurement of Urban Poverty: From the Metropolis to the Nation, 1880–1920', *Economic History Review*, 40 (1987), 208–27.

7 For critical analysis of Progressivisim in London see P. Thompson, 'Liberals, Radical and Labour in London 1880–1900', *Past and Present*, 27 (1964), 73–101; P. Thompson, *Socialists, Liberals and Labour – the Struggle for London 1885–1914* (London, 1967).

8 *The Liberal Magazine*, November 1893.

9 P.F. Clarke, *Lancashire and the New Liberalism* (Cambridge, 1971), 162–3.

10 *MCN*, 4 November 1893.

Policy differences in the ranks of Liberal leaders were, however, only one barrier to more collectivist municipal activity. Complex legislation governed the scope of the authority of municipal corporations. The Municipal Corporations Act of 1882 tightened central control of municipal government by more clearly delimiting the scope of municipal action. Municipal corporations had always required special private Acts of parliament for public improvement projects not covered by existing powers, but the Act of 1882 made it even more difficult for municipal corporations to develop large-scale improvements without resort to private legislation – which could prove both troublesome and costly. Moreover before the Manchester corporation could proceed on such a course it was required to call a meeting of ratepayers to authorise the action. A well-organised pressure group could easily pack such a meeting with a handful of zealots and in doing so frustrate the will of the council elected, with the exception of the aldermanic bench, on a city-wide franchise.[11] Even when a city like Manchester wanted to develop a relatively trivial new capital project, such as expanding its library service in 1887, complex legislation governing financial procedure could mean new powers were required. If the 'town's meeting' did approve the measure, the corporation still had to win the ear of local MPs to assist the corporation in the passage of any necessary legislation. Such a lengthy and costly procedure meant that the corporation's political leadership found it difficult to pilot any remotely controversial proposal. Even apparently poorly organised and newly formed pressure groups could frustrate the agreed policy on the corporation. When in 1885 the corporation intended to promote a private Act to extend the boundaries of the city and consolidate the rate levying authorities, the Manchester Ratepayers' Association was able to persuade just 69 people to attend the 'town's meeting' and oppose the Bill – yet they were easily able to defeat the puny 45 supporters of the Bill mustered by the council.[12] Only when the corporation agreed to withdraw the clauses the Ratepayers' Association objected to, was the Bill allowed to proceed to Westminster.[13]

This opposition to legislation to expand the city's municipal boundaries not only damaged the authority of the council but also threatened to have serious financial consequences. The desire to extend Manchester's boundaries was not simply an emotional desire to create a 'Greater Manchester', but a response to the growing suburbanisation around the city and the increasing need to co-ordinate effort to provide more efficient public services.[14] In 1879 the Thirlmere Water scheme threatened to bankrupt the corporation when parliament rejected the inclusion of Harpurhey and Newton Heath in an expanded city. Without the inclusion of further suburbs the

---

11 F.W. Hirst and J. Redlich, *Local Government in England*, volume two (London, 1903), 249; Seuss Law, 'Manchester's Politics', 30–32.

12 *MG*, 22 December 1885.

13 Manchester Ratepayers' Association, *Annual Report*, 14 January 1886, 3–5, MCL, P3416/15.

14 For a recent comparative analysis of the problems of local government finance see R. Millward and S. Sheard, 'The Urban Fiscal Problem, 1870–1914: government expenditure and finance in England and Wales', *Economic History Review*, 48 (1995), 501–35.

poorer districts of central Manchester were left to foot the bill for expensive capital investment in new public infrastructure.[15] Expansion of the city's boundaries in 1886 and 1890 relieved some of the pressures, but there was a growing recognition that the days of decreasing rates were over. Ald. James Harwood, who proudly boasted at the council's 1886 annual meeting of the corporation's success in bringing about a long-term reduction in rates, admitted 12 months later that the council could not afford further public improvements without extra charges to the rates. In that year the council's total debt was over £7 million, which had to be serviced by an annual sinking fund of over £150,000. From 1 January 1890 the council had to establish an additional sinking fund to service debts on the Thirlmere project. Financially the council had little room for manoeuvre – debt periods could not be extended as the maximum length of time for the repayment of debts was limited by statute to 60 years.[16] Hard choices had to be made.

Financial difficulties were arising at the very time when the city's Liberal leaders were, for the first time, facing a Conservative group offering a real challenge to traditional Liberal domination of the council. By 1885 the Conservatives had a majority of elected members, the Liberals retaining their nominal majority only through their domination of the aldermanic bench.[17] In the general election of the same year the Conservatives took five of the six parliamentary seats in Manchester. Conservative success was a product both of short-term Liberal disorganisation, following boundary changes, and long-term Conservative recovery, following the Conservatives' boycott of municipal politics after the city's incorporation. By the mid-1880s the Conservatives had powerful electoral organisations in many working-class districts of Manchester – such as East Manchester where the charismatic Conservative brewer Stephen Chesters Thompson had established a firm populist grip on local politics.[18] The Liberal municipal position was further undermined when the Home Rule crisis saw three aldermen and four Liberal councillors declare themselves for the Unionist side. This removed the Liberal Party's nominal majority and made it even harder for the party to direct council policy along Progressive or any other lines. A combination of tight municipal finances and declining electoral fortunes made the prospects of an adventurous and investment-led municipal policy from the Liberals an unlikely possibility. Worse still, a series of financial scandals so tarnished the reputation of the council in the 1880s that its leaders lost public credibility and confidence that they could be trusted to spend even modest sums of money for the public good.

Instrumental in exposing the financial scandals and petty corruption in the council were the elected citizens' auditors, who were empowered to make a

---

15 Seuss Law, 'Manchester's Politics', 39–44.

16 *MG*, 10 November 1886; *MG*, 10 November 1887.

17 The figures were – Liberals: 15 aldermen, 27 councillors; Conservatives: four aldermen, 30 councillors. See Seuss Law, 'Manchester's Politics', 292.

18 Chesters Thompson's organisational work helped the party to attract leading national figures, such as A.J. Balfour, to Manchester to stand as parliamentary candidates. For a detailed discussion see Seuss Law, 'Manchester's Politics', 157–64.

detailed inspection of the corporation's accounts. Some, such as Joseph Scott, developed his role as official scrutineer into a crusade against council corruption and mismanagement. After previous attempts at detailed investigation of council contracts and expenditure had been frustrated by officials' secrecy, Scott used his elected position to investigate every aspect of council work, publishing detailed accounts of his controversial findings in the local press. The corporation's officials did not make his job easy and suspicions remained that much had been concealed. When Scott investigated the all-powerful finance committee he discovered that all previous invoices had been removed, making detailed investigation of this aspect of financial procedure impossible.[19] However the catalogue of mismanagement and corruption that did bear investigation was damning enough. Council members had run up bills of over £500 on deputations and 'Pic-nics', £875 of public money had been spent on wine for members and one committee alone had managed to consume 3,500 cigars during the year – all at public expense.[20] Corruption seemed to be rife with one councillor and his officials allegedly taking commission on public loans, others illegally trading with the corporation in supplying chemicals, whiskey and provender, and the health committee facing a catalogue of complaints including an illegal payment made to a local charity.[21] Even Charles Rowley, the council's leading social reform advocate and famous in Manchester for his work for the relief of poverty in Ancoats, was charged with using his position on the art galleries committee to give his own small picture framing business a council contract. He subsequently declined to stand for re-election.[22]

Although personal scandals could damage individual careers it was the collective reputation of the corporation that suffered most. Ill-thought out policy-making was compounded by the use of public money in an attempt to conceal past mistakes. When market tenants challenged the council to refund charges illegally imposed on them by the markets committee, the committee responded by publishing, at ratepayers' expense, 10,000 leaflets condemning the action of the tenants in bringing the issue to light. Yet when the matter went to litigation the markets committee was forced to refund £5,000 in money illegally taken from the tenants in addition to a legal bill of £500. The council also used public money for more sinister political purposes. Faced with demonstrations and meetings of the unemployed the watch committee engaged shorthand writers and monitors to keep close tabs on the leading agitators and published notices, at public expense, defending the council's attitude to the unemployed. Even for those who had little sympathy for the unemployed agitation, such as Joseph Scott, this demonstrated a dangerous and repressive tendency in a supposedly Liberal city.[23]

---

19 J. Scott, *Leaves from the Diary of a Citizens' Auditor* (Manchester, 1884), 2.

20 Scott, *Leaves*, 5, 17–18.

21 Scott, *Leaves*, 9, 43–5.

22 *MCN*, 18 October 1884; Scott, *Leaves*, 30; *MCN*, 25 October 1884, *MCN*, 27 October 1884.

23 Scott, *Leaves*, 40, 45–6.

Scott had little confidence that the council could reform itself from within and felt that prospects for change were hopeless whilst senior members of the council – the largely Liberal aldermanic bench – exercised power without facing the necessity of re-election.[24] Radical Liberals shared this concern and, already alienated from the Liberal mainstream after the 1883 parliamentary by-election, formed, with a number of leading Conservatives, an all-party Ratepayers' Association to agitate for reform.[25] Thus when Joseph Scott's period of office as citizens' auditor came to an end, Radicals Richard Pankhurst, Stephen Norbury Williams and George Payne organised a joint deputation with Conservatives urging Scott to stand for re-election.[26] The cross-party nature of the Ratepayers' Association attracted a broad range of activists dissatisfied with the council's leadership. By the time of the Association's first annual meeting in January 1886, it claimed a membership of 1,450 and appeared to exercise significant influence, with many aspirants for municipal office joining its ranks. Although it is difficult to assess the degree to which the Ratepayers' Association actually assisted new candidates to secure election, it is clear that when the Association actively campaigned against a particular councillor the effect could be very damaging to his prospects of re-election. When Cllr. Charles Stewart, the Liberal councillor for New Cross, charged with illegal corporation trading, was brought out by the Liberal Association to stand for re-election, the Ratepayers' Association responded by nominating their own candidates in opposition. Fearing a split, the Liberal Association quietly dropped Stewart and replaced him with a Ratepayers' Association member, Henry Pingstone. In St. Clements' ward the Ratepayers' Association similarly opposed the long-standing Liberal councillor, Thomas Bazley, helping bring about his defeat after 12 years of office.[27] However Richard Pankhurst's move to London and the gradual reconciliation between the Liberal mainstream and the Radicals following the 1885 general election, soon left Radicals with less appetite for fighting internal party battles through municipal elections. Younger Conservative leaders such as Cllr. William Windsor and Stephen Chesters Thompson were clearly using the Ratepayers' Association to undermine the largely Liberal aldermanic bench, the body upon which the Liberal Party was reliant for their majority.[28]

Some senior Liberals, embarrassed by the action of their colleagues, saw the crisis as an opportunity to remove the worst abuses, and worst abusers, of the public purse. James Southern felt that few members knew of the abuses and accepted that many of the charges were 'probably unanswerable'.[29] His solution for restoring public confidence in the authority was to emphasise the need for greater accountability through a continuous audit of the council's accounts. Similarly veteran Liberal

24 Scott, *Leaves*, 3.

25 *MCN*, 27 September 1884; *MCN*; 10 October 1884.

26 *MCN*, 27 September 1884.

27 *Manchester Ratepayers Association Annual Report*, 14 January 1886, 3, 18–20, MCL, P3416/15.

28 *MCN*, 24 October 1885.

29 Scott, *Leaves*, 52–5.

alderman Abel Heywood welcomed the action of the citizens' auditor's exposures and frankly recognised that practices prevailed which many councillors were unaware of. As the bulk of council work was conducted through committees and no council member, except the mayor, could be on all committees, abuses in one committee could easily go undetected by those who were not members of that committee.[30] This reflected a long-standing complaint about the way in which decentralised council committee structures placed power in the hands of a few and the limited time for proper public scrutiny.[31]

The growing recognition of the inadequacies of the existing operational and decision-making process of the council was partly a product of continuing allegations of corruption and financial waste throughout the 1880s. The greatest scandal of the period came with the committee charged with responsibility for effecting public improvements. The improvement committee's apparent incompetence and financial waste in the construction and finishing of the prestigious Victoria Hotel refocused public attention on the inadequacies of effective scrutiny of council expenditure. The scandal forced the resignation of most of the improvement committee, created great public hostility and suspicion towards future major improvement schemes and made municipal policy-makers cautious about future large-scale investment in alliance with the private sector. Initial completion costs were estimated to be £25,000. Unfortunately the improvement committee, who were charged with responsibility for the project, failed to make any detailed examination of the estimates. By March 1881 the improvement committee revealed to a Local Government Board inquiry that, in fact, £57,000 would be required for the hotel's completion. In the event the final cost was more than double even this swollen estimation.[32]

A prestigious development was turning into a public farce. The workmanship of contractors left much to be desired. One tenant of the Victoria Buildings complained that toilet facilities were so inadequate that local youths were able to witness his female employees taking natural breaks.[33] The failure of the corporation to appoint a clerk of works or an engineer to supervise work on behalf of the improvement committee meant contractors completed work in whatever fashion they wished. As late as March 1886 the hotel's main tenant was still trying to persuade the committee to undertake closer supervision of contractors, although by this time

30 Scott, *Leaves*, 54.

31 R.G. Lawson, *The City Council Seen From the Inside* (Manchester, 1904), 8–9. T.C. Horsfall, 'The Government of Manchester', *Transactions of the Manchester Statistical Society, 1895–6* (13 November 1895), 1–28; T.C. Horsfall, *Ought Mayors and the Chairman of Committees of Town Councils be Appointed for Long Period of Time and be Paid Salaries to Enable Them to Give All Their Working Time to the Service of the Community?* (Manchester, 1903).

32 *The City Ledger*, March 1888.

33 Letter, T.J. Walmsley to W.H. Talbot, 1 April 1885, MCC, ICLB, 37, MCL, M9/63/3/24.

the worst excesses were already apparent.[34] Eventually the city council was forced to set up a committee of inquiry into the whole question of the Victoria Hotel.[35] There was little opposition to this move from Liberal ranks, with senior Liberals such as Ald. Harwood realising that an internal investigation was the only way to head off the possibility of a full Government inquiry.[36] Close inspection of the books of the improvement committee did little to restore the council's reputation.[37] A statement by the Liberal Unionist chairman of the committee, Ald. Hopkinson, that he had been unaware of additional expenditure brought howls of ridicule from his Conservative opponents and heightened public suspicion that there was no one in charge of the committee's purse strings.[38] The resignation of Hopkinson – and the subsequent decision of three-quarters of the 1886 improvement committee to decline renomination to the committee for the following year – took some of the pressure off the council. Following the death of former improvement committee chairman Ald. Grundy, it was decided to wind up the inquiry.[39] For the beleaguered city council members, however, further scandals were to follow.

The corporation's health committee shared with the improvement committee a responsibility for improving the sanitary condition of the city. Unfortunately it also shared the improvement committee's reputation for mismanagement and, worse still, endemic corruption. In November 1884 all candidates for the city council election declared themselves in favour of an inquiry into the committee's operations after the citizens' auditor discovered evidence of illegal payments, excessive expenditure and illegal use of public monies.[40] Another committee was established to investigate the allegation but after two years seemed to have made little progress. Conservative Cllr. Harry Mainwaring alleged that leading officials in the health department were intimidating other employees from giving evidence to an inquiry. Other Conservatives alleged that papers and books from the works had already been taken away and destroyed.[41] At each council meeting there were new allegations of victimisation.[42] Although an inquiry reportedly found no evidence to support the charges of corruption and illegal payments, Conservatives were unconvinced and kept up the pressure on council officials.[43]

---

34 Letter, J. MacGregor to W.H. Talbot, 15 March 1886, MCC, ICLB, 74, MCL, M9/63/3/24.

35 Significantly the committee included three of the city's most influential Conservatives, journalist N.C. Schou, Chesters Thompson and Windsor.

36 *MG*, 7 October 1886; *MC*, 7 October 1886.

37 *The City Ledger*, March 1888.

38 *MG*, 28 October 1886.

39 *MG*, 7 June 1888.

40 Scott, *Leaves*, 43–6.

41 *MC*, 3 February 1887; *MG*, 3 February 1887.

42 *MC*, 9 June 1887; *MG*, 9 June 1887.

43 When the superintendent of the Health Department released Liberal Richard Newton from a corporation contract in order to become a council candidate, Chesters Thompson succeeded in getting the committee minutes referred back for investigation. *MG*, 10 November 1887.

Unlike the chairman of the improvement committee, the health committee chairman Ald. Schofield chose to fight scandal allegations rather than step aside under public pressure. When Chesters Thompson, who was by now the Conservatives *de facto* group leader, demanded a full report on workmen who had been allegedly victimised, Schofield responded with disdain, revealing a determination to defend his committee from the encroaching power of full council. For Schofield, unless the council were prepared to allow committees to exercise their own judgement and allow them their confidence, local government would become unworkable:

> A committee appointed to do certain work must have the confidence of the Council, and was the time of the Council to be taken up if they happened to discharge a man? – (Hear, hear) ... He strongly deprecated the bringing of such matters before the Council instead of first getting the information from the Chairman of the Committee. If such proceedings were allowed to continue, they would spread through every Committee of the Corporation.[44]

The activities of committees were regarded as essentially private matters and the floor of the chamber was not seen as the place to pry into the administration of such business. Many members were, however, increasingly using council debates to challenge the council's leadership. Although the Conservatives had fewer elected councillors in 1888 than 1885, an increased number of Conservative aldermen, divisions in Liberal ranks over Home Rule and a more aggressive Conservative leadership made the old methods of private council management more difficult. Loyalty to one's committee, seen by some as the unwritten law of the council, was a concept now actively questioned.[45] Unpopular or distrusted committee chairmen like Schofield faced almost constant hostile questioning in the chamber, sometimes on relatively minor matters. During the council's July monthly meeting, Schofield was forced to report on former employees supposedly persecuted by his department. In August he faced hostile questioning on the allegedly unnecessary employment of a draughtsman.[46] The following month a Conservative councillor John Andrews raised the issue of an employee injured in the health committee's service, and the committee was forced to reconsider the case.[47] When the committee refused to change its decision the council again referred the matter back for yet further consideration.[48] Councillors had discovered the latent power of full council meetings to expose issues of concern and embarrass opponents. Committee leaders were being forced to provide detailed public justification for what had previously been regarded as private committee activities.

Part of the problem for Schofield was that, like Hopkinson, he was a Liberal Unionist. Seniority and experience had elevated them both to the chairmanship of important committees, but following the Home Rule crisis they lacked a large

44 *MG*, 5 July 1888.

45 *The City Ledger*, February 1888. .

46 *MG*, 2 August 1888.

47 *MG*, 6 September 1888, *MC*, 6 September 1888.

48 *MG*, 4 October 1888.

body of party support in the council chamber. Before 1891 Liberal Unionists in the chamber tended to vote with the Liberals far more than with the Conservatives, suggesting that some linkages with their former party remained.[49] However as Liberal Unionists they could not rely on the unquestioning support of Gladstonians. Conservative members had developed their strategy around highlighting the failings of Liberal and Liberal Unionist aldermen so there was no scope for co-operation here – and in any case there was only limited Liberal Unionist–Conservative collaboration in Manchester at any level before the 1890s. Schofield therefore hung onto his chairmanship somewhat precariously until his resignation in 1889. Following his death in 1891 a general reorganisation of committees finally brought an end to the atmosphere of corruption by formally dividing the committee into two new bodies.[50] Although Schofield had never been charged with corruption himself, the personalisation of committee authority in one man meant he was largely held to be responsible.[51] As scandals broke, council distrust of committee autonomy grew and increasingly tighter oversight of committee activity resulted.

Even if the two bodies responsible for public health and improvement had not been gripped by scandal in the late 1880s, other factors limited the prospects of innovative public improvement policies. Rather than introduce a large improvement rate, Manchester Corporation traditionally relied on profits from trading in gas to subsidise improvement programmes – representing essentially an indirect tax on gas consumers. In 1885 the council ruled that 10 per cent on the capital employed for the manufacture of gas be set aside for improvement purposes. By September 1886, however, it was clear that the economic depression with lower gas profits rendered payment of such a sum impossible without the gas committee collapsing heavily into debt. Moreover some councillors, both Liberal and Conservative, felt that guaranteeing sums to the improvement committee in this way only encouraged it to be less than prudent in its expenditure.[52] By rescinding the original resolution the finances of the improvement committee were less certain and directly linked to the economic fortunes of the gas retail market. The financial year 1886–87 brought little improvement in gas profits and because overall rates had recently increased, the levying of a special improvement rate to replace charges on gas profits was even less of a possibility, particularly following the excesses revealed by the Victoria Hotel debacle.[53] Tight restrictions on new capital investment in gas production meant that potential for dramatically increasing production and sales in the future was limited.[54] There were also limits to just how far the corporation could exploit its existing monopoly. With threatened competition from electricity suppliers, the days

---

[49] Seuss Law, 'Manchester's Politics', 300 (table VI).

[50] Full details of the revised committee structure and committee membership can be found in *The Official Handbook of Manchester and Salford and Surrounding District* (Manchester, 1891).

[51] *The City Ledger*, February 1888.

[52] See comments of J.W. Southern and W.T. Windsor, *MG*, 2 September 1886.

[53] *MG*, 4 August 1887; *MC*, 4 August 1887.

[54] *MG*, 3 January 1889.

of the committee raising large sums through exploitation of their near-monopolistic position were numbered. The issue of how to raise large sums for public improvement programmes was increasingly problematic.

Disputes over the levels and use of gas profits were, however, dwarfed by the allegations of corruption and bribe-taking in the gas department made during the summer of 1889. The scandal had its origins in Salford where one of Northern England's largest coal contractors, Ellis Lever, accused Salford Corporation's gas manager, Samuel Hunter, of accepting bribes. Encouraged on by Salford's gas committee, Hunter sued Lever for criminal libel. The case attracted nation-wide publicity. The eventual defeat of Hunter's libel action turned Lever into something of a public celebrity. In the months that followed, Lever embarked on a public crusade to cleanse gas contracting of corruption, and his attention soon turned to Manchester.[55] Salford Corporation found that it faced real difficulties in bringing legal proceedings against Samuel Hunter. Commission-taking left little documentary evidence and was, in any case, not a criminal offence until the passing of the Public Bodies Corruption Act in 1889. Salford Corporation's priority was to recover losses and discover the details of the corrupt contractors. In return for a petition of leniency, unsuccessful in the event, Hunter agreed to name those contractors from whom he had taken bribes. Among those named was Ellis Lever, who was then successfully sued by the Salford Corporation for £2,300.[56] Although this action destroyed the credibility of Lever as a crusader for public virtue, the case brought to light fresh evidence that corruption had been rife in Manchester Corporation's gas department, too. Hunter alleged that a former superintendent of the Manchester gas department had also received bribes from Lever. No longer able to ignore the allegations, the Manchester Corporation responded by setting up a special committee to investigate the claims, and resolved that those found guilty would be taken off the tendering list.[57] Once again, the main difficulty in conducting an inquiry was uncovering solid evidence upon which legal proceedings could be taken. Ald. Makinson and H.H. Howarth MP both reported allegations and 'information' they had confidentially received regarding a gas committee wood contract in 1882.[58] However Makinson gave the name of his informant only very reluctantly and Howarth simply refused to do so, giving little scope for further investigation. Sleaze allegations took up a large amount of the council's time but without more evidence they were unable either to prove or disprove any of the major claims. As Ald. Harwood observed 'they could not go to law upon every cock and bull story'.[59]

Many younger and newly elected councillors began increasingly to resent the failure of the council to deal with those committees accused of malpractice and to

---

[55] J. Garrard, 'The Salford Gas Scandal of 1887', *Manchester Region History Review*, 2 (1988–89), 1.

[56] Garrard, 'The Salford Gas Scandal', 2.

[57] *MC*, 3 April 1890.

[58] *MG*, 18 April 1890.

[59] *MG*, 8 May 1890.

tackle the apparent culture and proceedings of the council which allowed inefficient bodies to go unreformed. Central to this concern was the role of aldermen and the way in which they dominated the most important committees of the council due to an unwritten iron law of seniority. Back in 1884 Joseph Scott, the citizens' auditor, had placed much of the blame for corruption on the class of 'irresponsible aldermen'.[60] In 1885 the Ratepayers' Association made the abolition of aldermen a test question in the municipal elections of that year and reported that almost all new councillors had declared in favour of this abolition.[61] During the council's first full meeting of 1886 Conservative Cllr. Windsor unsuccessfully proposed a motion calling for the abolition of the office.[62] Two months later his Conservative colleague, Chesters Thompson, attempted to reduce aldermanic domination of committees by proposing that the council limit each committee to just four aldermen each, exclusive of the mayor, and was successful in having the matter referred to a special committee for further consideration.[63] Seuss Law has viewed these moves as evidence of increased party politicisation of the council and a response of the Conservatives to Liberal domination of the aldermanic bench.[64] However, just as many 'advanced' and progressive Liberals supported the Ratepayers' Association campaign against the largely Liberal aldermanic bench, many younger or newer Liberal councillors supported moves to reduce the influence of unelected members. Indeed some of the first moves to reduce aldermanic power came from within the Liberal ranks. The well-known 'advanced' Liberal and social reformer Ald. Walton Smith had proposed limiting aldermen to three committee assignments back in November 1885. Although unsuccessful, it spurred on Chesters Thompson who persuaded the council to replace aldermen on key committees with councillors from both parties.[65] When the council debated Windsor's motion calling for the abolition of aldermen Radical Cllr. J.H. Crosfield seconded the motion, further suggesting that there was co-operation between Conservatives and 'advanced' Liberals. Moreover it was at the suggestion of Liberal Ald. James Harwood that the whole issue be referred to special committee.[66] Recent scandals had produced irresistible pressure for some form of review. The improvement committee, the subject of the Victoria Hotel scandal, had a membership more than half made up of non-elected members. Other committees that had been the subject of criticism also had high proportions of aldermen and the three most prestigious committees, the watch, waterworks and finance committees, were also half composed of aldermen. Senior committee positions were almost exclusively occupied by unelected members. Of the 22 committees in 1886, 20 were chaired by aldermen. Even the deputy chairmanships were dominated by members

60 Scott, *Leaves*, 3.

61 Manchester Ratepayers' Association, *Annual Report*, 14 January 1886, 11–12, MCL, P3416/15.

62 *MC*, 7 January 1886.

63 *MG*, 4 March 1886.

64 Seuss Law, 'Manchester's Politics', 92–4.

65 *MCN*, 7 November 1885; *MCN*, 14 November 1885.

66 *MG*, 4 March 1886; *MC*, 4 March 1886.

of the aldermanic bench, with just seven deputy chairmanships held by councillors. Although some councillors had also faced charges of corruption and illegal trading, the domination of senior council positions by aldermen meant it was they who became the focus of much of the criticism.[67]

Clearly many Liberals, as well as Conservatives, felt that reform was necessary. Over a third of Liberal councillors present opposed the blocking of Windsor's motion calling for the abolition of aldermen. In the local press there was growing frustration with some of the older Liberal members. One Liberal correspondent to the *Manchester City News* accused many Liberals of becoming 'suddenly tainted with Toryism when they enter the Town Hall portals'.[68] Voting records on open contracting, the Victoria Hotel and health committee municipal trading seemed to suggest that whilst many – although not all – Liberal councillors were prepared to support greater openness and scrutiny of council affairs, the votes of Liberal aldermen were often cast in direct opposition to their elected Liberal colleagues.[69] Clearly all elected members were coming under increasing pressure from the press and public opinion to respond to the allegations of corruption and mismanagement. Even a newspaper, *The City Ledger*,, was established as a direct response to public concern about council corruption.[70]

The special committee on committee composition met twice, in April and May, but despite prolonged discussion, no firm conclusions were reached, not least because over one-third of the committee considering reducing aldermanic influence were themselves aldermen![71] Following further negotiations Chesters Thompson introduced a more modest suggestion than that originally proposed, namely that only five aldermen, exclusive of the mayor, should be placed on any one committee without a special resolution of council. This did not settle the aldermanic controversy. Ald. Bennet immediately attempted to get the watch committee exempted from the resolution and had he succeeded it seemed that the finance and waterworks committee were to seek similar exemptions.[72] Failure to obtain exemptions and the resultant removal of Ald. Brown and Hopkinson from the watch committee caused open hostility between aldermen and councillors. Ald. Brown, nominated for the more junior nuisance committee, felt that his new appointment was below his dignity and 'declined at his time to life to go back to it, especially after the way in which he had been treated that morning, in being removed from the watch committee on which he had served thirteen or fourteen years'.[73]

Differences between reformist councillors and the more traditionalist members of the aldermanic bench continued, but November 1886 represented the high tide

---

67 *MG*, 4 March 1886; *MC*, 4 March 1886.

68 *MCN*, 23 October 1886.

69 *MCN*, 23 October 1886.

70 *City Ledger*, 18 January 1888.

71 MCC, Special Committee Re-Constitution of Committees, Special Committee Minutes Vol. I, 80–82, MCL.

72 See comments of Chesters Thompson, *MCN*, 13 November 1886.

73 Ald. Brown, *MCN*, 13 November 1886.

of reaction against aldermanic authority. This was partly due to the effects of the Chesters Thompson resolution, partly due to Conservative divisions and partly due to the success of some aldermen in developing popular policy initiatives – particularly Ald. Walton Smith's work for slum clearance and council house building.[74] Tension between two of the leading Conservatives, Windsor and Chesters Thompson, had been evident when the latter refused to endorse Windsor's call for municipal councils to be directly elected. Hostility between the two became public when Windsor decided to contest a vacancy for the aldermanic bench, which, on the basis of seniority, was reserved for fellow Conservative George Moulton. Windsor opposed seniority promotion and condemned what he saw as the 'unprincipled alliance of the inferior members of both parties in the Council'.[75] Chesters Thompson, who as the leading Conservative Party manager probably helped to secure Liberal acceptance of Moulton, interpreted this as a reference to himself and issued a public rebuke to Windsor.[76] The Conservative leadership, further disappointed by the results of recent municipal elections, lapsed into mutual recriminations.

By 1889 the issue of the aldermanic domination of the council was of decreasing importance in local political debate. This was partly because by the end of the decade the Liberal Party had ceased to dominate the aldermanic bench. A quarter of the party's aldermen allied themselves to the Liberal Unionists, making their partisan loyalty far more questionable. Yet perhaps of most significance was the gradual increase in Conservative aldermen between 1885–89 and by the end of the decade there were as many Conservative aldermen as Gladstonian Liberals.[77] Moreover many of the leading Conservatives who had once been most critical of the principle of aldermanic power and 'seniority' were now sufficiently senior to join the aldermanic bench. Cllr. Windsor, who had once declared he objected to the position of alderman on principle, joined the aldermanic bench in August 1888. Cllr. Chesters Thompson followed him in 1891.[78] With the city's Conservatives gradually incorporated into the city's aldermanic elite, partisan reasons for attacking the bench were gone. Gladstonian Liberals were now in a nominal minority for the first time and could not afford the luxury of internal conflicts, whilst of the seven-strong Liberal Unionist group, just four were elected members, making future criticism of the non-elected members unlikely.

Despite the scandals of the 1880s, the resultant hostility to senior members of the council and the overwhelming damage to the prestige of the corporation, the decade was not without some policy achievements. The unhealthy dwellings committee, led by Liberal social reformer Ald. Walton Smith, demonstrated that a committee without a history of a scandal could develop innovative policies, provided that it

[74] Ald. Walton Smith became the chairman of the new Unhealthy Dwellings Committee responsible for housing and sanitary improvements.

[75] *MCN*, 4 December 1886.

[76] *MG*, 2 December 1886.

[77] Seuss Law, 'Manchester's Politics', 292 (Table I).

[78] *City Of Manchester Council Members form Incorporation* (annotated), 125, MCL, BR 352.OL12 M99.

could maintain the trust of a large section of the council and public. Progressive policy-makers forged co-operative links with voluntary and philanthropic organisations to promote new approaches to housing problems. By the mid-1880s Manchester's largely middle-class pressure groups had lost patience with private landlords who seemed either unwilling or unable to tackle the problem voluntarily. Commenting on the Royal Commission on Housing, the Manchester Domestic Mission pointedly called on landlords to fulfil their 'moral obligations' towards their tenants.[79] The Manchester and Salford Sanitary Association went further and called for a programme of municipal intervention to remove and repair dwellings and create new open space.[80] When Walton Smith brought forward a proposal to an unhealthy dwellings committee, the Sanitary Association enthusiastically supported the move and memorialised the council to accept the suggestion.[81] The support of the Sanitary Association was of considerable significance. Although it had among its activists those who would later become closely identified with the 'advanced' wing of the Liberal Party, such as W.E.A. Axon and T.C. Horsfall, it represented a much broader body of middle-class humanitarian opinion. The Bishop of Manchester served as its president and by convention the mayors of Manchester and Salford accepted vice presidencies. Other Liberals actively involved such as Oliver Heywood, Sir Thomas Bazley and Prof. Hopkinson were associated with the right of the party.[82] By 1885 political opinion had clearly moved in support of some form of municipal action to tackle the city's chronic housing problems and there was little opposition to the creation of a special committee for this purpose.[83] Interestingly the members appointed to the new committee were relatively junior members of the council – allowing the new unhealthy dwellings committee to remain largely untarnished by the scandals that affected the council's more senior leaders.[84]

The committee could not escape some of the consequences of scandal, however. Following the Victoria Hotel affair the council were keen to closely supervise the activities of the committee. Just two months after the committee's creation, the council ruled that no property could be officially condemned as unfit for human habitation and no structural improvement enforced until the plans and costings were submitted for approval to a full council meeting.[85] Some Liberal councillors

---

79 Manchester Domestic Mission, *51st Annual Report*, 1 June 1885, 24, MMUL (microfilm).

80 Manchester and Salford Sanitary Association, *Annual Report for 1884*, 35–8, MMUL (microfilm).

81 MCC, Memorial, 31 December 1884, Special Committees Letter Book I, 12, MCL, M9/77/1.

82 Manchester and Salford Sanitary Association, *Annual Report for 1884*, 3–4, MMUL (microfilm).

83 *MC*, 5 February 1885.

84 MCC, Council Resolution, 4 February 1885, Special Committee Letter Book I, 2, MCL, M9/77/1.

85 MCC, Council Resolution, 14 April 1885, Special Committee Letter Book I, 5, MCL, M9/77/1.

were particularly concerned about possible injustice to very small property owners who had invested what little capital they had in lower grade property to provide a guaranteed income, often as a form of retirement pension. For these individuals slum clearance meant impoverishment.[86] The problem for the council in criticising private landlords was that most of the unsanitary houses constructed in overcrowded courts and yards had been built under the jurisdiction of the corporation and under the corporation's own building code. Moreover the responsibility for building and planning was fragmented. As the building code was the responsibility of another committee – the highways committee – however active Walton Smith was in his own committee, he had no way of directly influencing future construction. It took agitation by the Sanitary Association before the highways committee reconsidered its own code.[87] Following this mobilisation of professional opinion a joint memorial was sent to the highways committee who appointed a sub-committee to produce an amended code.[88] Again it seemed as though the council was forming policy in reaction to public pressure rather than leading opinion.

Despite the formidable difficulties that the unhealthy dwellings committee faced, the complex legislation, the close scrutiny of the council, lack of resources and difficulties with other committees, significant results were achieved. By the summer of 1889, 696 houses had been either demolished or improved.[89] Unfortunately the sheer scale of the problem meant that it was increasingly difficult to satisfy the continuing demands for more rapid progress.[90] Moreover the council faced further embarrassments as it became clear that a number of the members of the corporation themselves were either directly or indirectly the owners of insanitary property. In the summer of 1888 Conservative Cllr. John Hinchcliffe was summoned by Walton Smith to answer for the state of property he owned. Hinchcliffe's failure to attend two meetings meant that the dispute over the future of the property lasted over six months.[91] Less than 12 months later senior Conservative Chesters Thompson faced the same problem when it was revealed that property that his brewing company had purchased was also the subject of a condemnation order.[92] As criticism increased the Sanitary Association redoubled its efforts both in terms of propaganda and in organisation. At a prestigious joint meeting with the Manchester Statistical Society,

---

86 *MG*, 17 March 1887, *MC*, 17 March 1887.

87 Manchester and Salford Sanitary Association, *Annual Report 1886*, 4–5, MMUL (microfilm).

88 Manchester and Salford Sanitary Association, *Annual Report 1886*, 5, MMUL (microfilm).

89 *MC*, 2 May 1889.

90 See Letter, G. Heap, *MCN*, 20 October 1888.

91 Letter, J. Hinchcliffe to Ald. Walton Smith, 16 July 1888, December 1888, MCC, Special Committee Letter Book I, 88, 101, MCL, M9/77/1.

92 Letter, S. Chester Thompson to Allison, 8 April 1889, MCC, Special Committee Letter Book I, 116, MCL, M9/77/1.

the details of an investigation of the sanitary condition of Ancoats were made public, further emphasising the work that remained to be done.[93]

Walton Smith was aware of the limitations of his committee's existing policy. Visits to Liverpool, Glasgow and Edinburgh had convinced him of the need to promote council built housing accommodation to replace that being demolished.[94] However as the costs of a limited corporation housing scheme in Ancoats became clear, Smith realised that he was moving too fast for some members of the council and was forced to reassure a full council meeting that his committee had no intention of proceeding beyond the pilot scheme – the hope being that 'when they had shown the practicability of their scheme private capitalists would save the Corporation the risk and trouble of further undertakings of a like nature in other parts of the city'.[95] After the scandals of the improvement and health committees the council was reluctant to allow any committee to take unnecessary financial risk if alternative private finance could be found. Where property owners were entitled to compensation for clearance schemes the problem was even more acute, with cases having to be referred to an official arbitrator to define the 'fair market value' payable by the corporation. There was little official guidance for the arbitrator to act upon, which naturally made the costs incurred unpredictable.[96]

The large body of cross-party support for a vigorous housing policy was diminished, however, not just because the complications were greater than some had imagined but also because of increased partisan conflict on the council. With Conservatives gradually co-opted on to the aldermanic bench in greater number the alliance of 'advanced' Liberals and Conservatives against the older leaders of the council dissolved and straightforward partisan considerations became more relevant. The partisan dispute over the appointment of a new deputy town clerk in January 1890 demonstrated just how deep party feeling ran.[97] Liberals felt that the Conservative group had deliberately plotted a partisan appointment and vowed to respond.[98] The dispute had revealed the growing weakness of the Gladstonian Liberal group, which, outnumbered 37 to 32, could not hope to defeat the Conservatives in a straight vote without practically the full support of the seven Liberal Unionists. The extension of the city's boundaries in 1890, therefore, represented something of a lifeline for the party. It helped the Liberals restore approximate parity with the Conservatives – and also introduced new Radical Liberal councillors providing the practical stimulus for a wider social reforming programme.

---

93 Manchester Sanitary Association, *Annual Report 1889*, 4–7, MMUL (microfilm).

94 Letter, W. Tatham to Ald. Walton Smith, 18 July 1889, MCC, Unhealthy Dwellings Letter Book 9, MCL, M9/78/2; MCC, Report of Committee Chair, 22 October 1889, Unhealthy Dwellings Letter Book, 19, MCL, M9/78/2.

95 *MG*, 4 December 1890.

96 Letter, A.D. Adrais to W.H. Talbot, 8 September 1890, MCC, Unhealthy Dwellings Letter Book, 59, MCL, M9/78/2.

97 *MG*, 9 January 1890.

98 *MC*, 6 March 1890; *MG*, 6 March 1890.

All of the seven new wards created by the city extension were essentially industrial suburbs and most already had a strong Liberal presence in local administration. Longsight was partly in the Liberal-held South Manchester parliamentary division and the party was able to find a well-known sanitary reformer as one of its candidates. In Blackley and Moston the Liberals already had a strong presence in local government and brought out former councillor Charles Rowley to stand alongside local candidates John Ward, an experienced Poor Law guardian and former chair of the local sanitary authority and George Stanley, who had experience on the Crumpsall School Board.[99] Gorton, well known for its Radical Liberal tradition, produced three Liberal candidates to stand on what amounted to a Lib–Lab platform. Housing and labour relations featured prominently in their campaign.[100] The adjacent ward, Openshaw, also selected Radical candidates, including J.H Crosfield, the former parliamentary candidate. In other new wards, Newton Heath, Miles Platting and Crumpsall, Liberal prospects were not so obvious, but large Irish populations in all these wards meant that the party had a strong base of support. It was not only the newly incorporated areas of Manchester that were selecting new candidates from amongst the 'advanced' section of the party. T.C. Abbott, the honorary secretary of the Sanitary Association, was selected as the Liberal candidate in St. Clement's and in St. Michael's the disgraced former alderman, William Brown, was rejected in favour of a new candidate, J.H. Wells.[101] It was, however, in the newly incorporated parts of the city where the Liberal Party made most of its gains – and where Radical Liberals were most conspicuous as candidates. In the five new wards that were contested, 11 of the 15 seats fell to the Liberals. In Gorton, where Liberal candidates stood on a particularly Radical platform, they took all three seats.[102] The newly amalgamated districts had brought many with more 'advanced' Liberal opinions into the council and allowed the party as a whole to again outnumber the Conservatives in the chamber.

The growth of the Conservative Party in the city council had aroused the concern of the Manchester Liberal Union who noted with some satisfaction that the first election in the newly expanded Manchester had 'lessened the danger that Tory domination would become paramount...'.[103] Over the next 18 months there was little change in the relative electoral position of the parties. By-election successes nationally and local electoral success brought a new air of cautious confidence to members of the Liberal Union.[104] Locally, Conservative divisions over licensing questions assisted this air of Liberal optimism. These divisions were in part a consequence of the business interests of leading Conservatives. The leader of the Conservative city council group, Ald. Chesters Thompson, was, by the early 1890s, the managing

99 *MCN*, 27 September 1890.
100 *MCN* 18 October 1890.
101 *MCN*, 27 September 1890; *MCN* 18 October 1890.
102 *The Official Handbook*, 311–13.
103 MLU, Secretary's Report to Annual Meeting, 6 May 1891, MCL, M283/1/1/2.
104 MLU, Annual Meeting, 7 April 1892, MCL, M283/1/1/2; *MG*, 3 November 1891.

director of the most powerful brewing company in the Manchester district.[105] Such was his influence locally that he had been dubbed the 'King of Ardwick' in the popular press.[106] His position as Balfour's principal party manager in Manchester gave him considerable influence in the wider party.[107] Liberals, however, were highly suspicious of Chesters Thompson. Not only had he done much to threaten Liberal hegemony on the council, many believed his political methods were, if not actually unlawful, highly disreputable and socially destructive. In 1892 the Liberal Party in East Manchester went as far as launching a unsuccessful election petition against Balfour and Chesters Thompson, alleging the use of public houses as bases to bribe the electorate.[108] For many Liberals licensing questions were a vital part of any social reform programme. When magistrates granted a licence to a notorious public house in Oldham Street, previously closed on police evidence, Liberals forced Chesters Thompson into a defence of the brewing interest. The subsequent debate saw the most senior Liberal Unionist on the council, watch committee chairman Ald. Mark, expressing sympathy with Liberal views and making an outspoken attack on the magistrates who had allowed the licence.[109] Chesters Thompson, dependent on Liberal Unionists for a majority on the council, was faced with a Liberal Unionist leader with whom he would find it difficult to do business.

The real difficulty for the Conservatives, however, came when George Scott, the manager of a newly built music hall in the centre of Manchester's most fashionable area, applied to the council for a dramatic licence, a precursor for a future application for a drinks licence.[110] For many Liberals and social reformers, the public and moral health of the city were under threat. The debate was not simply about the granting of a licence to one theatre – rather the new 'Palace of Varieties' became a test of public attitudes to temperance and social reform.[111] Both Ald. James Harwood, leader of the often conservatively inclined Liberal aldermanic bench and George Russell the recently elected Radical member for Longsight, were united in their denunciation of the drink interest. The issue gave the Liberal Party a rallying campaign issue which united almost all their supporters and an opportunity to embarrass the city's leading municipal Conservative, Chesters Thompson. At times the issue took the form of something akin to a Gladstonian-style crusade with Manchester's own 'grand old man' Ald. James Harwood leading the charge.[112] When a vote was finally taken the Conservatives split down the middle with 16 supporting the granting of the licence

105 *Spy*, 16, 24 July 1891.

106 *Spy*, 2, 17 April 1891. Chesters Thompson represented Ardwick ward on the city council.

107 Seuss Law, 'Manchester's Politics', see chapter five, 204–52.

108 See evidence in *MCN*, 19 November 1892.

109 *MC*, 3 December 1891.

110 *Spy*, 35, 5 December 1891.

111 MCC, Memorial, Manchester and District Temperance Association, Watch Committee Letter Book 9, 21 March 1892, 132, MCL, M9/70/2/9.

112 See speech in *MC*, 7 April 1892.

and 17 opposing. In contrast the Liberals were almost entirely united behind their leaders with 41 opposing the granting of the licence and just eight supporting it.[113]

Despite the greater sense of unity engendered in Liberal ranks by the temperance agitation, the party still faced a formidable problem. The tri-annual election for the aldermanic bench was set for November 1892 and, after the bad feeling created after the Liberals had used their new councillors to elect almost exclusively Liberal aldermen in 1890, many Conservatives were looking for revenge. Moreover the eight Liberal Unionist council members were now even less likely to vote unquestionably with the main Liberal groups, following a general election in which the party nationally were more closely tied to the Conservatives than ever. In early October, the Manchester Liberal Union, aware of the Conservative desire to elect several Tory aldermen to replace the existing Liberals, called upon ward organisations to fight every seat 'where there is a reasonable prospect of success'.[114] Somewhat unusually for a party which resisted being directed from the centre, 'recommendations and advice were freely offered by the Union.'[115] Fear of a major Conservative revival had forced the central committees to act.

The worst fears of the Liberal Union were not realised. The Conservatives, defeated nationally and divided locally gained just one Liberal seat in the municipal elections of that year. Once again the Liberals showed signs of decaying in the old central parts of Manchester with St. Anne's Ward, formerly Liberal Unionist, and St. John's, formerly Liberal, both falling to the Conservatives. Outside the centre, however, Liberalism continued to prosper with the once marginal Rusholme being gained from the Conservatives with an overwhelming majority, and the Radical grip on Longsight being further strengthened.[116] The result did, however, now mean that the Conservatives had one more member than the Liberals. In practice it seemed Conservative supremacy would be greater than this, as, in the aldermanic elections, nine retiring Liberal aldermen would be unable to vote, in contrast with just three retiring Conservatives. Absenteeism and a divided Liberal Unionists group, however, meant that only one Liberal alderman was actually defeated.[117]

The party politicisation of the council was assisted by the recruitment of councillors with specific agendas and programmes. From the extension of the city boundaries in 1890 there emerged a Radical group in the council who consistently supported the advancement of Labour and Progressive causes. By compiling a list of those who consistently voted for 'Progressive' measures between 1885 and 1895, it is possible to identify a significant pattern which gives important clues as to why Progressivism as an ideology quickly attracted the support of so many Liberals in the council group.[118] Of the hard core of 18 committed Progressives identified, only three were aldermen.

113 *MG*, 7 April 1892.

114 MLU, Executive Committee, 3 October 1892, MCL, M283/1/1/2.

115 MLU, Executive Committee, 24 November 1892, MCL, M283/1/1/3.

116 *The Official Handbook*, 358–60.

117 *MCN*, 12 November 1892.

118 See appendix four for details of this calculation.

Seven of the 18 were first elected in 1890, and a further five in 1891. All, with the exception of Cllr. J.H. Greenhow and W. Butterworth, represented largely working-class constituencies. Almost half represented constituencies newly incorporated within the city. In contrast, of the hard core of seven Liberals who were identified as the most consistent opponents of Progressive causes, five were aldermen by 1895, five had entered the council before 1886 and all bar one represented constituencies with a significant middle-class element. Four of the seven represented wards in the safe Conservative commercial parliamentary division of North-West Manchester. Three represented the old central wards of Collegiate and Exchange who had little resident population, and only one represented a newly incorporated area, and that was Cllr. H. Plummer who represented the largely middle-class suburban ward of Rusholme.

New councillors from the newly incorporated, largely working-class districts of the city clearly had a significant impact on the balance of the Liberal council group. Significantly their emergence on to the council predated the challenge of the Independent Labour Party by two years, giving them little chance to establish a new brand of politics before the ILP municipal challenge. As early as November 1892, the ILP took over a third of the vote in newly incorporated Harpurhey in a two-sided contest with the incumbent Conservative.[119] Such success in newly incorporated industrial suburbs naturally gave rise to the concern that the ILP were the greatest threat in the very areas in which the Liberals had been recently so successful, presenting the nightmare scenario of the party being squeezed by the Conservatives out of the older central commercial wards and by the ILP from the new working-class suburbs.

The 1893 municipal elections marked the first all-out assault by the ILP on the council. None of their candidates was elected but substantial ILP votes in Harpurhey and St. Mark's looked ominous to some Liberals.[120] Liberal candidates were clearly somewhat bemused by the new political conditions, although several, in an attempt to prevent defections and to outflank their new opponents, simply announced their agreement with most of the Independent Labour programme.[121] Privately, Ardwick Liberals admitted taking 'as many points as could be off the Labour Party's programme'.[122] Discussions in the Liberal Union committees, revealed that the nature of the ILP challenge required more than simply leaving local party workers to find their own solutions to the problem. Representatives from Harpurhey advocated coming to an arrangement with the ILP, but elsewhere, notably in South-West Manchester, this had already been attempted and had proved unsuccessful. ILP opposition to Liberal candidates in South Manchester constituency was blamed on the action of Liberals who had opposed ILP candidates in South Salford. Radical

119 *MG*, 2 November 1892.

120 *MG*, 2 November 1893.

121 See comments Cllr. Sherratt, *MCN*, 14 October 1893; Cllr. J.W. Southern, *MCN*, 4 November 1893.

122 MLU, Executive Committee, Report to Union Committee, 17 November 1893, MCL, M283/1/1/3.

Ald. J.H. Crosfield complained of Liberal co-operation with the Conservatives in other seats, including Gorton. Clearly a co-ordinated response was required. The Liberal Union defeated a suggestion that specific wards should adopt 'representatives of labour' and instead passed a resolution appointing a committee to consider the adoption of 'an advanced Municipal Programme for Manchester'.[123]

Ten years previously the idea of the then Manchester Liberal Association drawing up a programme for municipal representatives to follow would have been unthinkable, but by 1893, with a number of candidates already adhering to a programme, albeit that of another party, the changes that had taken place in the previous decade meant that the development of a Progressive Programme was the least controversial way forward. Following internal party negotiations which took over six months the Progressive Programme that finally emerged was an amalgam of themes which clearly reflected its dual heritage.[124] Its support of council action to tackle unemployment, to enforce a standard rate of wages and an eight-hour day for corporation workmen, betrayed clear ILP influence, although these were also important to Lib–Labs such as George Kelley, the secretary of the local trades council. Other elements of the programme, however, reflected either priorities that the Liberals were already pursuing, ones which had cross-party support or were proposals designed clearly for partisan benefit. The demolition of slum property, increased public open space and the 'energetic enforcement' of sanitary legislation had been part of the Liberal social reform platform since the mid-1880s.[125] Reform of rate collection and charges for gas and water were already being propounded by many Liberal candidates in the early 1890s. The municipalisation of tramways had attracted support from all sides of the political divide, mainly due to the tramway company's treatment of its staff, and by 1894 even the moderate *Manchester City News* was acknowledging the fact that the corporation might be forced by the power of public opinion to take action.[126] Incorporation of Manchester's industrial suburbs had already proved politically beneficial, increasing the party's numbers on the council and if further incorporation took place of other industrial townships there was no reason to suspect that the results would be any different, provided that the party acted before the ILP became too powerful in these areas. In any case a large increase in the city's size would probably have stretched the meagre resources of the ILP, preventing them fighting the new wards very effectively. It was also clear that municipal expansion was a method by which the 'advanced' section of the Liberal Party could outflank and outnumber both the remaining conservatively-inclined Liberals clinging on to seats in the central part of the city and the Conservatives who had largely taken over the older central areas. Expansion of the city also represented a way of reducing tension with the ILP. Socialist candidates were outspoken in their

123 MLU, Executive Committee, Report to Union Committee, 17 November 1893, MCL, M283/1/1/3.

124 MLU, Executive Committee, 16 July 1894, MCL, M283/1/1/3.

125 MLU, Executive Committee, 16 July 1894, MCL, M283/1/1/3.

126 *MCN*, 20 October 1894.

condemnation of the over-representation of the central wards, controlled as they saw it by middle-class commercial interests.[127] The geographical expansion of the city was a relatively uncontroversial way of diluting the influence of these central wards, without actually having to redraw central boundaries and deny long-standing aldermen their seats. It also gave the Liberals and ILP the opportunity to expand into new areas and increase their numbers without, necessarily, having to come into direct conflict with each other.

The Progressive Municipal Programme cannot, however, be simply seen as an opportunistic response to the challenge of the ILP[128] or even as a product of the changing general intellectual climate of the Liberal Party.[129] For a new programmatic style of politics and a more cohesive party system to emerge the old style Liberal elites with their informal system of party management and leadership had to be swept aside. The difficulties associated with informal, decentralised and highly personalised leadership were compounded by the historic difficulties of city government. Increasing statutory restrictions, heavy financial commitments and bureaucratic difficulties made it difficult for 'advanced' Liberals – even when in positions of influence – to tackle the grave social problems left by the legacy of rapid industrialisation. By the 1880s, however, the Liberal city fathers could only control and manage the council by packing the aldermanic bench. Radicals and Conservatives, largely shut out of the corporation's inner circle, highlighted the questionable public ethics of some leaders and exploited a series of scandals to wrest power from the all-powerful committee chairmen to the floor of the council chamber. In the short term this made council members nervous about the spending of any public money on public improvement projects, but ultimately brought more centralised cohesive policy-making, a process further assisted by increasing levels of party competition in the chamber.

Aldermanic scandals helped undermine both the old Liberal leaderships and foster greater partisanship. Firstly, it gave the Conservative leadership a position around which they could unite and attack the increasingly vulnerable Liberals. Secondly, following the 1885 general election debacle in Manchester and the Liberal Unionists' secession from the Liberal Party, both the Liberal council group and the Manchester Liberal Union were increasingly concerned to see that Liberal ascendancy was restored in the council chamber. Motivated by the fear that Conservative leaders would pack the aldermanic bench as the Liberals had once done, much greater effort was made by the party organisation to assist individual candidates during local elections and mobilise Liberal council members in support of

---

127 For example see comments of Patrick Murey, *MCN*, 20 October 1894.

128 As implied by J.Hill, 'Manchester and Salford Politics and the Early Development of the Independent Labour Party', *International Review of Social History*, 26 (1981), 171–201.

129 Clarke's work on Manchester Progressivism does not consider the important changes that took place in Manchester's municipal government in the period before C.P. Scott came to lead the local Liberal Union. P.F. Clarke, *Lancashire and the New Liberalism* (Cambridge, 1971), 153–97.

Liberal candidates for the aldermanic bench. The expansion of the city's boundaries in 1890 served to reinforce this trend with party allegiances increasingly overriding localist considerations. Moreover the new industrial districts brought into the council a much larger body of Radical Liberals with much more explicit and specific social reform agendas, reducing the influence of the more conservative Liberals, largely from the central commercial wards. Progressive politics was the product of both long-term intensification of party competition, short-term political manoeuvring and fundamental changes in the political composition and outlook of the Liberal council group. By the time a more cohesive Liberal group with a Progressive programme had emerged the party was no longer a sufficiently large force in the council chamber to be able to put its policies into effect. There remained the danger that the working-class electorates in Manchester's industrial suburbs, upon which the party seemed to be increasingly reliant, would grow tired of promises by the established parties who had hitherto shown only limited interest in labour issues, and instead turn to the politics of the ILP. Despite the creation of a more cohesive council group with a clear programme, free of past scandals, the Liberal Party's municipal future was still far from certain.

CHAPTER SIX

The 'Politicisation' of the Town Hall

Like Manchester, for much of the nineteenth century Leicester's municipal politics was characterised by one-party domination. Liberals led the council from incorporation and gradually made the central working-class wards their own. North and Middle St. Margaret's, West St. Mary's and All Saints' all regularly returned Liberals, with only one ward, St. Martin's, being safe Conservative territory.[1] The Liberal Party's near hegemonic position naturally had significant implications for the style of local politics and the policy priorities adopted by the council. Leicester was unusual in that the town and ward boundaries established in the late 1830s with the incorporation of the town remained constant for over 50 years. It was not until 1891 that the town's boundaries were extended to include the immediate suburbs. This meant that political organisations at ward level had remained geographically unchanged since the emergence of modern political associations in the 1850s.[2] By the 1870s the Liberal Party had a highly sophisticated political machine at ward level and one that could mobilise a substantial number of voluntary activists. Influenced by the Birmingham model, it was a system that, as in other towns, was heavily criticised by opponents, but brought substantial electoral dividends to the Liberal Party.[3] The dominant position that the Liberal Party had obtained made for predictable local election results. Indeed the Conservatives, frustrated by their failure to make a significant municipal breakthrough, experimented with the idea of standing as 'independents' in the hope of making a breakthrough. In 1886 even J. Herbert Marshall, one of the town's best-known Conservative figures, stood as an independent, although it was clear that the local Conservatives provided his electoral machine.[4] The decision of Conservatives not to fight elections on party political issues helped render municipal politics even less exciting for the electorate. Thus the 1885 elections were widely regarded as having created the least popular interest for many years.[5] The years that followed generated still less. For three years in the late 1880s – 1887 to 1889 – there were no contested elections at the beginning of November when a third of the council retired. Local compromises avoided the necessity and cost of elections, but there was a price to be paid for preserving the electoral calm.

---

1 Alan Little, 'Chartism and Liberalism: Popular Politics in Leicestershire 1842–1874', Unpublished PhD, University of Manchester, 1991, 289–90.

2 *LDP*, 4 November 1991.

3 R. Read, *Modern Leicester* (London, 1881), 259–62.

4 *LDP*, 2 November 1886.

5 *LDP*, 3 November 1885; *LDM*, 3 November 1885.

The failure of the Liberal Party to motivate and mobilise its supporters on relevant local issues meant that when elections came around it was difficult for the party to persuade its voters to turn out however mechanically efficient its organisation was. Apathy and uninterest, rather than the Conservative Party, was the main Liberal enemy. In 1886 the apathy of Liberal supporters was blamed for the surprise loss of three council seats. Complacency was also a problem. Many Liberals viewed the electorate's lack of interest as a sign that the Liberal Party was providing discreetly efficient local services and administration.[6]

Unlike Manchester, the 1870s and 1880s did not see a general Conservative revival in Leicester. Part of the reason for this may be that economic trends in the city favoured the growth of industries the leaders of which were strong supporters of free trade and Liberal politics. The emergence of the boot and shoe trade in the late nineteenth century created a class of elite manufacturers who, in general, attached themselves to the Liberal Party. Of the ten boot and shoe manufacturers who sat on the council in 1902, all were Liberals.[7] The local boot and shoe trade unions were also largely Liberal, at least until the 1890s, and the leader of the National Union of Boot and Shoe Operatives, William Inskip, became an active and high profile Liberal councillor in the town. In contrast Leicestershire's most prominent Conservatives came largely from non-industrial backgrounds and played only a limited role in municipal politics. The Manners family exercised great influence in Conservative politics to the north and east of Leicester, but was rarely associated with municipal activities. Lesser gentry such as the Packes, Halfords and Pells, although heavily involved in county politics, did little to promote a Conservative revival in Leicester. This probably reflected a long-term trend towards the withdrawal of the country gentry from urban municipal politics.[8] In the absence of the gentry, the Conservatives failed to attract significant numbers of senior industrialists into their ranks. Indeed the party failed to develop any significant links with senior industrialists until the Home Rule crisis saw the Liberal Unionist Faire family gravitating towards the Conservative Party. However the small scale of the Liberal Unionist secession in Leicester did little to revive Conservative fortunes.[9] The town's most famous Liberal Unionist, Thomas Fielding Johnson, well known for his philanthropic and educational work, played no role in municipal politics, preferring to stay aloof from the activities of the Liberal-dominated council.[10]

The reasons for the failure of the county's most senior Conservative and Unionist personnel to engage in municipal politics were complex. Clearly many of high social standing in the county would have found taking on the role of a small minority party in the council unattractive. Moreover the Conservatives on the council did

6 See 'Local Notes', *LDP*, 2 November 1886.

7 M. Elliott, *Victorian Leicester* (London, 1979), 161–5.

8 Little, 'Chartism and Liberalism', 290–93.

9 W. Pike and W. Scarfe , *Leicestershire and Rutland at the Opening of the Twentieth Century*, (Brighton, 1902) reprint, (Edinburgh, 1985), 169. See chapter four.

10 C. Howes, *Leicester – its Civic and Social Life* (Leicester, 1927), 43.

little to attract new recruits by the way they performed in the council chamber. Frequent divisions over tactics and a lack of clear leadership made it difficult for them to operate even as an effective opposition group. These divisions were brought sharply into focus in 1891, shortly before the first election under the new ward boundaries. The Liberals planned to turn the election into a straight battle of party strength. The Conservatives, however were divided on the approach they should take. J.F.L. Rolleston, the president of the Conservative Association, was highly critical of the 'shallow' partisanship in local politics, and preferred to emphasise the contribution that Conservatives had made to the past administration of the town. In doing so he attempted to associate the party with many of the town council's achievements and thus prevent the Liberals taking all the credit for the corporation's public improvements.[11] This approach contrasted sharply with that of the *de facto* leader of the Conservative group, J.H. Marshall. Marshall, who had once fought a municipal election unsuccessfully as an independent, demanded that the party take a much more aggressively partisan approach in opposition to the Liberal group. At a hustings meeting in Charnwood ward he launched a scathing attack against Liberal representatives who blindly followed their leaders and described Liberal aldermen as 'old ladies'.[12] These differences of opinion made for difficult election campaigns with the Conservative Party sending out confused and sometimes contradictory messages to the voting public. Leicester Conservatives had no figure akin to Stephen Chesters Thompson in Manchester who built a powerful political machine in his area and led the Conservatives into a successful onslaught against the Liberal majority. Years of frustration meant that some Leicester Conservatives had abandoned any real attempt to overturn the Liberal majority and instead hoped to gain election by being seen merely as effective administrators in a Liberal-led council. The consequence was that the ruling municipal elite faced little electoral challenge until the creation of a strong Independent Labour Party.

The Liberal municipal elite was in a formidable position. Not only did it face little challenge from other parties, but their own party, in the shape of the central Liberal Association, showed little disposition to interfere in municipal politics. It was not until the 1890s that the Association began to see itself as having a major role in managing local elections and even then was cautious about intervening in policy debates. Moreover few of the town's leading municipal figures took a high profile role in the Association. William Barfoot, who served as the Liberal Club's chairman of directors, was a rare example of a municipal figure taking a leading role in local party bodies, but few followed his example.[13] Even Barfoot's role was largely administrative rather than political; the senior alderman's primary concern was the provision of a new Liberal Club.[14] Unlike their counterparts in Manchester, the Leicester Liberal Association seems to have played little direct role in the financing

11 *LDM*, 22 September 1891.

12 *LDM*, 25 September 1891.

13 Leicester Liberal Club, Board of Directors, 9 March 1883, LRO, 10 D 62/8.

14 Leicester Liberal Club, Board of Directors, 19 May 1887, LRO, 10 D 62/8.

of local election campaigns. Long-established ward organisations took on the major role of raising subscriptions and finance for local elections, with local political management highly decentralised.[15] Councillors and aldermen operated largely independently of the central Association. In 1885 the Liberal Association's finance and general purposes committee even went as far as sending a deputation to meet the town's municipal leaders in order to try to persuade them to give a larger degree of support to the activities of the Association.[16] Even at times of crucial political developments there was often little co-ordination between the Liberal Association and the town council leaders. When parliament finally accepted proposals for the extension of the town's boundaries in 1891, the redrawing of electoral wards had potentially massive implications for the Liberal Party's organisation and position in local politics. Yet when the Liberal Association executive met to devise a Liberal plan for new boundaries, to submit to the public inquiry, the leading officers of the association were not informed of the position the Liberal council leadership would take on the matter. Eventually the Association asked its agent to produce a scheme independently of the town council in case the council group failed to submit one itself.[17] This was, in fact, a very rare move on the part of the Liberal Association. In general the Association saw itself as mainly responsible for parliamentary elections and rarely passed comment or resolution on matters pertaining to council activity. Ward committees and local officials were deemed to be exclusively responsible for the management of local politics. Moves to persuade the Liberal Association to take a lead in the promotion of labour candidates were blocked for the fear of damaging ward autonomy. The executive committee deemed it 'inexpedient to interfere with the free action of Ward Committees in the selection of Candidates', preferring instead to simply suggest that wards should 'favourably consider' the matter.[18] Similarly when many Radicals pushed for the adoption of a Progressive municipal programme, the executive committee decided to make no firm recommendation on the grounds 'that the Ward Committees should have full freedom of action in all Municipal matters'.[19] Only during periods of real crisis did the Liberal Association attempt to interfere in the conduct of municipal elections – although by 1895 competition from the ILP and demoralised activists forced the Association's hands. Apathy and disaffection following the general election saw the Liberal Party lose three municipal seats in the 1895 November municipal campaign, prompting one Conservative councillor to predict 'that if they worked with the same determination they had shown on that occasion for the next ten years Radical Leicester would be like Radical Manchester – a thing of the past'.[20] The central Liberal Association could not simply let the Liberal Party's grip on municipal power slowly wither in the hands of increasingly

---

15 East St. Margaret's Ward LA, Executive Committee, 30 September 1885, LRO, 11 D 57/5.

16 LLA, Finance and General Purposes Committee, 13 July 1885, LRO, 11 D 57/2.

17 LLA, Executive Committee, 20 July 1891, LRO, 11 D 57/2.

18 LLA, Executive Committee, 4 October 1893, LRO 11 D 57/3.

19 LLA, Executive Committee, 3 October 1894, LRO 11 D 57/3.

20 *LDP*, 2 November 1895.

inactive and demoralised ward committees. In early 1896 it appointed a permanent committee to oversee the activities of ward committees, to produce campaign literature and supervise the selection of local council candidates.[21] A meetings and literature committee was formed centralising responsibility for the organisation of elections and the question of adopting a Progressive municipal programme was again put back on the agenda of the local Liberal Association.[22]

This move to the centralised management of municipal elections, with the drawing up of a common electoral programme, was in great contrast to the highly decentralised structure of the council and the highly decentralised structure of local party organisation in the early 1880s and 1890s. The changes were not, however, the product of simply a short-term political crisis, but rather a reflection of the growing problems with the existing decentralised forms of municipal management. Liberal domination of the council meant that there was little partisan conflict over individual council policies. Only a very substantial Liberal split offered any real hope of the Conservatives seeing their agendas being adopted, unless, of course, Liberals shared those agendas. With no clearly defined opposition group that could challenge the majority, the most significant debates in the council came between members of the Liberal Party.

One-party domination of the council reinforced the decentralised nature of local politics, with councillors being seen primarily as advocates of a particular geographical area – their ward – rather than advocates of a party programme. Key decision-making took place largely in committee meetings with only highly controversial issues getting a public airing on the floor of the council chamber. As councillors and aldermen wanted a major say in the public monies spent in their area they clamoured to obtain seats on the key spending committees. As a result these particular committees were large and unwieldy. In 1886 the highways and sewerage committee had 30 members. There were moves to restrict numbers on the largest committees, but there were significant difficulties in the way of slimming down these bodies. Although it was generally recognised that committees were too large, junior members of council were worried that restrictions would deprive them of access to council patronage and spending and that small committees would lead to the centralisation of power in the hands of aldermen and senior officials.[23] Those who advocated introducing restrictions cited Birmingham as an example of an authority where small committees had led to more efficient administration – but the proposed restrictions were defeated by 20 votes to 18.[24]

The issue of committee size and structure, however, increasingly became a preoccupation with municipal leaders. Shortly before plans to extend the town's municipal boundaries – and thus the size of the council – went before parliament

21 LLA, Meeting of ward representative and honorary officers of the Association, 13 April 1896, LRO, 11 D 57/3.

22 LLA, Executive Committee, 9 October 1896, LRO, 11 D 57/3.

23 Legal precedent seemed to suggest that councillors could not be prevented from being members of any council committee they wished to join. *MFP*, 6 November 1886.

24 *MFP*, 13 November 1886.

another attempt was made to reduce committee sizes to what were regarded as more manageable levels. In 1890 a private meeting of council members agreed that the highways and sewerage committee be reduced to 19 members. Twenty-six members, however, had submitted their names with the hope of being included on the committee and it quickly became clear that junior members were the ones who were to be removed from the committee.[25] Predictably backbench opinion forced the council to reinstate the members who had been dismissed.[26] Local representatives, and particularly junior members of the council, felt they could not afford to be excluded for fear that their own areas would be overlooked by the spending committees. It was not until 1895 that a standing order was introduced limiting the size of committees to 21 members – the statutory limit for the watch committee. By then, as veteran Liberal Ald. Israel Hart observed, the issue had become an annual discussion when committees were appointed. Eventually, however, the enlarged council meant that most councillors felt that some restriction was necessary – if only to prevent the size of some committees expanding to such a degree as to make them unworkable.[27]

Disputes about committee size were central to political struggles in the council because of the centrality of committees to the work of the corporation. Each committee exercised a combination of executive and legislative power and had a wide range of discretionary authority in its designated area of responsibility. When the council was drawing up plans to expand its municipal boundaries, the sheer scale of work required before a parliamentary application could be made necessitated the establishment of a separate committee which could complete all the detailed and controversial work away from the public gaze of full council meetings.[28] When the Bill eventually went before parliament the council's parliamentary committee were solely responsible for its progress. In both cases one man – Thomas Wright – headed the committees concerned and took personal responsibility for the proposals. Not all members approved of single committees taking responsibility for such important matters. On the eve of the Bill's successful passage several Liberal councillors criticised Wright, who was by then a Liberal Unionist, for exceeding his authority in the negotiations that had taken place. Wright dismissed this as simply a party move designed to restrict Liberal Unionist influence in the council and prevent Liberal Unionist leaders becoming associated with a successful project.[29] It did, however, demonstrate that there was a limit to how much committees were to be allowed to manage important business without reference to full council. With a new council about to be elected on new boundaries, municipal leaders began to recognise the importance of the political parties in helping secure their position in council.

[25] *LDM*, 10 November 1890.

[26] *MFP*, 15 November 1890.

[27] *MFP*, 2 November 1895; *LDM*, 30 October 1895.

[28] See, for example, the draft report of the LTC, Borough Boundaries Committee, 21 September 1882, LRO, CM8.

[29] *LDM*, 1 July 1891.

Liberals had to restrain those opponents who were using their position at the head of important committees to enhance their own personal reputations.

The issue of committee authority came to a head shortly after the election of the new council in 1891. Demands for municipal expenditure increases from individual committees clashed with the generally held desire to keep down rates. Decisions over expenditure had hitherto been left largely to the discretion of individual committees and there were few formal restrictions on how much each committee could spend. Each spring individual committees submitted their 'estimates' for the general approval of council, but there was no formal mechanism to force committees to stay within these self-imposed expenditure limits. Although the finance committee was nominally responsible for the payment of council debts, their role was solely administrative – they could not actually refuse to pay the bills presented to them, however extravagant they were.[30] Historically large gas and water profits had been used to subsidise local government expenditure and keep local rates down. These profits, however, were unpredictable. High profits one year only encouraged committees to believe that if their expenditure did exceed the original estimates the extra sums could easily be absorbed by profits from this municipal trading. If profits then did not meet expectations the council was left with a considerable shortfall. By 1889 there was considerable concern that leaving committees to regulate their own expenditure only encouraged extravagant use of public money, with individual members pushing for expenditure on their wards in the hope of obtaining personal political benefit. Talk of strengthening the powers of the finance committee, or limiting committee budgets to specific sums, however, met with opposition from committee chairmen who felt their position could be undermined. More junior members also feared the centralisation of budgetary authority that these suggestions implied. The principle of seniority dictated that councillors could not expect to join the finance committee until they had recorded many years' service.[31] The matter was a pressing concern but the solution was not obvious. In the financial year 1889–90, the council paid £11,500 over and above the figure anticipated by its original estimates and expenditure was calculated to be rising by an average of £20,000 per annum. Even in the context of the general rise in municipal expenditure during the late nineteenth century, the figures were alarming. Part of the problem was that councillors often exhibited contradictory attitudes wanting to hold down overall expenditure yet pushing hard for expensive projects they were associated with. Cllr. Underwood, a leading critic of increasing expenditure, was at the same time a prominent supporter of the movement to improve communications with the west of the town and the town centre – proposals which included a new boulevard and river bridge costing up to £30,000.[32] Moreover there were aspects of the local rate which the council could not control – namely the school board portion of the rates. If they rose at the same time as the municipal rates, the impact on residents could be particularly heavy.

30 *MFP*, 2 March 1889.

31 *LDM*, 27 February 1889.

32 *MFP*, 29 March 1890.

While the Leicester Liberal Association discussed school board affairs, the absence of the Liberal Association from involvement in municipal politics meant there was no central policy-making body to determine policies for overall local expenditure.[33]

Matters came to a head when the plans for borough extension were announced. In order to persuade citizens outside the borough to support extension, the town had to provide generous rating concessions to newly incorporated areas while making lavish promises of increased expenditure on local services in these areas.[34] The consequences for local finances were serious. Israel Hart, the Liberal chairman of the finance committee, was forced to announce a large leap in the level of rates. For the previous two years, expenditure had comfortably exceeded the estimates and combined with interest on capital and increased educational demands, an increase in the basic rate of 10d was necessary.[35] Although a significant proportion of the rise was due to the changing method of levying rates brought about by the town's extension, the town's leaders could hardly admit this given that there had been overwhelming and cross-party support for the measure in the council chamber. Consequently politicians of all sides focused on the over-expenditure of committees as the cause of the crisis – and in particular on the highways committee which had overspent by some £6,000. This particular criticism was a little harsh, as much of the additional expenditure was a result of the committee having to fulfil commitments the council had made to the county council as a result of borough extension. The point was all but lost as the image of extravagant committees came to dominate public perceptions of municipal politics.[36]

The half-yearly returns for the year 1892-3 made even more depressing reading for the finance committee. In October 1892 Israel Hart lost patience and launched an astonishing attack on his fellow members for permitting committees to overspend, blaming councillors for being too keen to associate their names with prestigious – but expensive – municipal projects.[37] The local Radical press joined in the condemnation of councillors who advocated improvements 'with the utmost complacency' and with little regard for the extra costs they would impose upon the public purse.[38] Figures revealed that estimates had been exceeded by 10 per cent and that urgent action was needed to halt a complete collapse in local finances. Realising just how serious the situation had become, the finance committee negotiated a flexible agreement that when estimates were reached, no more expenditure should be sanctioned.[39] Although this did not mean the finance committee had a veto on expenditure – curiously committees would be allowed to overspend if they deemed it 'necessary' – it opened the way for a much greater degree of scrutiny and control of council accounts by

---

33 LLA, Executive Committee, 20 July 1891, LRO, 11 D 57/2.

34 See chapter eight.

35 *MFP*, 19 March 1892.

36 *MFP*, 2 April 1892.

37 *Wyvern*, 28 October 1892.

38 See 'Stray Notes', *MFP*, 29 October 1892.

39 *LDM*, 28 September 1892.

full council.[40] It is difficult to judge how successful these moves were in the long term. Education made up a large proportion of the original increase and, of course, the council had no influence over the rate the school board set.[41] Moreover a rise in gas profits the following year assisted a downward pressure on the rates evident in subsequent periods.[42] The significance of the development, however, was that it demonstrated how a crisis could force councillors to put aside sectional interests and bring forward measures which increased centralised control of municipal finances. An outcry over the level of rates reflected very badly on all members of the ruling group and forced councillors to accept limitations on expenditure for their own particular areas and projects.

The problems of a highly decentralised form of committee government were also made very clear in another political controversy that broke in the early months of 1892. The small free libraries committee took a decision to discourage racing and gambling enthusiasts from coming into the municipal library to consult the sporting sections of newspapers. By blacking out certain types of sports coverage from the newspapers the committee hoped to take a stand against gambling and, in the words of one councillor, raise the 'moral character' of the people.[43] Movements for the suppression of gambling may have been popular amongst certain elements of Nonconformist opinion but this type of municipal censorship attracted widespread anger. The move had been taken without consultation with other members of council and the controversy broke in the press with many councillors unaware of the committee's policy. The issue of the 'blacking brush' – municipal censorship – soon became a major issue in a by-election in Westcotes ward, formerly a safe Liberal seat. Conservative candidate Thomas Mann placed protests against press censorship at the forefront of his campaign, alongside the issue of increasing rates, and came very close to recording an amazing success, going down by just ten votes. The *Leicester Daily Mercury* felt the free library committee should share the blame for the result – for 'treating grown men as children'.[44] Even the Radical *Midland Free Press*, which itself refused to publish racing coverage on the grounds that it encouraged gambling, scolded the free library committee for acting in accordance with a 'vicious principle' in censoring newspapers.[45] Once again the action of a committee had brought the whole council into public disrepute. Many Liberals were naturally frustrated that their party was again being blamed for the indiscreet action of a committee over which they had little direct control. As in Manchester, however, the notion that committees should operate semi-autonomously within their own sphere of competence was a powerful one and for some any direct condemnation of a committee's action by councillors outside was regarded as an unjustifiable interference with the private

40 *LDM*, 26 October 1892.
41 *MFP*, 29 October 1892.
42 *MFP*, 30 September 1893.
43 *MFP*, 30 January 1892.
44 *LDM*, 18 March 1892.
45 *MFP*, 30 January 1892.

business of a committee. Thus when the matter first came before full council, it was simply referred back to committee for further consideration. Continued public outcry and Liberal electoral embarrassment, however, meant that further action had to be taken. Ald. William Inskip led the Leicester Trades' Council in opposition to the censorship and eventually persuaded enough Liberal colleagues to pass a resolution condemning the committee's action.[46] This controversy, although at face value a trifling matter, revealed how the whole council could easily be held up to ridicule as a result of indiscreet actions by a small committee. The price of allowing committees such a large degree of discretion had proved very costly to the council's reputation.

The independent authority of committees and committee chairmen was also being undermined by other factors. On several occasions suspicions were aired that some senior committee members were using the privacy of committee work to promote their own private interests free from public scrutiny. As long ago as April 1886 Thomas Wright, the leading advocate of borough extension, was alleged to be using his 'knowledge' of council business to advance his own land-holding interest in those areas to be incorporated.[47] Arthur Wakerley, a renowned city architect, served in senior positions on the highways and sewerage committee, charged with providing investment for public improvements in the suburbs where he had substantial property-owning interests.[48] In 1894 Wright again faced allegations that he had misused his public position, this time to secure public finance for the improvement of a private drive in Stoneygate.[49] The decision had been endorsed in a private committee meeting and, again, the matter had not been scrutinised by full council. When a resolution was put forward to the next full council meeting calling for a ban on public funding for private roads, Wakerley led opposition to the move, which was then subsequently defeated.[50] Many backbench Liberals, however, were increasingly unhappy about property developers voting for the application of public money to improvement schemes on private estates behind the protective closed doors of committee.

The new year saw several councillors bringing forward proposals to open up all committee meetings to the press in an attempt to promote greater scrutiny of this type of expenditure. The objection was not just that these meetings were held in private but that when votes were taken they were not recorded, making it impossible for electors to form a judgement about the extent to which representatives were acting according to self-interested motives. Although these particular proposals were defeated the support expressed for the measures made it clear that committee chairmen could no longer go on running their committees as something akin to private businesses. It is also significant that the committee that was subject to the allegations of improper conduct was the highways and sewerage committee – the one on which many

46 *MFP*, 2 April 1892.

47 *LDM*, 21 April 1886.

48 J. Farquhar, *Arthur Wakerley 1862–1931* (Leicester, 1984), 22.

49 *LDM*, 31 January 1894.

50 *MFP*, 2 December 1893.

younger members of council cut their teeth. Many did not want to be associated with the possible misdeeds of more senior members and consequently wanted to make it quite clear through the press who the 'guilty' parties were.[51] A further attempt to open up the council to press scrutiny 12 months later also failed, but this can perhaps be explained in part by the attitude of the press. Unless there was an obvious scandal the press had little interest in examining the detail of council procedure, believing that few readers would be interested in the dull day-to-day activity of committee business.[52] Junior councillors protested that long reports from committee chairs squeezed out the comments of other municipal representatives and consequently restrictions were placed on the length of speeches.[53] Although the press was not a very useful ally in the campaign to open up committee business, it indirectly helped the process by which committee chairmen were prohibited from dominating the business of full council through the tactic of 'talking-out' all opposition. Thus more time was freed up for the scrutiny of committee business on the floor of the council chamber. By 1895 the balance of power had shifted from the private committee to a more centralised form of municipal management closely overseen by backbenchers during full council meetings. A recognition of the inefficiencies of large committees, the problems of financial management and the suspicion that members were misusing their committee privileges all contributed to the decay of committee power and the growth of central control. Significantly too this trend was accompanied by a growth in political partisanship and greater party oversight of municipal activity.

The first election to the newly extended borough in 1891 revealed just how important parties were to municipal representatives despite their frequent protestations – by some Liberals as well as Conservatives – that partisanship should not be allowed to interfere with municipal business. The domination that the Liberal Party had achieved was a source of great pride to the party leadership. When registration agent Thomas Smith, the man credited with the success of building up a strong local association, resigned in March 1892 his colleagues treated him as little short of a departing hero.[54] The 1891 election marked the high tide of Liberal triumph in municipal politics. After several years of weakly contested elections the Liberals were called upon to rebuild and overhaul their organisation in the face of what was expected to be a strong Conservative challenge in the newly created wards. Although the issue was never publicly discussed, the prospect of a forthcoming general election was also probably a significant factor in the rising enthusiasm for local elections. On the Liberal side there was little shame in admitting theirs was a party fight. Barfoot admitted that the Liberals 'had endeavoured to make the struggle a test of the strength of parties' and regretted that 'personalities' still influenced local politics in some areas.[55] Some even went as far to suggest that the election marked the

51 *MFP*, 3 February 1894.

52 *MFP*, 2 March 1895.

53 *MFP*, 2 January, 1894.

54 LLA, Executive Committee, 14 March 1892, LRO, 11 D 57/3.

55 *LDP*, 4 November 1891.

emergence of Leicester as the capital of Liberalism in the Midlands.[56] Even taking into account the post-election euphoria it is clear that most Liberal activists saw the election as an opportunity to renew their local organisation and to score a significant party political victory over their opponents. With ward associations adopting a much more partisan stance this naturally had some effect on the political behaviour of their local municipal leaders. It was no longer enough to be seen merely as an advocate of a particular area – local committees also demanded partisan loyalty.

Aldermen, as well as councillors, were expected to show loyalty to their political colleagues. When they failed to do so other senior Liberals, and ward associations, made their feelings clear. When Charles Rowlett dropped his allegiance to the Liberal Party in 1895 and stood for re-election as a Conservative, two personal friends – both Liberal aldermen – spoke publicly in support of his re-election.[57] Although the aldermen could defend their action by claiming their support was merely given on personal grounds, the Liberal Association was enraged that two of its senior members were prepared to speak in support of a Conservative candidate.[58] Significantly it was not only Liberal Association officials who were infuriated by the aldermen's actions. Perhaps the most outspoken attack on the two aldermen, however, came from their fellow alderman Thomas Wright, who had himself once left the party to join the Liberal Unionists.[59] Increasing demands for loyalty to party did not come exclusively from the Liberal camp. One year after the Rowlett controversy it was the Conservatives who were warning members of their party against making public criticism of Conservative candidates and being disloyal to their party's cause.[60] By the 1890s neither party was prepared to allow its senior members to embrace other parties' candidates, whatever the ties of friendship or municipal fellowship which existed between them.

Partisan rivalry was not new but its increasing intensity reflected Conservative frustration at being excluded from the increasingly centralised decision-making processes of the council. As in Manchester, there were constant complaints that the Liberal Party were packing the aldermanic bench to further strengthen their grip on the council. Although the aldermanic bench was supposedly elected on the basis of seniority, in fact aldermanic elections were carefully orchestrated by the Liberal leadership to ensure their own nominees were elected. In 1886 there were even complaints that the Liberal leadership had circulated cards instructing their

---

56 *LDP*, 4 November 1891.

57 *LDP*, 2 November 1895.

58 Shortly after Rowlett's successful re-election the Association passed a strongly worded resolution condemning the aldermen concerned and implied that tough action would be taken if there was a similar occurrence. LLA, Finance and General Purposes Committee, 11 November 1895, LRO, 11 D 57/3.

59 'It was quite time the Liberal members of the Town Council told the Liberal Aldermen that their duty was not to go out of their way to lecture other constituencies, and throw cold water over the efforts of Liberals in other parts of the town to their own.' *LDP*, 2 November 1895.

60 *LDP*, 3 November 1896.

members how to vote.[61] Following the extension of the borough boundaries in 1891 the Liberal group held a private meeting collectively to nominate candidates and the agreed list was then circulated to all members in order to remind them how to vote.[62] Indeed it is clear that the use of private party meetings to arrive at decisions before council met was a key feature of Liberal management of the authority. Much of the day-to-day business of the council was conducted in this way and on most major decisions private party meetings usually preceded important votes. This approach had obvious advantages for the party leading the council. Decisions could be arrived at in private, minimising the risks of public party splits on the floor of the council chamber. As Liberal domination was so great decisions of group meetings were effectively decisions of the council.

Not all Liberals approved of conducting business in this way. When a private Liberal meeting controversially decided to nominate Israel Hart as mayor for a third time, one Liberal member attempted to mitigate the effects of collective decision-making by calling for a vote by ballot for future elections.[63] This would have made it much more difficult for party leaders to hold dissident backbenchers to account when voting against decisions arrived at by a majority in private meetings. The re-election of Hart following the screening of possible candidates by private Liberal group meetings was particularly controversial because it seemed that party leaders had used private meetings to eliminate alternative candidates. The Conservatives were particularly angry that they had not been consulted and took the unprecedented step of voting against the mayoral candidate and accusing Hart of 'buying the office, by his hospitality'.[64] From 1886 the election of the mayor via private Liberal group meetings became the focus of partisan conflict in the council, with Conservatives angry at their exclusion from what was supposed to be a non-partisan office. In 1887 a major dispute was averted with the election of Liberal Unionist Thomas Wright as mayor, a figure respected on both sides of the chamber.[65] Two years later, however, controversy erupted again when one councillor cheekily asked three months before the mayoral election whether the Liberal leaders had already selected the mayor for the following year.[66] The Liberals, fearing another embarrassing battle over the nomination, which would do little for the 'dignity' of the position, agreed to allow the Conservatives to bring forward a nominee.[67]

Conservative protests were in part the product of frustration at being unable to make any real impact on council decision-making. The difficulties of finding any willing candidates for the mayoralty gradually diffused party conflict on this issue and in 1894 the parties resolved to hold a joint private meeting to arrive at

---

61 *MFP*, 13 November 1886.

62 *MFP*, 14 November 1891.

63 *LDM*, 5 November 1886.

64 *LDM*, 9 November 1886.

65 *MFP*, 12 November 1887.

66 *MFP*, 3 August 1889.

67 In the event the Conservative nominee declined to accept the office, with the result that a Liberal again took the position. *LDM*, 29 August 1889.

an agreed nomination.[68] On other issues, however, the Liberal Party continued to meet in private session and arrive at policy decisions in advance of full council meetings. The Conservatives continued to feel closed out of key decision-making. Conservative leader J.H. Marshall even attempted to introduce a standing order designed to prohibit municipal leaders from arranging private meetings to predetermine policy decisions. Marshall recognised that he could not prevent small informal gatherings of Liberals, but what he objected to was the system of formal pre-council group meetings, called by written circular, to arrive at policy decisions.[69] The key difficulty for Marshall, however, was that his party steadfastly refused to co-ordinate their activities at all. Thus when Marshall spoke out against the use of private meetings to decide policy, one of his own backbenchers turned on him, and denied that he had any right to speak for the Conservatives. Marshall's appeals for the Conservatives to be given a share of official council positions were similarly condemned by a member of his own group as 'derogatory to the dignity of the party'.[70] Leicester Conservatives were still divided between those who felt that they should organise their party more tightly to fight the Liberals and those who held on to the belief that municipal representatives should be largely independent of party machines once they had secured election. Thus, although there were periodic bouts of partisan frustration from the Conservatives, co-ordinated opposition was rare. Indeed many Radicals were concerned that the lack of a party opposition had damaging effects on the Liberal group. One member went as far as to suggest the formation of 'an extreme left, or group, like the Radicals who sit below the gangway in the House of Commons'.[71]

The Liberal municipal leadership, however, was trying to avoid just this type of division. The growing tendency of councillors and aldermen to accept collective party decision-making reflected the concern that the council was too highly factionalised. The financial problems of 1891–92 made an eloquent case for centralised supervision of policy-making and collective party decision-making. There was also the fear of the consequences of a serious split in the party. Indeed the growth of party involvement in municipal activity can be traced back to the aftermath of the 1884 battle over the nomination of parliamentary candidates. In September 1887 the Liberal Association drew up new rules for the election of ward committees, tightening central control and giving local officers greater influence over the selection of their committees, rather than allowing a completely open system of nomination.[72] Thus although the central Liberal Association remained at arm's length from the Liberal leadership, the extra responsibilities given to ward officers gave them an elevated position in the local hierarchy. Naturally this had implications for the relationship between ward

68 *MFP*, 10 November 1894.

69 *LDP*, 26 July 1893.

70 *LDP*, 26 July 1893.

71 'Stray Notes', *MFP*, 31 August 1889.

72 LLA, Meeting of Ward Officers and Superintendents, 22 September 1887, LRO, 11 D 57/2.

officers and local municipal representatives. Municipal representatives had to be increasingly aware of the views of these more powerful local officers if they were to retain their position as ward representatives. In 1892 the central Liberal Association issued a statement which made it clear that they regarded themselves as the final arbiters of disputes over candidate nomination, and further emphasising the degree to which municipal nominees were expected to be accountable to their local ward party.[73]

With the council so dominated by one party, there was little prospect of independents getting elected and there was little to be gained by Liberals attempting to secure election in opposition to powerful local party machines. Even if they were successful in gaining election they were unlikely to be accepted into the Liberal group and thus could have little influence on council policy. Moreover evidence suggests that voters saw local elections as partisan conflicts. In 1891 all council seats came up for election to the newly expanded town, with three vacancies coming up in each ward. The vast majority of electors voted straight for party slates, rather than splitting their votes between parties or 'plumping' for one candidate. Exceedingly popular candidates could attract extra support but in general the figures suggest that around three-quarters of a successful candidate's votes came from voters who supported all three candidates of that party. For example, William Inskip, the popular trade unionist with a large personal following, polled over 10 per cent more votes than his nearest Liberal colleague, yet 732 of his 1,016 supporters still voted for the entire party ticket. Interestingly those who voted straight for the complete Conservative ticket generally accounted for a lower proportion of individual candidates' votes. This suggests that those voting for Conservative candidates were less likely to see the election in purely party terms. In Castle ward, for example, the lowest individual Conservative vote was 808, yet only 403 electors voted for both Conservative candidates.[74] This trend may reflect the attitude of some Conservative leaders who wished to keep 'politics' out of municipal elections. However, it is clear that the Conservatives did not have the benefit of quite such strong party machinery and disciplined body of electors as the Liberals. The reluctance of Conservatives to turn local elections into a partisan battle clearly made it more difficult for them to mobilise their supporters and gave weight to the arguments of those such as Marshall who advocated a more aggressively partisan approach.

The growth of centralisation, partisanship and the decline of committee government were rapid processes. However, many of the older facets of council management remained. The willingness of the Liberals to offer the Conservatives the mayoralty indicated a desire to place this office above party politics. There was a strong feeling that the mayor should be a unifying figurehead representing the whole of the town. Indeed the initiation of the mayor was a major ceremonial event, supposedly bringing together all citizens of the town, with those appointed to nominate the mayor chosen to represent different aspects of Leicester's people –

73 LLA, Executive Committee, 21 January 1892, LRO, 11 D 57/3.

74 *LDP*, 4 November 1891.

including one for 'the working-class population'[75] Unfortunately those who sat in the mayor's chair did not always live up to their image as representatives of all classes. When Israel Hart made disparaging comments about shoe workers and betting – suggesting that their wages should be reduced if they had sufficient to 'indulge in the luxury of gambling' – he brought the mayoral role seriously into question.[76] Several thousand people assembled in the Market Place to protest at his comments and the incident marked a significant break between the mayor and those Liberal councillors associated with the shoe trade unions. Moreover it placed the mayor's private business affairs under close scrutiny. Trade unionists accused him of holding shares in a tramway company where men worked 85 hours a week for low wages, and, even more damaging in Nonconformist Leicester, having a pecuniary interest in the Oadby Racecourse Company.[77] Such incidents placed the notion of mayoral dignity and impartiality under severe strain. More skilled politicians, however, could use the position to their advantage, avoiding controversy and concentrating on patronising hospitals and charities – becoming the personification of the active and benevolent citizen. When Arthur Wakerley became Leicester's youngest major in 1897, he made support for charitable and religious organisations central to his mayoral year.[78] By using the office in this way the mayor could be seen to be representing all parties and denominations, even though Wakerley was one of the most loyal Liberal Party servants. Taking up the mayoralty certainly did not imply a retirement from party politics – Wakerley stood for parliament in both 1895 and 1900.[79]

Other factors limited the degree to which party politics could engulf the council. Both parties periodically had difficulties in obtaining candidates for public office. Indeed the Liberal Party's offer of the mayoralty to the Conservatives was in part a reflection of the fact that few on the council were prepared to finance the office from their private funds as had become the custom. Over time there had been a gradual increase in mayoral 'hospitality' and patronage with the result that only wealthy individuals could contemplate taking up the office. When a mayor of relatively modest means was elected in 1890 there were a number of comments made about the reduction in mayoral hospitality that this would entail.[80] Indeed even the Radical press sometimes found it necessary to comment on the likely level of generosity that the mayor would indulge in.[81] Unlike other towns, such as Manchester, the council provided no rooms for the mayor to entertain official guests, leaving individual office holders to provide accommodation for visiting dignitaries. Wakerley, for example, had to do a large amount of entertaining in his relatively small London Road home.[82]

75 *LDM*, 9 November 1889.

76 *LDE*, 2 April 1894.

77 *LDE*, 2 April 1894.

78 Farquhar, *Arthur Wakerley*, 17–18.

79 Farquhar, *Arthur Wakerley*, 61–4.

80 *MFP*, 15 November 1890.

81 *MFP*, 10 November 1894.

82 Farquhar, *Arthur Wakerley*, 19.

More seriously, for both parties, was the problem of finding suitable people to serve at a junior level on the council. The Conservatives, probably because of their modest position on the authority, found it especially difficult. Even at times of triumph, such as 1886 when they took seats from the Liberals, Conservative Party leaders felt that the difficulty in obtaining candidates was the main limitation they faced.[83] The failure of the Liberals to find effective candidates was also a contributory factor to their organisational problems of the 1890s. After poor results in 1895 the Leicester Liberal Association asked ward committees to produce reports in April of each year detailing the candidates who would be available for the following November elections.[84]

Despite growing partisanship in many aspects of council life, some local ward committees prized an individual's administrative and business abilities above loyalty to party. In 1887 St. Mark's ward Liberals justified their decision not to contest the second seat in the ward on the grounds that the Conservative who had been nominated for it was 'a thorough business man and a valuable addition to the Council'.[85] A year later they allowed both sitting Conservatives to return unopposed declaring that St. Mark's 'was a small ward, and it became increasingly difficult for them to find an efficient representative' while praising the business qualifications of the Conservatives.[86] St. Mark's, an almost exclusively middle-class commercial district, did not have a social and economic structure typical of the town, but similar attitudes could be found elsewhere. Even as late as 1895 some Liberal ward associations preferred to stress the administrative abilities of their candidates rather than specific policy commitments.[87] This concern for obtaining candidates with strong business and administrative capabilities was partly a reflection of the growing complexity of municipal activity. Indeed there was a concern, following the expansion of the town in 1891, that new councillors were too concerned with obtaining specific advantages for their own areas to be concerned with the overall health of municipal administration or municipal finances. Thus those with business, financial and administrative skills were particularly valued. Also, as parties struggled to find candidates from within their own ranks they were forced to look to those whose partisan convictions were less certain.[88] In such cases the parties had to stress in their election campaigns the professional capabilities of these figures as they had few distinctive policy positions.

---

83 See editorial, *LJ*, 5 November 1886.

84 LLA, Meeting of Ward and Honorary Officers of the Association, 13 April 1896, LRO, 11 D 57/3.

85 *LDP*, 22 October 1887.

86 *LDP*, 20 October 1888.

87 See, for example, reports from Abbey Ward, *LDM*, 1 November 1895.

88 Both parties suffered defections from their ranks in this period. Arthur Wakerley went from the Conservatives to the Liberals and Charles Rowlett went from the Liberals to the Conservatives. Several Liberals also allied to the Liberal Unionists after 1886, although the most prominent, Thomas Wright, eventually returned. See chapter four.

As issues of industrial relations came to dominate the political agenda in the 1890s there was, however, a growing reluctance amongst municipal candidates to emphasise their business careers in political campaigning. It was not only Independent Labour and Socialist candidates who attacked their opponents for representing the interests of a middle-class industrial elite. In 1891 Charnwood Conservatives attacked their Liberal opponent on these very same grounds.[89] Part of the reason for the reluctance of manufacturers and businessmen generally to stress their business success was the increasing level of public scrutiny of the industrial relations record of major employers. During the 1894 parliamentary by-election in Leicester one of the Liberal Party candidates, publisher William Hazell, faced very close scrutiny of his firm's employment practices by the Leicester trade unions, even though his business premises were located far away in Aylesbury.[90] The criticism Hazell attracted naturally sounded a warning to councillors not to boast too freely of business successes for fear of opponents exploiting the stories of disaffected employees during election campaigns. Such scrutiny could not only damage their political reputation but also their livelihoods.

Interestingly the council itself encouraged greater scrutiny of employment practices through its own contracting policies. In February 1891, following pressure from the trades council, the Radical Club and other working-class political organisations, William Inskip persuaded the council to establish a committee charged with investigating the rates of wages paid by the corporation and its contractors.[91] The special committee surveyed the prevailing rate of wages in 13 large towns and concluded that the corporation was indeed paying the 'standard' rate of wages prevalent in the district. The committee did, however, recommend that the council add a clause in all council contracts forcing contractors also to pay this standard rate.[92] Although the resolution was passed, problems of enforcement remained. Only by a detailed inspection of contractors' activity could council officials determine whether workmen were indeed being paid in accordance with this provision. If contractors broke the clause, there was little the council could do to enforce it. In 1895 trade unionist Cllr. H.H. Woolley proposed that in addition to a standard rate of wages clause, each contract should also include a system of penalties for those firms who failed to pay the standard rate. Some even went as far as to suggest that any firm found breaking the clause should be banned from tendering for future council contracts. Such was the anger at contractors who broke the clause that Woolley's resolution met with only one recorded opponent.[93] The consequence of this resolution was to bring discussion of individual contractors' business operations before the public scrutiny of full council meetings. Individual businesses were being

89 *LDM*, 30 October 1891.

90 *LDM*, 1 September 1894.

91 LTC, 24 February 1891, LRO, CM 1/24.

92 LTC, Workmen's Wages and Contracts Committee Report, 28 July 1891, LRO, CM. *WT*, 31 July 1891.

93 *MFP*, 4 May 1895.

opened up to public examination in ways which some feared could seriously threaten the reputation of the businesses concerned.[94] Charles Rowlett was appalled by the implications of the clause and soon after left the Liberal Party.[95]

What is remarkable, however, is that Rowlett was alone in opposing the penalty clause, demonstrating that the vast majority of municipal representatives had accepted the need for closer regulation of municipal work. Most were aware how the council would be damaged if it were associated with 'sweating'. The decision had implications that went beyond the immediate activities of the council. If municipal leaders were to demand scrutiny of council contractors' work they could hardly refuse to accept closer public scrutiny of their own businesses. Hazell's difficulties in the 1894 by-election demonstrated just how difficult it was for an employer to disprove allegations of operating an 'unfair' house.[96] Increasingly it was much safer for employers to promote a party programme rather than try to rely on their business reputation as a means of securing election. Successful business skills and the ability to generate profit from municipal enterprises were increasingly failing to impress the voting public. Although profits from municipal trading in gas and water had long been used to subsidise the rates, by 1892 many were coming to question who the real beneficiaries of this subsidy were. Liberal trade unionists, like William Inskip, regularly attacked the gas committee for generating profits at the expense of poor consumers – and then granting wealthier property owners most of the benefits through lower rates.[97] Although the business and professional classes dominated the council, it was clear that many in the electorate were suspicious of those who made too much of their entrepreneurial reputation. For trade unionists profit had become too closely associated with exploitation.

Despite the many changes in council management between 1885 and 1895 the Liberal majority remained intact and the Liberal Party's ward organisation was a long way from collapse. In the spring of 1895 the Liberal Party held 48 of the council's 72 seats, and 33 of its 48 elected councillors.[98] Significantly the Leicester Liberal Association took an increasing interest in municipal elections with local ward officials helping integrate council leaders into the party's decision-making processes. When things went wrong – as they did in 1895 – the central Liberal Association acted to reinvigorate local ward groups and thus municipal politics. By 1895 Liberal municipal leaders were no longer a semi-independent elite but rather a partisan body grappling with progressive ideas. The pressures of public improvements forced the council to adopt new management structures, taking power from individual committees and centralising policy-making functions. This

---

94 See the discussion of Water Committee contracts in the *MFP*, 30 November 1895.

95 'Would any man in a large way of business, any man with any regard to the dignity of his business, tender for Corporation work if such a humiliating condition as this penalty clause were imposed. He thought that all respectable firms accustomed to high-class work would gradually withdraw from contracting.' *LDM*, 1 May 1895.

96 *LDM*, 1 September 1894.

97 *MFP*, 19 March 1892; *WT*, 10 April 1891.

98 *LDE*, 28 March 1895.

allowed the party leadership to balance demands for increased public spending with a general determination to keep down local rates. Despite the fact that the Liberal Party remained in a dominant position and the emergent ILP offered only a limited challenge, having just two councillors in 1895, Liberal leaders did not lose sight of Progressive ideas. Many in the Liberal Association encouraged discussion of the Progressive programme, while the municipal leadership were happy to encourage intrusive industrial relations regulations, demanding that council contractors pay a standard rate of wages. However, while Liberal leaders were alive to the political and managerial challenges they faced, the Liberal electorate often fell short of the ideal of the active citizenry. In a town managed by Liberals since incorporation and which still had a large Liberal majority, the complacency and apathy of Liberal electors may have been the principal threat to the Liberal Party's future. Both the party's major reverses in 1886 and 1895 were widely blamed on the apathy of the Liberal public following a general election. Despite the dynamic changes of the decade and the growth of more integrated collective decision-making processes, the Liberal Party faced the same basic difficulty – how to interest the public in municipal affairs and how to persuade Liberals of the importance of voting when election results seemed so predictable.

PART IV
The Town and the Suburbs

CHAPTER SEVEN

Manchester's Suburban Radicalism

The drift of middle-class suburbia towards Conservatism has traditionally been seen as an important feature in the development of class-based politics in late nineteenth-century Britain. Yet this process was neither inevitable nor universal, with Liberals in Manchester illustrating how suburban support could be maintained by adopting a new language of Progressivism and public improvement. This language was not designed solely to attract working-class support, but also addressed the aspirations of the rising group of clerks, shopkeepers and small traders in the suburbs. In contrast, most existing literature concentrates on how Gladstone's support for Irish Home Rule and land reform seemingly accelerated the growth of class-based politics, by driving English 'Villadom' into the arms of the Conservatives in defence of their property rights.[1] For some, 1892 was the first general election to be fought 'to a great extent upon class'.[2] Long-standing Nonconformist suspicion of Roman Catholicism and a growing sense of Imperialist egotism, it is alleged, further acted to prise 'Villadom' from a Gladstonian Liberal Party allied to, and apparently politically dependent upon, Irish Nationalists.[3] Indeed some have suggested that the core values of middle-class suburban Nonconformists – the bedrock of Liberal support – were changing, with social ambitions and economic self-interest were taking over from religious convictions as the chief motivational force in their public lives.[4]

Current interpretations of the suburban middle class have been shaped by the attitudes of Victorian Conservatives who often saw suburbia as their 'natural' territory. In 1885 the Conservative Party campaigned for the creation of single-member suburban constituencies with the hope that they could create Conservative 'islands'

---

1 H. Perkin, *The Origins of Modern English Society 1780–1880*, reprint (London, 1971) 431–35; G. Crossick, 'The Emergence of the Lower Middle Class in Britain: A Discussion', in G. Crossick (ed.), *The Lower Middle Class In Britain* (London, 1977); J. Parry, *The Rise and Fall of Liberal Government in Victorian Britain* (Cambridge, 1986), especially 304–6.

2 P. Magnus, *Gladstone* (London, 1954), 394.

3 R. Blake, *The Conservative Party From Peel To Thatcher*, paperback edition (London, 1985), 160. For the background to the Home Rule crisis see W.C. Lubenow, *Parliamentary Politics and the Home Rule Crisis* (Oxford, 1988); A.B. Cooke and J. Vincent, *The Governing Passion: Cabinet Government and Party Politics in Britain, 1885–1886* (Brighton, 1974); M. Barker, *Gladstone and Radicalism: The Reconstruction of Liberal Policy in Britain, 1885–94* (Brighton 1975); T.A. Jenkins, *Gladstone, Whiggery and the Liberal Party, 1874–1886* (Oxford, 1988).

4 M. Ostrogorski, *Democracy and the Organisation of Political Parties*, vol. one (London, 1902) 621; J.F. Glaser, 'English Nonconformity and the Decline of Liberalism', *American Historical Review*, 63 (1957–58), 352–63.

in the larger Liberal boroughs.[5] Yet their success in this type of constituency was patchy. Liberals in Manchester illustrated how suburban support could be maintained by adopting a new language of Progressivism and public improvement. Existing literature tends to view Manchester Progressivism primarily as a Liberal method of attracting working-class support.[6] However, it also addressed the aspirations of the rising group of clerks, shopkeepers and small traders in the suburbs. Hastily built suburbs often lacked basic social infrastructure and facilities. Therefore, far from being hostile to increasing public expenditure on local services, many in suburbia were the most vehement advocates of public investment in public health, tramways, branch libraries and schools. These were services that were regarded as just as essential for the health and welfare of middle-class suburbia as the inner-city slums. Liberal Progressivism succeeded amongst the suburban middle class by addressing aspirations that were shared across classes of the late Victorian city.

Liberal success in suburban politics is important because it challenges important assumptions about the long-term decay of British Liberalism. Although there is disagreement about the degree to which the Liberal Party suffered from the rise of class-based politics, the middle-class flight from Liberalism has become an important part of subsequent explanations for Liberal decline. Clarke's work on Lancashire emphasises how successfully the Liberal Party attracted working-class support by transforming itself into a social democratic party. A consequence of this transformation was, in his view, the loss of substantial middle-class support, as typified by the movement of the cotton barons towards Conservatism.[7] However it is questionable whether these groups were representative of the wider middle class and wider suburbia. Thompson's work on London has been particularly influential in illustrating how suburban Liberalism apparently went into decline in the latter years of the nineteenth century.[8] However, middle-class and suburban politics need to be viewed in the wider context of the political culture of the region and the locality. Whilst 'Villa Toryism' may have typified some of the London suburbs, in South Manchester Liberal Radicalism continued to be a vigorous and successful political force, supported by a progressive and Nonconformist culture. Engels's famous depiction of the geographical division of Manchester into distinct residential zones, from the urban proletariat around the centre to the upper bourgeoisie on the fringe,

---

5 See J. Garrard, *Democratisation in Britain* (Basingstoke, 2002), 94–6.

6 P. Clarke, *Lancashire and the New Liberalism* (Cambridge, 1971); J. Hill, 'Manchester and Salford Politics and the Early Development of the Independent Labour Party', *International Review of Social History*, 26 (1981), 171–201.

7 P.F. Clarke, *Lancashire and the New Liberalism* (Cambridge, 1971); P.F. Clarke, 'The end of Laissez Faire and the Politics of Cotton', *Historical Journal*, 15 (1973), 493–512.

8 P. Thompson, *Socialists, Liberals and Labour – The Struggle For London, 1885–1914*_(London, 1967). Thompson identifies a sharp decline in the fortunes of the party after 1892, and considers the lack of a viable electoral standpoint, working-class electoral base and financial backing as major reasons for this pattern. These trends are all viewed as the product of a rise in class-based voting patterns.

can blind us to the social diversity of suburban life.[9] By studying the development of Manchester's largest suburban community and analysing the local politics of its most affluent township, it is possible to analyse how Radical and Progressive Liberalism[10] could prosper in the suburbs and why it may have suffered less from the rise of 'class politics' than some areas predominantly working-class in social composition.

The parliamentary constituency of South Manchester, the largest in the city, represented 'classic' nineteenth-century suburbia. Stretching from the older All Saints in the north to the newly developed Fallowfield in the south, it contained a large portion of leafy Moss Side, lying outside the city council boundaries, the exclusive private estate of Victoria Park and the suburbanised village of Rusholme. It was an almost exclusively residential constituency 'largely composed, not of work people, but of clerks, shopkeepers, and others of the middle class'[11] and was regarded as 'the most aristocratic of the divisions'.[12] If class politics were to mean anything, one would expect this to be the most Conservative division in Manchester. Yet in 1885 it was the only one of the six parliamentary divisions in Manchester to return a Liberal MP. In 1886 the South Manchester Liberal Association suffered a larger secession of Liberal Unionists than any other area of the city, and yet the sitting Liberal member was comfortably returned in the election of that year. Indeed, it was not until the nation-wide Liberal debacle in 1895, where the party collapsed to just 177 seats at Westminster, that the South Manchester Liberals tasted defeat, and then only narrowly at the hands of a Liberal Unionist.[13]

Part of the explanation for this success must be that South Manchester was the chosen residence of a large number of Manchester's most influential Liberals. Spiers, in his study of the exclusive estate of Victoria Park, draws attention to the important influence of a group of Liberal professionals with a close public interest in the growing educational institutions of South Manchester.[14] Significantly, John Slagg, MP for Manchester 1879-85, and Sir Henry Roscoe, MP for South Manchester 1885-95, both made their homes in South Manchester and patronised local educational and cultural institutions. Other senior local Liberals such as Edward Donner and R.D. Darbishire were actively involved in local civic society, including the nearby Victoria University.[15] However, perhaps the two most influential figures in South Manchester Liberal politics of the period were C.P. Scott, the editor of the leading

---

9 F. Engels, *The Condition of the Working Class in England*, reprint (Chicago, 1984) 78–9.

10 Liberals on the left of the party used a variety of political descriptions during the period. In general the term 'Radical' was used most frequently in parliamentary elections, while 'Progressive' gained wider currency in local government after the use of the term at the London County Council elections in 1889.

11 *MG*, 18 November 1885.

12 *MG*, 27 November 1885.

13 F.W.S. Craig (ed.), *Parliamentary Election Results 1885–1918*, second edition (Aldershot, 1989) 152.

14 M. Spiers, *Victoria Park, Manchester* (Manchester, 1976), 5–6, 51–2.

15 Spiers, *Victoria Park*, 51–2.

Liberal newspaper the *Manchester Guardian*, and Edwin Guthrie, a fellow Radical, president of the South Manchester Liberal Association and a key influence on the policy of the Manchester Liberal Union. Both were staunch advocates of labour representation and felt that the Liberal Party's future depended upon its ability to incorporate working-class interests.[16] Their influence in Liberal ranks can be seen through the Manchester Liberal Union's adoption of a Progressive Municipal Programme in the run-up to the 1894 local elections.[17] Far from being concerned with the narrow self-interest of the middle-class suburban property owner, it attempted to address the major claims of trade unionists by advocating corporation action to tackle unemployment, improved housing and the demolition of slum property, ground value taxation and the vigorous enforcement of the sanitary legislation. Although some 'suburban concerns' were addressed – greater municipal control of the tramways being one – the Progressive Programme presents the apparent paradox of middle-class suburban Liberals taking little interest in their own constituency's problems and instead focusing on the concerns of the urban industrial working class. If middle-class communities in suburbia were becoming more self-interested by the late Victorian period, it becomes difficult to explain how suburban politicians advocating policies which would seemingly materially disadvantage their constituents could remain a strong force in local suburban politics. The phenomenon of the arch Radical, Edwin Guthrie, leading a successful Liberal Association in the most affluent middle-class suburb demands further investigation. Was the shock defeat for South Manchester's Liberal MP at the 1895 general election a sign that there were tight limits to how much left-wing politics suburban communities would accept?

A clue to the reason for the enduring strength of Liberalism in South Manchester lies in the history of the suburb itself. Manchester's suburbia, as with many other older industrial cities, was not a creation of the 1880s. Manchester could trace the beginnings of its suburban development back to the first decades of the nineteenth century.[18] Unsurprisingly its early residential structure was dominated by that of the city's economic and political elite. The most fashionable suburb of all, Victoria Park, included many prominent Liberals involved in the Anti-Corn Law League, including James Kershaw and George Hadfield. Both Kershaw and Hadfield made their mark locally. Hadfield was a prominent Congregationalist and resident in the park throughout his time representing Sheffield in parliament. Kershaw had a distinguished career not only in the League and in parliament as MP for Stockport, but also in local government serving as an alderman of the city between 1838–50 and mayor 1842–3.[19]

---

16 Manchester Liberal Union minutes (hereafter MLU), Union Committee, 16 July 1894, Manchester Central Library (hereafter MLU), M283/1/1/3; MLU, Union Committee, 26 July 1894, MCL, M283/1/1/4.

17 MLU, Progressive Municipal Programme statement, 16 July 1894, MCL, M283/1/1/3.

18 F.M.L. Thompson (ed.), *The Rise of Suburbia* (Leicester, 1982), 6.

19 Spiers, *Victoria Park*, 51–5.

Quite apart from their influence in formal politics, Manchester's mid-Victorian suburban Liberal elite spent much of their time and money supporting the spiritual work of the Nonconformist churches. By the early 1890s no part of the city was provided with more Nonconformist places of worship. The major Nonconformist denominations – the Baptists, the Congregationalists and the Wesleyan Methodists – each had at least one place of worship in each of the major suburban areas of South Manchester – Chorlton-on-Medlock, Rusholme and Moss Side. Smaller dissenting congregations such as the Unitarians, Primitive Methodists, United Methodists, Welsh Calvinistic Methodists, Presbyterians, Salvationists, Armenians and Swedenborgians were also well represented.[20] There were few Roman Catholic churches – probably because of the relatively small Irish community – but the substantial Welsh population was well catered for by several Welsh Baptist and Methodist institutions. The prestige of South Manchester as a residential location attracted some of the best-known Nonconformist leaders in the city – including the ardent Liberal Rev. Arnold Streuli of Moss Side, the Rev. Thomas Finlayson of Rusholme and the Rev. John Trevor of Chorlton – the latter of whom became the founder of the Labour Church Movement and a key figure in the Manchester and Salford Independent Labour Party.[21] Clearly the South Manchester suburbs of the 1880s and 1890s were not ones in which residents were deprived of political or religious guidance. Although constantly changing physically through building development, the suburbs had deep Liberal and Nonconformist traditions. There seems little evidence that the early suburban residents substantially abandoned their traditional political and religious loyalties.

By the 1880s some of the older suburbs closest to the city centre were undergoing significant social change. Victoria Park was no longer the most fashionable part of the city and many, including senior Liberals Sir Henry Roscoe and Edward Donner, left for the newly developed Fallowfield on the southern edge of the parliamentary division.[22] In the place of Manchester's leading merchants and professionals came the lower-middle classes identified by the *Manchester Guardian.* This change seems similar to a general trend of this period – namely the general 'social deepening' of suburbia identified in other British towns.[23] Yet if 'class politics' was becoming more significant in suburban politics, one may expect the new lower-middle-class voters of suburbia to be more likely to support the Liberal Party than the generally wealthier elite they were gradually replacing.[24] By the 1885 general election the party had

---

20 *The Official Handbook of Manchester and Salford 1892* (Manchester, 1892).

21 L. Smith, 'John Trevor and the Labour Church Movement', Unpublished MA thesis, Huddersfield Polytechnic, 1985, 28–30.

22 Spiers, *Victoria Park*, 51–5.

23 *MG*, 18 November 1885; S.M. Gaskell, 'Housing and the Lower Middle Classes, 1870–1914', in G. Crossick (ed.), *The Lower Middle Class in Britain* (London, 1977), cited in Thompson, *The Rise*, 17.

24 Some have suggested that the lower-middle class were disproportionately inclined to support Unionist 'jingoism' – see R.N. Price, 'Society, Status and Jingoism: The Social Roots of Lower Middle Class Patriotism, 1870–1900', in Crossick (ed.), *The Lower Middle*

established Liberal clubs covering the four major areas of the new South constituency – Oxford Road, Rusholme Road, Moss Side and Longsight. At municipal level Liberal candidates had made significant progress. All Saints' Ward, in the north of the constituency, had been Conservative for many years, yet had recently been taken comfortably by a Liberal. In the adjacent St. Luke's Ward the Liberals claimed over 60 per cent of the vote, and significantly the new South Manchester parliamentary division included the parts of these wards regarded as the most 'Liberal'. The newly incorporated Rusholme and Moss Side also had a tradition of electing Liberals to local public bodies.[25]

South Manchester Liberals chose Owen's College academic Sir Henry Roscoe as their parliamentary candidate who, although politically inexperienced, developed a reputation for being in the 'advanced' section of the party.[26] Roscoe was steeped in Radical family traditions.[27] He had little time for the more unpredictable left-wing critics of the Manchester Liberal establishment, like Richard Pankhurst who resigned from the party in 1883 to stand for parliament as an Independent Radical, but instead worked to ensure that Radical agendas gradually became party of the Liberal mainstream.[28] This approach did not dilute the Radicalism of the local party or make it afraid to tackle issues of property rights and class privilege. Roscoe's academic colleague Prof. Williamson, addressing Liberal campaign meetings, described himself as 'an enthusiastic Radical reformer', openly attacking the notions of 'respectability' and snobbery that were associated with middle-class suburban life.[29] Roscoe's own Radicalism was a little more understated, but he was a strong supporter of more working-class MPs and social reform, and a strong critic of the failures of the education system. He saw that in failing to provide a meritocratic system in which talented people from all backgrounds could rise, education was both unjust and ineffective – an issue that had some resonance with parts of the upwardly-mobile suburban electorate.[30]

Roscoe's 1885 victory in South Manchester was of vital importance in that it saved the Manchester Liberals from losing all parliamentary representation. The lack of a large Irish constituency in South Manchester meant that, unlike other areas of the city, there was not an organised body of Irish Nationalists to vote *en bloc* against the Liberal candidate. Moreover South Manchester had a relatively high proportion of affluent Liberal residents prepared to support – with their wealth and spare time – the

---

Class, 89–112 – but in Manchester most lower-middle-class residential areas were principally Liberal.

25 *MG*, 18 November 1885; *MG*, 3 November 1885.

26 *MC*, 27 November 1885.

27 Sir Henry Roscoe was the grandson of the famous Liverpool Radical MP, William Roscoe. Sir Henry's wife was a daughter of Edmund Potter, the Liberal MP for Carlisle 1861–74. One of Sir Henry's daughters married C.E. Mallet, the Liberal MP for Plymouth.

28 Roscoe defeated Pankhurst for the chair of the Victoria University's convocation in 1882. E. Thorpe, *Sir Henry Enfield Roscoe* (London, 1916), 90–92.

29 *MG*, 10 November 1885.

30 *MG*, 20–21 November 1885.

party organisation in the division. There can be little doubt that Manchester Liberal Party organisation was generally very unprepared for the 1885 general election.[31] A strong body of wealthy support in the area allowed for rapid reorganisation and the formation of a new divisional campaign body. [32]

If there had been significant dissatisfaction with Sir Henry Roscoe's brand of Radicalism, one might have expected many middle-class suburban voters to take the opportunity of the Home Rule crisis to move into Liberal Unionism or switch to the Conservatives. Some Unionists did accuse Roscoe of acting like Gladstone in cynically setting 'class against class' but the issue did not become a central feature of the campaign.[33] The Liberal Party suffered some defections from its ranks, including veteran alderman Sir Alfred Hopkinson[34], however any advantage the Conservatives might have obtained from the division in Liberal ranks was largely nullified by the failure of Liberal Unionists and Conservatives to agree upon a joint candidate for South Manchester. Liberal Unionists were eventually forced to withdraw in favour of a Conservative and then lost further credibility when correspondence in the local press revealed that several leading figures who claimed to have left the Liberal Party over Home Rule had, in fact, already deserted the party before the 1885 general election.[35] No attempt was made to shield Roscoe from the Home Rule controversy despite the fact he represented a constituency that might be expected to generate the largest number of dissidents. [36] Rather, local Liberals seemed to be using Roscoe's popularity to win over waverers. The gamble paid off. Far from a net loss of support, in January 1887 the South Manchester Liberal Association was able to report an increase in subscriptions and was second only to the commercial North-West division in terms of the total income they attracted.[37] By the summer of 1888 even the funds of the central Liberal Union had recovered and the executive committee could 'note with satisfaction that no indications are discernible of any increase in the number or power of the dissidents'.[38]

Home Rule continued to dominate the terms of the political debate over the next decade and, although Roscoe's parliamentary majority fell in 1892, Liberals continued to perform well in suburban municipal elections.[39] The once largely

---

31 MLA, Joint Consultative Committee, 17–18 June 1885, MCL, M283/1/1/2. The party had recently fought an expensive by-election, was short of funds and seemed to underestimate the significance of the new constituency boundaries.

32 MLU, Financial Statement, 3 February 1886, MCL, M283/1/1/2.

33 C.M. Wharton speaking at Longsight, *ME*, 2–3 July 1886.

34 *MG*, 30 June 1886; Spiers, *Victoria Park*, 53–5.

35 *MC*, 30 June 1886, *ME*, 2–3 July 1886.

36 MLU, General Council, 7 May 1886, MCL, M283/1/1/2.

37 MLU, Financial Statement, 24 January 1887, MCL, M283/1/1/2.

38 MLU, Secretary's Report, 22 April 1887, MCL, M283/1/1/2; MLU, Annual Council Meeting, 2 May 1888, MCL, M283/1/1/2.

39 The marginal nature of the three central wards, St. Luke's, All Saints' and Rusholme, meant that previously contests were rare with Liberals and Conservatives usually coming to an agreement about the representation of the districts.

Conservative All Saints' ward fell to Liberal Alexander McDougall by almost 500 votes in 1890. Two years later the Liberals inflicted a crushing defeat on the sitting Conservative councillor for Rusholme, Samuel Royle, winning by 708 votes to 478. St. Luke's saw no contested elections before 1893 when the Liberals easily fended off an ILP candidate. In Longsight's first election as part of the city of Manchester in 1890, it returned two Liberals and just one Conservative.[40] By the time the central Manchester Liberal Union adopted a Progressive Municipal Programme to fight off the ILP, South Manchester Liberals were already campaigning on Progressive issues showing little fear of the reaction they might receive from supposedly more conservative-minded suburban voters.[41] Indeed suburban Liberals went beyond the Progressive programme and campaigned vocally for the disestablishment of the Welsh Church, another Irish Land Bill, Local Veto legislation and the abolition of the House of Lords.[42]

The policies of leading municipal candidates followed this Radical trend. Alexander McDougall attributed his large majority in the All Saints' Ward election of 1890 to the strong views he held on temperance and social reform.[43] In the only other contested election of that year, one of the Liberal candidates in Longsight, Dr. Russell, made the pulling down of unsanitary property his electoral platform, and was elected second of six candidates – only being out-polled by the well-known former chairman of the Longsight Local Board.[44] This despite the fact that many middle-class residents in South Manchester were small-scale property owners in central Manchester, which they were dependent on renting out for a supplementary income – property which was often in poor condition due to lack of capital for repairs and which would be clearly at risk from Russell's proposal. A further sign of the Radicalism of the South Manchester Association came with the election of the working-class trades council president, Matthew Arrandale, as the Liberal candidate for All Saints in a municipal by-election of June 1895.[45] Arrandale's Radicalism, like that of Roscoe, and many other Liberal municipal representatives, combined social reform with what are often regarded as typically 'Nonconformist' ethical concerns. Like the ILP, Arrandale was an advocate of the eight-hour day, municipalisation of the tramways and improved housing to be provided by the corporation. Like the traditional Nonconformist Radicals, he was concerned with moral and spiritual issues such as the drink question and Sunday trading.[46]

South Manchester Liberals went into the 1895 general election with an agreed set of Radical priorities and considerable confidence. Home Rule, Welsh Disestablishment,

40 Election results from *The Official Handbook of Manchester and Salford*, series (Manchester, 1884–96).

41 MLU, Union Committee 16 July 1894, MCL, M283/1/1/3; MLU, Union Committee, 19 December 1894, MCL, M283/1/1/3.

42 MLU, Union Committee, 19 December 1894, MCL, M283/1/1/3.

43 *MG*, 3 November 1890.

44 *MG*, 3 November 1890.

45 *The Official Handbook of Manchester and Salford* (Manchester, 1896).

46 Arrandale election speech, *MG*, 30 October 1895.

registration reform, Local Veto and reform of the House of Lords continued to be the central planks of Roscoe's programme.[47] Despite the candidature of the Marquis of Lorne, the Queen's son-in-law, for the Liberal Unionists, South Manchester Liberals saw little to fear. Liberal Unionists were now clearly an adjunct of the Conservatives making them less of the covert threat they once were.[48] Registration surveys by the party indicated that local Liberalism was in a stronger position than ever before.[49] George Birdsall, vice-president of the Association, declared that 'victory for Sir Henry was certain'.[50] Yet by the evening of 14 July 1895 the longest-held Liberal division in Manchester had fallen to a Conservative-backed Liberal Unionist. The victory of a Liberal Unionist was a major surprise. Radical politics had been successful on three occasions at parliamentary level. Much of the party's programme had been endorsed in previous elections. House of Lords reform and Home Rule were well-worn issues. Registration reform did not involve a matter of principle and was relatively uncontroversial. Welsh disestablishment was potentially controversial, but the policy was widely supported by the large Welsh community in South Manchester.[51] Little attempt was made by Conservatives to attack Roscoe on the issue, perhaps fearing a Welsh backlash. Local Veto was controversial, although it had not prevented Roscoe's return on previous occasions. The South Manchester Liberals thus went into the 1895 election with broadly the same Radical programme, as that they had utilised successfully in 1885, 1886 and 1892.

The Liberal defeat in South Manchester should be seen therefore as a setback rather than a disaster. It represented the narrow loss of a marginal Liberal seat in a year when many much 'safer' seats were lost to the Unionists on much larger swings from the Liberals. The retirement of Gladstone alone could have been enough to remove sufficient voters from the Liberal camp to make retention of the seat more difficult.[52] Defeat brought no great loss of confidence to the local party. Roscoe was happy to reassure his supporters 'that when this wave of Tory reaction has passed away South Manchester will again return a Liberal member'.[53] The prediction turned out to be correct – the seat returned to the Liberals in 1906 and was retained in 1910. In what was regarded as the most aristocratic division in the city leading Liberals not only embraced Radicalism but were able to carry its doctrines to electoral success. South Manchester's large Welsh population, strong Nonconformist traditions and caucus of influential Radicals helped sustain a strong local Liberal presence. These

---

47 Sir Henry Roscoe's election address, George Birdsall Cuttings Book (hereafter GBC), 117, MCL, f379.4273 Bil.

48 C.P. Scott, speech at Free Trade Hall, *MG*, 5 July 1895.

49 South Manchester Liberal Association cutting, GBC, 175, MCL, f379.4273 Bil.

50 South Manchester Liberal Association cutting, GBC, 175, MCL, f379.4273 Bil.

51 See the 'Welsh Meeting Moss Side Liberal Club' circular letter, 17 January 1895, GBC, 183, MCL, f379.4273 Bil.

52 Lorne also ran a very innovative campaign, making use of direct mail to voters through low-cost telegrams, see *MG*, 15 July 1895; Lord Lorne Circular Letter, 12 July 1895, GBC, 191, MCL, f379.4273 Bil.

53 Letter, H. Roscoe to G.D. Birdsall, 15 July 1895, GBC, 192, MCL, f379.4273 Bil.

features alone, however, could not produce electoral success unless the messages advanced by Liberals had an appeal to new voters in the rapidly expanding suburban electorate. If middle- and lower-middle-class voters of the 1890s had voted primarily on grounds of material self-interest, defence of property rights and low taxation, it is difficult to see how Liberals could have triumphed at all, and particularly difficult to see how Radical or advanced Liberals such as Roscoe could have achieved repeated success. Yet Radical Liberalism was shown to be electorally successful in this suburban constituency, while in other more industrial working-class Manchester constituencies the electorate seemed more reluctant to embrace it.

A suspicion exists, however, that it might be misleading to consider South Manchester an exclusively 'suburban' constituency by the mid-1890s. The introduction of labour candidates appears to indicate that the working-class electorate in the constituency was becoming more influential, particularly in All Saints' and St. Luke's wards – those nearest the city centre. Perhaps what is required is not a survey of the whole constituency, where the concerns of the growing working class dominate the language of politics, but rather a more specific analysis of local politics in a part of the constituency unquestionably dominated by the middle and lower-middle class. Perhaps only by disaggregating the politics of such an area from wider constituency politics, can one discover whether there were any distinctive features of the politics of suburbia and why Radical Liberalism had a hold over these more materially affluent parts of suburbia. The idea of attempting to identify an area as 'typical' of affluent suburbia is in itself problematic. South Manchester's suburban estates were by no means identical. Longsight had a strong industrial influence, due to its association with the railway and engineering works located nearby. Victoria Park, by the 1890s, was no longer the fashionable suburb of 20 years previously and had only a very small number of residents – albeit very wealthy residents. Moss Side, however, seemed to typify what is traditionally regarded as suburbia – an almost exclusively residential area outside the boundaries of the city with 'green lanes and stately avenues of trees'.[54] During the 1890s local politics were vigorously fought out over the future of the suburb, fuelling debates which revealed much about how local politicians looked upon where they lived, their relationship with the nearby city and the rights of local property owners, who were faced with increasing rates to pay for public improvements.

By the early 1890s Liberalism was emerging as the dominant political force in Moss Side. Local politics, however, were not officially conducted through the agency of political parties. Elections to the school board, the board of health and, later, the district council saw all candidates standing as independents, although leading Liberals were influential in forming 'Progressive' slates of candidates for all these bodies, raising issues that echoed many of the themes of municipal and parliamentary candidates in other parts of South Manchester. The headquarters of

---

[54] J. Wynne, a Moss Side Local Board of Health member's description of the township during a public meeting opposing the amalgamation of Moss Side with the City of Manchester, GBC, 30, MCL, f379.4273 Bil.

local Liberalism was the Moss Side Liberal Club with influential patrons including Jacob Bright MP, Charles Schwann MP, Edwin Guthrie and J.A. Beith. Many Nonconformist ministers also lent their public support to the club with Rev J.A. McFadyen, Rev. Charles Roper, Rev. J.H. Holyoak and the Rev. R. Cheney among its patrons.[55] Liberal politics had strong roots in the community and yet outside parliamentary elections there was little scope for its health to be tested publicly. The decision of the owners and ratepayers of Moss Side to oppose, by a clear majority, the amalgamation of the district with Manchester in the mid-1880s left the area in an anomalous position, with the existing local government left mainly in the hands of the local board of health. Most Moss Side residents were, however, dependent on Manchester Corporation or the Manchester School Board for the provision of major public services such as gas, public libraries, public baths and elementary education. Moss Side had none of these public facilities provided locally. The politics of the 1880s were to be dominated by calls from Liberals demanding the amalgamation and the modernisation of the suburb and the concurrent opposition of the local board of health to these demands.[56] Before the 1890s local Liberals had shown little interest in challenging the existing system of local government in the district, either as a body or by using prominent local Liberals in 'non-partisan' campaigns. This may have been because several existing members of the local board were known to have Liberal sympathies.[57] Alternatively, some may have been reluctant to engage in elections which took place under the archaic Sturges Bourne system with its denial of the secrecy of the ballot and in-built bias towards property owners through plural voting – either for the fear of defeat or, like the Liberals of nearby Levenshulme, because they did not wish to give legitimacy to a system of voting so open to corruption.[58] However the most likely explanation is that the administrative nature of much of local board work gave little scope for controversy – this at least seems to have been the case until 1892 when the issues of amalgamation and sewerage improvements could not be delayed any longer and involved decisions with significant financial implications for local ratepayers.[59]

The issue of public improvements in Moss Side was raised partly as a consequence of pressure from within the suburb and partly due to the action of the Manchester Corporation in pointing out the failure of adjacent local authorities to act to improve sewage treatment and discharge facilities.[60] When the Moss Side Local Board did submit a scheme to the Local Government Board for authorisation, the matter was referred back for reconsideration with a gentle hint that Moss Side should further assess its relationship with the city of Manchester before an irrevocable and expensive decision was taken. At the lowest estimate the scheme proposed by the Moss Side

55 *South Manchester Chronicle*, 5 April 1894.

56 See Local Board cuttings, GBC, 11–13, MCL, f379.4273 Bil.

57 *MG*, 3 November 1885.

58 *South Manchester Gazette*, 4 April 1890.

59 See Local Board cuttings, GBC, 11–13, MCL, f379.4273 Bil.

60 City Council report, GBC, 12, MCL, f379.4273 Bil.

Local Board would treble the debt of the board, which, it was argued, would place the board in a much worse position when it eventually decided to negotiate with the city on the incorporation question. Higher debts meant a less favourable deal for the ratepayers if a differential rate for an incorporated Moss Side was to be negotiated.[61]

Growing public criticism of the local board's scheme prompted a number of Liberals to challenge the re-election of existing members. Two prominent members of the local Liberal Club and the Moss Side District Liberal Association, George Birdsall and Richard Chiswell came forward as 'Progressive Candidates'.[62] Although their election address claimed that they had come forward as candidates in response to a requisition 'from owners and occupiers of ALL SHADES OF POLITICAL OPINION [sic]', their most prominent sponsors were all Liberals.[63] Their central complaint against the board was that nothing had been done to provide modern facilities for the suburb – the district had no free library, deficient school accommodation, no public baths, and insufficient provision against fire and poor sewerage. The issue of amalgamation itself was not mentioned, although following the defeat of the Progressive candidates under a system of voting biased toward property owners, the amalgamation issue was soon to become the main feature of the Progressive platform. The four retiring members of the local board gradually became the focus of growing dissatisfaction with public services in the suburbs and Progressives, although unsuccessful, took a significant share of the vote in the local elections.[64] Criticism intensified when it became clear that at least £60,000 would be required to finance the board's own sewage treatment scheme – and this for a population of just 23,500 people.[65] The leading Progressives, including the Liberal Club chairman, Reuben Spencer, formed themselves into an Amalgamation Committee and approached the local board with a memorial calling upon the Board to summon a public meeting to discuss the issues of amalgamation. Their request was initially rejected, but eventually the board was forced into granting a public poll in order to kill off the issue.[66]

The intervention of a number of large property owners, concerned at the level of rates in Manchester and the abolition of plural voting, which incorporation would mean, soon turned the language of the battle into a conflict between landlord and tenant. Obsessive concern about the level of rates was depicted in the press as a sign of backward and self-interested property owners defending a class privilege.[67] The

---

61 Decision of the Inspector of the Local Government Board cutting, GBC, 13, MCL, f379.4273 Bil.

62 Local Board election address of Birdsall and Chiswell, GBC, 7, MCL, f379.4273 Bil.

63 Local Board election address of Birdsall and Chiswell, GBC, 7, MCL, f379.4273 Bil.

64 *South Manchester Chronicle*, 8 April 1892

65 Sewerage question cutting, GBC, 35, MCL, f379.4273 Bil.

66 Local Board cutting, GBC, 24, MCL, f379.4273 Bil.

67 'By Our Special Commissioner' cutting, GBC, 28, MCL, f379.4273 Bil.

benefits of reduced gas prices, lower school fees and public libraries were being resisted by a self-interested landlord class concerned that they would be faced with an increase in taxation that could not be passed on to tenants. Progressives argued that in order to defend their position, landlords were forced into the defence of an archaic Sturges Bourne plural voting system. The Amalgamation Committee attributed the previous poll majority of 815 against amalgamation to the preponderance of property votes – around 300 property owners had between them 700 votes. In addition proxy voting was seen as being wildly misused – it was alleged that over 60 votes were held as proxies at just one address.[68] Revelations in the *Manchester Guardian* that Anti-Amalgamationists had issued a private circular to property owners, urging them to use their influence over the votes of their tenants, seemed to confirm Liberal suspicions that a vested interest was standing in the way of progress.[69]

The result of the poll only gave added strength to those who argued that 'landlordism' was resisting modernisation. Those opposing amalgamation secured victory, but with a tiny majority of 22. Immediately the Amalgamationists attempted to focus attention on how property owners had used their plural votes to defeat the will of the majority of voters. Alongside the result the local press published a statement claiming that just 255 property owners in Moss Side held a total of 620 votes, immediately casting doubt on the political validity of the result.[70] Scrutiny of the votes cast showed that owners' plural votes had turned a large majority for the Amalgamationists into a small majority for their opponents. Ratepayer-qualified voters had polled 1,700 to 1,416 in favour of amalgamation negotiations. In contrast ownership-qualified voters had voted 408 to 113 against. Given that a considerable number of owners were also qualified as ratepayers, the charge that plural voting had cost the Amalgamationists victory seemed justified.[71] It was clear that the narrowness of the result had cast serious doubt upon general public support for the scheme. The *South Manchester Chronicle* declared that the poll had only demonstrated local preference for amalgamation and it attacked the local board for failing to come to the defence of the householder against the landlord.[72] What had begun as a debate about public improvements quickly resolved itself into one about sectional interests and political democracy, highlighting that even in suburbia the tenant could suffer, like the tenant in Ireland, at the hands of the self-interested landlord. Although more materially prosperous than many residents of Manchester, the Moss Side clerk or shopkeeper was often still not a property owner with the security that came with it. Opposition to selfish landlordism consequently became the central theme of Progressive campaigners.

Debates about public improvements also had a religious dimension. The conflict over educational facilities in Moss Side illustrated how denominational differences

---

68 Amalgamation Public Meeting, GBC, 68, MCL, f379.4273 Bil.

69 Letter of 'Property Owner,' *MG*, 7 January 1893, GBC, 32, f379.4273 Bil.

70 Poll cutting, GBC, 15, MCL, f379.4273 Bil.

71 Amalgamation poll cutting, GBC, 57, MCL, f379.4273 Bil.

72 *South Manchester Chronicle*, 27 January 1893.

could be equally important in defining the terms of the political debate, and the extent to which religious affiliation was an important force in political mobilisation. The poor public provision for elementary education in Moss Side had long concerned local Liberals and Nonconformists. In 1887 Sir Henry Roscoe, responding to a local request, offered to assist in the matter and place the issue before the Education Department in Whitehall.[73] When Whitehall officials investigated the matter they found a deficiency of some 2,398 school places in the township and in 1893 ordered the formation of a local Moss Side School Board.[74] As the Progressives had attacked the local board for its record in local education in previous local board elections, the battle for the school board quickly resolved itself into a similar conflict with battle lines being drawn between supporters of the local board and its Progressive critics. Religious differences, rather than cutting across these divisions, largely reinforced them. Local board leader James Blair, originally selected as a Church school board candidate, was the Progressives' and Amalgamationists' chief opponent. He was supported by his controversial local board colleague, Nathaniel Rowley, who also came forward for the Church party.[75] In contrast the leading Progressive, George Birdsall, came forward as one of the 'Unsectarian' candidates.[76]

The Unsectarian candidates' election committee membership gives a strong indication of how close the alliance between Progressive Liberals and Nonconformists was. It included ministers from all the major Nonconformist denominations in Moss Side and many active Liberals, including city councillors and the president of the South Manchester Liberal Association, Ald. Edwin Guthrie, who represented Moss Side on the county council.[77] Public meetings for the Unsectarian candidates were held at all the major Nonconformist places of worship and education – the Baptist Church schoolroom, the Ridgeway Street Mission Hall, the New Church Society schoolroom, the Primitive Methodist schoolroom and the schoolroom of the Welsh Calvinistic Church.[78] Apart from Richard Chiswell, the only notable Amalgamationist absentee from the Unsectarian campaign was the Churchman, Rev. Dr. John Garrett, who decided to stand independently, although in doing so spent much of his time attacking the other church candidates for neglecting their duties as members of the local board. However much this was supposed to be an election about education, the Church candidates were not allowed to escape from their associations with the local board, with electors being reminded that of the original five Church candidates, four were members of the local board and two were allegedly not even Anglicans![79] The result of the contest was an overwhelming victory for the Unsectarian group with all five of their official candidates securing election together with their Amalgamationist

---

73 Letter, A.D. Johnson to Jas. Flanagan, 23 December 1886; Sir Henry Roscoe to Jas. Flanagan, 21 January 1887; Moss Side Letters, MCL, M158/1/1/1–2.

74 Moss Side School Board cutting, GBC, 93, MCL, f379.4273 Bil.

75 Nomination cutting, GBC, 18, MCL, f379.4273 Bil.

76 Public meeting cutting, GBC, 100, MCL, f379.4273 Bil.

77 *Election Committee for Unsectarian Candidates*, GBC, 94, MCL, f379.4273 Bil.

78 Public meeting cutting, GBC, 100, MCL, f379.4273 Bil.

79 John Garrett election address, GBC, 95, MCL, f379.4273 Bil.

colleague, independent Churchman Rev. Dr. Garrett. Just two of the local board's Church candidates were elected and one independent.[80]

It is important to see how the difference in the franchise between the local board and school board election influenced the result. The former was much more limited and allowed for plural voting. The latter was essentially a householder franchise, which allowing for cumulative voting, ensuring the protection of minorities. Indications from the Amalgamation poll clearly suggested that the former system heavily disadvantaged the Progressive ratepayer and gave greater influence to property owners who overwhelmingly supported the position of the local board and the status quo. Moreover the cumulative vote is well known to advantage the well-organised campaign group which tries to allocate votes to their candidates in roughly equal proportions, in order to avoid wasted surplus votes and to maximise the candidates elected. The large number of Progressive–Unsectarian meetings was probably indicative of a stronger organisation supporting their side, and the inclusion of a number of leading Liberals on the Unsectarian election committee suggests that they had access to a very wide range of organisational expertise.

The more democratic household franchise was seen by the Progressives as a great opportunity to defeat the entrenched property-owning conservative influence on the local board – a feeling that was strengthened after the success of the Unsectarian candidates in the school board elections. With the coming of district councils and the household franchise, Progressives could break through into local politics whether or not Moss Side was amalgamated with the city. Local Liberals, such as William Axon, approached the election with the belief that the old order would be swept away with the old electoral system.[81] The local board was vulnerable on a range of issues, but significantly the Progressives chose to turn the election into a referendum on the issue of the Moss Side destructor – the proposed erection of a large mechanical furnace for the disposal of refuse. Understanding local residents' concerns about the possible effects on the district of air pollution, leading Progressives moved to form a 'Committee of Ratepayers and Property Owners for Opposing the Erection of a Destructor in Moss Side', electing William Axon as their chairman.[82] The committee became a rallying point for all those opposed to the local board, selecting candidates for a Progressive slate almost exclusively from ranks of active Moss Side Liberals. Of the nine successful Progressive candidates, eight were publicly active in local Liberal politics, either through the district association, the divisional association or the Moss Side Liberal Club.[83]

The campaign against the destructor took two forms. First the local board was accused of being self-interested in attempting to adopt a patented design from one of their own members. Secondly the Progressives posed as popular defenders

80 Election results cutting, GBC, 121, MCL, f379.4273 Bil.
81 Moss Side Election Notes, William Axon Papers, MCL, M158/2/1/1.
82 Moss Side Election Notes, William Axon Papers, MCL, M158/2/1/1.
83 See District Council and Liberal Association cuttings, GBC, 160–61.

of Moss Side's suburban character, opposing a polluting machine.[84] Although the Progressives took care not to openly charge the board with corruption – the suggestion of impropriety being struck out of Axon's speaking notes – they could and did play on popular suspicion of the Board's actions by attacking its secretive decision-making.[85] The district council election results repeated the pattern seen in the school board election with the Progressives sweeping to an overwhelming victory. Of the 12 newly-elected councillors, nine were elected from the Progressive slate, and only two from the slate representing the old local board.[86] The Progressive manifesto, combining calls for public improvement with a healthy dose of populism, was everywhere triumphant.

The Progressive success was a Liberal Party success in all but name. Its candidates were overwhelmingly Liberals, the candidates' committees were dominated by Liberals, they met at the local Liberal Club and they were supported by a movement synonymous with British Liberalism in the nineteenth century – the Nonconformist churches. Local Liberal Progressives campaigned against the sectarian influence of the Established church and the dominance of local government by a property-owning elite and for effective public improvements and the protection of the suburban environment. However it is important to see that the Liberal defence of suburbia was not a defence of the privileges of a suburban elite, but rather part of their approach to public improvement. By the late 1890s public improvements began to materialise with Moss Side gaining its own board school, public library and newsroom.[87] The Progressive appeal was, in part, a 'class' appeal, however it was not an appeal to a secure affluent middle class but rather to a lower-middle class, insecure in its social status and requiring the public provision of important services, like many of the city's working population. In Moss Side this appeal had an important religious dimension. The area's Nonconformist population required board schools not just for convenience and to end school fees but also to ensure that their children could enjoy education free from Anglican dogmas. For these people Progressivism addressed their interests and their desire for a more democratic, open and inclusive local politics. It met their aspirations for a healthier lifestyle outside the urban slums, while also addressing their needs for improved access to education and local public services. They required local government that was prepared to raise rates and squeeze property owners in order to raise the sums for investment in public services. Progressivism provided just that type of politics.

It would be a mistake, however, to believe that the suburban Liberal outlook of Moss Side excluded interest in labour questions. It is true that no Liberals from a working-class background were elected to the new urban district council, but this is not too surprising at a time when the Manchester City Council could boast of

---

84 *The Ratepayers' Candidates' Election Address*, Moss Side UDC Broadsides, MCL, LB3.

85 William Axon election letter, 5 November 1894, Axon Letters, MCL, M158/2/1/12.

86 Election results cutting, GBC, 121, MCL, f379.4273 Bil.

87 *Moss Side District News*, 8 May 1897.

only two working-class Liberal councillors – the trade council leaders, Matthew Arrandale and George Kelley.[88] Moreover, the social make-up of Moss Side and the failure of the ILP to challenge the Liberal dominance never really forced the Moss Side Liberals to face up to the issue of labour representation in the same way as their colleagues in the city of Manchester.[89] The Progressive candidates put forward for the first Moss Side District Council election were a combination of 'shopocracy' and professionals, and included a journalist, a science teacher, an architect, an engineer, two butchers, an auctioneer, a contractor and a publisher.[90] This did not, however, imply a general disinterest in the problems of working-class residents. Edwin Guthrie, on his retirement from the aldermanic bench of the county council, stood for re-election as a councillor on a platform that advocated minimum wages clauses in all council contracts.[91] The proceedings and lectures of the Moss Side Liberal Club indicates considerable grass-roots enthusiasm for labour issues and demonstrates that Liberals were alive to a possible ILP threat.[92] The language of the debate was one which saw labour issues as being primarily about the development of a society based on merit rather than privilege – a message that resonated as much, if not more, with the lower-middle-class Moss Side suburbanite as the Longsight railway worker:

> Liberalism's true aim was to give the working man the same social advantages as the rich man. ... the Liberal Party are anxious that no barrier should be placed before the labourer, but every man should have a fair and equal chance of success.[93]

Democratic reform was depicted as being as much in the interests of suburbia as anywhere else, with the aim of democratic legislation 'not legislation for the poorer classes of the community but legislation for all classes'.[94] This did not mean, however, that the party was fearful of supporting controversial proposals – Moss Side Liberals even came out in favour of land nationalisation.[95]

Liberalism in Moss Side, like that in the South Manchester parliamentary division as a whole, had developed into a Progressive and at times extremely Radical creed.

---

88 *The Official Handbook of Manchester And Salford 1893–4*, (Manchester, 1894).

89 See chapter on C.P. Scott and Progressivism in P.F. Clarke, *Lancashire and the New Liberalism* (Cambridge, 1971), 153–97; J. Hill, 'Manchester and Salford Politics and the Early Development of the Independent Labour Party', *International Review of Social History*, 26 (1981) 171–201.

90 *The Ratepayers' Candidates' Election Address*, Moss Side UDC Broadsides, MCL, LB3 MCL.

91 Election meeting cutting, GBC, 166, MCL, f379.4273 Bil.

92 Speaker's comments 'Liberalism and Labour' cutting, GBC, 164, MCL, f379.4273 Bil.

93 Speaker's comments, 'Liberalism and Labour' cutting, GBC, 164, MCL, f379.4273 Bil.

94 Registration meeting cutting, GBC, 166, MCL, f379.4273 Bil.

95 Henry Aldridge, speaking at the Moss Side Liberal Club, Meeting cutting, GBC, 195, MCL, f379.4273 Bil.

Part of the explanation for this Radicalism must be the influence of a number of wealthy Radical Liberals who chose to reside in the area, patronising local Liberal associations and clubs, helping to set a Radical agenda in local politics. The presence of a formidable cadre of 'advanced Liberals' – Edwin Guthrie, William Axon, George Birdsall – clearly assisted the emergence of a Progressive agenda in local politics. However the Progressives may not have emerged so strongly had it not been for the Anglican-dominated local board acting, it seemed, with the interests of wealthy property owners as their chief concern and resisting demands for public improvements and public unsectarian education. With the coming of the school board and the urban district council elections, opposition to old local board members was consolidated and a more democratic electoral system allowed for the emergence of a Liberal-dominated Progressive majority on both local public bodies. The Progressive appeal was one designed to appeal to the concerns of the lower-middle class dependent on the wealthier property owner for their residence, board schools for their children's education and public services for their education and entertainment. Although materially better off than the average Manchester resident, their needs were substantially different from the super-rich who resided in the exclusive dwellings of areas like Victoria Park. Suburban Liberalism was successful, not because it spoke the language of a privileged group, but, somewhat paradoxically, because it attacked a privileged group – the largely Anglican property-owning class who resisted the public improvements prized by many of the lower-middle class.

A recent national survey of Liberalism at the 1895 general election has revealed that the Liberal platform had a much greater coherence at this time than has sometimes been suggested.[96] Similarly, there were few signs of fundamental disagreements amongst Manchester Liberals, either on issues of nationalisation, property ownership or any other subject associated with 'class politics'. Suburban Liberalism could afford to be Radical because either, as in the case of Welsh disestablishment, a large number of Nonconformist Liberals supported such stances on religious or ethical grounds, or, as in the case of labour representation, it could be depicted as a further step toward a meritocratic liberal society, threatening only the privileged classes, not the hard-working shopkeeper or clerk. Although some public improvements, such as board schools and public libraries, were costly and benefited the poorer ratepayers the most, they could equally appeal to the Nonconformist who resented Anglican domination of local government and education and the educated clerk who placed value on self-improvement and literary culture. South Manchester Liberalism, typified by Sir Henry Roscoe, presented itself as an enlightened, meritocratic and moral force opposed to a self-interested and unenlightened property-owning elite. 'Radical Villadom' came to dominate local politics because it addressed many of the key concerns of suburban South Manchester's largest social group – the

---

96 P. Readman, 'The 1895 General Election and Political Change in Late Victorian Britain', *Historical Journal*, 42 (1999) 467–93.

mainly Nonconformist lower-middle class. As the new century dawned, Liberalism continued to be a powerful political force in Manchester's southern suburbs.[97]

[97] Even after the First World War Manchester Liberalism continued to be electorally and organisationally stronger in middle- and mixed-class suburban constituencies. See B. Jones, 'Manchester Liberalism 1918–1929: the electoral, ideological and organisational experience of the Liberal Party in Manchester, with particular reference to the career of Ernest Simon', Unpublished PhD thesis, University of Manchester, 1997, 32–3, 310–11.

CHAPTER EIGHT

Incorporation – An Agent of Radicalism?

Manchester's suburban electorate had a long Radical tradition dating from the creation of suburbs in the mid-nineteenth century. Leicester's suburbia developed much later, presenting late nineteenth-century party managers with the challenge of developing political institutions in almost entirely new communities. Indeed the particularly rapid withdrawal of the Leicester middle class to surrounding residential suburbs has been seen as a significant development in the growth of class consciousness in the town and, indirectly, to the strength of the Independent Labour Party.[1] Geographical separation from the poor and from town centre Nonconformist leadership produced, it has been argued, new middle-class attitudes, concerned more with material wealth and status than philanthropic and ethical endeavour.[2] If accurate this view would seem helpful in explaining the late nineteenth-century 'crisis' in Leicester Liberalism and the growth of class-based politics in the twentieth.

Initial impressions of Leicester politics would seem to suggest there is much in this type of explanation. The affluent middle-class suburb of Stoneygate, to the south-east of Leicester, became synonymous with the middle-class flight from Liberalism when a number of Stoneygate Liberals led the way in the creation of a breakaway Liberal Unionist Association, and then allied themselves with the Conservatives to wrest the local town council seats away from the Liberal Association.[3] Some Radicals viewed this particular suburb with great suspicion. Even J.A. Picton, the borough MP, admitted 'that the average Liberalism of Stoneygate was not of a very advanced type'.[4] These attitudes naturally annoyed some Stoneygate Liberals, one even accusing Picton of pandering to class prejudice.[5] Certainly there were considerable tensions between some Stoneygate Liberals and the more Radical wing of the party. However whether this represented class prejudice, personal envy, or a general hostility to the new suburban estates is open to question.

Criticism of suburban developments and suburbanites as conservative, dull and uninspiring is as old as suburbia itself. Indeed antipathy to suburban life has

---

1 R.A. McKinley and C.T. Smith in R.H. Evans (ed.), *The Victoria History of the County of Leicester*, IV (1958), 231–5.

2 H. Baynton and G. Pitches, *Desirable Locations – Leicester's Middle Class Suburbs* (Leicester, 1996), 7.

3 *LDP*, 4 November 1891.

4 Letter, J.A. Picton, *LDM*, 10 July 1886.

5 Letter, T.H. Downing, *LDM*, 10 July 1886.

tended to distort both popular and academic views of suburbia and its citizens.[6] It is an antipathy that is not peculiar to Britain and is also strong in the United States.[7] Suburbs were often regarded as uniform cultural and aesthetic deserts – places 'without any society: no social gatherings or institutions: as dull a life as mankind ever tolerated'.[8] They were places where, according to the caricature, the middle classes allegedly cut themselves off from wider society, abandoning public life for the nuclear family, and duty for the pursuit of personal ambition.[9] Recent historical research has tended to challenge this stereotype. Dyos's study of Camberwell illustrated how, far from being uniform, this particular London suburb developed as a mosaic of estates.[10] Speirs's work on Manchester's Victoria Park depicted a vibrant, complex and socially aware community with a population intimately engaged in local public life.[11] Even famous high-class suburbs such as Edgbaston and Mayfair have been shown to be far more socially mixed than previously thought.[12] Similarly, sociologists have further demonstrated how modern suburbs developed as complex cultural hybrids with only superficially uniform characteristics.[13]

It is therefore important to look beyond prejudices against suburbia, and ask if the antipathies and stereotypes reflected something more than personal and local rivalries. Hostilities to a particular suburb, in this case Stoneygate, need to be placed into a broader context. Moreover, Stoneygate – and its municipal ward, Knighton – were not necessarily typical of Leicester suburbia and declining Liberal support in this area would not necessarily indicate a suburban Liberal crisis. In order to assess the relevance of the Liberal programme to suburbia it is vital to assess how the leaders of the various suburban communities behaved and the political priorities they held. Following incorporation into the county borough of Leicester, the new suburbs had a significant impact on municipal politics and the priorities the town council pursued. Evidence from local elections suggests that residents of the new suburban estates were not highly materialistic or atomised from the wider community but, like those in Manchester were full participants in local public life. In many cases suburban residents came together to form strong community institutions and to put pressure on the municipal authorities for infrastructure improvements and new public amenities – such as public libraries and local swimming baths. As in Manchester,

---

6 R. Harris and P. Larkham (eds), *Changing Suburbs: Foundation, Form and Function* (London, 1999), 3.

7 D. Thorns, *Suburbia* (London, 1972), 3.

8 Sir W. Besant in 1909, cited in D. Olsen, *The Growth of Victorian London* (London, 1976), 210.

9 For discussion see Olson, *Growth*, 214–15, and Thorns, *Suburbia*, 14–16.

10 H.J. Dyos, *Victorian Suburb: A Study in the Growth of Camberwell* (London, 1961).

11 M. Speirs, *Victoria Park, Manchester* (Manchester, 1976).

12 D. Cannadine, 'Residential differentiation in nineteenth century towns: from shapes in the ground to shapes in society', in J. Johnson and C. Pooley (eds), *The Structure of Nineteenth Century Cities* (London, 1982) 235–51, esp. 239–51; D. Cannandine, 'Victorian cities: how different?', *Social History*, 2 (1977), 457–87.

13 R. Silverstone (ed.), *Visions of Suburbia* (London, 1997), 6–7.

this demand for the collective provision of municipal services to the suburbs gave Liberal politicians a common platform in local elections and helped make growing rate demands more palatable for suburban residents.

The chief problem in making a detailed study of Leicester's suburban estates is, again, in identifying those areas which can be regarded as 'typical' – for, in general, Leicester's suburban estates were characterised only by their great diversity. In some Midland towns, such as Nottingham, the growth of suburbia developed around a suburban railway network, giving estates a physical cohesion. However in Leicester public rail services played little part in creating suburbs. Indeed until the opening of the Manchester, Sheffield and Lincolnshire Railway at the end of the century, Leicester possessed just two genuinely suburban stations, both serving Humberstone Road to the north of the town centre.[14] Leicester suburbanites therefore depended mainly on private carriages and horse buses to provide access to smaller, more dispersed suburbs. Suburban development in Leicester was thus not confined to any one particular area. The only areas of the town that did not see major suburban growth before 1900 were those areas in which physical and geographical conditions made it too difficult or unattractive. Thus, development to the west of the town along the river did not take place until much later – the necessary flood control and sewage treatment works not being complete until 1891 – whilst development alongside railway lines was unpopular because of its association with low-grade housing.[15] Elsewhere small-scale developments sprang up all around the old town.

These suburbs, which developed so rapidly in the late nineteenth century, were neither exclusively middle class nor exclusively residential. Belgrave, to the north of Leicester, was already a bustling industrial framework knitting village by mid-century and by 1900 had become a mixed class industrial suburb of some 12,000 people.[16] North Evington, to the north-east, was an almost entirely new settlement created by local architect, developer and Liberal councillor, Arthur Wakerley. Wakerley, a pioneer of modern town planning, aimed to create not a residential estate, but rather a model self-sufficient suburb, with its own housing, shops, churches, markets and factories all in close proximity.[17] By 1914 the area provided employment for over 5,000 people in 31 different trades.[18] In contrast, the Knighton suburbs – and, in particular the more exclusive Stoneygate estate – contained no significant industrial

14 J. Simmons, *Leicester Past and Present: Volume II The Modern City* (London, 1974), 113–14.

15 R. Rodger in D. Nash and D. Reeder (eds), *Leicester in the Twentieth Century* (Stroud, 1993), 6.

16 J.D. Martin and P. Wilson, 'Belgrave', in R.H. Evans (ed.), *Victoria History*, IV, 420–27.

17 J. Farquhar, *Arthur Wakerley 1862–1931* (Leicester, 1984), 29–39; J. Martin and R. Bird, 'Evington', in R.H. Evans (ed.), *Victoria History*, IV, 436; R. Rodger in D. Nash and D. Reeder (eds), *Leicester*, 6–9.

18 Farquhar, *Arthur Wakerley*, 29–30.

or commercial areas.[19] The population of the parish increased by nearly 1,000 from 1871 to 1881, with some of the largest and most ornate residences in the county springing up within its bounds.[20] Inevitably Stoneygate became well known because of the wealth displayed in the building of these homes, although many more modest properties also existed.[21] Indeed the Knighton area, of which Stoneygate was only a small part, consisted of a wide variety of residential properties, including a large number of smaller homes, to the north of the Clarendon Park Road, housing mainly working-class families. Despite its image, Knighton was not an exclusively residential area, and perhaps because it lacked a suburban railway station, it was surprisingly self-sufficient in local services, with its own shops, board school and public library by the end of the century.[22] Leicester 'Villadom' was socially and functionally mixed and did not always live up to the ideal image portrayed by developers. Working-class demands for affordable suburban housing forced developers to reduce the quality of construction, with poorer properties located close to large villas. Even in prestigious estates such as Clarendon Park, there were complaints of 'shaky shanties and band box buildings'.[23]

Just as the suburbs were not isolated residential estates without public amenities, nor were they bereft of religious and social institutions. Indeed, religious organisations redoubled their efforts to attract new suburban congregations, faced with depleted attendances in the town centre. Several attempted to develop a network of recreational, educational and sporting associations to ensure that their congregations continued to place the church at the centre of their social lives.[24] Many Nonconformist denominations embarked on entirely new chapel-building programmes. In Belgrave, between 1894 and 1905, all three major Methodist denominations – the Wesleyans, Primitives and United Methodists – constructed new chapels or mission halls to supplement the two existing chapels built in the early years of the century.[25] Knighton also had a strong Nonconformist presence and had had a Wesleyan congregation since 1816. A Congregational chapel opened in 1886, followed by a Primitive Methodist establishment a year later. A new Baptist chapel opened in 1894 and before the First World War a further two Congregational and Baptist chapels appeared.[26] If the level of church building can be taken in any way as a proxy of Nonconformist allegiance, it must be clear that the suburban population largely retained their commitment to the 'free' churches. Prominent Liberal Unionists, such as Knighton town councillor Samuel Faire and educational

---

19 For brief details of the development of these areas see J. Martin and R. Bird, 'Knighton' in R.H. Evans (ed.), *Victoria History*, IV, 446.

20 Simmons, *Leicester Past and Present: Volume II*, 116.

21 A. Abisror, 'Stoneygate – A Leicester Victorian Suburb 1891–1914', Unpublished MA thesis, University of Leicester, 1994, 64.

22 Simmons, *Leicester Past and Present: Volume II*, 116.

23 *LJ*, 10 September 1886.

24 D. Nash, 'Leisure and Consumption', in Nash and Reeder (eds), *Leicester*, 194–5.

25 J. Martin and P. Wilson, 'Belgrave', in Evans (ed.), *Victoria History*, IV, 420–27.

26 J. Martin and R. Bird, 'Knighton', in Evans (ed.), *Victoria History*, IV, 446.

benefactor Thomas Fielding Johnson represented a continuing Anglican tradition in the suburbs but, by the end of the nineteenth century, Nonconformist places of worship heavily outnumbered those of the Established church in the suburban districts. Indeed Nonconformist concerns were felt not just through the churches, but in the very establishment of the new estates. Worries over the baneful influence of the drink trade meant that when the new suburbs of North Evington and Stoneygate were planned, neither were afforded a public house, reflecting the temperance principles of the developers and those expected to move into the new suburbia.[27]

The political orientation of the suburbs was not, of course, simply a reflection of the pre-existing attitudes of those who moved there. Many residents found that the quality of life in the new developing districts did not meet their expectations. Arrangements for public sanitation and water supply were often primitive and where water and sewerage schemes existed they had often not kept up with the pace of development. Most of the new suburbs were located outside the boundaries of the town and thus responsibility for improvements lay with local boards of health. Elected by the Sturges Bourne system on a multiple franchise that varied based on individual property holding, they had traditionally limited responsibilities, limited resources and often were reluctant to pursue expensive improvement schemes. Inevitably, therefore, as the town spilled over its municipal boundaries, there were demands that the municipality should expand its boundaries to meet the new conditions and address the sanitary problems of the districts in the shared watershed. Initial proposals for municipal extension came from the Conservatives as early as 1867, although this may have been a ploy to dilute 'Radical' Leicester with Conservative representatives from the more rural areas around the town.[28] The first serious attempt to expand the municipal boundaries was made in the early 1880s when it became clear that a comprehensive sewerage scheme would be necessary for the whole of the Leicester drainage area if Leicester was not to suffer from pollution from the surrounding suburbs. In 1880 the town council appointed a borough boundaries committee to investigate and bring forward detailed proposals.[29] Although the town council may have found borough extension attractive for other reasons – not least for the extension of rateable value and prestige that came with it – the need to deal with the Soar valley's sewage seems to have been the major justification. It was this, and its financial implications, which dominated local debates on the issue.[30]

There were two major barriers to municipal expansion – one practical and one political. The main practical difficulty was the lack of ordnance plans and geographical surveys for much of Leicester's suburban area – so that although the first general proposal for expansion was made in 1880, the first application for parliamentary

---

27 Simmons, *Leicester Past and Present: Volume II*, 122.

28 M. Elliott, *Victorian Leicester* (London, 1979), 148–51.

29 LTC, Borough Boundaries Committee, 31 May 1880, LRO, CM8.

30 In 1882 the committee advised the council to limit the extension scheme solely to the natural drainage area of Leicester on the grounds that incorporation of other areas would be difficult to justify politically. LTC, Borough Boundaries Committee, 21 September 1882, LRO, CM8.

approval could not be made until five years later.[31] The main political difficulty was that the boards of health for the out-districts were very reluctant to hand over power to the corporation and quietly dissolve. This was partly because of a desire to protect their own local identity and partly because many were Conservative-dominated and were consequently reluctant to be absorbed into Liberal-controlled Leicester. Thus while Leicester drafted detailed proposals for borough extension, neighbouring local sanitary authorities, like the Billesdon Union, drew up their own sewerage schemes in an attempt to ward off the unwelcome approaches from Leicester.[32] If the Local Government Board in Whitehall had agreed to sanction such schemes, it would have greatly diminished Leicester's arguments for incorporation.

Within Leicester the battle over incorporation resolved itself into a partisan conflict between the Liberal and Conservative council leaders. Ald. Thomas Wright, the Liberal chairman of the borough extension committee, was opposed by Ald. Winterton and Cllr. Millican, the leaders of the minority. Conservatives argued that the Liberals had brought the proposals forward for partisan benefit, that the rating clauses were unjust and that extension was designed to secure private advantages to Liberal land speculators. Inside the council chamber it was an unequal struggle, the overwhelming Liberal majority ensuring the proposals were passed by 33 votes to nine.[33] Outside the chamber, the electorate also followed the Liberal leadership and a poll of the town gave the extension proposals a two-thirds majority.[34] This did not, however, deter Conservative opponents who took their battle to Westminster. Winterton and Millican both appeared before a special parliamentary hearing and made strenuous efforts to undermine the town council's case. The appearance of these senior members of the council against their own corporation bill was probably a major reason for its rejection. Allegation that Wright, the leading promoter of the bill, had acquired land with the intention of obtaining private profit from the adoption of the scheme also sullied the waters. Wright strongly denied the Conservative allegations but the damage had already been done.[35]

Politically the episode is interesting for two reasons. Firstly, the determination of Liberal politicians to bring forward an extension bill, in the face of Conservative hostility, suggests they were not afraid that the incorporation of the suburbs would seriously damage their majority on the council. Secondly, many Conservatives felt the only way to maintain political influence in suburbia was through the existing local board system. With the continual expansion of suburbia, however, the practical difficulties of small boards of health managing major improvement schemes soon became obvious. Unlike large corporations, such authorities could not spread the cost of improvements over a large number of ratepayers and so major projects meant sharp increases in the rates. Worse still they could not raise capital at the preferential

31 LTC, 24 February 1884, LRO, CM1/20, LTC, 28 July 1885, LRO, CM1/20.
32 LTC, Borough Boundaries Committee, 3 September 1885, LRO, CM8.
33 LTC, Borough Boundaries Committee, 28 July 1885, LRO, CM8.
34 *LA*, 6 February 1886.
35 *LA*, 24 April 1886.

interest rates available to larger authorities – thus while Leicester corporation could raise capital at 3.5 per cent, smaller authorities could pay as much as 5 per cent.[36] Had local boards been successful in keeping their rates substantially below those of the borough they may have been able to fend off criticism, but while borough rates remained relatively stable in the early 1880s, the surrounding sanitary authorities, faced with increasing suburbanisation, were forced to make substantial increases. Between 1882 and 1885 Leicester's basic rate dropped from 5s 4d to 4s 10d. Meanwhile in Belgrave, rates rose from 1s 11d to 5s 6d in the five years from 1877 to 1882.[37] Increasing rate demands on the township and the shoddy construction of local sewers helped turn the once exclusively Conservative Belgrave Local Board into one on which the Liberals enjoyed a majority for the first time.[38] Belgrave was not, however, unique and the upward trend in suburban rates was witnessed in all the major 'out-districts'. In 1890, while the borough rate for St. Margaret's parish in the town was 5s 2d, Belgrave had a 6s 2d rate, Humberstone a 6s 8½d rate, Evington a 6s 11¼d rate, and Aylestone a 7s 7½d rate. Only Knighton had a basic rate lower than that of Leicester and it could not remain lower for long if major sewerage works were to be undertaken. Although even advocates of incorporation admitted these basic figures were a little misleading, given the different methods of assessment in the various districts, the basic trend was clear. Between 1886 and 1890, Evington's basic rate rose by 129 per cent, Knighton's by 77 per cent, Aylestone's by 20 per cent, Belgrave's by 12 per cent and Newfoundpool's by 43 per cent.[39] Faced with such hard economic realities, Conservative opposition to the principle of incorporation began to evaporate. The experience of Belgrave demonstrated that local ratepayers would not tolerate Conservative or 'independent' local boards who continued to increase rates while making only half-hearted attempts to deal with the problems of sewage and sanitation. Thus when proposals for borough extension next came before the Leicester town council they met with just three opponents.[40]

Conservative opposition was divided between those who accepted the principle of incorporation, but wanted to negotiate the best deals for their respective areas, and those who continued to maintain outright opposition. Incorporation meant that the most urban – generally the wealthiest – parts of the rural sanitary districts would be removed, leaving rural sanitary authorities with a much reduced rateable area. This was of little concern to urban and suburban Liberals who accused Conservatives of regarding 'the urban parishes as a sort of "milch cow" for the rural districts'.[41] Municipal expansion also threatened a substantial loss of revenue for the county council, who opposed the plans and called for the payment of compensation for

36 *LDM*, 27 February 1886.
37 Elliott, *Victorian Leicester*, 151.
38 *MFP*, 8 March 1884.
39 *LDM*, 30 July 1890.
40 *LDM*, 30 July 1890.
41 Letter, John Wignall, *LC*, 21 March 1891.

the loss of rateable value. As there were few precedents for such a claim, it was uncertain what attitude central government would take.[42]

There was also a significant partisan dimension to county council opposition. The first county council election of 1889 had seen the return of a large Conservative majority and was naturally hostile to any growth of Liberal influence in the county. However, while the Liberal Party did poorly in rural districts it enjoyed significant success in Leicester's suburbs. To the north of the city the Liberal Party had launched an all-out assault on the Humberstone division and secured an impressive victory, mainly by attacking the Conservative 'magisterial' local government which had gone before. In Belgrave and Thurmaston – a two-member division – the Liberal nominees took both seats with large majorities, on an anti-compulsory vaccination and sanitary reform platform.[43] In South Leicester the Harborough Liberal Association decided not to encourage partisan contests – but even here Liberals performed well. Ald. Thomas Wright, the leading proponent of municipal incorporation, now a member of the Liberal Unionists, came forward as an independent candidate.[44] The Clarendon Park and Knighton Liberal Association, however, were alarmed at the prospect of a Unionist candidate being successful and supported S.A. Marris, a member of the district highway board, in opposition to Wright.[45] The contest developed into a straight party fight and in a very heavy poll Marris took the seat with a majority of 15.[46] Despite the fact that Knighton was the wealthiest Leicester suburb, and the organisational centre of Leicester's Liberal Unionists, the Liberal Party had demonstrated the continuing strength of its following.

The differences between Marris and Wright, however, exposed divisions in Knighton Liberal ranks. Despite the fact that the Liberal town council group were almost unanimously behind the extension proposals, Marris later broke ranks with prevailing Liberal opinion, claiming his election reflected the wishes of Knighton to stay out of the municipality.[47] This was a rather curious claim as there was little discussion of the amalgamation issue during the 1889 election contest – suggesting that continuing personal differences with Wright may have coloured his behaviour.[48] An alliance of Marris's Liberals, local clergymen and disaffected Conservatives formed an influential lobby against the borough extension, which the town council could not ignore. Mainly because of this powerful lobby, Knighton extracted particularly favourable amalgamation terms from the town council. In an attempt to appease local opinion it was agreed that initially, at least, Knighton residents would be exempt from payment of school board rates and that they should be free from any reassessment of rateable value for a period of ten years. The first concession

42 *MFP*, 11 April 1891; Simmons, *Leicester Past and Present: Volume II*, 119.

43 *LDP*, 15 January 1885; *LC*, 19 January 1889.

44 Although Wright's election committee seems to have been composed chiefly of prominent Conservatives and Liberal Unionists. *LC*, 19 January 1891.

45 *LDM*, 28 October 1888.

46 *LC*, 19 January 1889.

47 *LC*, 21 March 1891.

48 *LC*, 19 January 1889.

was on the grounds that the area had already privately provided substantial school accommodation. However, the fact that Knighton residents were still to be allowed to vote in school board elections caused considerable resentment, provoking strong criticism from the Liberal school board chairman, James Ellis.[49] The second concession was equally controversial. It meant that even though Knighton was a rapidly developing suburban district, with property values increasing accordingly, local residents would pay rates based on old assessments, conducted when the district was little more than an agricultural village. Opponents of incorporation hinted darkly that local speculators – some members of the town council – were promoting incorporation on generous terms for simply selfish reasons.[50] Although scarcity of evidence makes evaluation of these claims difficult, it is known that in other areas Liberal council members had substantial financial investments in the suburban property market. Arthur Wakerley bought up large amounts of land in North Evington with the expectation that the area would soon be brought into the borough and its value thus increased. Indeed in the 1897 municipal elections he was directly accused of using his knowledge of council business to secure private profit in land deals.[51] For residents of Knighton, however, these additional clauses were highly beneficial. Knighton residents could enjoy all the benefits of being part of Leicester without facing substantial increases in local taxation. Necessary local improvements could be effected with little cost to those who would most benefit.

The town council's campaign for incorporation was a long process and illustrates the commitment of Liberal leaders to suburban concerns. Liberal council leaders mobilised the full resources of the town council in support of the movement.[52] The town clerk effectively operated as campaign organiser and adopted sophisticated techniques to persuade large ratepayers to accept the proposals – such as approaching waverers through their tenants.[53] All such pledges were recorded and then produced before the parliamentary committee in order to illustrate public support for the council's proposals.[54] Careful preparations were made for the vestry meetings ensuring the council proposals were carried overwhelmingly. Shortly before crucial meetings, areas were closely recanvassed and new pledges obtained.[55]

The campaign to persuade the suburbs to accept incorporation was conducted at several levels. Liberal council leaders were anxious to reassure middle-class residents that wealthier members of the community supported amalgamation and would benefit

---

49 *LC*, 28 February 1891; *LC*, 7 March 1891.

50 *LC*, 21 March 1891.

51 Rodger in Nash and Reeder, *Leicester*, 2; Jones in Nash and Reeder, *Leicester*, 92–3.

52 See, for example: Letter, J. Storer to J. Thornhill Harrison [copy], 19 December 1890, Leicester Town Clerk's Letter Book 102, 14–16, LRO, 22 D 57/102.

53 Letter, J. Storer to J. Stafford [copy], 19 December 1890, LTCLB 102, 17, LRO, 22 D 57/102.

54 *LC*, 28 February 1891.

55 Letter, J. Storer to H. Simpson Gee [copy], 3 January 1891, LTCLB 102, 101, LRO, 22 D 57/102.

from it. When large-scale petitions were organised from Humberstone, Evington and Aylestone in favour of amalgamation, rather than quote the numbers of residents in favour, the rateable value that the residents represented was reported instead. Thus in Aylestone those in favour of the scheme were said to represent £12,222 of a total rateable value of £14,739. In Humberstone supporters of the proposals represented £8,678 of a £11,775 total, while in Evington supporters represented £8,169 of a total £12,593 rateable value.[56] From the outset the council had been determined to ensure that wealthier residents of each district were signed up first. Concessions for some areas, such as Knighton, were combined with reassurances and promises of improved local services, sanitation and branch free libraries. Wealthier areas shared the problems of poor sewage and sanitation treatment and despite the substantial investment in individual properties, work on public infrastructure had not kept pace with land development. Sewerage arrangements in Knighton were described by one advocate of amalgamation as being 'as bad as bad could be' – and this in Leicester's most 'exclusive' suburb.[57] Skilful political manoeuvring, exploiting concerns about rising rates and poor sanitation, and generous concessions saw public support for incorporation grow. By the time Knighton residents came to vote on the subject the issue was no longer in doubt and the amalgamation proposals were carried by more than two to one.[58]

Other than the county council, the Belgrave local board of health was the most significant public body to oppose the extension scheme. After a brief period of Liberal control the board had reverted to Conservative leadership. Local boards, however, with their Sturges Bourne system of election, were only very imperfect reflections of wider public opinion. Indeed the board's action in failing formally to consult local ratepayers on the issue did little to persuade the parliamentary hearing that their opposition had the support of the wider electorate. When the board presented a petition with its official seal stating their grounds for opposition, it was revealed that it had not followed the correct procedure and had brought forward its opposition without consulting local ratepayers.[59] This opened them to charges of acting illegally, and of having no mandate from their electorate. The episode naturally provided much ammunition for Liberal propagandists.[60]

The endorsement of extension plans by parish vestry meetings further gave weight to the amalgamationist cause. A resolution in favour of amalgamation was passed at the Aylestone vestry meeting, even though the majority of those present were from the more conservative 'old village' rather than the new suburban estates.[61]

56 *LDM*, 30 July 1890.

57 *LJ*, 3 April 1891.

58 *LJ*, 10 April 1891.

59 Under the Borough Funds Act local authorities who wished to spend public money in opposition to proposed legislation were required to obtain permission from ratepayers via a public meeting and, if requested, by a public poll.

60 See comments of J.L. Ward, the former Liberal chairman of the board. *LC*, 11 April 1891.

61 *LC*, 18 April 1891.

Only in Knighton was there any major difficulty, and that largely arose because of Marris's continuing crusade against Wright. The first vestry meeting held to discuss the proposals ended in scenes of disorder, with Marris's supporters facing a barrage of opposition.[62] At the second meeting Wright decided to attend in an attempt to avoid a damaging defeat. The tactic worked, placing the amalgamationists in a good position to win the subsequent district poll.[63] Favourable rating clauses and offers of improved public services had once again won the day. The Bill's opponents, in contrast, could offer the suburban public very little. Their claims that incorporation would mean higher rates rang a little hollow when the existing largely Conservative sanitary authority had been forced to increase rates to cope with the demands of suburban expansion.

The proposals for municipal expansion became closely identified with the Liberal town council, although the issue never became a purely partisan conflict for several reasons. Liberal county councillor S.A. Marris led the unsuccessful movement against amalgamation in Knighton. Thomas Wright, who did so much to spearhead the progress of the Bill, became a Liberal Unionist in 1886 and did not return to Gladstonian ranks until after the 1892 general election. Moreover there were good reasons why municipal expansion could be of benefit to both Liberal and Conservative elites. Many lived in the suburbs and would thus benefit from the municipal improvements and higher property values that would come with being incorporated into the town. Both parties had within their ranks building developers who would clearly benefit from investment in local public infrastructure. Liberal Arthur Wakerley and Conservative Orson Wright may have had little in common politically but both had substantial commercial interests in seeing further suburban development.[64] Yet while the issue within the town itself did not divide residents on straightforward partisan lines, the Liberal town council's advocacy of the proposals in opposition to the Conservative county council and Conservative Belgrave local board meant that the Liberal Party were inevitably seen as the scheme's principal supporters – and by implication the strongest advocates of public investment for municipal improvement.

The most time-consuming aspects of the campaign involved the detailed negotiations with neighbouring local authorities. Disputes over sewerage arrangements in Aylestone and Knighton meant that negotiations with the Blaby sanitary authorities were always problematic and on one occasion broke down completely.[65] The county council, in addition to demanding compensation, called for the exclusion of a number of districts from the scheme.[66] Negotiations failed and the town council went to parliament faced with a county council prepared to

[62] *LC*, 21 March 1891.

[63] *LC*, 4 April 1891.

[64] Rodger in Nash and Reeder (eds), *Leicester*, 3.

[65] Letter, J. Storer to Messrs Dyson and Co. [copy], 20 December 1890, LTCLB 102, 20–22, LRO, 22 D 57/102.

[66] *MFP*, 11 April 1891.

lead the other public bodies in outright opposition.[67] Talks with the Belgrave local board were no more successful, although here the town council took a tougher approach and faced down their opponents in the knowledge that they had limited public support from Belgrave itself. Belgrave residents were reminded of the costs associated with remaining outside the borough and the pledges continued to roll in.[68] Similar tactics were tried when the Knighton authorities began to raise opposition – the town clerk urging Wright to contact the press and warn local residents how much sewerage and public work schemes would cost them if the district remained outside the borough.[69]

As with most schemes of this kind some form of compromise was inevitable if extension was to proceed. The final agreement, accepted by parliament, brought almost all of Aylestone and the majority of Belgrave into the borough together with around a third of Knighton and Evington and smaller proportions of Humberstone and Braunstone. In all, the scheme introduced around 33,000 new residents into the borough and increased its total area by over one-third.[70] Although the final arrangements were the product of political deals, the new boundaries were not without logic. The area the town council had wanted to include had been significantly reduced, although municipal officials were generally satisfied, as those areas that had been excluded were largely agricultural rather than suburban in character.[71] Although this meant that some new suburbs would be excluded, in practice the great suburban expansion of the 1880s was slowing up a little, leaving few major anomalies.[72] Financially the promotion of the scheme had not been unduly costly to the council, although they were required to pick up the bill for the cost of parliamentary opposition incurred by the neighbouring local authorities.[73]

The real costs of incorporation were yet to be fully realised. In order to persuade residents of the benefits of incorporation council leaders were forced to make liberal promises and generous rating concessions. Wright made the provision of free libraries, new sewers and sanitary improvement central to the incorporationist campaign. These were measures that would bring direct and measurable benefits to the suburban quality of life and increase suburban property values.[74] Even during the course of the Bill through parliament, there were concerns that the full

67 Letter, J. Storer to Messrs Dyson and Co. [copy], 2 February 1891, LTCLB 102, 302, LRO, 22 D 57/102.

68 Letter, J. Storer to T. Wright [copy], 12 January 1891, LTCLB 102, 148–9; J. Storer to Dyson and Co., 23 January 1891, LTCLB 102, 240, LRO, 22 D 57/102.

69 Letter, J. Storer to T. Wright [copy], 1 April 1891, LTCLB 102, 690, LRO, 22 D 57/102.

70 Simmons, *Leicester Past and Present: Volume II*, 119–22.

71 Letter, J. Storer to S.J.Storer [copy], 20 April 1891, LTCLB 103, 2, LRO, 22 D 57/103.

72 Simmons, *Leicester Past and Present: Volume II*, 122–23.

73 Letter, J. Storer to Messrs Dyson and Co. [copy], 17 April 1891, LTCLB 102, 819–21, LRO, 22 D 57/102.

74 *LDM*, 30 July 1890.

costs of promised improvements had not been calculated accurately. Hitherto, like Manchester and many other local authorities, Leicester was dependent on municipal trading profits to subsidise public improvements and the general district rate. Central to the health of its finances was the profitability of gas retail. However in the early 1890s the gas committee was coming under increasing pressure to abolish rents on gas meters – widely regarded as a punitive tax on small consumers. While the extension scheme made its way through the corridors of Westminster, the possibility of the abolition of gas meter rents alarmed those who knew that without meter rents there would be a substantial cut in gas profits. Municipal officials warned the town's political leadership of 'the present rather precarious position of matters in connection with Finance' and successfully persuaded the council to defer abolition until after the next November local elections.[75] This did, however, leave the Liberal leadership with a problem for it seemed that small gas consumers were being asked to subsidise the municipal extension plans and the rates of suburban residents. The fact that this controversy developed at the same time as a significant labour dispute in the gas department only served to heighten public hostility towards council management of its financial affairs.[76]

Radicals, although generally in favour of incorporation and sanitary reform proposals, viewed the concessionary rating of wealthier suburban areas as thoroughly objectionable. Middle-class Liberals who remained ratepayers in the central area also regarded the concessions as unjust. Nonconformist leader Rev. J. Page Hopps went as far as coming out in opposition to the Bill because of the privileges being conferred on suburban residents.[77] Radical opposition to suburban privileges may, however, have only served to demonstrate to suburban residents just how good the deal being offered was. Some Clarendon Park residents openly resented the amounts they had to contribute to the Blaby Union and accused rural areas of exploiting the suburban districts.[78] Many openly admitted that their support for incorporation was self-interested and that in supporting the Bill they hoped to secure municipal programmes of sanitary works to increase the value of their properties at public cost.[79] Far from being opponents of public expenditure, the underdeveloped nature of suburban estates meant suburbanites knew the importance of attracting investment. Many, however, were shrewd enough to realise that incorporation offered the opportunity to obtain improvements at significantly lower cost.

While Liberal opinion was divided on the justice of the rating settlement, the Conservatives began to see municipal extension as an opportunity to secure

---

75 Letter, J. Storer to E. Wood [copy], 16 March 1891, LTCLB 102, 585, LRO, 22 D 57/102.

76 *LDM*, 25 March 1891.

77 'People like me are rated up to the hilt, and over it, while richer men are absurdly under rated. I do not believe in buying off their opposition by the granting of a long leave of immunity. The Bill is tainted with injustice, and I for one shall vote against it.' Letter, J. Page Hopps, *LDM*, 3 April 1891.

78 Letter, 'Clarendon', *LDM*, 1 April 1891.

79 Letter, 'Clarendon', *LDM*, 31 March 1891.

representation in areas generally less well organised by the Liberal Party than the wards of the old town. Municipal extension required the complete redrawing of the old ward boundaries and the complete reconstruction of each party's electoral machinery. Leading Conservative Cllr. J.H. Marshall predicted 'a very considerable increase' in Conservative representation and called on the party to bring pressure on the independent electoral commissioner, charged with drawing up the new boundaries, in order 'to get such alteration as they thought would be advantageous to their party'.[80]. The public discussion of these matters illustrates that, by this time, both parties saw municipal elections in partisan terms. When the town council met to discuss the proposals for new wards, the Liberal and Unionist groups could not even agree on the composition of a committee to report on the issue. Ultimately the matter was left with the evenly balanced parliamentary committee, but the nature of the discussion revealed just how much was at stake for all concerned.[81]

Predictably, when the parliamentary committee finally reported it produced not one report but two. The Conservative 'minority' scheme attempted to divide Leicester primarily along the lines of economic characteristics, clearly separating the more urban working-class areas from the more mixed class suburbia. Unfortunately for them, this proposal fell apart when the presiding electoral commissioner declared that his remit was to unite the prosperous parts of the town with the more working-class areas, creating wards of mixed population.[82] The Conservatives, who believed that their best hope lay in the creation of new middle-class divisions, were appalled. J.F. Rolleston, the leading Conservative negotiator, likened the proposed merging of the Evington and Humberstone districts to 'joining Mayfair with Whitechapel' – Evington being regarded as 'a health resort' while Humberstone had a reputation for run-down housing and poor sanitation.[83] Although in this case the commissioner agreed to divide the districts in question for geographical reasons, the wards that finally emerged were more akin to the more socially mixed wards favoured by the Liberals.

There remained the general issue of how to balance the representation of people and property across the town – 'how to give property and numbers their due representation'.[84] There was no suggestion that population should be the sole criterion for the distribution of representation. Indeed great significance was given to rateable value in determining the scale of representation. Thus the commercial centre of Leicester and the most prosperous suburbs obtained the greatest proportion of councillors to electoral population. Although all 16 newly created wards were given three representatives each, the number of electors per ward varied greatly. Thus the central commercial ward of St. Martin's had just 1,391 electors on the new municipal roll compared with 2,677 for the nearby, but heavily working-class, Newton ward.

80 *MFP*, 21 March 1891.

81 *LDM*, 1 July 1891.

82 *MFP*, 1 August 1891.

83 *LC*, 1 August 1891.

84 *MFP*, 1 August 1891.

Wyggeston ward, a mixed working-class and lower-middle-class district to the north of the centre had an astonishing 3,353 burgesses, while suburban Knighton had just 1,066 and Aylestone just 986. Although this over-representation of the suburbs could partly be justified by the expectation that the population in the suburban districts would expand rapidly, this cannot explain all the anomalies. Latimer ward, an almost exclusively working-class suburb near Belgrave, had 2,959 electors, despite the fact large areas were still available for residential development.[85] Property values, not people, were the major determinant of a ward's size and representation. Consequently the commercial heart of Leicester and the southern suburbs were significantly 'over-represented' while the urban central wards were significantly 'under-represented' in terms of electoral population. Although almost all wards were socially mixed to some degree, the generous representation of the commercial heart of the town and the more affluent suburbs seemed to provide the Conservatives with a reason for confidence.

No attempt was made to conceal the fact that certain 'deserving' classes of voters would be granted additional representation. Thus although Thomas Smith, the Liberal agent, argued for a mixing of classes in the various wards, he also made it clear that he argued for additional representation in parts of the town based on the social standing of its current and future residents. He, for example, argued for special consideration for the western part of the town where boot and shoe manufacturers were moving over to factory production and constructing new residential estates for newly recruited workpeople. These new style factory operatives were regarded as a special case for generous representation because of their anticipated industrious characteristics.[86] Similarly the Conservatives were particularly keen to protect the St. Martin's ward – the central commercial ward – from being divided into adjoining working-class districts. This was partly because it furnished them with a large proportion of their existing representatives – five of its six representatives were Conservatives – but also to protect the general representation of business, commercial and professional classes. Therefore the small St. Martin's ward survived in an amended form, despite the professed desire of the electoral commissioner to create mixed wards. The economic power of the district and the desire to protect the representation of a 'minority' proved crucial.[87]

The Liberals felt they had the most to lose from the new arrangements. James Ellis, concerned about the changes, urged the party to fight all the new seats in an attempt to thwart the danger of a serious Conservative assault.[88] Liberals on the town council were so unhappy with some of the new wards that they even considered an appeal to the home secretary over the issue. Unfortunately this was not a viable option as the new arrangements came into force as soon as they were published in

---

85 *Burgess Rolls for the Borough of Leicester 1891–2*, LRO DE3278/172 SRI.

86 '...the man who idled Monday, Tuesday and Wednesday each week was no use to himself or to his master, and now as the employers would have to have their men on the premises they would naturally make the selection of the best artisans'. *LDM*, 31 July 1891.

87 *LDM*, 31 July 1891.

88 *MFP*, 29 August 1891.

the London press. If the home secretary had allowed alterations to the scheme, they could not have come into force before the scheduled 1891 election and, clearly, a second election on a third set of boundaries would have caused much confusion.[89] Thus the matter was allowed to drop, but Liberals remained dissatisfied. However much Liberals like Thomas Smith believed that distinctions should be made between the industrious and idle working-class communities, the scale of the electoral inequality between the richer and poorer areas of the town that the redistribution scheme implied was unacceptable. The redistribution was roundly condemned by the Association's agent as 'a scheme which favours the classes at the expense of the masses'.[90]

Despite concerns that the affluent areas of the town had been treated far too favourably, the Liberal Association had little, in general, to fear from 'over-representation' of the suburban districts. The party had done well in the suburban county council elections of 1889 and had rudimentary organisation in most suburban areas. As early as December 1890 the Leicester Liberal Association agreed to co-operate with the local county divisions in holding a conference to discus joint tactics – mainly in view of a possible general election, but also, no doubt, to discuss the implications of municipal expansion.[91] By the time the new ward boundaries were announced there were already separate Liberal Associations in Belgrave, Knighton and Aylestone, which were then grafted onto the Leicester Liberal Association's own organisation, and which took responsibility for municipal elections in their respective districts.[92] Particular care was taken to ensure that the new ward organisations for the new divisions were elected with due regard to local feeling – Smith warning all local groups that unless the new committees were seen to represent all classes of the community, they would not command general support.[93] The smooth transition of Liberal organisation into the new arrangements was in great contrast to the problems experienced by the Conservatives. J.F.L. Rolleston, the president of the Leicester Conservative Association, preferred the party to stick with its existing municipal strategy, 'compromising' on representation to avoid contests and doing everything possible to keep explicit partisan conflict out of council politics. In contrast, Marshall, the unofficial leader of the Conservative council group, had grown frustrated with 'their President going cap in hand to the other party' and called for the Association to fight all possible seats.[94] As the responsibility for deciding which seats to fight lay primarily with local ward committees, direct conflict between the two men was averted, but clearly with such disagreement at senior level the prospects of success were diminished. With each local association following its own course during the

89 *LDM*, 26 August 1891.

90 Letter, T..Smith, *LDM*, 26 August 1891.

91 LLA, Executive Committee, 3 December 1890, LRO, 11 D 57/2.

92 *LDM*, 27 August 1891.

93 Letter, T. Smith, *LDM*, 27 August 1891.

94 *MFP*, 26 September 1891.

election campaign there was little prospect of a united and co-ordinated approach – essential if resources were to be used effectively.

Although the Liberal Association did not meet formally to develop policy for the all-out municipal elections of 1891, the policies their candidates advocated were largely a natural extension of the pledges made during the campaign for municipal extension. No collective manifesto was issued and individual candidates were left to develop their own campaign themes, but in practice the need for public expenditure for investment in public infrastructure soon became the central platform of most candidates. In some areas, such as Knighton, the campaign for public improvements had a distinctively Nonconformist flavour, with calls for non-denominational education and the provision of a board school.[95] In Aylestone, straightforward public health issues held sway, with calls for municipal action to improve sanitation and housing.[96] Some areas were even more ambitious. Belgrave Liberals adopted a wide-ranging platform, calling for free branch libraries, swimming baths, allotments, public open space and municipal housing for their newly incorporated suburb.[97] Thus, although there was no formal policy-making body for Liberals to agree a common municipal platform, a consensus had emerged in favour of more municipal spending to support important public facilities in the suburbs. It was a platform that appealed both to existing residents of suburbia, who saw it as an opportunity to obtain improved local facilities at little cost to themselves, and to those who lived in the old town, but also aspired to move out to the suburbs. Again, this new consensus was not an exclusively Liberal consensus, as the successful Liberal Unionist campaign in Knighton ward followed broadly the same lines, but as the Liberal town council had promoted extension, they inevitably became closely associated with the programme of municipal improvements that came in its wake.[98] There was no obsession with retrenchment and low public expenditure. Like their colleagues in Manchester, Leicester Liberals spent much of their time in the 1890s making the case for increased expenditure and arguing that retrenchment in education, public health and housing represented a false economy. Nor was this pressure for increased municipal expenditure coming simply from one section of the party. James Ellis, the president of the Liberal Association, made advocacy of public expenditure for improvement a central feature of his address during the election campaign.[99]

As the tone of the Liberal campaign was largely set by individual candidates, it is tempting to believe that the new candidates recruited to contest the enlarged borough significantly affected the general platform adopted. Indeed in Manchester this was a very significant factor in the adoption of an interventionist Progressive Municipal Programme. However, close study of Leicester's Liberal candidates suggests that the policies advocated by retiring councillors and new candidates were largely

95 *LDM*, 10 October 1891.

96 *MFP*, 17 October 1891.

97 *MFP*, 31 October 1891.

98 *LDM*, 9 October 1891.

99 *LDM*, 28 October 1891.

indistinguishable.[100] The most prominent advocates of municipal interventionism were generally the same figures who had piloted the municipal extension proposals through Westminster, or had been actively involved in the creation of the suburban districts, such as Arthur Wakerley.[101] Although the recruitment of new, often younger, candidates may have shifted the ideological balance within the Liberal group slightly to the left, the general social profile of Liberal candidates was little changed, with only two unequivocally working-class candidates selected – the trades council representatives William Inskip and Joseph Woolley.[102] Moreover it is easy to overstate the significance of a change in personnel as very often new, younger, candidates had a long history of activity within the party and were steeped in local municipal traditions. In De Montfort ward, for example, the party struggled to find a candidate and eventually adopted James Ellis's son, Herbert. Herbert could hardly have been more closely associated with the 'traditional' Liberal Party in Leicester, being a member of the Society of Friends and having a grandfather who represented East St. Mary's ward on the first reformed corporation.[103] Although shared traditions do not necessarily imply loyalty to particular political views, clearly these shared social and political backgrounds were less likely to produce candidates with highly divergent views.

Liberal advocacy of public expenditure and improvement was a natural outgrowth of the campaign for municipal extension and the electoral evidence suggests it was a platform that attracted considerable support. After the November 1891 elections, the Conservatives were reduced from 11 to seven seats, and the Liberal Party's domination of the council chamber became overwhelming.[104] The election left the Conservatives, who had hoped to benefit from extension, in a desperate condition. After threats of mass Conservative resignations the Liberals agreed to elect two of the Conservative Party's most senior councillors as aldermen, although it seemed like an action taken more from sympathy than recognition of merit.[105] Although the Liberal Party faced both Independent Labour and renewed Conservative challenges in subsequent years, the basic pattern of municipal politics for the rest of the century had been set. Of the 16 Leicester wards only two – De Montfort and Knighton – consistently returned Conservatives in the years 1891–96. Even here the limited number of contests in these apparently marginal wards indicates that the Liberals compromised and waived their right to fight seats in return for their solitary Knighton councillor being allowed a free run when his term of office expired. The central wards of St. Margaret's and Charnwood divided fairly evenly between the

[100] Unfortunately it is not possible to provide a detailed breakdown of voting patterns within the Liberal group because of the limited nature of Leicester Town Council voting records for the period under consideration.

[101] *LDM*, 10 October 1891.

[102] *MFP*, 31 October 1891.

[103] *LDM*, 20 October 1891.

[104] *LDM*, 3 November 1891.

[105] *LDM*, 9 November 1891.

parties, but the remaining districts – including the suburbs of Belgrave, Evington and Aylestone – all consistently returned Liberals during this six-year period.[106]

The fears that suburbia was slipping away from the Liberals had not been realised. In 1891 even in the most affluent ward, Knighton, the Liberal Party was only narrowly outpolled by the Conservatives in overall vote share and took one of the three seats.[107] Suburban success, however, had been bought at a price. The favourable suburban rating clauses and the lavish promises of public improvements meant that future management of municipal policy would be difficult. Moreover just as the Liberal-dominated town council had become synonymous with the successful completion of municipal extension, it also became synonymous with its future failings. Even at the height of the party's municipal successes some councillors were uneasy about the promises made and the expectations they had generated. One Aylestone ward councillor made a desperate plea for patience, arguing that local improvements could only be justified when the suburban population expanded to a higher level.[108] However once expectations had increased, local suburbs became increasingly impatient for the promised municipal action. Local councillors came under pressure to deliver on promises, particularly when other areas were perceived as having obtained the benefits of public improvements before their own. When new sewerage proposals were brought forward in 1892, there was an outcry from local councillors when South Knighton was omitted. Consequently the council leadership were forced to pledge that additional proposals for South Knighton would be brought forward within the month.[109] Although this pledge no doubt pleased South Knighton residents, other areas began to resent what they saw as priority being given to wealthier districts. Thus Liberal councillors in Newfoundpool used the extra expenditure in South Knighton to argue for a better deal for their own area.[110] Belgrave Liberals lobbied hard for a branch library, pointing out how it had been one of the promised benefits of incorporation, yet it was four years before the expansion of branch free services came before the council. Once Belgrave had raised the issue, representatives of other areas demanded action for their wards. When proposals for new branch libraries emerged from committee, only Aylestone Park, Clarendon Park and St. Leonards were included, enraging councillors from the other suburbs of Belgrave, North Evington and New Humberstone.[111] Again there was the suspicion that the wealthier districts were obtaining priority, much to the annoyance of Radicals.

All these demands placed upward pressure on municipal expenditure. With each new suburb competing for resources, each new municipal development in one area brought demands for action in another. Increased rates in the wake of municipal

---

106 See appendix three.

107 *MFP*, 7 November 1891; *LDM*, 3 November 1891.

108 *MFP*, 7 November 1891.

109 *LDM*, 27 April 1891.

110 *LDM*, 13 October 1891.

111 *LDM*, 27 February 1895.

expansion sounded the alarm for some Liberals. The Radical press put the short-term financial crisis down to the complacency of municipal leaders who had long enjoyed a steady income from gas and water profits and called for a period of 'economy' after the recent expansion in municipal activities.[112] Politically, however, this had become more difficult than ever. Pledges to the suburbs had to be redeemed. The Liberal council group had such a large majority that members could not easily be coerced into following a party whip and the decentralised structure of party organisation meant that local representatives needed the support of their ward committees to secure election – not the central party organisation. Thus local representatives from suburban districts became, for a time, as much advocates of particular local interests as members of a political party. Advocacy of municipal improvement programmes had proved popular and was often essential for both the political status and public health of suburban districts.

The difficulties associated with resolving these conflicts become one of the most important challenges for municipal leaders. The Conservatives, although often highly critical of alleged Liberal extravagance, had also been associated with a major expansion of municipal activity. It was, after all, a Conservative leader who played a major role in bringing gas and water enterprises under municipal control.[113] The issue of the suburbs rendered a much more interventionist municipal policy necessary, both for the public health of the new suburban districts and in order to justify municipal incorporation of those districts. Favourable rating clauses gave suburban residents the opportunity to have their district infrastructure developed and the expense shared with the whole town. Liberal suburbanites could therefore hardly oppose this type of expansion in municipal activity. Far from being obsessed with municipal economy, election results indicate widespread support for this extended municipal activity, which brought the direct benefits of improved local facilities and higher land values. Liberal determination to develop the suburbs was in part a response to the housing problems of the town and fitted in well with the growing working-class aspirations for suburban existence. However expenditure on the suburbs naturally caused resentment from those who continued to live in the overcrowded town centre. This perhaps goes some way to explaining why the Leicester Independent Labour Party, and to some degree the Radical press, adopted at times a somewhat old-fashioned platform of retrenchment, campaigning against municipal extravagance, in the mid-1890s.[114] The competition between the suburbs for resources, however, naturally maintained the upward pressure on expenditure, but as suburban residents were the main beneficiaries, protests from the suburbs were muted. Far from the middle and upper elements of the working class retreating to suburbia to escape the high taxation of the Liberal town council, suburbanites embraced the Liberal town council for the opportunity it provided for the provision of public infrastructure at lower cost than would otherwise have been possible with the old sanitary authorities. Suburbia could

---

112 *MFP*, 25 February 1893.

113 Elliott, *Victorian Leicester*, 157–60.

114 Elliott, *Victorian Leicester*, 157–60.

not be persuaded to join the town without generous promises of improved public services. Liberals were therefore forced to adopt a more interventionist policy to meet these demands. In doing so they established a powerful political base in suburbia and became closely associated with the collective provision of public services of all kinds – water, sanitation, gas, free libraries, public allotments and open spaces. Thus there was a close relationship between the process of municipal incorporation and the growth of collectivism. In contrast to Liberals in Manchester, the Leicester's Liberal leadership had adopted an interventionist progressive municipal programme almost by accident. It was, however, a programme that could only be implemented at the cost of generous concessions to wealthier districts. Thus, somewhat ironically, in Leicester it was the Liberal Party's traditional working-class supporters who were most critical of the growth of municipal collectivism.

PART V
The Challenge of Progressivism

CHAPTER NINE

Manchester and the Rise of Progressivism

Manchester has a good claim to be the birthplace of the modern British Labour movement. It provided the location for the first Trades Union Congress, it played a large part in the formation of the Independent Labour Party and it was home to the pioneering Labour Church Movement. Yet 'Cottonopolis' did not become a staunch supporter of Socialist and independent labour politics until well into the twentieth century. Indeed the major cotton trade unions of the north-west became synonymous with opposition to independent labour politics after famously opposing the formation of the Labour Representation Committee at the 1899 Trades Union Congress.[1] In his seminal work on the ILP, Howell spent little time analysing the Manchester party, regarding the limited progress it did make as largely a product of labour and trade union loyalties, rather than a result of its socialist programme.[2] Part of the reason for the difficulties in establishing an independent labour movement in Manchester was the economic and cultural fragmentation of the working class. By the late nineteenth century the depiction of Manchester as 'Cottonopolis' was only partly accurate. The large cotton warehouses springing up around the major railway stations paid testimony to the emergence of Manchester as a leading distribution centre, but by the end of the century most of the cotton spinning and production had moved to towns on the periphery of the city.[3] This clearly had profound implications for the city's labour politics. The Conservative cotton union leader James Mawdsley often attempted to use his influence to sway Manchester cotton workers during election times. However the decline of cotton production in central Manchester deprived him of a constituency and threatened to weaken Conservative influence in many working-class neighbourhoods in Manchester. In 1891 one cotton operative estimated that only 266 spinners were left working in the North-East parliamentary division – once an area dominated by cotton production.[4]

The diversification of Manchester's industrial base brought new challenges to those concerned with organising the working class. Major infrastructure projects such as railway improvements and the Manchester Ship Canal brought waves of unskilled

[1] J. Hill, 'Working Class Politics in Lancashire 1885–1906, A Regional Study in the Origins of the Labour Party', Unpublished PhD thesis, University of Keele, 1969, 4.

[2] D. Howell, *British Workers and the Independent Labour Party 1888–1906* (Manchester, 1983), 221–5.

[3] A. Kidd, *Manchester*, second edition (Keele, 1996), 106–11.

[4] Letter, 'Cotton Operative', *MG*, 5 October 1891.

labourers into the city. The old small trades in the workshops of Ancoats and the tailors' shops of Strangeways continued to exist alongside the new railway and engineering works of Gorton and the chemical plants along the city's waterfronts.[5] Significant ethnic and racial divisions reinforced the city's fragmented and diverse labour market. Manchester's substantial Jewish and Irish communities are well known, but the city also became home to a thriving Italian community and various nationalities from Eastern Europe. These ethnic loyalties and differences were used by both major parties to rally electoral support. Stephen Chesters Thompson successfully built up a strong Conservative East Manchester constituency with populist appeals to the 'loyalist' and Unionist sympathies of the indigenous population and in opposition to the alleged dangers of Irish Home Rule. The Liberals, in contrast, derived much support from the Jewish traders of North Manchester and from the Irish of North and North-East Manchester – with North Manchester quickly becoming the safest Liberal seat in the city.[6]

Independent labour politicians also faced a Liberal Party at least nominally committed to a form of Progressivism that seemed to offer a viable alternative way of securing direct labour representation, obviating the need to create a new political party for the purpose. Led by C.P. Scott, Manchester Liberals devised a Progressive Municipal Programme and made direct attempts to increase the number of working-class representatives elected under the auspices of the party.[7] Although several writers have been somewhat sceptical as to how far the Liberals were genuinely committed to a Progressive agenda, the New Liberalism of the Edwardian era can claim to be as much a product of Manchester as London.[8] It is also important to recognise, in all the excitement of the New Liberal agenda, that by 1895 Manchester was a city in which the Conservatives seemed to be in the political ascendancy. With the Liberal Unionists as allies, the Conservatives enjoyed a majority on the city council and in 1895 won five of the Manchester's six parliamentary seats, including overwhelmingly working-class divisions such as South-West and North-East Manchester. Thus the growth of the ILP threatened the Conservative position as much as that of the Liberals.

As in Leicester, and in other areas like Bradford, the growth of the Independent Labour Party was associated with the increasing appetite of local trade unions for direct labour representation.[9] The development of New Trades Unions, in forging new trade associations in formerly unorganised trades, provided not only a potential source of support for an independent party, free from the party political guidance of older unions, but also acted as important training grounds for a new generation

---

[5] J. Hill, 'Manchester and Salford Politics and the Early Development of the Independent Labour Party', *International Review of Social History*, 26 (1981), 171–201.

[6] See F.W.S. Craig (ed.), *British Parliamentary Election Results1885–1918*, second edition (Aldershot, 1989), 149.

[7] P.F. Clark, *Lancashire and the New Liberalism* (Cambridge, 1971), 162–3.

[8] Howell, *British Workers*, 229.

[9] J. Reynolds and K. Laybourn, 'The Emergence of the Independent Labour Party in Bradford', *International Review of Social History*, 20, (1975), 313–46.

of political organisers. Leonard Hall, responsible for much of the ILP's early organisation in Lancashire, gained considerable political experience from his work in organising the navvies' union and before the age of 30 had worked in the labour movement for nine years.[10] Some of the New Trades Unions were the product of special efforts by established unions, whilst others emerged almost spontaneously as a result of industrial disputes – for example a dispute over alleged employee fraud persuaded the Manchester tramway guards to form a union.[11]

Much of the enthusiasm for establishing New Unions, however, diminished after a damaging strike in the municipal gas department. The National Union of Gas Workers and General Labourers had, by the autumn of 1889, established a large branch amongst the Manchester gas employees. Calls for improvements in wages and conditions fell on deaf ears, provoking a mass walk-out. Corporation officials responded by devising elaborate plans to help beat the stoppage and taking on an entirely new workforce. Most senior Liberals on the council supported the action of their officials believing the strike to be largely the result of 'agitators'.[12] There was, however, evidence of significant public support for the strikers. When John Burns came to Manchester to address a meeting in support of the gas workers he attracted a crowd estimated to be over 25,000.[13] Many Liberals outside the council were more sympathetic to the union's claim than those who held offices in it. William Mather sparked controversy by offering to mediate while the traditionally Radical South-West Manchester Liberal Association passed a resolution calling for their colleagues on the council to re-employ the striking workers.[14] These pleas were to no avail. The collapse of the union's resistance did much to slow the momentum of the New Unions and the Socialist League who had supported the strike. William Bailie, the secretary of the local Socialist League, felt that the identification of the Socialist movement with the strike damaged the union's cause in the eyes of the public. The strikers could all too easily be depicted by their opponents as being misled by dangerous agitators. Bailie attempted to distance the League from the New Unions, even claiming that when socialists joined trade unions, 'they abandoned socialist agitation, because they knew that socialism was entirely distinct from these, and its advocacy might retard the success of the union movement'.[15] The credibility of local union leaders was also severely damaged – not only because of the failure of the strike, but because of their own bad organisation and timing. As the Manchester union had been affiliated to the national union for a little less than the mandatory six-month probationary period when the dispute broke, those thrown out of work were not even entitled to strike pay.[16]

---

10 *Labour Prophet*, February 1894, III/26.

11 *Commonweal*, 3 August 1889.

12 *MG*, 5 December 1889.

13 *MG*, 9 December 1889.

14 *MG*, 11 December 1889; *MEN*, 11 December 1889.

15 Letter, W. Bailie, *MG* , 17 December 1889.

16 *MG*, 23 September 1889.

Although there was significant public sympathy for a body of relatively poorly-paid workers, there was also a strong feeling amongst many Liberals that the New Unions were being misled and mismanaged by extremist groups. Consequently the Liberal Party made attempts to recruit influential New Union leaders into their own party. John Kelly, the leader of the Lurrymen and Carters' Union was asked by his local Liberal Association to oppose Alf Settle, a Salford SDF councillor, in a municipal by-election. Kelly initially spurned these advances and gave Settle his support.[17] Yet three months later, much to the disgust of local Socialists, Kelly re-appeared as a Liberal candidate in Ordsall Ward, Salford. Kelly's defection seems to have been as much on personal as political grounds, but the move strengthened ties between the Liberal Party and one of the most powerful New Unions. Many local Liberals also became closely associated with attempts to organise trade unions for women and white-collar workers. Local MPs H.J. Roby and William Mather chaired meetings of the National Union of Shop Assistants and became prominent supporters of measures to limit the hours of retail workers by statute.[18]

Between the Liberal Party and the independent socialist groups stood the Fabian Society. The Manchester branch was formed in 1890 and two years later had a membership of 124. The organisation represented an eclectic group of socialists who widely disagreed as to socialist strategy. Some, such as J.W. Scott of North-East Manchester, were active members of local Liberal Associations as well as being active in the equivalent local groups of the Fabian Society. Indeed, J. W. Scott's branch in North-East Manchester supplied Fabian activists to C.P. Scott in the 1891 parliamentary by-election in the division.[19] Others, such as former Liberal Richard Pankhurst, maintained close links with Liberal leaders while supporting the formation of an independent labour party. Other Fabians were much less compromising, with figures such as William Johnson, Secretary of the Shop Assistants Union, campaigning for the removal of all Liberal Party officials from local Fabian membership.[20] These tactical differences over 'permeation' were not, of course, unique to Manchester, but rather reflected a national debate as to how Fabians could best achieve their political goals.[21] What is remarkable is that the Manchester Fabian Society abandoned the notion of Liberal permeation very early. By the spring of 1892 they were already supporting the creation of an independent labour electoral association and prohibiting Liberals who held official party positions from being members of the local society.[22] Thus in an important sense the Manchester Fabians were not so much an adjunct of the early ILP but rather its forerunner.

Although the New Trades Unions and socialist societies provided a limited base of support for a fledgling ILP, the Manchester and Salford Trades Council did the

---

17 *WT*, 17 July 1891.

18 *Clarion*, 23 April 1892.

19 Letter, J.W. Scott to C.P. Scott, 28 September 1891, JRULM, CPSC 119/78.

20 *WT*, 16 January 1892.

21 M. Bevir, 'Fabianism, Permeation and Independent Labour', *Historical Journal*, 39 (1996), 179–96.

22 *WT*, 19 March 1892; *WT*, 30 April 1892.

most to stimulate wider public discussion of direct labour representation. It did, after all, represent by far the largest single group of organised trade unions in the city. Its role in nominating candidates for public office in alliance with the Liberals made it the inevitable focus of working-class grievance over labour representation. The trades council had long been allowed by the Liberal Association to nominate a working-man representative for the local school board, but had become increasingly frustrated at being given such a small share of the representatives on a body of crucial importance for working-class education and self-improvement. Every time the school board elections came round the Liberal Party organised a conference in which all sympathetic religious organisations were invited – the Nonconformist churches and the Roman Catholics – together with trades council representatives. The conference then elected a committee with the difficult and controversial task of selecting candidates.[23] The curious cumulative vote system used in school board election gave minority and dissident groups the opportunity to break out of caucus control. Provided they were well enough organised and could persuade their supporters to concentrate their votes on just one candidate, they could elect nominees without recourse to a broader political alliance. In order to avoid chaos the various Nonconformist denominations generally preferred to co-operate, but all wanted their own representative on the school board. However if the Liberal and Nonconformist coalition fielded too many candidates this would only result in their votes being spread too thinly with a consequent loss of seats. The determination of the Nonconformist denominations to maintain their own positions made it impossible for the Liberal Party to accommodate many more trade unionists. Thus although the party were keen to negotiate with the trades council, party organisers such as J.A. Beith steadfastly refused to increase the number of candidates the party were set to field for fear of courting disaster.[24]

The trades council offered four names to the Liberal committee for consideration, but only one, George Kelley, was accepted. Kelley contacted the committee expressing his dissatisfaction at the failure of the party to consider his colleagues, but could not persuade its members to receive a trades council deputation to discuss the issue. The trades council felt snubbed and resolved to refuse to co-operate further with the election committee. The Liberals, clearly having misjudged just how much offence they had caused, sought to reopen negotiations, but this time the trades council refused. This was a dispute purely about labour representation, with ideology playing no part in the disagreement. Two of the trades council representatives nominated for the school board, Kelley and Slatter, were committed Liberals and long associated with the local party.[25] The key significance of this dispute, however, was that it prompted a major representative body with significant resources to work towards the creation of independent labour electoral machinery in the city. Trade societies affiliated to the trades council were not obliged to support the new Labour Electoral

23 Letter, S. Woodcock to C.P. Scott, 24 July 1891, JRULM, CPSC 119/69.

24 Letter, J.A. Beith to C.P. Scott, 28 July 1891, JRULM, CPSC 119/70.

25 *WT*, 28 August 1891.

Association which emerged from the dispute, but the snub given by the Liberals was such that in the first six months of the LEA, 16 societies chose to affiliate.[26]

The Liberal school board election committee adopted a programme that the trades council would have found easy to support. The abolition of school fees for every elementary school became central to the Liberal platform. Only differences over representation kept the sides apart. Officials on both sides were blamed for the breakdown in relations between the two parties and the Liberal Association secretary Benjamin Green came in for particular criticism.[27] The subsequent election demonstrated that although the trades council could present a significant challenge to the Liberal Party, it would struggle to get its candidates elected. C.P. Scott's wife polled more votes than the three independent labour candidates combined.[28] Improvements in Liberal Party organisation helped ensure that all their 'Free Board School' candidates were elected and further emphasised the importance of effective party machinery in cumulative vote contests.[29] The trades council's defeat, however, only seemed to spur it on to yet more energetic activity and within months the number of trade societies which had affiliated to the LEA had increased to 30, with very few refusing to join outright.[30] Relations with the Liberal Party further deteriorated when the city council refused to allow the trades council rooms in the town hall for their regular meetings. This refusal had great symbolic significance for union leaders who saw themselves as being deliberately excluded from the official public life of the city, at a time when middle-class philanthropic organisations were freely allowed to use municipal buildings.[31] The gradual breakdown in relations between the trades council and the Liberal Party made many trade unionists increasingly receptive to the idea of an independent labour party and new socialist ideas.

Advocates of independent labour representation were fortunate in having three outstanding public supporters who helped shape the nature of the early ILP in the city. Leonard Hall of the Navvies' Union provided the practical organisational expertise. Robert Blatchford, or Nunquam of the *Clarion* newspaper, was the popular and flamboyant public face of local socialism. Already well known for his work at *Bell's Life* and the *Sunday Chronicle*, Blatchford made his *Clarion* into one of the most lively popular journals of the day.[32] John Trevor, the founder and *de facto* leader of the Labour Church Movement, helped provide Manchester socialism with a strong ethical and religious dimension. Trained as a Unitarian minister in Manchester, Trevor became disillusioned with the attitudes of existing churches towards working-class participation in religious activities and founded a movement that exercised an important influence over many northern towns. Although the

---

26 *WT*, 9 October 1891.

27 *Spy*, 21 November 1891, 33.

28 *WT*, 21 November 1891.

29 MLU, Annual Meeting Secretaries Report, 7 September 1892, MCL, M283/1/1/2.

30 *WT*, 30 January 1892.

31 *WT*, 30 April 1892.

32 *Spy*, 24 April 1891, 3.

movement did not last long into the twentieth century, its ethical teachings supported the political work of the ILP, with Trevor viewing the movement as having an important role in giving a central focus to the work of the SDF, trades councils, socialist societies and the ILP.[33] By the spring of 1892 the plethora of independent labour and socialist groups demanded the need for some level of co-ordination. In some areas independent labour electoral associations had been set up in competition with those of the trades council, and some, such as the North Manchester group, refused to affiliate to the trade council's LEA despite lengthy negotiations.[34] In order to try to bring these groups together Trevor persuaded Blatchford to call a meeting with the aim of establishing one body to co-ordinate the campaign for independent labour representation. Blatchford's position as a flamboyant socialist personality clearly contributed to the success of the initiative. Around 1,000 people attended the first meeting with about 700 supporters allegedly offering their names as potential party members.[35]

The presence of figures like Hall, Trevor and Blatchford in Manchester clearly brought significant benefits to the local movement for independent labour representation. However all three tended to give a greater priority to the national movement than to the detail of party management and organisational development in Manchester itself. Trevor spent much time and money on his *Labour Prophet*, attempting to use it as a vehicle for creating a genuinely national movement. The *Labour Prophet* lost money almost continuously and it had to be heavily subsidised by Trevor's own private wealth. Trevor was particularly keen to spread his message in the capital and in 1895 decided to move south for a time to promote the movement in London.[36] By the general election of that year Trevor was becoming increasingly frustrated with the ILP who, he felt, did little to support Labour Church work. He became particularly critical of church members who seemed to see the ILP as their only sphere of political operations. As the ILP fell short of Trevor's ideas of building an ethical socialist commonwealth, he became far more interested in promoting the Labour Church Movement as a national organisation and far less interested in the day-to-day operations of the ILP in Manchester.[37]

Manchester's other major ILP leaders took up prominent roles in the national party. Local ILP organiser Alfred Settle took the chair of the first NAC meeting, which was held in Manchester.[38] The 1894 NAC elections saw both of Manchester's best-known local activists, Leonard Hall and Fred Brocklehurst, gain election.[39] Although this did not take Manchester's ILP leaders out of local politics entirely, it did provide them with a heavy burden of political work – particularly the work involved in

---

33 L. Smith, 'John Trevor and the Labour Church Movement', Unpublished MA thesis, Huddersfield Polytechnic, 1985, 2–3, 40.

34 *WT*, 13 February 1892; *WT*, 5 March 1892.

35 *WT*, 28 May 1892.

36 *Labour Prophet*, May 1895, IV/41.

37 *Labour Prophet*, July 1895, IV/43.

38 ILP NAC, 15 March 1893, 3–5, ILPC, BLPES, ILP1/1/1 – M890/1/1.

39 ILP NAC, February, 13, ILPC, BLPES, ILP1/1/1 – M890/1/1.

trying to secure sufficient finance to support the work of the NAC. The leaders of the Manchester ILP were effectively trying to help establish a national party before they had had the opportunity to consolidate their own electoral position in the difficult territory of an economically and ethnically divided city. At this stage the Manchester and Salford ILP depended almost exclusively on voluntary workers to establish local party organisation as none of the local party organisers were paid employees of the party. Leonard Hall worked as the general secretary of the Lancashire and Adjacent Counties Labour Amalgamation – a federation of mainly New Unions and trade societies.[40] Fred Brocklehurst took up the general secretaryship of the Labour Church Movement and his duties frequently took him away from the city.[41] Robert Blatchford was much in demand as a national political figure and commentator, in addition to being editor of the weekly *Clarion*. Having nationally important figures running the local ILP was clearly not an unmixed blessing, with local party leaders only being able to devote limited time to the Manchester party.

The determination of local ILP leaders to launch outright attacks on Liberal heartlands in Manchester and refuse any talk of electoral accommodations had significant implications for the relationship between the two parties. To a large extent the network of socialist and LEA groups that had existed before 1892 determined ILP strategy. In several areas the local ILP already had a basic party organisation, such as Harpurhey where activity focused around the Fabian Institute in Rochdale Road.[42] The scale of the Independent Labour vote in those wards the party fought was sufficient to suggest that a breakthrough in some areas of the city was a realistic possibility. The 1892 election saw the fledgling party do poorly in St. George's, a Radical Liberal stronghold in South-West Manchester, but in the other two wards it fought, New Cross and Harpurhey in North-East Manchester, each ILP candidate took over 1,000 votes.[43]

The ILP had emerged on the local political scene at a critical time in the city council's history. Following the general election the Liberal Party could no longer depend on the Liberal Unionists in the city council to maintain a nominal majority. Before the municipal election of that year the Liberals had 49 members to the Conservatives 47 but the eight Liberal Unionists effectively deprived the Liberals of a majority for the first time since the city's incorporation. The city Liberal leadership was alarmed at the new situation and had called for all local associations to fight all seats where there was 'a reasonable prospect of success'.[44] The ILP's intervention in the election forced the Liberal Party to fight a rearguard action in seats they regarded as safe and would probably otherwise have been uncontested. This, of course, meant the diversion of Liberal resources away from marginal wards. Rather than gain seats,

[40] *Clarion*, 14 October 1893.

[41] *Labour Prophet*, January 1893, 2/13.

[42] *Clarion*, 22 October 1892.

[43] *The Official Handbook of Manchester and Salford 1893* (Manchester 1893), 358–60.

[44] MLU, Union Committee, 3 October 1892, MCL, M283/1/1/2.

the elections of 1 November actually saw one net gain to the Conservatives. This loss was recovered in a by-election later that month, but the new Conservative and Unionist majority gradually began to assert its authority and replaced two Liberal aldermen with Unionist nominees.[45] Although party discipline on the council was not rigorously enforced, the Liberals found themselves in a clear minority for the first time ever and under strong pressure from a new political force in one of their strongest constituencies – that of North-East Manchester.

North-East Manchester, with its large Irish population, was widely regarded as the most marginal seat in the city. The Liberal Party long recognised the need to field a candidate with broad appeal to the substantial working-class constituency, as well as Irish nationalist supporters. Charles Rowley, famous in the area for his self-help social reform work through the Ancoats Brotherhood, would have been a popular choice. Rowley was keen to be the Liberal candidate but the 'top end wirepullers' were all too aware of his somewhat crotchety reputation and put a block on his candidature.[46] Radical grass-roots opinion feared that Alex Forrest, a local merchant with a reputation for being on the right of the party, would take the candidature if organised attempts to find an alternative were not forthcoming. William Holland, the head of the local party organisation and a leading local employer, was reluctant to look beyond Forrest, but local party officials approached C.P Scott.[47] Scott's triumph in securing the nomination marked a significant victory for the 'advanced' portion of the party. Scott was, of course, well known for his strong Home Rule sympathies. He was also a powerful advocate and patron of New Unions, such as William Johnson's National Union of Shop Assistants, whose North-East Manchester branch had close Liberal Party ties and was actually based in the local Gladstone Club in Rochdale Road.[48] When a government re-shuffle brought about a by-election in North-East Manchester during October 1891, the Liberal Party naturally anticipated victory in this highly marginal division. The election was one of the most hotly contested ever seen in Manchester, dominating the local press for several weeks and developing into an important symbolic test of the health of Manchester Liberalism. Large-scale factory tours were organised and football fans were even treated to the sight of Conservative candidate, Sir James Ferguson, kicking off the local derby match 'clad in sober morning costume'.[49] C.P. Scott's narrow defeat represented a major blow to Liberal prestige. Both candidates had made a specific pitch for working-class votes but the failure of the Liberal Party to capture perhaps the most Irish and working-class constituency in the city was particularly galling to C.P. Scott who placed so much importance on the Irish and working-class electorate.[50] Many Liberals were wholly bemused and frustrated at the failure of working-class electors to support

45 MLU, Union Committee, 24 November 1892, MCL, M283/1/1/3.

46 Letter, C. Rowley to C.P. Scott, 6 December 1889, JRULM, CPSC 118/134.

47 Letter, W. Johnson to C.P. Scott, 21 July 1891, JRULM, CPSC 119/20.

48 Letter, W. Johnson to C.P. Scott, 1 October 1891, JRULM, CPSC 119/83; 6 October 1891, JRULM, CPSC 119/84.

49 *MC*, 5 October 1891.

50 *MG*, 9 October 1891.

'their party'. Jacob Bright's wife, Ursula, expressed the annoyance of many middle-class Liberals when privately noting 'how dreadfully ignorant and dull the working classes of Manchester are!'[51] More experienced politicians such as Schnadhorst and Holland viewed the defeat philosophically and felt it would be reversed at the general election.[52] Yet within 12 months Scott had again gone down to defeat, despite his advocacy of popular labour measures such as a national pensions scheme and statutory regulation of hours in the retail trade.[53] The frustrating serial defeats of the Liberal Party in North-East Manchester damaged Liberal electoral credibility and led some to look to a possible independent labour candidate as a way of breaking the narrow Conservative hold on the seat.

Following promising municipal election results in North-East Manchester, the ILP began to concentrate its efforts in this area of the city. In September 1893 the party launched a separate constituency branch association in the division which quickly proved a great asset to the city party.[54] Branch officials succeeded in attracting city-wide attention when they were arrested for making an allegedly illegal street collection for locked-out miners. Somewhat inadvisably the city council's watch committee decided to go ahead and prosecute the ILP officials, but then were forced into an embarrassing climbdown after a Liberal rebellion at the following meeting of the full council. ILP commentators rejoiced in the victory, believing that the propaganda generated was certain to improve ILP prospects in the coming municipal elections.[55] The watch committee then lost even more friends by attempting to outlaw street demonstrations by local anarchist groups. Many Liberals, as well as ILP members, were appalled at the apparent restriction of free speech the move implied and joined in protests against their Liberal Party colleagues on the council. The North-East Manchester ILP had not only exposed the somewhat repressive tendencies of local city council leaders, but had also succeeded in dividing many Radical Liberals from some of the Liberal city fathers.[56] Having recorded such important successes in just a few months of its existence, it was almost inevitable that the local ILP would soon develop parliamentary ambitions in this key constituency.

The decision of the ILP to fight North-East Manchester was a disaster for C.P. Scott's own ambitions in the constituency. Once Leonard Hall had conditionally accepted the offer of the candidature, the prospects for the Liberal Party in a three-cornered contest seemed bleak.[57] Initially Scott made conciliatory moves towards the ILP, advising his party colleagues that the new party should simply be seen as the unofficial left wing of the Liberal Party, but predictably Hall, who wanted no

51 Letter, U.M. Bright to C.P. Scott, 9 October 1891, JRULM, CPSC 119/94.

52 Letter, F. Schnadhorst to C.P. Scott, 9 October 1891, JRULM, CPSC 119/96; Letter, W. Holland to C.P. Scott, 13 October 1891, JRULM, CPSC 119/100.

53 *MCN*, 2 July 1892.

54 *WT*, 9 September 1893.

55 *WT*, 16 September 1893.

56 *WT*, 25 November 1893.

57 *Clarion*, 9 December 1893.

compromise, ridiculed these comments.[58] Scott was indeed a genuine supporter of increased labour representation and therefore his subsequent decision to resign the Liberal candidature can be seen as one driven by political principle. However, Scott was also no doubt aware that a three-cornered contest would do little to satisfy his ambitions to obtain a seat at Westminster. Richard Pankhurst, the former Radical and now a staunch ILPer, paid tribute to Scott as 'a high-minded, public spirited man' offering 'a rare and precious precedent of disinterested devotion to the public service'.[59] Scott encouraged the Liberal Party in North-East Manchester to support the ILP candidate. However, the ungenerous response of many members of the ILP to Scott's decision did little to persuade Liberals that the ILP were potentially friendly allies. Hall's accusation that Scott's true reason for withdrawing was simply the belief that he could not win the seat seemed genuinely to hurt the *Manchester Guardian* editor.[60] Hall, in turn, was offended by Scott's apparent suggestion that the ILP were less committed to Irish Home Rule than the Liberal Party. Although Scott tried to smooth relations between the two parties, it was clear that his hopes of conciliating the ILP were failing.[61]

Scott's motives for withdrawing may not have been entirely selfless as other constituencies were interested in him as a possible candidate. The 1891 by-election had helped Scott establish a powerful political reputation and immediately following his resignation Arthur Symonds of the National Reform Union offered to find him a constituency with better prospects.[62] Wisely, for fear of being branded an opportunist, Scott declined to make an immediate decision, although his eventual choice of Leigh proved much more electorally rewarding than North-East Manchester.[63] Unfortunately C.P. Scott's withdrawal from North-East Manchester was interpreted by many as a sign of Liberal weakness. The local Liberal Association was left with no candidate and yet was being expected to support a party that seemed increasingly hostile to it. Many Radicals were clearly confused at the reaction of the ILP to their accommodating overtures. Others felt that if the ILP was indeed to be regarded as simply an 'advanced' section of the Liberal Party, then perhaps they should be a member of it rather than the official Liberal Party. The loss of senior Radicals such as L.D. Prince, the president of the Hulme Radical Association, to the ILP only served to highlight the atmosphere of confusion and impending crisis.[64]

The response of the ILP towards Liberal offers of co-operation was typified by events surrounding the selection of school board candidates in 1894. Liberals attempted to forge co-operation while the ILP were determined that they would only co-operate if Liberals surrendered completely to their demands. The Progressive

58 *WT*, 6 January 1894.

59 Letter, R. Pankhurst to C.P. Scott, 24 March 1894, JRULM, CPSC 120/15.

60 Letter, C.P. Scott to R. Pankhurst, 3 April 1894 [copy], JRULM, CPSC 120/21; *Clarion*, 31 March 1894.

61 Letter, C.P. Scott to R. Blatchford, u.d. [copy], JRULM, CPSC 120/23.

62 Letter, A.G. Symonds to C.P. Scott, 25 March 1894, JRULM, CPSC 120/16.

63 Letter, A.G. Symonds to C. P Scott, 28 March 1894, JRULM, CPSC 120/17.

64 *Clarion*, 13 January 1894.

Liberal committee responsible for managing the elections invited representatives of all local labour organisations to attend its deliberations, including the ILP, the Labour Church and the SDF. Controversy arose, however, on the issue of religious education. The Nonconformist groups present defeated a socialist resolution for secular education in schools and when a socialist proposal for free school meals was ruled out of order on the grounds the issue was outside the board's control, the socialists walked out.[65]

Local Liberal activists were divided on just how to respond to socialist tactics. Harpurhey ward officials continued to insist on the importance of avoiding conflict between Liberal and ILP candidates. Many branches, however, felt any attempts to conciliate the ILP were doomed to failure. ILP opposition to Liberal candidates in some areas of the city was deemed to be motivated mainly by personal dislike – such as that against James Southern in South Manchester. Radicals in South-West Manchester made numerous attempts to come to some form of electoral agreement with the ILP, but after continual snubs they came to the conclusion that further effort was not worthwhile. With apparently no possibility of the Liberal Party reaching an understanding with the ILP at municipal level, the only alternative was for Liberals to take a more confrontational approach and fight the ILP on their own ground. Ardwick Liberals had already experimented with stealing the ILP's thunder by 'including [in the Liberal manifesto] as many parts as could be of the Labour party's programme'.[66] Consequently a committee was appointed to consider the adoption of 'an advanced Municipal Programme for Manchester', although the Union declined to direct the traditionally semi-autonomous ward associations to adopt labour representatives at future elections.[67]

Following C.P. Scott's dramatic withdrawal from North-East Manchester, a degree of panic began to spread through Liberal ranks. The 1893 municipal elections saw eight ILP candidates come forward in Manchester, with the socialists doing particularly well in New Cross and helping defeat one of the two Liberal candidates.[68] Events left Liberals in North-East Manchester particularly divided. Some not only supported the new ILP candidate, as Scott had advised, but also subscribed to ILP funds. This support allowed the socialists to issue 15,000 election pamphlets in the spring of 1894.[69] Others saw the danger that the ILP could pose to the Liberal Party if Liberals encouraged it through well-meaning sympathy for increased labour representation. Edwin Guthrie led moves in Manchester to persuade Liberals to face up to the dangers the ILP posed to the integrity of the party. First he urged the Manchester Liberal Union to consult the national party leadership and the Labour Electoral Association in order to secure more labour candidates for the Liberal

65 *LL*, 21 April 1894.

66 MLU, Union Committee, 17 November 1893, MCL, M283/1/1/3.

67 MLU, Union Committee, 17 November 1893, MCL, M283/1/1/3.

68 *The Official Handbook of Manchester and Salford 1894* (Manchester, 1894), 337.

69 *Clarion*, 5 May 1894.

Party at the general elections.[70] In the absence of Gladstone as a figure who could command the loyalties of all Liberals there was a real fear that the trickle of ILP defections could develop into a flood. However, despite a warning from Guthrie that 'the Liberal Party will suffer disintegration unless steps are taken to forestall and undermine the action of the ILP', consultations with Schnadhorst proved largely unproductive.[71] A Manchester deputation to the National Liberal Federation obtained little other than a promise to consider the suggestion that local associations should be consulted on the issue.[72] It was clear that Manchester Liberals would have to find their own local solutions to the ILP problem.

Part of the solution proved to be the adoption of the Progressive Municipal Programme, although by the time it was used in a municipal campaign the ILP already had a foothold on the city council. The Liberal Party's adoption of the Progressive Municipal Programme marked a move away from local politics in which individuals with party labels fought elections to a system in which parties with specific programmes contested battles over policy differences. Although the Progressive Municipal Programme was not binding on all candidates, it did offer a benchmark against which the opinions of potential Liberal candidates could be tested. The programme was ambitious. It called for an eight-hour day for corporation workmen 'where practicable', a large increase of working men on public bodies, greater municipal control of corporation tramways, ground value taxation and widespread demolition of slum property.[73] Although less collectivist than that of the ILP, the Liberal proposals contrasted sharply with the type of politics the party had pursued in municipal government in the 1880s – a time when the council had obtained a reputation for corruption and mismanagement.[74] Indeed in one sense the Liberals were fortunate in that they had lost their council majority. Had they been in control a large number of the more conservative Liberal aldermen – James Harwood for example – would probably have opposed many of the programme proposals. However, as the party was now effectively in opposition Liberal Party divisions were less obvious. Those Liberals who disagreed with the programme could simply ignore it.

The ILP were, of course, all too aware of the differences that existed between more conservative Liberal representatives and the Progressives, personified by Edwin Guthrie and C.P. Scott. The ILP did all they could to try to associate current Liberal representatives with those involved in the scandals of the 1880s. Housing and building control was a particular focus for criticism. The council's failure to promote widespread housing and sanitary improvement was blamed on the fact that the council's buildings by-law committee was largely composed of Liberal and

70 MLU, Union Committee, 16 July 1894, MCL, M283/1/1/3.

71 MLU, Union Committee, 26 July 1894, MCL, M283/1/1/4.

72 MLU, Union Committee, 19 December 1894, MCL, M283/1/1/4.

73 MLU, Progressive Municipal Programme, 16 July 1894, MCL, M283/1/1/4.

74 See chapter five.

Conservatives who had a financial interest in the construction trade.[75] The council also continued to come into conflict with the ILP and trade unions on the use of streets and public parks for demonstrations, particularly on Labour Day.[76] However, despite populist campaigns against local municipal leaders, the ILP's electoral progress was much more limited than the panicky Liberal reaction may have suggested. As with ILP branches elsewhere, the party faced the key difficulty of how to finance its political activities, particularly as it was attempting to fight as many municipal seats as possible. Various fund-raising schemes were tried, including an unsuccessful co-operative trading society.[77] It soon became clear that the ILP were making only limited progress in the key North-East Manchester constituency where Scott had allowed them a free run. In New Cross Ward, with its large Irish electorate, Irish politicians continued to look to the Liberal Party as their main political allies. A summer by-election in New Cross Ward saw a largely unknown Irishman, standing on a Liberal–Progressive platform taking almost double the number of votes as the ILP candidate, with Irish electors reportedly voting solidly for their countryman.[78] The suggestion often made by Liberals that the ILP were not wholly committed to Home Rule clearly did significant damage to the socialists in Irish neighbourhoods. There were also significant tensions in the trade union movement between the largely Irish Liberal supporting trade unions and those unions that were increasingly coming under the influence of the ILP. When leading Liberal Irishman Daniel McCabe turned up to a Sunday trade union demonstration with his Gasworkers and General Labourers' Union, his political opponents tried to force him to march at the back. The largely Irish union naturally felt slighted, rolled up its banner and left. Suggestions in the national labour press that the Irish action simply reflected the Irishman's 'national gift of perversity' were hardly calculated to improve relations with the Irish community.[79] Indeed it may have been the Irish community in North-East Manchester who were behind Liberal Party moves to reject C.P. Scott's advice and bring out an alternative Liberal candidate to run against the ILP. One group was even reportedly audacious enough to try to persuade Richard Pankhurst to come out as a Liberal candidate against Leonard Hall.[80]

When the ILP finally made a significant municipal breakthrough on the city council it was mainly at the expense of the Conservatives rather than the Liberals. In 1894 the ILP took two Conservatives seats by adopting popular local miners' union representatives as candidates. One of the seats won, Openshaw, was actually located in the Lancashire Gorton parliamentary division, outside the Progressive guidance of the Manchester Liberal Union. Liberals in Gorton had been divided ever since the adoption of a rather conservative railway magnate as Liberal parliamentary candidate

[75] *LL*, 31 March 1894.

[76] *Clarion*, 12 May 1894.

[77] *LL*, 16 June 1894.

[78] *Clarion*, 30 June 1894.

[79] *LL*, 19 May 1894.

[80] *LL*, 16 June 1894.

in 1885; by the 1890s the local mining unions had proved rich recruiting grounds for the ILP.[81] The other ward in which the ILP was victorious was Bradford, another area where miners were influential, helping to elect colliery checkweightman J.E. Sutton to the city council and breaking long-standing Conservative domination of the ward. In neither case did the Liberal Party field a candidate. In the seven cases where Liberal and Labour candidates came into direct conflict, the Liberal candidates polled more votes in all but one. Overall two Liberal losses were counterbalanced by two Liberal gains – a remarkably creditable performance in a year where municipal elections across the country saw the Conservative Party heavily in the ascendancy.[82]

Older unions, like the miners, played a more significant role in securing independent labour representatives on public bodies than the celebrated New Trades Unions. The trades council became a particular focus of ILP political attention with socialists gradually trying to persuade the council not only to support independent labour representatives, but also to take a more active role in the general political life of the city – by organising the annual Labour Day demonstration at the beginning of May, for example. The Liberal leaders of the trades council increasingly felt under pressure, with G.D. Kelley threatening to resign after accusing the ILP of trying to 'nobble the Council'.[83] By 1895 the council's executive committee probably had as many committed ILP partisans in its ranks as Liberals. Liberals largely resisted moves for the council to get involved in May Day demonstrations, but by 1895 they only defeated moves for the council to organise the demonstration by 42 votes to 41.[84] Liberal trade unionists that remained, however, made it impossible for the council ever to become a completely compliant ally of the ILP. The chairman, Liberal Matthew Arrandale, appealed to trade union loyalties to prevent the council splitting on partisan lines, but there were signs that many unions were very unhappy with the growing ILP influence within the body.[85] After the 1895 general election there were a large number of trade union secessions from the council, reversing the generally upward trend in membership since the early 1880s.[86] Hostility to political partisanship within the council meant that the ILP were never able to fully capture its key offices, with trade union loyalties and records of service being more important for promotion within the council than party political views. Kelley, despite his distaste at ILP influence, continued to serve as secretary and in 1897–98 the trade unionists of Manchester even elected a Conservative as their chairman.[87]

The Manchester and Salford ILP were not, in any case, without their own internal divisions and on several occasions these divisions threatened severely to undermine

---

81 See chapter one for the background of the 1885 controversy in Gorton.

82 *MG*, 2 November 1894.

83 *MG*, 22 March 1893.

84 E. Frow and R. Frow, *To Make That Future Now! A History of the Manchester and Salford Trades Council*, (Manchester, 1976), 35–6.

85 *MG*, 28 March 1893.

86 *Manchester and Salford Trades Council Annual Report*, January 1896, MCL, 331.88 M30 LHN.

87 Frow, *To Make That Future Now!*, 35–42.

their electoral effectiveness. In order to maintain democratic control over their elected representatives, the ILP's executive committee adopted rigorous regulations as to the responsibilities of their chosen candidates. Representatives were required to provide regular reports on their activities, submit their election address to the party's executive committee for approval and even leave a signed resignation letter in the hands of party officials in case the party decided to withdraw their support for the candidate.[88] To a large extent these conventions reflected trade union traditions of delegate democracy, but these types of rules were wholly alien to those who had joined the ILP from the Radical wing of the Liberal Party. Radicals traditionally valued local ward autonomy over central control and had fought long battles against the centralising authority of the old Liberal Association and Reform Club. Yet when the St. George's ward branch refused to co-operate with the new rules on just these grounds the ILP executive committee seemed genuinely surprised. St. George's, although only one of 16 branches, was potentially a strong working-class ward for the ILP and even after the branch was suspended from the party its candidate still managed to take over 600 votes in the municipal election of that year.[89] Indeed the conflict was regarded as so significant that Tom Mann intervened in the dispute on the side of the executive committee.[90] St. George's refused to accept Mann's direction and appealed to the NAC to be allowed to affiliate directly to the national party. Such a move would clearly have created a very dangerous precedent and wisely the NAC ruled in favour of the Manchester and Salford executive eommittee, effectively confirming the branch's expulsion from the party.[91] Revelations about the apparent illiberality of ILP internal procedures and the centralised control of the party by an executive committee did little to make the ILP attractive to Liberals dissatisfied with their own party. Moreover the St. George's branch did not let matters rest, launching into attacks on Keir Hardie's *Labour Leader* and accusing it of becoming a mouthpiece for those trying to establish dominance over the local party.[92] The paper responded by trying to smear the dissident candidate in St. George's ward with alleged associations with an employers' organisation.[93] Just when the party was beginning to enjoy a limited amount of electoral success, its leading local figures appeared to be at daggers drawn.

Leonard Hall, by now president of both the Manchester and Salford and Lancashire and Cheshire ILP, became the focus of criticism. This criticism was aimed not only at his powerful role in the party, but also at his behaviour as a Navvies' union organiser. During the height of the St. George's ward controversy a leading ILP organiser from Levenshulme, A.F. Winks, wrote to the NAC's elections and constitution sub-

88 *LL*, 20 October 1894.
89 *MG*, 2 November 1894.
90 *Clarion*, 27 October 1894.
91 ILP NAC, 4 December 1894, 70–71, BLPES, ILP 1/1/1 M890/1/1.
92 *LL*, 27 October 1894.
93 *LL*, 3 November 1894.

committee making unspecified allegations about Hall's activities.[94] At the same time Robert Blatchford began using his newspaper to air vocal opposition to the structure of the Manchester and Salford executive, and, in particular, to the powerful position of president, which Hall occupied. In December the *Clarion* launched a stinging attack on the party's lack of internal democracy accusing the executive committee of being 'too small, and its connection with the party … too distant and too slight'.[95] Nunquam's attacks were the spur for Hall to resign his presidency of the Manchester party.[96] Other members of the executive committee were, however, angry at what they saw as Hall being forced out and little over a month later Hall was persuaded to return to his position at the party's annual general meeting. A key factor in the return of Hall was the support of Keir Hardie who valued Hall as an important figure resisting the domination of the popular Blatchford over the Lancastrian party. Hardie used the *Labour Leader* to write articles in support of Hall and blamed 'unscrupulous gangs of schemers and plotters in Manchester working with might and main to disrupt the ILP movement there'.[97] Liberals were blamed for trying to foster the divisions that had become all too apparent – a curious statement, given that many of the dissentients were desperately trying to regain their membership of the ILP after their branch had been expelled.

Hardie had leapt to the support of Hall largely for reasons of internal party politics – he could hardly have known much of the allegations made against Hall or other local Manchester leaders. The complaints against Hall, however, did not go away and his position in the navvies' union also came under public scrutiny. Several former colleagues issued a damaging statement, accusing Hall of causing splits in the union and misappropriating union funds. Hall was forced to come forward with a detailed rebuttal of the claims, but the rebuttal only seemed to stimulate more gossip about the local ILP leader.[98] Suggestions that Hall had offered to repudiate the ILP movement and work for a Conservative newspaper even reached the NAC, who eventually decided to instigate a full investigation to clear Hall's name once and for all. Part of the problem was that in denying the allegations of financial wrongdoing, he had to admit that he had been forced to repay small sums of money to the London-based navvies' union from which his own union had split. Although there was no suggestion he tried to benefit privately from the funds, the repayment seemed to acknowledge an element of impropriety. The NAC could only say that any discrepancies were 'of a very trivial character' and dismissed the major allegations.[99] Although the NAC had come out in support of Hall it was clear that the Manchester

---

94 ILP NAC, Elections and Constitution Sub Committee, 17 November 1894, 48–51, BLPES, ILP 1/1/1 M890/1/1.

95 *Clarion*, 8 December 1894.

96 *LL*, 1 December 1894.

97 *LL*, 19 January 1895.

98 *LL*, 25 August 1894.

99 ILP NAC, Sub Committee, 14–15 December 1894, 78–84, BLPES, ILP 1/1/1 M890/1/1.

president feared for his position, and sought Hardie's advice.[100] Hardie's support was probably crucial in protecting Hall's position. However Hall's rather controversial past, and his at times abrasive character, had done much damage to his candidature and the party in Manchester, forcing him to admit that he seemed 'to make enemies faster than friends'.[101]

To a very large extent the Manchester ILP had placed their future in the hands of Leonard Hall. He was their parliamentary candidate in a key constituency and took personal responsibility for much of the organisational work of the Manchester party. The allegations against Hall had been highly damaging and although there were no further public disagreements in the first few months of 1895, rumours began circulating that Hall would not contest the general election. In May the *Manchester City News* reported that Richard Pankhurst was to take over Hall's candidature in North-East Manchester.[102] No official announcements were made but a little over two weeks later Hall prompted further speculation about his future by moving out of the city to a new address outside Stockport.[103] Again there were suggestions that Hall was at odds with several members of the Manchester party. Following the constitutional disputes of the previous year, the local ILP had established a rules revision committee to agree once and for all the structure of the local party organisation. After deliberating for four months it achieved little agreement, at which point Hall refused to take any further part in its deliberations.[104] Finally, at the end of June, Hall did what many of his opponents had expected him to do and resigned his candidature – ostensibly because he felt there were insufficient funds to fight the election.[105] It was clear, however, that this was not the only reason for his resignation. Local ILP activists had been told by the Conservatives that they had information about Hall's union record that they would release during the election campaign if he were to go to the polls. This was interpreted as meaning that the Conservatives had obtained a private navvies' union report printed in 1892 that was highly critical of Hall's conduct. It is impossible to say what the precise nature of the allegations were, or indeed if they were true, but the threat of their release seemingly contributed to Hall's decision to stand down. George Beresford, an ILP organiser in North-East Manchester certainly believed that rumours of a Conservative 'trump card' prompted the resignation.[106] Hall's withdrawal so shortly before the election left the ILP in an impossible situation, with the local party facing a complete loss of credibility.[107] The ILP had been handed a golden opportunity to take a seat in Manchester by Scott's Progressives, yet just weeks before the poll were left with no candidate.

---

100 Letter, L. Hall to K. Hardie, 20 November 1894, BLPES, FJC 94/205.

101 Letter, L. Hall to K. Hardie, 23 November 1894, BLPES, FJC 94/207.

102 *Clarion*, 18 May 1895.

103 *Clarion*, 1 June 1895.

104 *LL*, 4 May 1895.

105 *Clarion*, 29 June 1895.

106 Letter, G. Beresford to K. Hardie, u.d., BLPES, FJC 95/149.

107 *LL*, 6 July 189.

The electoral situation in Manchester was complicated by the decision of Richard Pankhurst , the former Radical, to contest nearby Lancashire Gorton as an ILP candidate. Gorton had been shown to be promising ILP territory with municipal victories for the party in Openshaw. Hall's resignation in North-East Manchester seemed to offer the opportunity of an accommodation between the ILP and the Liberal Party. Some Liberals hoped that in return for the Liberals withdrawing from Gorton, the ILP would lift their threat of fielding a candidate in North or North-East Manchester where they, in any case, no longer had a candidate.[108] Richard Pankhurst, never a doctrinaire politician, was open minded about the situation, hinting to Keir Hardie that the party should consider negotiating to secure the withdrawal of the Liberal candidate from Gorton providing this could 'be done consistently with the principles and dignity of the party'.[109] Grass-roots opinion on both sides, however, precluded any such arrangement. The executive committee of the Gorton Liberal Association was strongly in favour of bringing forward a Liberal candidate, agreeing unanimously to field a candidate.[110] The ILP in North-East Manchester were also in no mood to compromise after for so long expecting to challenge the sitting Conservative MP.[111]

Astutely Richard Pankhurst realised that his only real prospect of success was by stressing his Radical Liberal rather than socialist credentials during the course of the election campaign. Although he was unable to persuade the Liberal executive committee not to field a candidate against him, he caused a sensation by persuading the official Liberal candidate, James Brierly, to withdraw.[112] Just like C.P. Scott two years before, Brierly saw little point in opposing an ILP candidate if this meant allowing a Conservative in, especially when the ILP candidate in question had such remarkably similar views to the 'advanced' section of the Liberal Party. Having pulled off this major coup Pankhurst did all he could to display his loyalty to Liberalism in order to attract Liberal votes. At a meeting in Longsight he declared himself to be 'the strongest Liberal candidate in the north of England', and challenged his remaining Liberal opponents to demonstrate how his programme differed from 'the Liberal progressive programme' officially endorsed by the Manchester Liberal Union.[113] Pankhurst was simply stressing the notion that the ILP was merely an 'advanced' Liberal Party – something that many Liberal Progressives believed. Indeed, this was an argument Liberals had often previously used in unsuccessful attempts to negotiate electoral pacts with the ILP. As the campaign progressed it became increasingly clear that the local Liberal Party executive had been completely out-manoeuvred. When

108 *MEM*, 10 July 1895.

109 Letter, R. Pankhurst to K. Hardie, 9 July 1895, BLPES, FJC 95/116.

110 *MG*, 4 July 1895.

111 *MG*, 16 July 1895.

112 *GR*, 13 July 1895.

113 *MG*, 16 July 1895.

Pankhurst eventually persuaded the sitting MP, William Mather, to subscribe to his candidature, the humiliation of the local Liberal Party executive was complete.[114]

Scott, Mather and Brierly all genuinely supported an increased number of working men in Westminster and were not afraid to endorse socialist candidates if electoral logic suggested that by fielding a Liberal candidate the Conservatives would be successful. However, the 1895 election demonstrated the problems of this type of electoral generosity towards the ILP. The ILP, despite their emphasis on a democratic and participatory party structure, were actually as dependent on key political personalities and leaders as other parties. Hall's fall from grace left a vacuum in the leadership of the Manchester ILP. Pankhurst provided much of the resources for the Gorton ILP, but his appeal was as much to Liberal as socialist sympathies, and because the Gorton ILP lacked any real party organisation the branch were heavily dependent on him as a political personality.[115] In North-East Manchester the Liberal Party was once again defeated, but the ILP were humiliated taking little over 6 per cent of the vote in a seat they had once boasted of winning. Pankhurst did much better in Gorton and clearly inherited many Liberal supporters, but still went down to the Conservatives by some 1,600 votes.[116] If nothing else the election demonstrated the inadequacy of Liberals simply leaving the field open for the ILP to tackle the Conservatives. Even when the Liberals were in close political agreement with the ILP candidate on major issues and their former local MP and candidate endorsed the ILP candidate, they could not persuade sufficient Liberals to support a socialist. Moreover Gorton demonstrated that many Liberal Party officials were not prepared to support ILP candidates at any price and would split the party rather than accept the advice of figures like Mather and Brierly. Liberals were seen placarding local walls calling for their fellow party members to abstain from voting for Pankhurst and some even declared their support for the Conservatives.[117] The election had destroyed any immediate hopes of a future electoral agreement between the parties. Hardie reminded his party supporters that official Liberalism viewed the ILP 'with demonic hatred' while local leaders blamed the Liberal Party for the re-emergence of a Conservative parliamentary majority in Manchester.[118]

The Manchester Liberal Party's loss of two of its three seats in the city had little directly to do with ILP intervention in the election. The party's Manchester South seat was won by a Liberal Unionist in a straight fight, but the Unionist majority was only 78 votes in what was by then a marginal constituency. The loss of South-West Manchester probably had much to do with the retirement of popular Radical MP Jacob Bright, and in any case the ILP were very weak in this constituency after closing down the powerful St. George's branch which made up such a large part of

114 *GR*, 13 July 1895.

115 *Clarion*, 17 August 1895.

116 Craig, *British Parliamentary Election Results*, 150, 317.

117 *Clarion*, 27 July 1895.

118 *LL*, 27 July 1895. The Conservatives won five of the six parliamentary seats in the city.

the division. The ILP's only degree of success had come in a constituency, Gorton, where the Liberal Party had been historically divided and where sympathetic miners' unions could give the party at least some organisational focus. The labour press could do little to hide the fact that the election had proved a great disappointment to the rank and file of the ILP.[119] The lack of effective constituency organisation was the party's main handicap. In Gorton, despite recruiting over 100 new members during the course of the campaign, the ILP found it difficult to match the effectiveness of the established parties. Workers, of course, found it disproportionately difficult to be placed and stay on electoral registers and without effective registration committees, it was unlikely the ILP would be able to make much progress against well financed and professional party machines.[120]

There were also other problems in establishing a party based on the form of 'democratic centralism' of the ILP. Figures like Richard Pankhurst and L.D. Prince who had moved from Radical Liberalism to ILP socialism did not fit in easily with the culture of the new party. Whereas Radicalism traditionally favoured decentralisation, pluralism and constructive dissent within the party, ILP socialism stressed the need for collective discipline in accepting centrally agreed policies and rules. Thus it was not surprising that after the 1895 general election more internal troubles broke, just as they had done 12 months before. The dispute focused on L.D. Prince, who as one of Manchester's citizens' auditors, was perhaps the most important ILP elected representative in the city. Over a decade before Joseph Scott had demonstrated the power of the office of citizens' auditor by exposing a series of scandals and mismanagement in the city council that brought fundamental changes to the operation of the authority.[121] Prince, who had long been something of a loose cannon in the Liberal party, was clearly seen as a potentially dangerous adversary by the council. Traditionally the work of citizens' auditor was done without charge, although the office holder was entitled to payment. When Prince came to present the council with a bill of £150 for his services, several senior council figures responded with an explosion of vitriol, accusing Prince of using the money to swell ILP coffers.[122] This also provoked unsubstantiated allegations about other aspects of Prince's financial affairs, with suggestions of impropriety in his dealings with ILP accounts. A detailed ILP investigation found that Prince had no charges to answer, but censured him for 'not loyally obeying the orders of the executive committee in this matter.'[123] Prince, clearly angered by the failure of his party to give him unqualified support after the charges had been found to be groundless, responded by resigning his position as citizens' auditor without consulting the ILP executive committee. In a party where elected representatives were regarded as elected delegates, directly responsible to the party leadership, this move was regarded as the ultimate sin. At the

119 *LL*, 27 July 1895.

120 *Clarion*, 17 August 1895.

121 See chapter five.

122 *Clarion*, 14 December 1895.

123 *LL*, 7 December 1895.

party's annual general meeting the following month Prince was not only suspended but also expelled from the party for failing to consult the local party's executive.[124] A figure who could have been a major thorn in the side of the Liberal municipal establishment was thus permanently lost to the ILP.

For the ILP loyalty to the labour brotherhood was all, but taken to extremes the culture it engendered could be counterproductive. It meant that many of those from the Liberal Radical tradition were permanently marginalised, with dissenters from collectively agreed positions having little role to play. This culture discouraged any thoughts of co-operation with those of other parties, like C.P. Scott, who did genuinely support a much greater level of labour representation in Westminster. It also antagonised those Progressive Liberals, like Edwin Guthrie, who turned from being moderately sympathetic to the broad goals that the ILP represented to believing that the ILP must be fought and defeated if the Liberal Party was to survive. The possibility of a Progressive alliance as envisaged by C.P. Scott and others, was also undermined by the failure of the ILP to put up a sufficiently strong performance where the Liberal Party did stand down in their favour, such as at Gorton. The early successes of the ILP helped ensure that Progressive Liberals gradually became predominant in the Manchester Liberal Union. With C.P. Scott as president of the Union and editor of the city's leading Liberal newspaper, Manchester soon came to symbolise much of the New Liberalism of the next century. However, with the exception of a few isolated instances, the ILP did not emerge before 1900 as the great threat to Manchester Liberalism that many anticipated. When ILP strength was tested at the polls, as in November 1894 and July 1895, the party performed less well than commentators expected. This was, after all, a time when the Liberal Party at national level was in something of a crisis and when disputes over the national party leadership in the wake of Gladstone's resignation brought serious questioning of its future role. It was not until a strong labour party emerged in 1900, locked into a nationally agreed Progressive Alliance, that a Progressive Alliance at local level could come back onto the agenda. Even then there were major doubts as to whether it was viewed by Labour politicians as anything more than a short-term marriage of convenience, with Liberal generosity being exploited by a Labour Party prepared to concede little in return.[125] Moreover it is wrong to accord C.P. Scott and the ILP the sole responsibility for turning the Liberal Party towards a Progressive agenda. The Progressives could only be successful in the 1890s because of the changing

124 *Clarion*, 25 January 1896.

125 Two recent writers regard the Liberals as having simply abandoned many working-class areas of Manchester to Labour after 1906. See B. Jones, 'Manchester Liberalism 1918–1929: the electoral, ideological and organisational experience of the Liberal Party in Manchester, with particular reference to the career of Ernest Simon', Unpublished PhD thesis, University of Manchester, 1997, 33, 310–11, and S. McGhie, 'Liberal Politics in Manchester, Oldham and Stoke-on-Trent, 1906–1922', Unpublished PhD thesis, Manchester Metropolitan University (forthcoming). For a short assessment of the national implications of the Gladston–MacDonald pact see T. Lloyd, 'Lib–Labs and "unforgivable electoral generosity"', *Bulletin of the Institute of Historical Research*, 48, (1975), 255–9.

nature of Liberal politics in the 1880s. The creation of a relatively decentralised party structure following the creation of single-member constituencies allowed the 'advanced' section of the party to become increasingly influential at local level, effectively taking over several constituency associations. The Home Rule crisis removed several senior 'moderate' Liberals from the party while municipal scandals brought in a new generation of political leaders on the city council. In 1885 the party was seemingly hopelessly divided, struggling to win just one parliamentary seat, despite its success at national level. Ten years later the party's national leadership was hopelessly divided, but the Manchester Liberal Union were largely united behind a Progressive programme and had largely seen off a strong ILP challenge. Although the city's Liberal Party was a long way off regaining its mid-century supremacy, Manchester Liberalism remained intellectually vibrant and electorally significant.

CHAPTER TEN

The Labour Challenge in Leicester

The two MPs elected for Leicester in 1906 personified the two rival elements of the late Victorian and Edwardian British Labour movement. Henry Broadhurst, member for Leicester since 1894, was a staunch supporter of Liberal–Labour politics, representing the tradition that had dominated the town's working-class allegiances for much of the late Victorian period. His nominal ally, James Ramsay MacDonald, represented a party, in the ILP, that had for more than a decade attempted to wrest 'Radical Leicester' away from Liberalism towards a socialist future. By 1906 the Leicester ILP had became an important player in Leicester politics. It had persuaded the local trades council to become one of the first to affiliate to the newly formed Labour Party of 1900 and by 1912 the local party had as many as 800 paid-up members.[1] In some respects Leicester represented ideal territory for the ILP. Howell has noted how ILP branches were more likely to be successful in towns with a relatively self-confident working class actively engaged in a network of pre-existing voluntary organisations, such as trade unions, friendly societies and Nonconformist groups. Where these types of communities faced an environment of growing industrial conflict, the prospects for the development of a strong local ILP were good.[2] Leicester certainly had a strong network of voluntary organisations, a powerful Nonconformist tradition, and highly unionised industry. During the early 1890s the major trades, hosiery and boot manufacture, underwent significant structural changes, with moves to mechanisation and factory production, leading to rising industrial tension.[3] This suggests that the reason for the success of independent labour politics in twentieth-century Leicester can be traced directly to the rising industrial tensions of the late nineteenth. However, even those who place great emphasis on the relationship between structural changes in the economy and the growth of support for independent labour politics are cautious about suggesting that the early ILP derived a broad base of support from these processes. Lancaster notes just how narrow the ILP following was in 1895 – 'essentially rooted in the skilled section of the two local major trades'.[4] Indeed far from taking control of

---

1 D. Cox, 'The Labour Party in Leicester: A Study in Branch Development', *International Review of Social History*, 6 (1966), 200, 207.

2 D. Howell, *British Workers and the Independent Labour Party* (Manchester, 1893), 278.

3 B. Lancaster, 'Breaking Moulds: The Leicester ILP and Popular Politics', in D. James, T. Jowitt and K. Laybourn (eds), *The Centennial History of the Independent Labour Party* (London, 1993), 43–62.

4 B. Lancaster, *Radicalism, Co-operation, Socialism* (Leicester, 1987), 132.

the trades council, by the winter of 1895 the council had resolved not to support labour candidates of any description in municipal elections.[5] It is therefore a matter of debate whether Labour's twentieth-century successes do indeed owe very much to the structural economic changes of the late nineteenth.

With historians more reluctant to ascribe the rise of the Labour Party to purely structuralist causes, there has been an increasing focus on the role of the Liberal Party as a bulwark against the development of class politics, and the importance of the measures it took to resist competition on the left. Howell, for example, sees the 'strength and quality' of local Liberalism as a key factor in the ILP's potential for success.[6] As with other radical groups, ILP support seems to have been highly volatile in Leicester. Crushing disappointments often followed dramatic successes for the ILP. After obtaining an impressive poll in the 1894 parliamentary by-election and winning a safe Liberal council seat in early 1895, the subsequent general election and municipal elections brought only disappointment. The ILP was not, of course, the first challenge to mainstream Liberal orthodoxy in the town. Numerous radical and socialistic groups operated on the fringe of Liberal politics during the 1880s. Often ILP and socialist support grew from within Leicester's existing Liberal, Radical and Chartist traditions. The Leicester Secular Society, in particular, provided an interesting link between the radical and Chartist traditions of the 1840s and the contemporary Radicalism and socialism of the late Victorian period. Formed in 1853, the society became one of the first established political organisations to offer a platform to socialist thinkers, in the shape of the Fabian Society.[7] In 1889 F.W. Reade, Annie Besant and Hubert Bland were amongst those who spoke to the Leicester group.[8] Fabian speakers proved an attractive addition to the Secular Society's programme and by 1891 figures such as George Bernard Shaw were bringing in record audiences to the organisation's Sunday lectures.[9] From 1885 Leicester had a branch of the Socialist League, whose campaigning style of street corner oratory also revived memories of the Chartist agitation some 40 years previously.[10] In addition to these fledgling socialist activities there was also a substantial branch of the London and Southern Counties Labour League in Leicester dedicated to organising the unskilled trades. A mass meeting addressed by League leader John Simpson in September 1890 attracted a crowd estimated at 2,000, and, through its network of groups based around public houses, the League exercised an important influence on labour politics in the town.[11] Liberal trade unionist leaders such as William Inskip and the trades council were strong supporters of this 'new

5 *MFP*, 19 October 1895.

6 Howell, *British Workers*, 278.

7 F.J. Gould, *The History of the Leicester Secular Society* (Leicester, 1900), 10, 31. LRO, 10/D/68/17.

8 Sunday Evening Lectures Bill 1889, Leicester Secular Society scrapbook, LRO, 10/D/68/6; *Commonweal*, 26 January 1889.

9 Secular Society Report 1891, Leicester Secular Society scrapbook, LRO, 10/D/68/6.

10 Lancaster in James, Jowitt and Laybourn (eds), *The Centennial History*, 79–82.

11 *WT*, 11 September 1890.

unionism' and assisted in the organisation of Leicester corporation workers.[12] The strong trade unionist and labour culture in Leicester was supported not only by the established Radical *Midland Free Press*, but also by an emerging labour press, begun by anarcho-socialist Thomas Barclay, which went on to publish an influential local socialist journal, the *Pioneer*.[13]

Despite all this labour and socialist activity on the fringe of party politics, local mainstream trade unionism largely remained loyal to the Liberal Party. Indeed the local trades council served as an important recruiting ground for Liberal Party activists, while providing a means by which trade union leaders could rise to more senior positions in business and local government. Thomas Smith, the first general secretary of the National Union of Boot and Shoe Operatives, went on to become agent of the Leicester Liberal Association from 1878 to 1892.[14] His successor at the NUBSO, George Sedgewick, served as a Liberal member of the Leicester School Board, became a local magistrate and was eventually appointed a government Inspector of Factories in 1886.[15] Some trade unions clearly found it difficult to retain experienced staff. Edward Kell, a Liberal town councillor and school board representative, quit his post as a union organiser for a position in business, after his union refused to raise his salary.[16] Kell, however, typified the close relationship that existed between the Liberal Party and the trades council in the 1880s, obtaining election to public office as the joint nominee of the two bodies. The promotion of Smith, Sedgewick and Kell, however, removed three of the most prominent Liberal trade unionists from local union ranks, leaving the way for new leaders to emerge in the 1890s, many of whom were less closely associated with the Liberal Party. With the Liberal Party's trade unionist elder statesmen gone it was much more difficult for the party to influence the day-to-day management of trade unions. The Liberal Party continued to promote its most loyal working-class supporters rapidly within its own ranks, but in doing so helped diminish their influence over day-to-day shop floor opinion. William Inskip, the Liberal secretary of the NUBSO, made rapid progress up the ranks of municipal government to become an alderman, but with growing tensions between socialists and Liberals within local branches, he found it increasingly difficult to steer his union's grass-roots supporters away from the influence of the ILP.[17]

The alliance fostered between the Liberal Association and the trade council was not solely the product of a belief that co-operation would secure mutual benefits in the form of increased numbers of elected representatives. Both Liberal leaders and Liberal trade unionists saw co-operation between political elites and trade unions as a way of helping to preserve the industrial peace. In particular, Liberals on both

---

12 *WT*, 19 June 1891.

13 Lancaster, *Radicalism*, 112–13.

14 LLA, Executive Committee, 14 March 1892, LRO, 11 D 57/3.

15 C. Howes, *Leicester: Its Civic, Industrial and Social Life* (Leicester, 1927), 201.

16 *WT*, 29 August 1890.

17 *MFP*, 6 May 1893.

the management and trade union sides of industry saw the creation of arbitration boards as a way of reconciling the interests of trade unions and shareholders. Inskip viewed arbitration as a way of avoiding costly strikes, while drawing attention to the legitimate grievances of those in his trade.[18] Similarly most employers supported the formation of an arbitration system – indeed Liberal Ald. Kempson, who had made his fortune in the hosiery trade, only accepted the mayoralty of the town in 1890 on the condition that the council would support his efforts to establish such a system.[19] Although the hosiery unions were a little reluctant to accept the creation of the board, they eventually followed their colleagues in the boot trade in supporting the board, which elected Inskip as its first secretary.[20] Both Liberal trade unionists and Liberal manufacturers had staked their reputations on support for arbitration mechanisms. Liberal–Labour co-operation thereafter depended significantly on the success of arbitration procedures.

Liberal–Labour relations, however, came under strain well before increasing industrial unrest exposed the problems of arbitration. In 1892 the local SDF brought forward two independent labour candidates. One was heavily defeated but the other, trade unionist Israel Beck, was forced to withdraw from his candidature after Liberals allegedly threatened him with legal action for a minor breach of electoral law.[21] The incident naturally left a considerable degree of ill feeling against the Liberals on the part of the SDF, at a time when there was an increasing breach between the trades council and the Liberal Party on the issue of labour representation and the treatment of municipal workers. Following the extension of the borough in 1891 the town council suffered a financial crisis with all council committees coming under pressure to reduce expenditure. When the largest spending committee, the highways committee, contemplated sacking up to 40 workers to meet spending targets members of the trades council were predictably enraged. Inskip, by then a senior alderman, attempted to defend the authority's decision by arguing that the council must operate in the same way as a private business when it was short of funds.[22] This enraged not only socialist members of the trades council, such as Beck, but also political waverers such as George Banton, the newly elected chairman. The issue highlighted the apparently divided loyalties of Liberal–Labour representatives and the issue of whether trade unionists would be better served running candidates independently of the ruling council group. Just two years earlier the trades council had warmly endorsed the long-held practice of running candidates under Liberal auspices with little opposition.[23] The policy had proved electorally successful with, in 1891, the election of all three trades council candidates, two at the head of the poll.[24] The issue

18 *WT*, 21 November 1890.

19 *WT*, 3 October 1890.

20 *WT*, 17 April 1891.

21 The SDF allegedly issued election literature without the correct imprint. *Wyvern*, 28 October 1892; *Wyvern*, 4 October 1892.

22 *MFP*, 15 April 1893; *MFP*, 29 April 1893.

23 *WT*, July 1891.

24 *WT*, 14 November 1891.

of municipal redundancies, however, brought the problem of divided loyalties to a head. The trades council contacted the Liberal Association with the request that they be allowed greater autonomy in the selection of candidates and be allowed to select a larger proportion of the Liberal slate. Initially the Liberal Association seemed willing to negotiate, appointing a committee to consult with the trades council. However for the Liberal Association to have accepted the trades council's demand to have a free hand in selecting candidates for certain wards would have meant the association having to re-write its own rule book. The association was based on the principle that ward groups were the sole arbiters of local affairs and only they could decide upon candidates. Thus all the central association could do, constitutionally, was urge wards to 'favourably consider' the claims of labour candidates.[25] Liberals had no objection to trades council candidates in principle, but they did object to giving the trades council special recognition and signing over wholesale responsibility for nominating municipal candidates. Ald. Israel Hart typified the attitudes of many members of the Association:

> If the Trades Council had a particular desire that any one of their body should take the part of representative of the ward on the Town Council there was no reason in the world why they should not attend the [Liberal Association ward] meetings and propose a candidate, and if he was acceptable to the burgesses there would be no difficulty at all in having him elected.[26]

The key difficulty was that most Liberal ward associations chose their candidates well in advance of the November round of elections and by the time negotiations between the trades council and the Liberal Association had concluded few vacancies remained. A dispute in Belgrave typified the problem. Belgrave ward Liberal Association, regarded as a Radical stronghold, received a request to nominate Richard Cort, the Liberal president of the local shoe trade union, as a 'progressive candidate' – but only after the Liberal ward committee had already decided upon a candidate.[27] Moreover many resented what they saw as an attempt, by an outside body, to impose candidates on the ward association. As former local board chairman J.L. Ward observed, local wards had fought to win their independence from the oligarchical control of the old central Liberal Association and were reluctant to allow another body to impose a candidate upon them. Others warned darkly about the consequences of surrendering to the 'tyranny' of class interests.[28] The Liberal constitution gave local ward associations a special place in party organisation, making them sovereign bodies charged with representing all local people. Demands that a special organisation representing a class interest be given special status could not be squared with the principle that local representative organisations should be charged with defence of the general public interest.

---

25 LLA, Executive Committee, 4 October 1893, LRO, 11 D 57/3.

26 *LDM*, 6 October 1893.

27 *LDM*, 18 October 1893.

28 *LDM*, 18 October 1893.

The trades council responded by nominating their own candidates in defiance of the Liberal Association. Socialist T.F. Richards suggested the council should take an 'Irish party' approach, using their position to undermine the Liberal majority.[29] The Liberal Party heavily defeated a trades council candidate in suburban Aylestone, but in Belgrave the trades council nominee collected 290 votes, helping defeat the Liberal candidate who went down by just two votes to the Conservatives. The result left Liberal municipal leaders with mixed feelings. While some attacked the trades council for maliciously undermining Liberal prospects, others, including the chairman of Freeman, Hardy, Willis, the town's leading footwear manufacturer, called for speedy action to heal relations between trade unionists and the Liberal Party.[30] Although some manufacturers were keen to build bridges, influential members of the town's largest union, the NUBSO, were gradually drifting away from the leadership of Inskip and his Liberal colleagues. Shortly before the 1892 municipal elections H.H. Woolley, the secretary of the Leicester No 1 branch, announced his support for the fledgling ILP and the ill-fated ILP–SDF candidature in that election.[31] Although the ILP remained small there were signs that it was attracting significant members of former Liberal working men and even exercising considerable influence within Liberal working-men's clubs. Its first group, for example, met in the Gladstone Working-Men's Liberal Club in Charles Street.[32] Loyalty to Liberal traditions, however, inhibited some working-class leaders from embracing the ILP too enthusiastically. George Banton, despite his growing sympathy for the new party, paid warm and generous tributes to Gladstone when the Grand Old Man retired from office for the final time.[33] The Leicester ILP, from the start, was a diverse movement encompassing radicals of all hues and when, in December 1893, it elected to merge with the local SDF, it became imbued with yet another political tradition.[34]

The growth of grass-roots ILP support within the major unions and the electoral conflict between the Liberal Party and the trades council paved the way for a possible Independent Labour candidate at parliamentary level. In March 1894, J.A. Picton announced his intention of retiring and socialists in the trades council saw a possible opportunity.[35] The ILP, however, seemed to be in no position to field a candidate. When Keir Hardie visited the newly opened Independent Labour Club in June he was distinctly unimpressed, with the *Labour Leader* reporting glumly that the ILP had 'no organised existence in Leicester'.[36] The trades council therefore seemed to have been left to make its own arrangements – the principal difficulty being that of finding a candidate. Ideology and political affiliation, surprisingly, played little part in the council's attempts to find a candidate. Former independent labour municipal

29 *LDM*, 30 September 1893.

30 *LDP*, 2 November 1893.

31 *WT*, 29 October 1892.

32 *WT*, 5 November 1892.

33 *LDM*, 7 March 1894.

34 *WT*, 16 December 1893.

35 *LDM*, 3 March 1894.

36 *LL*, 2 June 1894.

candidate, Richard Cort, advocated Liberal William Inskip as a possible candidate.[37] When it became clear that the Liberal Association were contemplating the selection of veteran Lib–Labber Henry Broadhurst as their candidate, the trades council became even more interested in Inskip. Many felt that if Inskip was offered the trades council nomination, and he accepted, the Liberals would not attempt to bring forward Broadhurst, as Broadhurst was likely to decline rather than fight an old colleague he had known for over 15 years. The trades council hurriedly telegraphed Broadhurst urging him not to accept a Liberal nomination until their members had been allowed to consider the matter and vote on the issue.[38] Inskip, however, knowing that Broadhurst was a possible candidate, refused to take the bait. As he had already provisionally accepted the candidature for nearby Northampton, he had a ready-made excuse to decline the offer, and in declining the invitation he made it clear that he continued to favour co-operation between the trades council and the Liberal Association.[39] Significantly, however, perhaps having learned from the episode of the municipal redundancies, he was heavily critical of the Liberal Association for failing to include more working men in the decision-making bodies of the local Liberal caucus.[40] Yet, with no other candidate in mind and with the Liberal Association about to adopt a candidate with excellent working-class credentials, the trades council seemed to have been completely outflanked by an excellent tactical move. The Liberal Association had found a candidate that supporters of labour representation could hardly oppose and yet had been forced to concede no ground whatever to the trades council who were themselves demanding the right to name a candidate.

The Liberal Association's reluctance to open up the nomination process to allow some form of joint nomination with the trades council was the product more of practical political concerns than prejudice. Open-ended nomination procedures had their risks. Recent experience had demonstrated that the search for new parliamentary candidates often opened up divisions in Liberal ranks – the nomination of Richard Chamberlain ten years earlier being the classic example. Therefore not only did the Liberal Association exclude other organisations from the process of nominating a new candidate, they also limited the influence their own grass-roots membership could have on the process, in an attempt to manage the candidate selection process as carefully as possible. A special sub-committee was appointed to receive nominations and make recommendations to the Liberal executive. Only then would the executive committee put the carefully screened names before the general committee of the Association.[41] In the event the general committee were offered no choice at all – even though five candidates were formally nominated and another eight applications

[37] As it was known that Inskip was already seeking a parliamentary seat, the move was not, perhaps, as paradoxical as it might seem. *LDM*, 7 March 1894.

[38] *LDM*, 14 March 1894; *LDP*, 14 March 1894.

[39] Inskip later withdrew from his candidature in Northampton after his union, the NUBSO, attempted to add nationalisation to his electoral programme. See A. Fox, *A History of the National Union of Boot and Shoe Operatives 1874–1957* (Oxford, 1958), 196–9.

[40] *LDM*, 20 March 1894.

[41] LLA, Executive Committee, 6 March 1894, LRO, 11 D 57/3.

received from those hoping to be considered for the vacancy. Nominees included Irish leader Michael Davitt and the well-known Nonconformist minister Rev. J. Page Hopps, but all were rejected in favour of Henry Broadhurst. The sub-committee came out strongly in favour of Broadhurst and the executive passed his name to the general committee who unanimously endorsed his candidature.[42] Broadhurst was, no doubt, a popular figure who may have won an open selection contest in any case. However, by vesting the selection procedure in a small committee and offering no alternative to their members, the Liberal Association leadership avoided the possibility of the alternative candidate being able to rally grass-roots support and thwarting the leadership's aim of appointing an approved labour candidate. With one of the country's leading labour politicians representing Leicester in parliament, the charge that Leicester Liberals were unsympathetic to labour representation could carry little weight.

Had the two sitting MPs carried on until the dissolution, the trades council may well have acquiesced in the Liberal Party's selection. However, when the second member, James Whitehead, announced his intention of resigning, it was decided to call a joint by-election. With a Radical labour candidate already selected, local Liberal tradition dictated that the party should support a 'moderate' Liberal for the second vacancy. A number of local municipal leaders were suggested as possibilities, including former Liberal Unionists Thomas Wright and H.S. Gee.[43] In all 11 nominations were received, and with several senior figures from the local Association potentially in competition, this time the selection procedure had to be more open.[44] After several candidates refused to accept nomination the contest eventually resolved into a fight between Israel Hart, the very well-known and somewhat conservative municipal leader, and Walter Hazell, a printer from Aylesbury with business links to Leicester. Hart had been mayor of the borough on four occasions and naturally started favourite. Hazell in contrast was, in the words of the *Leicester Daily Mercury*, 'comparatively unknown to the electors'.[45] Hart's reputation for conservatism, however, did not go down well with Radicals, and in a secret ballot, Hazell caused a surprise by narrowly defeating his local opponent 194 to 191.[46]

There is little doubt that Hazell was the choice of most Liberal trade unionists. Even George Banton, the socialist-leaning trade council president, declared he was 'personally satisfied' with the result and suggested the council should accept the decision of the Liberal Party.[47] Although there had been a suggestion that the organiser of the shoe trade union may come forward, the union prohibited their employee from seeking nomination.[48] It is likely, therefore, that no further action

42 LLA, Executive Committee, 15 March 1894, LRO, 11 D 57/3; LLA, '650', 21 March 1894, LRO, 11 D 57/3.

43 *MFP*, 18 August 1894.

44 LLA, Executive Committee, 16 August 1894, LRO, 11 D 57/3.

45 *LDM*, 21 August 1894.

46 LLA, Executive Committee, 20 August 1894, LRO, 11 D 57/3.

47 *MFP*, 25 August 1894.

48 *MFP*, 25 August 1894.

would have been taken by the trades council had it not been for the intervention of the ILP's national leadership. Tom Mann, the general secretary of the ILP, led a deputation of local supporters from the newly formed Labour Club and the Christian Socialist Society to a trades council meeting in an attempt to persuade the council to take a more active role. The national ILP could offer just what the trades council lacked – a possible candidate in Joseph Burgess, the editor of the *Workman's Times*, and funds for the campaign.[49] The labour press had accumulated a by-election fund of some £200 and Mann made it clear that with trades council support he would do all he could to make it available to a potential Leicester candidate.[50]

The ILP had to handle the election very carefully. Even the ILP candidate recognised he could not be seen to oppose Broadhurst. Therefore Burgess made it a condition of his candidature that his supporters should support both labour candidates. It was hoped that Liberal trade unionists would be prepared to support both labour men. Liberal trade unionist waverers would, after all, be able to support an Independent Labour candidate without abandoning completely their loyalty to the Liberal Party. Despite this position most Liberal trade unionists continued to oppose Independent Labour candidates outright. When the trades council finally invited Burgess to come forward with a view to being a candidate, 17 of the 38 trade council members attempted to block the move. The prospect of the trades council uniting behind the two labour candidates was bleak.[51]

Despite the obvious ideological differences between the ILP and the Liberal Party, the election campaign was fought out more over personalities than issues. This was perhaps inevitable in that the local trades council was in the uncomfortable position of supporting both an ILP and a Liberal–Labour candidate – and had a membership heavily divided by partisan differences. The trades council could unite their membership only by calling upon their membership to support candidates on the basis of their social class. Consequently Walter Hazell became the focus of trades council and ILP attacks. Hazell's publishing business came under microscopic scrutiny, with members of the Typographical Association being persuaded to come forward to denounce his employment practices and wage levels.[52] In response Hazell and the Liberals were forced to provide detailed rebuttals of the allegations. Hazell was no 'sweater'. Indeed some evidence suggests that his wage rates were actually higher than the union's standard rate and he had a reputation for providing social and recreational facilities on generous terms to his employees.[53] However, by focusing on Hazell's employment practices, the ILP successfully highlighted the key difference between the two labour candidates and Hazell – namely their contrasting social statuses. The ILP could not denounce Liberalism wholesale as the ILP's allies, the trades council, were calling for their members to support both labour candidates

49 *LDM*, 22 August 1894.

50 *MFP*, 25 August 1894.

51 *LDM*, 22 August 1894.

52 *Clarion*, 1 September 1894.

53 *LDM*, 27 August 1894.

– including Liberal Henry Broadhurst. By focusing on the contrasting social status of the Liberal candidates, the trades council was attempting to isolate Hazell from the Liberal trade unionists. Hazell was left in a difficult situation. If he did not respond to the allegations, the mud would stick. If he did respond, he only highlighted his status as a capitalist employer.

Liberal trade unionists were also left in a difficult position. Remaining loyal to the party meant defending the employment practices of an individual of which they knew little. Inskip, who had earlier been asked by the trades council to be a candidate, called upon trade unionists to reject the advice of the council and support the two Liberal candidates. Many other Liberal trade unionists followed Inskip's lead, including George Kell, the former president of the NUBSO, Charles Harris, the former president of the trades council, and W.H. Lowe, the secretary of the shoe clickers' trade society.[54] Publicly the two Liberal candidates worked together, but privately Broadhurst and Hazell seemed to have little respect for each other. Broadhurst was placed in a potentially embarrassing situation in being asked to defend a candidate whom the Typographical Society strongly opposed. National party leaders were also frustrated at the way in which revelations about Hazell were damaging the Liberal Party's reputation. Schnadhorst later admitted privately to Broadhurst that he 'shd. [sic] not have weeped if Hazell had been beaten' and reassured him that he had his 'knife into that gentleman'.[55] Liberal unity was clearly little more than a façade. Liberal Party managers had again attempted to ensure the party remained united by selecting candidates that represented both wings of the party. While this did prevent a split in Liberal Party organisation, a substantial amount of ill feeling remained. The Conservatives were well aware of this and taunted the Liberals for supporting an alleged Liberal Unionist as parliamentary candidate.[56]

The trades council, although containing a heterogeneous mix of political views, issued a manifesto intended to bind Liberal–Labour and socialist supporters together in support of the labour candidates. Although discussion of policies played only a small part in the campaign, the trades council did adopt the language of Progressivism in its campaign calling for support for 'the advanced labour platform'. Despite frequent references to nationalisation and socialism in the platform speeches of Burgess, the trades council's own platform concentrated on reassuring electors that Burgess remained committed to the Liberal Party's Newcastle Programme and temperance reform.[57] Faced with a town with such strong Liberal traditions, labour candidates of all hues had to reassure Radicals of their continuing loyalty to old Liberal maxims. This platform sat somewhat uncomfortably with the traditional socialist oratory of the many ILP speakers who visited Leicester in support of Burgess's candidature – such as Keir Hardie, Jabez Chaplin, Fred Brocklehurst and

54 *LDM*, 27 August 1894.

55 Letter, F. Schnadhorst to H. Broadhurst, 31 August 1894, BLPES, Broadhurst collection IV/40.

56 Hazell was unenthusiastic about Irish Home Rule. *MFP*, 1 September 1894.

57 *Clarion*, 1 September 1894.

Bruce Glasier.[58] Burgess was well aware of the somewhat anomalous position he had accepted. Initially he had been very reluctant to take up the candidature at all for fear of being accused of undermining Broadhurst's chances. Unlike hard-line advocates of the 'Manchester clause', Burgess was not implacably opposed to Lib–Lab candidates and therefore was an ideal ILP candidate for Leicester, where the trades council insisted on supporting both Socialist and Liberal labour candidates.[59] This approach did not make Burgess very popular with more hard-line members of the ILP who did not want to be associated with Lib–Lab candidates of any description. When the Leicester ILP wished to re-adopt Burgess for the subsequent general election the local branch were even worried that under tougher ILP rules for candidate selection, Burgess's candidature could be invalidated because of this more open-minded approach to Lib–Lab candidates.[60]

Burgess was, predictably, heavily defeated, but the 4,409 votes he collected marked the emergence of the Leicester ILP from political obscurity. Significantly, too, there were signs that many voters were placing their perceived class interest above that of their partisan interest. Of Burgess's 4,409 votes only 1,517 were plumpers, while almost 2,000 voted for the labour trades council ticket of Burgess and Broadhurst. Thus Burgess's large poll cannot be seen as a rejection of Liberalism or an endorsement of the ILP's socialist ideology – particularly as the trades council's platform owed so much to Liberal traditions. Instead what had emerged was a small but significant class-based labour vote – voters who looked not so much to Liberal or socialist party labels, but rather to candidates' working-class credentials. The result sent shock waves through Conservative and Liberal ranks. The *Leicester Daily Mercury* blamed the result on a failure of Liberal organisation and educational efforts rather than on the failings of individual candidates, but accepted that party leaders had been insufficiently responsive to 'advanced' opinion.[61] The Liberal Association similarly saw failings in political education as being the main reason for the increasing ILP vote and responded by setting up a special committee for educational work and for the organisation of lectures.[62] Surprisingly, given the nature of the election, many saw the growth of socialist ideology as the key threat to Liberal working-class support. In response the general committee of the Liberal Association passed a resolution condemning the ILP's programme of nationalisation, warning of the danger of the threat to individual freedom that the ILP programme posed. With the municipal elections rapidly approaching many feared that the ILP tide would not only diminish the party's working-class following, but also drive moderate Liberals into the hands of the Conservatives. Several Liberals drew up plans for a Progressive municipal programme and the general committee agreed to refer the proposals to

58 *LL*, 1 September 1894.

59 Letter, J. Burgess to K. Hardie, 16 August 1894, BLPES, ILP collection 94/178.

60 Letter, C.H. Wryman to the National Administrative Council, 29 March 1895, BLPES, ILP collection 95/70.

61 *LDM*, 29 August 1894.

62 LLA, Executive Committee, 20 September 1894, LRO, 11 D 57/3.

ward groups for consideration. Others suggested again opening up negotiations with the trade council in the hope of restoring relations – although with a strong ILP presence in the council the prospects of this succeeding were clearly limited.[63]

The key difficulty for the trades council was that the election had revealed just how politically divided local trade unionists were. The Liberal Party was no longer the dominant force in the trades council, but neither could the ILP command a sustained majority. At the first meeting of the council following the by-election a number of Liberal trade unionists, including Inskip, faced a hostile motion condemning their action in failing to support the agreed trade council slate of Broadhurst and Burgess. Some ILP representatives pushed divisions even further by trying to get the council immediately to endorse ILP candidates in the forthcoming municipal elections. Banton used his chairmanship to steer a middle course allowing further consultations short of committing the council to any one party.[64] It was clear that the only way the trades council could continue to operate in political contests was if it tried to remain above the party battle, and only gave discretionary support to labour candidates where Lib–Lab and ILP candidates did not come into conflict. This presented the ILP with a considerable difficulty. Without access to the organisational support of the trades council and the shop floor influence it wielded, the ILP were forced to organise separate branch organisations like the other parties. Without finance the ILP faced great difficulties in building the type of voluntary ward organisations necessary to combat their rivals. Several ILP members even suggested that the party should try to cultivate the support of wealthy middle-class Liberals to help finance a more effective party machine. This move was rejected for fear of the control which such middle-class individuals might seek to exercise over the party, but the discussion revealed just how chronic the problems of organising separately from the trade council were.[65] During the parliamentary by-election 700 people had handed in their names to join the party at just one eve of poll meeting. The difficulty was how to turn this outpouring of support into an effective political machine.[66] The Liberal Party, aware of the ILP's difficulties, went on the offensive, not only with its educational work, but also by trying to highlight the difficulties in the way of starting a rival political party. J.A. Picton, the former Radical MP, argued that Liberal organisation in Leicester was more open and democratic than many other towns and that 'Labour will find it easier and quicker to democratise and annex that [Liberal] association than to start a new one.'[67] Others tried barbed flattery to attract ILPers back to the Liberal Party, suggesting that 'in the ranks of that [ILP] party they had some of the most excellent Liberals'.[68]

---

63 LLA, General Committee, 20 October 1894, LRO, 11 D 57/3.

64 *LDM*, 12 September 1894.

65 *LDM*, 13 September 1894.

66 *LL*, 8 September 1894.

67 *LDM*, 17 September 1894.

68 *LDM*, 3 October 1894.

Leicester's senior Liberals saw the ILP's rise as the product of a unique combination of local circumstances that could be met by the Liberal Party demonstrating a commitment to labour representation and by allowing labour men to have a greater role within their organisation. James Ellis saw the crisis as a problem of success – after a long period of prosperity in the town's main trades, a general depression combined with the mechanisation of the shoe industry had caused a level of unemployment and uncertainly that the relatively prosperous town had not previously experienced.[69] The crisis could therefore be explained as the product of unique phenomena, rather than as a fundamental problem in the structure and organisation of Liberal politics in the town. Moreover those Liberals in the trades council who had remained loyal to the party showed no signs of being attracted away to the ILP in large numbers. When Liberal trade unionist J.H. Woolley was invited by his party to stand in Westcotes ward he made much of his continuing Liberal allegiance. Current trade council policy committed the council to support all labour candidates of all parties. As the ILP had heavily criticised the Liberal trade unionists for not supporting the trades council candidates in the parliamentary election, the ILP were under pressure to support Woolley in Westcotes, whatever his party affiliation. Firstly the ILP tried to persuade Woolley to run independently of the Liberal Party. When this failed the ILP tried to change the council's policy yet again, so that in future the council would only be able to support candidates independent of all parties.[70] However, by the time the policy change came up for discussion the municipal election campaign had already started and in at least one ward – Latimer – the trades council had already held meetings in support of a sitting Liberal trade unionist councillor.[71] The council was in danger of opening itself up to ridicule. Fifteen months earlier they had decided to support only those candidates who stood independently of the Liberal and Conservative Parties, but after heavy reverses agreed to support Liberal candidates in addition to those of the ILP. After the problems of this position had been revealed in the parliamentary by-election they were now returning to a position of supporting only entirely independent labour candidates – candidates free of any party affiliation. Many trades council delegates feared that the council was simply becoming a political football for partisan interests and that it was in danger of breaking up.[72] Although the resolution to support only independent labour candidates was passed, the Liberal Party did have a trades council-endorsed candidate in the 1894 municipal elections – as for the trade council suddenly to repudiate a candidate they had already started to campaign for would have been even more embarrassing.

The decision of the trades council left the fledgling ILP to fight the municipal elections alone with only a very rudimentary local organisation. T.F. Richards, the well-known shoe trade union leader, fought the working-class Wyggeston ward, but

69 LLA, Executive Committee, 20 September 1894, LRO, 11 D 57/3; *LDM*, 29 September 1894.

70 *LDM*, 5 October 1894.

71 *LDM*, 11 October 1894.

72 *LDM*, 5 October 1894.

in a straight fight with a Liberal fell over 300 votes short of success.[73] In Latimer ward the ILP's performance was even more disappointing. Even though the Liberal Party in the ward split and two Liberal candidates entered the fray, the official Liberal candidate won comfortably by 250 votes.[74] The Liberals, clearly bracing themselves for a much worse result, had amazed themselves, while the ILP seemed to have gone into dramatic decline. It seemed that without the support of Liberal trade unionists, independent working-class candidates would struggle. Just 30 activists attended an ILP election night meeting in dramatic contrast to the several hundred people who had offered their names in support of the party during the parliamentary by-election.[75] There were a few reasons for optimism. The average ILP vote share in the wards they contested was larger than in Halifax or Manchester – although this figure was obviously boosted by the fact they only fought two wards.[76] Crucially, however, the election demonstrated that without the support of the national ILP, its charismatic national leaders and without the active support of the trades council, the prospects for ILP candidates were limited.

By-elections, however, gave the ILP an opportunity to concentrate their organisational resources in one ward, catch their opponents unawares and score important propaganda victories. Thus within a month of T.F. Richards's defeat in Wyggeston, a by-election caused by an aldermanic promotion afforded Richards a second chance and, on a lower turnout, he was able to record a notable victory.[77] Unwisely their Liberal opponents based their campaign on the claim that an ILP victory would mean higher rates – unwise because following the expansion of the town boundaries the Liberal Party themselves had been forced to raise rates substantially.[78] Once again, however, town-wide elections revealed the organisational weakness of the ILP. The cumulative voting system of the school board elections, designed to favour minorities, did give the ILP another elected representative.[79] The subsequent board of guardians election, however revealed just how difficult the ILP found it to fight elections across the town. The election seemed tailor-made for the ILP. A number of Liberal guardians 'elected from the aristocratic part of the town' objected to a rise in outdoor relief for elderly persons over the winter months, and the ILP hoped to exploit this decision.[80] Organisational problems, however, brought heavy defeat. Tensions between rival factions in the trades council prevented that body playing any forward role in ILP organisation – even on issues of general interest to the labour movement. When the trade council president tried to persuade delegates to help organise a demonstration in support of the unemployed, the move was rejected on the grounds that it might once again open up partisan hostilities within

[73] *LDP*, 1 November 1894.

[74] *LDM*, 2 November 1894.

[75] *LDM*, 1 November 1894.

[76] *LL*, 10 November 1894.

[77] *LL*, 1 December 1894.

[78] *Clarion*, 1 December 1894.

[79] *Clarion*, 15 December 1894.

[80] *Clarion*, 29 December 1894.

the council.[81] The council had become politically enfeebled – placed in a position where it could not take a role in any project deemed to have partisan overtones.

Deteriorating industrial relations in the shoe industry produced the conditions that helped sustain the ILP through this difficult period. Liberal employers and trade unionists continued to base their industrial relations policies on the system of arbitration boards established to resolve conflicts between the employers' federation and the NUBSO. The credibility of this approach depended on the boards successfully negotiating mutually satisfactory settlements. However with the boot industry undergoing substantial structural change with the ending of outwork and mechanisation, which undermined the craft status of the lasters, industrial relations deteriorated.[82] Liberal trade unionists, such as Richard Cort, president of the Leicester No 1 branch of the NUBSO, openly criticised Liberals in the employers' federation for using mechanisation as an excuse to drive staff beyond reasonable limits and discharge labour.[83] The crisis came to a head in March 1895 when employers, concerned that increasingly militant unions were not prepared to respect arbitration agreements, signalled their intention to abandon the arbitration framework, and called a 'lock out'.[84] The dispute lasted three months and left local Liberal leaders politically disorientated. Some senior Liberals, such as Ald. Lennard, were clearly embarrassed by their own employers' federation. Some called for new forms of arbitration and urged employers to provide agricultural land to absorb those workers laid off from the boot industry by new machinery.[85] With rising tensions on the streets, two boot manufacturers on the watch committee of the town council resigned, worried that they should be seen as controlling the forces of law and order during the dispute.[86] Initially the ILP were cautious about trying to obtain political advantage from what was potentially a ruinous conflict. When Burgess came to Leicester to speak in support of the unions, he stressed that he would say nothing that would raise tensions or prolong the dispute. As time went on, however, the ILP became aware of the opportunity the boot 'lock out' presented. A municipal by-election in Castle ward gave the ILP an excellent opportunity to test public opinion on the issue. The Liberal candidate J.E. Thompson adopted a curious approach, criticising his own party on the council for not looking after the interest of the ward. Burgess came to Leicester to assist the ILP effort and quickly turned the election into a plebiscite on industrial relations in the boot trade. By giving Israel Beck, a shoe rivetter, the ILP candidature, the party placed the dispute at the forefront of the public mind. The result was a stunning victory for the ILP, with the Liberal candidate coming a very distant third behind the Conservative.[87]

81 *MFP*, 9 February 1895.

82 For details see Lancaster, *Radicalism*, 101–7.

83 *MFP*, 9 March 1895.

84 *MFP*, 9 March 1895.

85 *MFP*, 16 March 1895.

86 *MFP*, 23 March 1895.

87 *MFP*, 13 April 1893; *MFP*, 20 April 1893.

There were however, significant limitations on just how much the ILP could exploit such disputes. When union leaders negotiated a compromise, which preserved a localised system of arbitration but imposed a guarantee bond on unions that used it, most Liberal trade unionists, such as Inskip and Cort, were satisfied with the resolution.[88] ILP leader T.F. Richards was far less happy and criticised other union leaders for accepting the terms. By this time, however, grass-roots opinion had shifted strongly against a continuation of the dispute, and in several factories workers met to pass resolutions condemning Richards's comments.[89] Although the ILP were able to exploit temporary anger against employers they could not mobilise support for a long-term battle against the employers' federation.

Nor did growing militancy in the hosiery industry threaten a major revolt against Liberalism. Shortly before the general election of that year it was thought that a strike by hosiery operatives, determined to resist a reduction in wages, would assist Burgess's candidature.[90] It was a difficult election for the Liberals not only because of the strike, but also because of the increasing differences between the two Liberal candidates. Despite shows of public unity, the Conservatives again taunted Hazell about being 'unsound' on the Home Rule question.[91] Hazell's personal unpopularity was clearly the major reason for Liberal difficulties. While Broadhurst took 9,792 votes, Hazell polled just 7,753, beating the Conservative by just 99 votes or 0.3 per cent of the total poll.[92] The reduced margin seems to have come almost exclusively from a rise in the Conservative vote, rather than through the conversion of Liberals to the ILP. The ILP candidate did little directly to reduce the Liberal majority as his vote actually fell from 15.7 per cent to 13.7 per cent. Industrial disputes of the previous six months seem therefore to have done little to advance the ILP's medium-term electoral prospects.

Part of the explanation for the success of the Liberal Party in heading off the ILP challenge lies in the type of platform the Liberal candidates adopted. Both Broadhurst and Hazell, for instance, placed the taxation of land values prominently in their election addresses and hinted that this could be seen as a step towards the complete nationalisation of land. Following criticism of Hazell in the by-election for his industrial relations record, the town's 'junior' member spent much time stressing the responsibilities that employers had towards their employees and the importance of revised Liberal factory legislation.[93] Even J.F. Rolleston, the Conservative candidate, adopted increasingly collectivist views, prompting one commentator to remark 'Radicals themselves could hardly find a more advanced politician, if they could only disentangle him from the many folds of the British flag, in which

88 Lancaster, *Radicalism*, 101. *MFP*, 27 April 1895.

89 *MFP*, 27 April 1895.

90 *LL*, 13 June 1895.

91 *MFP*, 11 May 1895.

92 F.W.S. Craig (ed.), *British Parliamentary Election Results 1885–1918*, second edition (Aldershot, 1989), 136.

93 *MFP*, 6 July 1895.

he is perhaps a little too fond of burying himself.'[94] For many the feature of the election was not an ideological battle between Liberalism and socialism, but instead a growing consensus of the need to adopt collectivist solutions to industrial and social problems.[95] Following his second defeat in Leicester even Burgess had to acknowledge that the Liberal Party contained many of socialistic views and that a major problem for the ILP was that many voters felt they were more likely to get socialistic legislation from the Liberal Party than from waiting for the eventual success of the ILP. The ILP candidate, however, remained open-minded as to future strategy. Burgess even hinted in a private conversation that if the ILP could not obtain socialistic measures through the local Liberal Party, an 'understanding' with the Conservatives could be the answer.[96] This suggestion was hardly likely to gain him marks from hard-line ILPers, or win him many friends in the Liberal Party who were always anxious to depict the ILP as a Conservative 'stalking horse'.

The Liberal Party's flirtation with land nationalisation and other collectivist measures may have stemmed the earlier flow of Radicals to the ILP but it alarmed some of the party's middle-class supporters. Most of the city's major manufacturers still supported the Liberal Party at this time. Indeed the ILP was keen to emphasise the middle-class nature of Liberal support and associate the party with manufacturing interests, claiming that of the 119 boot manufacturers in the Leicester district, 112 were Liberals.[97] Although this was possibly an exaggeration, Liberals did depend heavily on the support of manufacturers. Non-partisan newspapers felt that Liberals had suffered substantially from the party's association with 'the somewhat arrogant demands of "labour"'.[98] There is, in fact, little objective evidence of major employer defections from Liberal ranks, and the swing to the Conservatives in the 1895 general election was no larger than in comparable towns.[99] The general election did seem, however, to indicate that the threat from the ILP was less than had been previously feared and therefore demands to adopt labour and collectivist programmes seemed to have less urgency. When the option of adopting a progressive municipal programme came before the Liberal Association's executive committee the following October, enthusiasm for the project seemed substantially reduced. The committee ruled that wards should be allowed full freedom to decide how to fight the municipal elections, rather than be forced to accept a programme adopted centrally.[100]

The ILP's electoral reverses in Leicester came as a dramatic shock to the party's activists. Burgess privately believed that he was 'certain to win'.[101] ILP expectations were far in excess of what was realistically achievable. Slowly party organisers

---

94 *Wyvern*, 12 July 1895.

95 *Wyvern*, 12 July 1895.

96 *MFP*, 20 July 1895.

97 *MFP*, 6 July 1895.

98 *Wyvern*, 19 July 1895.

99 In nearby Derby, for example, the Liberal Party lost both its seats on a much larger swing to the Conservatives.

100 LLA, Executive Committee, 3 October 1895, LRO, 11 D 57/3.

101 Letter, J. Burgess to T. Mann, 8 July 1895, BELPS, ILPC 93/110.

realised that having substantial networks of support in the NUBSO was not enough if the ILP were to become a mass party. Consequently the months following the election were taken up with the establishment of a registration committee that would concentrate its efforts in the municipal ward where the party had representatives.[102] The initiative, however, did little to save the Castle ward seat of Israel Beck, won in such dramatic fashion during the industrial dispute of the previous spring. Following the humiliating Liberal defeat earlier in the year, the Liberal Party decided not to put up a candidate and remained officially neutral between the Conservative and ILP candidates. Whether by accident or design this allowed the Conservative to win by 30 votes.[103] Many ILPers accused Liberals of voting for the Conservative in order to wreck the ILP. Bitterness between the two party leaderships reached a new high and Beck was even seen to attend Conservative League meetings some time later in opposition to Liberal candidates. This was, of course, just what the Liberals wanted, with their propagandists able to suggest that support for the ILP helped only the Conservatives.

The key difficulty for the ILP was that it had never been able to capture the trades council and consequently it lacked the level of financial and voluntary support required to challenge the major parties. When the trades council did decide to contest municipal elections with completely independent candidates – such as the Abbey ward by-election of 1895 – the election cost large amounts of money, produced little electoral success, and few trade council members actively supported their own candidate. Shortly before the November round of municipal elections in 1895 the trades council again reviewed its policy towards municipal contests and yet again changed tack, deciding to take no official position on municipal elections until the council could consistently agree on which candidates to support. It was widely acknowledged that to have a large portion of trade council members actively opposing their own official nominees only placed the council in a 'silly and ridiculous' position.[104] Although the council did agree to try to find candidates for the board of guardians' election, a substantial minority remained opposed to fielding candidates in any capacity. Significantly, too, the hosiery union delegates, the second largest group on the council, had been mandated to oppose any independent political action. With the two major unions in the town at odds over political representation, there was little prospect of the ILP turning the trades council into an electoral tool – despite taunts from the Liberal press that the council was allowing itself to become 'the cat's paw of the Socialists'.[105]

The main threat to the Liberal Party appeared to be the Conservatives and not the ILP. In the November election of 1895 the Liberal Party lost three seats – all in straight fights with the Conservatives.[106] The defeats were not, however, seen as

102 *Clarion*, 5 August 1895.

103 *LDP*, 2 November 1895.

104 *Wyvern* , 13 December 1895.

105 *Wyvern* , 13 December 1895.

106 *LDP*, 2 November 1895.

the result of moderate Liberals leaving the party owing to the growth of collectivist policies, but rather the consequence of apathy and complacency arising from Liberal domination of the council. Ward organisations were deemed to be at fault and the Liberal Association executive committee quickly went into consultation with ward organisations to find ways of improving the effectiveness of ward committees.[107] These moves brought greater central control over candidate selection and by diminishing the independent authority of the wards allowed the issue of a Progressive municipal programme back on to the local political agenda.[108] Indeed perhaps the greatest difficulty the ILP faced was developing a relevant local political programme which highlighted important and fundamental policy differences between the two parties. Their main cry, when in alliance with the trades council, had simply been that of demanding more labour representation, but with the Liberals having already adopted several working men as councillors, and one as a member of parliament, this cry was not as potent as in other towns. On the two other favourite issues of the ILP – municipal pay and the problem of unemployment – the Liberal-dominated council had a relatively sound record. As early as the summer of 1891 the town council passed a resolution committing the authority to ensuring all council contractors were obliged to pay the current standard rate of wages to their employees.[109] Although this proved to be a difficult policy to enforce it demonstrated an early determination on the part of the council not to be associated with 'sweated' labour.[110] The council also responded promptly to suggestions from the Local Government Board that local authorities should adopt a programme of public works during the winter months to absorb the surplus labour created by seasonal unemployment.[111] The subsequent public works schemes played a significant role in reducing seasonal unemployment in Leicester with, in 1894, over 2,300 people registering for temporary municipal work during the winter period. The scheme proved to be of particular benefit to those in the shoe trade, who were particularly vulnerable to unemployment – 1,045 of the 2,310 out of work in February 1894 came from this trade, compared to just 180 from Leicester's second largest industry, hosiery.[112] The shoe trade union, was, of course, the bedrock of ILP support. With so many of their members obtaining work through the paternalistic action of the Liberal corporation, tension between shoe trade employees and the Liberal elites – and union militancy – was likely to diminish. Indeed the schemes to tackle unemployment were deemed such a success

---

107 LLA, Executive Committee, 3 December 1895, LRO, 11 D 57/3; LLA, Meeting of Ward Officers and Hon. Officers of the Association, 13 April 1896, LRO, 11 D 57/3.

108 LLA, Candidates Sub-Committee, 6 July 1896, LRO, 11 D 57/3; LLA, Executive Committee, 9 October 1896, LRO, 11 D 57/3.

109 LTC, Workmen's Wages and Contracts Committee, 28 July 1891, LRO, CM.

110 See chapter eight.

111 LTC, Unemployed Workmen's Committee, 15 December 1892, LRO, CM.

112 LTC, Labour Committee Report, 27 February 1894, LRO, CM. This contrast may also have been a reflection of the fact that the hosiery industry was becoming increasingly dominated by female employees, less likely, perhaps, to have been able to do the type of heavy manual work often involved in public works schemes.

that each year they became more ambitious. In 1895, the town council and the board of guardians drew up plans for a land purchase scheme to provide regular work for those displaced from industry.[113]

Faced with a paternalistic Liberal corporation, flexible enough to put aside the problems of rising rates to deal with the unemployed question, the ILP found it difficult to focus public attention on issues of substantial grievance outside the sphere of industrial relations. This led to ILP councillors taking up positions which sometimes seemed absurd even to their own members. T.F. Richards, for example, voted against a programme of municipal technical education on the grounds that the money could be better spent on relief for the unemployed. Many ILPers, however, committed to extending educational opportunities for the working class, were appalled and the local ILP newspaper *Pioneer* launched a stinging attack on the 'consummate stupidity and ignorance' of their own member.[114] The difficulty was exacerbated by the fact that the ILP and the trades council expected their councillors to vote, like trade union delegates, on the basis of a collective mandate. Consequently public conflicts between ILP municipal representatives and the labour organisations were by no means uncommon – indeed sometimes major rows broke out over relatively trivial subjects such as electric lighting contracts.[115] If the ILP's small number of representatives were to be successful they had to forge an effective partnership with local activists, but in reality the ILP was shown often to be as factionalised as their much larger Liberal counterparts. Even on issues of industrial policy there were significant differences, and especially on the role of arbitration in the boot industry.[116]

There are many reasons for the limited success of the ILP in Leicester before the turn of the century, not least of which was the economic character of the city. John Trevor's depiction of 'Shanty Town' Manchester in the labour press contrasted sharply with the relative prosperity of Leicester.[117] Although Leicester's lodging houses did the town little credit, there was little in the way of the appalling living conditions present in many industrial cities of the period. Many unemployed workers were attracted to Leicester in search of work, causing some housing problems, but the ILP found it difficult to attract support from migrant workers.[118] Despite ILP campaigns amongst the unemployed, many were not on the electoral register.[119] Moreover the ILP's main source of support was in a craft union in the boot trade which had suffered a large degree of unemployment through industrial restructuring

113 LTC, Unemployed Committee, 26 March 1895, LRO, CM.

114 *Pioneer*, 2 February 1895.

115 *Wyvern*, 9 March 1894.

116 *Pioneer*, 2 February 1895.

117 *Clarion*, 20 August 1892.

118 See, for example, the discussion of unemployed migrants in the *LDM*, 30 January 1889; *LDM*, 13 February 1889.

119 Lancaster, *Radicalism*, 131. For a recent discussion of the uneven nature of the post-1867 franchise see J. Davis and D. Tanner, 'The Borough Franchise after 1867', *Historical Research*, 69 (1996), 306–27.

and mechanisation. These craft workers had to compete in the local labour market with the new migrants, causing tensions between different sections of ILP support.

One way of diverting attention from these conflicting material interests was to try to build a common fellowship and spirituality in the labour movement, and it was here that Leicester socialists were most successful. During the 1890s the Rev. John Clifford emerged as one the most prominent ministers of religion in the town, professing a Christian socialist gospel and working with the Christian socialist societies to distribute socialist pamphlets to all places of worship in Leicester.[120] Clifford's influence soon stretched well beyond the confines of Leicester's socialist movement. The Rev. J.E. James of Wycliffe Congregational Church, in a largely working-class district of the town, was very impressed by the Labour Church movement and called a meeting to establish a branch in Leicester. Angry at the 'foolish worship of respectability which still holds a large place in our churches', James became one of the most outspoken critics of the failure of Nonconformist churches to involve the working class in their daily life.[121] The rise to prominence of these socialist and labour theologians coincided with something of a crisis for Liberal Nonconformists. Radicals felt that Leicester was fast losing its reputation as the 'metropolis of dissent', not because of a decline in congregations, but because of a temporary absence of outstanding Radical Nonconformist leaders able to sway political and ethical opinion in the way the Revs. Joseph Wood and J. Page Hopps had in previous decades. During the 1895 general election Radical Nonconformists had been notable by their absence from the political platform.[122] Moreover there were signs that Leicester's Nonconformist churches were struggling to recruit and retain talented ministers. Of the six major Congregational churches in 1895, only one had a pastor who had been in office before 1893.[123] For the first time the 'metropolis of dissent's leading preachers were figures who placed socialist and labour issues at the head of their theological thinking.

By 1896 the ILP in Leicester were demoralised by electoral defeat and by their failure to capture the trades council and use it as a vehicle to promote independent labour representation. Unlike the Manchester ILP, the Leicester group did not have a charismatic local figure prepared to stand for parliament, with Burgess as much a 'carpet-bagger' as Broadhurst.[124] Leicester socialists had broken the Liberal Party's overwhelming grip on local labour politics, yet they were forced to accept the election of a local Lib–Lab MP who became one of the Liberal Party's most potent weapons against ILP progress. The most significant impact the ILP had on Leicester

[120] *Labour Prophet*, September 1893, 11/21.

[121] *MFP*, 24 August 1895.

[122] *MFP*, 31 August 1895.

[123] *Wyvern*, 30 August 1895.

[124] It is possible that, as Labour's appeal was one which emphasised the shared working-class community experience of the worker and MP, Labour 'carpet-baggers' were significantly less effective at mobilising class-based support than local Labour candidates. See J. Lawrence, *Speaking for the People, party, language and popular politics in England, 1867–1914* (Cambridge, 1998), 228–9.

Liberals was on the way in which it forced them to rethink their priorities, address specifically labour concerns and take a much more sensitive view of local industrial relations. The adoption of Broadhurst represented a masterstroke of Liberal strategy, and the adoption of Hazell a near disaster. The doctrine that one Radical and one moderate should share Leicester's parliamentary representation was so powerful that it coloured perceptions of electoral reality. Hazell's vote was consistently poorer than that of Broadhurst, and the numbers that voted for the unofficial Burgess–Broadhurst trade council slate marked the emergence of a small but significant class-based vote for labour candidates. Hazell, despite adopting the position of the socially concerned employer, found it difficult to attract working-class support and was unpopular with his own party. Thus his defeat in 1900 at the hands of a Conservative was not surprising – a defeat which paved the way for James Ramsay MacDonald to join Broadhurst as the town's second MP in 1906. However, it is questionable whether rising industrial tension in the boot and shoe industry contributed very much to the long term rise of the Labour Party in Leicester. Following the industrial dispute of 1895 the NUBSO, the bedrock of ILP support, went into decline. Between the end of 1904 and the end of 1906 the union lost 3,000 members in Leicester and the Leicester branches became heavily indebted to the union's central office.[125] Without the support of a strong and prosperous local trade union the ILP's organisational difficulties would continue.

The Liberal Party's key challenge after 1892 was how to maintain the support of both industrialists and workers at a time of industrial tension and when the traditional conciliatory institutions, arbitration boards and the nonconformist churches, were themselves becoming ideologically divided by battles between capital and labour. The fact that the Liberal Party held together and largely maintained its position was the product of skilful political management, an open-minded attitude to policy development and the strength of Radical traditions in the town. Despite Keir Hardie's often quoted objective of wanting to 'smash' the Liberal Party, the Leicester ILP had to accept grudgingly the endorsement of a Lib–Lab candidate in order to maintain unity in the local labour movement. When the *Pioneer* freely quoted Gladstone paying tribute to trade unions as 'the bulwarks of modern democracies', it was acknowledging the fact that neither wing of the labour movement could completely escape its heritage of Liberal influence and cultural attachment.[126] As the 1894 by-election demonstrated, many of the traditional Liberal themes of temperance, disestablishment and land reform had so much resonance with the working-class electorate that they had to form part of the ILP programme. The ILP struggled to break free from this legacy at a time when local Liberalism was both aware of the challenge the ILP represented and prepared to meet the challenge by adopting collectivist policies and selecting a Lib–Lab MP. In Leicester the 'strength and quality' of local Liberalism offered the ILP only limited opportunities to make a

---

125 Fox, *A History of the National Union of Boot and Shoe Operatives*, 239–48.

126 *Pioneer*, 15 July 1901.

major impact on local political life until the debacle of the 1900 general election and the Gladstone–MacDonald pact gave Leicester its first Socialist MP.

CONCLUSION

CONCLUSION

The Road to New Liberalism

Britain's modern highly centralised political system has a tendency to distort the way in which recent political history is viewed. The politics of Westminster are often the focus for research, with local and regional politics largely neglected. The limitations of this Westminster-dominated approach have unwittingly been highlighted by recent work on Victorian Liberalism and the Home Rule crisis. Parry, by focusing on events at St. Stephen's, concludes that Gladstone's actions in early 1886 were disastrous for the party, and marked the end of the Victorian Liberal Party.[1] Similarly, Jenkins views the crisis as marking the end of the Liberal ascendancy, undermining the party's long-term electoral position.[2] These views contrast sharply with the patterns identified in the major urban centres of Manchester and Leicester, where Liberalism continued to be a vibrant force. The Liberal Party was dependent on industrial towns and cities for its national electoral position. It is therefore essential to understand the dynamics of urban politics in order to appreciate the transformation of British Liberalism. Electoral reform, the perceived failure of urban local government, and the decentralisation of urban political authority created an environment where Radical local politics could grow. These processes, in turn, reflected broader urban trends. The growing complexity of the industrial urban economy, the rise of the professions and the developlemt of suburbia had created a larger and more diverse urban elite. By the 1880s there was a growing awareness of the political limitations of existing forms of urban governance and representation. In this atmosphere Liberalism advanced by combining its traditional language of moral reform and political representation with the new collectivist demands of urban society.

Many interpretations of the period are, of course, coloured by historians' attitudes to the men who suffered most from the Home Rule split – Chamberlain and Hartington. Chamberlain's interesting and complex character still stimulates controversy.[3] For so long Chamberlain was perceived by many in the Radical section of the party as an exciting and dynamic figure capable of leading the party into the twentieth century. More importantly he represented a new direction for the party. His

1 J. Parry, *The Rise and Fall of Liberal Government in Victorian Britain* (Yale, 1993), 306–31.

2 T.A. Jenkins, *The Liberal Ascendancy 1830–1886* (London, 1994), 222–6.

3 See M. Hurst, *Joseph Chamberlain and West Midlands Politics* (Oxford, 1962); P. Fraser, *Joseph Chamberlain; Radicalism and Empire, 1868–1914* (London, 1966); R. Jay, *Joseph Chamberlain: A Political Study* (Oxford, 1981); P. Marsh, *Joseph Chamberlain, Entrepeneur in Politics* (London, 1994). R. Quinalt, 'John Bright and Joseph Chamberlain', *Historical Journal* 28 (1985), 623–46.

'Unauthorised Programme' of July 1885 was significant not so much for the threat it posed to Gladstone's authority, but rather for the fact that it marked Chamberlain out as a pioneer of what was to become known as New Liberalism.[4] Heralded as marking the end of laissez-faire Liberalism, it was the first formal party programme ever issued for a British general election, and therefore can be seen as something of a watershed in modern political development. It is not surprising, therefore, that twentieth-century Liberal historians have viewed the loss of 'Radical Joe' and the Unionist split as a significant step in the decline of the Liberal Party, preventing the party developing into a 'modern' social democratic party. In a period when the mass popular press had made national politicians more familiar than ever before to their electorate and helped personalise the political conflict, it is reasonable to attach considerable importance to personalities and the ideas they represented.[5] However, this should not be done at the cost of ignoring constituency-level politics and neglecting the continuing significance of the locality.

Clearly the defection of Chamberlain was a blow to the Liberal Party and its Radical section, but one can exaggerate the importance of Chamberlain to the Liberal movement. Although his 'Unauthorised programme' was mild in content, the Radical language used probably alienated as many voters as it attracted.[6] Similarly the loss of Chamberlain did not necessarily undermine the position of the vast majority of Radicals who stayed within the Liberal Party. The defection of a large section of Liberal Whigs in the House of Lords probably made it easier for Radical ideas to gain acceptance amongst the national leadership and may help to explain why Gladstone was prepared to accept the National Liberal Federation's Radical Newcastle Programme of 1891.[7] Thus the overall effect of the Home Rule crisis was probably to shift the balance of power in the national party slightly to the left. Had Chamberlain stayed within the Liberal Party's ranks it is not at all clear that he would have made an effective party leader or done very much to attract working-class support. He was a pioneer of collectivist social policy and his work on the Birmingham City Council was well known. He was not, however, the only pioneer of collectivist social policies. From 1889 Rosebery, the man who would eventually succeed Gladstone, became synonymous with collectivist reform on the London County Council.[8] Although Chamberlain boasted that his Unauthorised Programme marked the end of laissez-faire, in many respects it was already dead. 'Gas and water socialism' was an established fact in most large towns and cities. It is also important

---

4 D. Judd, *Radical Joe: A Life of Joseph Chamberlain*, reprint (Cardiff, 1993), 116–17.

5 H.C.G. Matthew, 'Rhetoric and Politics in Great Britain, 1860–1950' in B. Kinzer (ed.), *The Gladstonian Turn of Mind: Essays presented to J.B. Conacher* (London, 1985), 35, 45–6.

6 P. Marsh, *Joseph Chamberlain: Entrepreneur in Politics* (London, 1994), 185.

7 T. Heyck, 'Home Rule, Radicalism, and the Liberal Party, 1886–1895', *Journal of British Studies*, 13, (1974), 66–91.

8 R. James, *Rosebery* (London, 1963); D. Hamer, *Liberal Politics in the Age of Gladstone and Rosebery* (London, 1972).

to recognise that the Unauthorised Programme was actually quite limited in its scope. Its most Radical element was its provision allowing local government the power to acquire land for smallholdings – a provision for which the Government had already indicated some sympathy.[9] Indeed it is not at all clear that a Chamberlain-led Liberal Party would have been able to prevent the formation of an independent labour party, or even have attracted greater aggregate support. Significantly his programme made little reference to industrial relations or specifically labour questions. Chamberlain, a successful middle-class entrepreneur, had little time for policies that smacked of Marxist-style socialism – even the LCC's Progressive Programme caused him alarm.[10] Had he attempted to develop the party into one which appealed explicitly to the self-interest of a particular class there can be little doubt that the Liberal electoral coalition would have broken up.[11] Moreover the antagonism between the Liberal Party and the ILP during the 1890s was not solely, or even primarily, of an ideological character. Personal, social and organisational differences also played their part in the disputes. It is unlikely that Chamberlain could have done very much to bring the sides together. Never very much of a conciliator, his impetuous and dictatorial leadership style may have persuaded some labour leaders that the party was serious about social reform, but it was unlikely to lead to harmonious co-operation between the Liberal Party and the ILP.[12]

The ramifications of the Home Rule split went, of course, beyond the loss of Chamberlain. The defection of Hartington deprived the party of a senior statesman and contributed to the movement of Whig Liberals into Conservatism.[13] Many Whig and centrist Liberals looked to Hartington as a leader able to moderate the demands of the Radical wing.[14] Without Hartington, many feared the party would move rapidly to the left, thus encouraging many Whig Liberals at Westminster to follow Hartington's example. This reinforced the Conservative majority in the House of Lords and ensured that future Liberal governments would face a consistently hostile upper chamber – at least until the passing of the 1911 Parliament Acts.[15] It is important, however, not to assume that the loss of high profile Westminster leaders was necessarily replicated at regional and local level. If the Home Rule split was indeed a nation-wide calamity for the Liberal Party it is difficult to explain how the

---

9 M. Balfour, *Britain and Joseph Chamberlain* (London, 1985), 145–6.

10 Judd, *Radical Joe*, 177–8.

11 Some, of course, regarded this as desirable, believing that the 1890s demonstrated the weakness of 'moral' appeals in the face of self-interested class-based programmes. See R. Jay, *Joseph Chamberlain: A Political Study*, (Oxford, 1981), 146–7.

12 Balfour, *Britain*, 221–2, 292–6.

13 P. Jackson, *The Last of the Whigs: a political biography of Lord Hartington, later eigth Duke of Devonshire* (London, 1994).

14 P. Fraser, *Joseph Chamberlain, Radicalism and Empire* (London, 1966), 58.

15 See R. Jenkins, *Mr. Balfour's Poodle* (London, 1968); C. Weston, 'The Liberal Leadership and the Lords Veto', *Historical Journal* 11 (1968), 508–37.

party was able to recover sufficiently to allow Gladstone to regain office just six years later.[16]

Part of the explanation lies in the fact that the crisis at Westminster was not always felt so sharply within individual constituency associations. In Leicester the crisis broke at a time when the local Liberal Association was preoccupied with the issue of compulsory vaccination. For several weeks the Association largely ignored the Home Rule question. Few felt strongly enough about the issue to leave the party and those who did were never sufficiently numerous to establish an electorally viable Liberal Unionist party in the town. When one leading Liberal Unionist decided to return to Gladstonian ranks after the 1892 election, the local Liberal Unionist group effectively collapsed. Similarly, in Manchester the Liberal Unionists were never strong enough to form an effective party organisation, even though the defection of Liberal Unionists in the city was said to be larger than in any other English borough, with the exception of Birmingham. Although Liberal Unionists' defections cost the Liberal Party its majority on the city council, the Liberals regained their majority by the mid-1890s. Evidence from other towns reinforces the view that Liberal Unionism had only very limited grass roots support. In Leeds the Home Rule question did little to undermine the strength of local Liberalism and in some respects the party was more powerful in the summer of 1886 than at any time previously. Liberal Unionist organisation in the major urban centres of Leeds, Bradford and Huddersfield was very limited, while in the county constituencies of West Yorkshire it was practically non-existent.[17] Certainly there is little evidence of more support for Liberal Unionism in rural areas. Until the disastrous election of 1895 Liberalism seemed to be enjoying something of a resurgence in the county constituencies.[18]

All this suggests the need to look beyond Westminster and the Home Rule crisis to develop a broader picture of the Liberal Party in the late nineteenth century. Despite the growing importance of national political personalities, local issues and local politicians continued to be important, especially in urban politics where personal contact between the elector and candidate was more likely. Although loyalty to the employer and one's own factory was less important in determining individual votes than previously, in some areas it continued to be important.[19] Mill owner William Holland continued to exercise a strong influence over local politics in North-East Manchester where most of his premises were located. Richard Peacock, the railway and engineering magnate, had largely created the industrial suburb of Gorton from a small village and such was his power he was able to override the wishes of the local Liberal Association to become the party's official parliamentary candidate in

[16] Albeit, of course, supported by the Irish Nationalists.

[17] A.W. Roberts, 'Leeds Liberalism and Late Victorian Politics', *Northern History*, 5 (1970), 153, 147.

[18] J. Howarth, 'The Liberal Revival in Northamptonshire, 1880–1895: A Case Study in Late Nineteenth Century Elections', *Historical Journal*, 12 (1969), 82.

[19] For a discussion of the influence of factory culture on local politics see P. Joyce, 'The Factory Politics of Lancashire in the Later Nineteenth Century', *Historical Journal*, 18 (1975), 525–53.

the division. For the Conservatives the brewer Stephen Chesters Thompson became known as the 'King of Ardwick' because of the power his chain of public houses gave him in East Manchester. In Leicester many boot and shoe manufacturers adopted a paternalistic leadership style, partly to assist their ascendancy to municipal leadership and partly as a component of their industrial relations strategy. Yet despite the continuing importance of local personalities, by 1880 the character of local party organisation was the key factor in determining the nature of local Liberalism. Local representative institutions were the means by which local political elites established and maintained their legitimacy. It was changes to these institutions, prompted by franchise extension, corrupt practices legislation and the boundary review, that brought about the most far-reaching changes in the composition of local Liberal elites and the nature of local Liberalism.

Radical progress in local Liberal politics was no doubt assisted by rapid urban economic change. The small group of largely Unitarian families who personified 1850s Liberal politics in Leicester and Manchester invariably struggled to retain control of the movement as urban economic elites expanded and diversified.[20] The growth of just one industry could transform the economic landscape of a market town like Leicester. The rise of Leicester's boot and shoe industry during the 1860s saw the town's population increase by almost 40 per cent inside a decade and rapidly replace hosiery as the town's leading industry.[21] Manchester's economy underwent a dramatic diversification too, although not, as is sometimes supposed, as a direct result of the cotton famine. Although cotton did suffer cyclical depressions, for example during 1877–79, 1884–85 and 1891–93, Lancashire continued to dominate world production until the outbreak of the First World War.[22] Indeed it was the continuing wealth of the region that contributed to its economic diversification. Between 1861 and 1881 there was a 60 per cent rise in the number of attorneys and solicitors working in the city centre and a massive 300 per cent rise in the number of accountants and commission agents.[23] Manchester's financial sector underwent a particularly rapid transformation. In 1872 the 12 banks making up the new Manchester Clearing House had a collective annual turnover of £69 million. By 1896 that figure had nearly trebled to £191 million, making Manchester home to the largest provincial clearing house in the country.[24] The opening of the Ship Canal stimulated another wave of inward investment into Manchester, with Trafford Park becoming the world's largest industrial estate. It is impossible to quantify precisely what particular changes the influx of new elites brought to Manchester's politics – especially as the wealthiest

20 For a study of the cultural and ethical influence of early nineteenth-century Unitarianism see H. Wach, 'A "Still, Small Voice" from the Pulpit: Religion and the Creation of Social Morality in Manchester, 1820–1850', *Journal of Modern History*, 63 (1991), 425–56.

21 M. Elliott, *Victorian Leicester* (London, 1979), 21–2.

22 J. Walton, *Lancashire: A Social History 1558–1939*, reprint (Manchester, 1994), 201–3.

23 A. Kidd, *Manchester*, second edition (Keele, 1996), 105.

24 Kidd, *Manchester*, 107–8.

tended to live in private rural estates and took little interest in the day-to-day political process.[25] What is clear is that the old Liberal families like Heywood of Manchester and Biggs of Leicester, who had dominated the politics of the mid-century city, had largely disappeared from urban politics by the 1880s, to be replaced by a more diverse political elite. Although the new Liberal Associations that developed in the 1870s were to a greater or lesser degree 'representative oligarchies,' they were more inclusive than their predecessors. In order to provide themselves with legitimacy the Associations had to recruit widely from the expanding urban elite, thus giving Radicals a better opportunity to exercise significant political influence, especially after the electoral changes of 1884–85.

Constituency boundaries were often a major determinant of the type of Liberal Associations and urban politics that emerged after 1885.[26] In Manchester the Radicals, long marginalised in the old Liberal Association, found that the division of the parliamentary borough into separate constituencies gave them a significant opportunity to expand their influence. Radical influence in a particular constituency clearly depended to a large degree on the social characteristics of the area. Thus Radicals were much more successful in working-class constituencies with a large Irish population such as North-East Manchester than business constituencies like North-West. There were, however, limits to local party autonomy. Party managers in the central Manchester Liberal Union were still powerful and could effectively wreck the candidature of anyone they strongly opposed – such as Crosfield in Gorton. Yet despite the continuing influences of the central Manchester party bodies, by 1892 the more decentralised nature of the new party structures meant that the centre and left of the party were well in the ascendancy, with all the city's Liberal MPs describing themselves as Radicals. In contrast to Manchester, Leicester's centralised party organisation experienced few changes during this period, with the town's parliamentary borough and old Liberal Association remaining intact after the redistribution of seats. Indeed because the Leicester Liberal Association's primary concern was the organisation of the county constituencies the Association tended to neglect the problems of its own town organisation, with those on the left of the party often feeling excluded from the decision-making processes. Moreover two-member constituencies, like Leicester, tended to institutionalise differences within the party by reserving one seat for 'Radical' Liberals and one for 'moderate' Liberals. This type of arrangement naturally had profound implications for party management and later made it more difficult for the party to frame programmes upon which all sections could agree. The arrangement made the party particularly vulnerable when the ILP offered the electorate a second 'Radical' candidate in the hope of persuading

25 Walton, *Lancashire*, 232–3.

26 For background of the politics behind boundaries and redistribution see J. Garrard, *Democratisation in Britain* (Basingstoke, 2002), 94–6; M. Chadwick, 'The Role of Redistribution in the Making of the Third Reform Act', *Historical Journal*, 19 (1976), 665–83; J. Dunbabin, 'Some Implication of the 1885 British Shift towards Single-Member Constituencies: A Note', *English Historical Review*, 109 (1994), 89–100.

Liberals to reject their 'moderate' Liberal representative in 1894.[27] Clearly, then, whether or not a parliamentary borough was or was not divided into single-member constituencies could have significant implications for Radical influence in local Liberal politics.[28] Even in cities like Liverpool, where Whigs traditionally had dominated urban Liberal politics, the division of party organisations following the creation of single-member constituencies undermined those on the right of the party.[29] Indeed it is not too fanciful to posit a relationship between the increasing marginalisation of Whig influence in local parties after 1885 and subsequent Whig defections to the Liberal Unionists. Both Liverpool and Manchester saw Whigs become increasingly marginalised by the creation of single member constituencies and both saw significant defections to the Liberal Unionists in 1886. In these cities, it was not just Radicals who would have benefited from the decentralisation of party decision-making but also, crucially, Irish Nationalist groups.

This increasing Radical influence in local politics naturally raises the question of whether the Liberal largely Nonconformist middle class remained generally loyal to the party after 1886. The Home Rule crisis is widely regarded as having accelerated urban and suburban middle-class defections from the party, particularly in the Metropolitan area.[30] Thompson's well-known survey of London constituencies suggests that the middle class were largely indifferent to Nonconformist influence and, fearful of Liberal collectivism, drifted increasingly towards class-based support for the Conservatives after 1886.[31] Clarke suggests that even the issue of free trade in the Edwardian period did little to stem the tide of defections to the Conservatives by Manchester's middle class.[32] These conclusions, however, need to be treated with some caution. Thompson's study was based on a division of constituencies into social classes based on aggregate social and economic data. Although this is a valid approach, still used in political science, it does have its limitations, as few constituencies are socially or religiously homogenous. Moreover Thompson's data suggests that after the collapse of the Liberal Party in 'middle-class London' between 1895 and 1900 some of these areas actually began to return to the party in 1906 and 1910.[33]

More recently scholars have questioned just how much the problems of Liberals and the Progressive Party in London really did represent a rise in class voting. Both

---

[27] B. Lancaster, *Radicalism, Co-operation and Socialism* (Leicester, 1987), 110–33.

[28] Again the social and economic composition of the single member constituencies is clearly important here, but the very fact of a redrawing of boundaries forced the reconstruction of local party organisations threatening the position of existing elites.

[29] N. Collins, *Politics and Elections in Nineteenth Century Liverpool* (Aldershot, 1994), 199.

[30] Jenkins, *Liberal Ascendancy*, 222.

[31] P. Thompson, *Socialists, Liberals and Labour – The Struggle for London 1885–1914*, (London, 1967), 295–6.

[32] P.F. Clarke, 'The End of Laissez Faire and the Politics of Cotton', *Historical Journal*, 15 (1972), 511–12.

[33] Thompson, *Socialists*, 301–3. (Appendix A).

Jeffrey and Pennybacker have challenged traditional assumptions that the lower-middle class was a force for Conservatism, arguing for a more sophisticated, issue-based understanding of metropolitan politics.[34] In any case it should not be assumed that the pattern of politics in London was necessarily typical of urban Britain as a whole. As Cox has observed, the majority of London suburbs began as well-established towns, some of which could trace their origins to medieval times.[35] Many originally had a significant number of residents from the landed aristocracy.[36] Although systematic studies of other British towns and cities are limited, recent research has tended to emphasise the resilience of Liberalism in suburbia and amongst the lower-middle class. Savage has noted the strength of Edwardian Liberalism in suburban Preston, despite Labour's progress in other parts of the town.[37] Similarly, Doyle's work on Norwich and Jones's research on Manchester have served to demonstrate the continuity of the Liberal tradition in suburbia well into the 1930s.[38] Bernstein, too, has stressed how Liberal emphasis on 'traditional' Nonconformist and ethical issues helped the party to retain a significant middle-class base – even though he ultimately sees the party as a victim of 'class politics'.[39]

Clarke's work on Manchester certainly implies that the upper elements of the commercial middle class were increasingly alienated from Liberalism. It would be unwise, however, to view the political opinions of the most senior members of the Chamber of Commerce as representative of wider middle-class opinion. The late Victorian urban economy was producing an increasingly complex middle class, including a growing array of rising professionals, clerks, small tradesmen and shopkeepers. It was these individuals who numerically dominated the suburban electorate and who played a crucial role in determining Liberal fortunes. Indeed these changes may have done more to erode and blurr class distinctions than reinforce them, especially in suburban constituencies where there was increasing evidence of social mobility. Recent historical geography has questioned whether nineteenth

34 T. Jeffrey, 'The suburban nation: politics and class in Lewisham', 189–216, esp. 189–92, and S. Pennybacker, '"The millennium by return of post": reconsidering London Progressivism 1889–1907', 129–62; both in D. Felman and G. Stedman Jones (eds), *Metropolis London* (London, 1989).

35 R. Cox, 'The old centre of Croydon: Victorian decay and redevelopment', in A. Everitt (ed.), *Perspectives in English Urban History* (London, 1973), 186, cited in J.M. Rowcliffe, 'Bromley: Kentish Market town to London suburb 1841–1881', in F.M.L. Thompson (ed.), *The Rise of Suburbia* (Leicester, 1982), 81.

36 C. Miele, 'From aristocratic idea to middle-class idyll: 1690–1840', in A. Saint (ed.), *London Suburbs* (London, 1999), 31–60.

37 M. Savage, *The Dynamics of Working Class Politics – The Labour Movement in Preston* (Cambridge, 1987), 150.

38 B. Doyle, 'Urban Liberalism and the "lost generation": politics and middle class culture in Norwich 1900–1935', *Historical Journal*, 38 (1995), 617–34; B. Jones, 'Manchester Liberalism 1918–1929: the electoral, ideological and organisational experience of the Liberal Party in Manchester, with particular reference to the career of Ernest Simon', (unpublished University of Manchester Ph.D. thesis, 1997), 32–3, 310–11.

39 G. Bernstein, *Liberalism and Liberal Politics in Edwardian England* (Boston, Mass., 1986), esp. 1–5, 135–65, 197–201.

century urban industrial communities really were becoming increasingly segregated on class lines. On closer examination, many new suburban communities of the mid-nineteenth century have been found to be less socially homogenous than once thought – with surprisingly little evidence of urban social segregation increasing over time.[40] Moreover where significant geographical social segregation has been observed, empirical research has tended to locate it as much in ethnic and religious cleavages as those purely of class.[41]

Assessing middle-class allegiance to religious Nonconformity is problematic. Britain's only official religious census can be of little help in assessing the character of suburban estates developed after 1851. Indeed although many have characterised the late nineteenth century as a period of growing secularism, it is unclear just how far and in what ways the movement had advanced in the years before the First World War.[42] Evidence from metropolitan suburbs suggests that churches with particular 'prestige', such as those in wealthier suburbs, could continue to be influential.[43] Similarly the scale of Nonconformist church building in suburban South Manchester and Stoneygate, Leicester suggests that Nonconformity remained a significant influence in suburban areas. Even where declining church attendance has been observed it should not necessarily be taken as evidence for a decline in the political importance of religious and denominational issues. Cultural historians such as Bebbington have illustrated just how significant denominational differences were in local public affairs.[44] Religious and denominational loyalties continued to be of crucial importance in determining the way many votes were cast and some elections – particularly school board elections – were fought exclusively on denominational lines.[45]

Moreover it is far from clear that the rapidly expanding suburban middle class were generally hostile to the collectivist political tendencies of the time. Suburban Liberal programmes tended to combine traditional denominational and Nonconformist concerns with campaigns for improvements to local municipal

---

40 R. Dennis, *English Industrial Cities in the Nineteenth Century – A Social Geography*, reprint (Cambridge 1986), 238–49.

41 C. Pooley and R. Lawton, 'The Social Geography of nineteenth century British cities: a review', in D. Denecke and G. Shaw (eds), *Urban Historical Geography – Recent Progress in Britain and Germany*, (Cambridge, 1998).

42 C. Brown, 'Did urbanisation secularise Britain?', *Urban History Yearbook* (1988).

43 J. Morris, *Religious and Urban Change: Croydon 1840–1914* (Woodbridge, 1992), 182.

44 D.W. Bebbington, 'Nonconformity and Electoral Sociology 1867–1918', *Historical Journal*, 27 (1984), 633–56. See also D.W. Bebbington, *The Nonconformist Conscience: Chapel and Politics, 1870–1914* (London, 1982).

45 D. Bebbington, *The Nonconformist Conscience: Chapel and Politics, 1870–1914* (London, 1982), D. Bebbington, 'Nonconformity and Electoral Sociology 1867–1918', *Historical Journal* 27 (1984), 633–56; J. Morris, *Religious and Urban Change: Croydon 1840–1914* (Woodbridge, 1992), B. Doyle, 'Urban Liberalism and the "lost generation": politics and middle class culture in Norwich 1900–1935', *Historical Journal*, 38 (1995), 617–34.

services. Middle-class suburban communities were often constituted with few public amenities and local residents often looked to the local municipality to invest in schools, libraries, sewers and roads for their own benefit. These new communities were often more vocal in their demands for municipal services than less privileged inner-urban areas and looked to Radical municipal interventionism to supply their needs. The Progressive municipal programmes that developed in the mid-1890s were in part a by-product of these new demands. Liberal electoral victories in Moss Side, Manchester and Belgrave, Leicester demonstrated just how successful policies of municipal interventionism could be. The policies of rigid economy practised by the more 'moderate' or Whiggish elements of the party were of little interest to those who lacked basic local facilities. By the mid-1890s even Liberals in cities not known for municipal Radicalism, such as Leeds, recognised the need for increasing municipal expenditure for suburban improvement programmes.[46] Moreover many suburban communities, far from being bereft of Nonconformist and Liberal influences, often had more Nonconformist churches and Liberal clubs than central working-class districts. Suburbia often contained residents sufficiently affluent to generously endow new Nonconformist churches in formerly Anglican-dominated areas. This could lead to religious competition which spilled over into local politics – as in the case of Moss Side where many Baptists strongly supported the Liberal Party in their attempts to rid the local board of health of Anglican domination. Denominational loyalties and demands for the 'development' of suburbia meant that a large portion of the middle class remained loyal to the Liberal Party and reinforced its moves towards a more Radical and collectivist municipal agenda.

The main brake on Radical influence in urban politics was often the Liberal leadership of the local municipal corporation.[47] The existence of the aldermanic bench allowed for the survival of centre-right Liberals who might have otherwise been rejected either at the polls or by the increasingly Radical local associations. By the mid-1880s it was openly acknowledged that Manchester's Liberal aldermen voted with the Conservatives as often as they voted with the main body of Liberal councillors – even on what seemed clearly party political issues. In Leicester the huge size of the Liberal majority and the tiny Conservative opposition inevitably led a degree of complacency and inertia. Other towns show a similar pattern. In Leeds moderate Liberals on the town council frequently broke ranks and voted with the Conservatives against Progressive plans for increased public expenditure.[48] Even in Liverpool, where Liberals found themselves in a small minority on the municipal authority, the Liberal group took up a 'moderate' position of non-partisanship for much of the period.[49] The reason that 'moderate' and Whig Liberals could continue

---

46 E.P. Hennock, *Fit and Proper Persons: Ideal and Reality in Nineteenth century Urban Government* (London, 1973), 253–7.

47 For an outline of the political constraints on innovative policy making see J. Moore and R. Rodger, 'Municipal Knowledge and Policy Networks in British Local Government, 1832–1914', *Yearbook of European Administrative History*, 15 (2003), 29–58, esp. 37–43.

48 Roberts, 'Leeds Liberalism', *Northern History*, 5, 136.

49 Collins, *Politics*, 201.

to exercise a major influence over council politics was often because the influence of local parties over municipal representatives was very limited – at least until the 1890s. Fraser, in his seminal work on municipal politics, identifies the growth of party organisation as a key factor in undermining the power of old urban elites.[50] However, party organisations often took only a limited role in municipal politics, aside from endorsing candidates and running periodic election campaigns. Even in powerful local government bodies with extensive resources, such as the London County Council, there was significant hostility to the introduction of formal party politics.[51]

Urban Liberal Associations clearly saw their role primarily in terms of securing the election of members of parliament, with local municipal elections often only being seen as a means to this end. Only when the ineptitude of municipal elites threatened to undermine the whole party did local Liberal Associations begin to get more actively involved in the management of municipal politics. In Manchester a series of financial scandals were exploited by Radical Liberals and Conservatives to force the removal of several of the city's most prominent 'moderate' Liberals. The Manchester Liberal Union reacted by trying to tighten its oversight of council management in order to head off the unthinkable prospect of the Conservatives gaining a majority on the council – something that many feared would do much damage to the party's wider electoral credibility. Liberals in Leicester suffered from no such threat, enjoying a very substantial majority. However, it was just this majority that was the main source of the party's problems. With no central policy-making body, power was decentralised to small committees. With councillors responsible to no one except their own small ward associations, the interests of wards came before the interests of the town as a whole, rendering efficient financial management impossible. Councillors and committees could pursue their own projects freely without recourse to financial discipline with the result that expenditure increased so rapidly the council was faced with a financial crisis when out-districts were amalgamated with the borough. Eventually council committees were compelled by circumstances to surrender more control of their financial affairs to the central finance committee in order to avoid further embarrassment. At the same time disputes over municipal candidate selection saw the Liberal Association tighten its rules for the management of local ward organisations and formalise is relationship with the Liberal council group. These moves paved the way for the adoption of a more programmatic style of local politics with candidates fighting on collectively agreed agendas, rather than primarily pressing the claims of ward or parochial interests. The introduction of a new generation of councillors also speeded up the removal of the older 'moderate' Liberal elites. In the early 1890s both Manchester and Leicester expanded their municipal boundaries to include many of the new suburbs around the old town boundaries. The new Liberal entrants to the councils inevitably diluted

[50] D. Fraser, *Urban Politics in Victorian England* (Leicester, 1976), 282.

[51] K. Young, *Local Politics and the Rise of Party: The London Municipal Society and the Conservative intervention in local elections, 1894–1963* (Leicester, 1975).

the strength of the remaining 'moderate' elements of the party and, in the case of Manchester, brought a significant number of new Radical leaders into the council chamber. Although it took Radicals longer to penetrate town halls than it had to influence local party organisation, by the early 1890s Liberals in both Manchester and Leicester were embracing the language of Municipal Progressivism. Of course, this was in part a response to the threat of the ILP but it was also a natural outgrowth of the increased Radical influence in municipal and local party politics.

Although a national party, the ILP's success differed dramatically by region and by locality.[52] The party failed to win a single seat in 1895 and generally performed poorly in by-elections thereafter. The Midlands was a particularly weak area for the party with Leicester standing out as something of an ILP 'island' in a region otherwise dominated by the two major parties.[53] Leicester's uniqueness can largely be explained by the success of the ILP in taking over the town's leading trade union in the boot and shoe industry at a time of deteriorating industrial relations. The Leicester Liberal Association, largely unaffected by the 1884 redistribution of seats, was less open to Radical influence and it was not until the party suffered a reverse in the 1895 municipal elections that a Progressive Municipal Programme came seriously on to the Association's agenda. However the Association's leaders were politically astute, courting working-class popularity by adopting Henry Broadhurst as a Lib–Lab parliamentary candidate and introducing minimum wages for the municipal workforce. These moves meant that even in Leicester ILP influence in other trade unions and in local politics was limited. The ILP could gain much short-term electoral capital by exploiting trade disputes and the activities of unpopular 'moderate' Liberals, but they could not offer a sustained assault on Liberal hegemony in the town. The ILP found the going even more difficult in Manchester, with its fragmented labour market and culturally diverse working-class population. Despite being known as the home of some of the most famous socialist personalities of the time, the ILP struggled to come to terms with the large Irish population who prized Home Rule above all other political priorities. Any prospect of a significant breakthrough was wrecked by a dogmatic refusal to co-operate with Radical Liberals, many of whom instinctively shared much of the ILP agenda. Even when C.P. Scott generously, if somewhat naively, withdrew from a marginal parliamentary constituency in favour of an ILP representative, the ILP were not sufficiently strong to pose a serious challenge to the Conservatives. Liberal dreams of a Progressive

---

52 For discussion see D. James, T. Jowitt and K. Laybourn, *The Centenary History of the Independent Labour Party* (London, 1993); K. Laybourn and J. Reynolds, 'The Emergence of the Independent Labour party in Bradford', *International Review of Social History*, 20 (1975), 313–46; D. James, *Class and Politics in a Northern Industrial Town: Keighley 1880–1914* (Keele, 1995); J. Brown, 'Attercliffe, 1894: How One Local Liberal Party Failed to Meet the Challenge of Labour', *Journal of British Studies*, 14 (1975), 48–77; J. Howe, 'Liberals, Lib–Labs and Independent Labour in North Gloucestershire, 1890–1914', *Midland History*, 11 (1986), 117–37. See also M. Savage, 'The Rise of the Labour Party in local perspective', *Journal of Regional and Local Studies*, 10 (1990), 1–16.

53 Howell, *British Workers*, 231.

alliance in the 1890s died when it became clear that the ILP were not prepared to co-operate with the Liberal Party and that even if Liberals did stand down in their favour, the ILP would not be strong enough alone to defeat Conservative candidates.

By the mid-1890s Liberals in Leicester and Manchester both faced competition on the left. This was a new experience for Liberals. However much Radicals had been divided from the party previously, the various factions continued to shelter under the Liberal umbrella.[54] In the 1860s Leicester's Liberals were hopelessly divided between rival claimants for the town's two parliamentary seats, but the feuding groups remained loyal to the Liberal faith and eventually an accommodation was found. In the 1880s Manchester Radicals established their own separate organisation – the Manchester Radical Association – in protest at the 'closed' nature of the Liberal Association, but there was no question of them establishing a rival party. Indeed even when Radical leader Richard Pankhurst joined the ILP he continued to profess his loyalty to Liberal principles. However the ILP would never 'return' to the 'Liberal Umbrella'. The emergence of an electoral competitor on the left of politics therefore seemed to suggest that, perhaps for the first time, the Liberal Party no longer represented the most 'advanced' and democratic opinion of the age.

Yet at local level Liberalism in Manchester and Leicester remained vibrant. Not only did the party continue to represent a large proportion of trades unions, but it also continued to hold sway in many of the often largely middle-class suburbs. The 'Liberal Umbrella' continued to shelter a very diverse collection of political interests, as indeed it always had. Although assessments of party vitality are inevitably coloured somewhat by subsequent events, there were few signs that Liberalism in Manchester and Leicester was in long-term decline. The New Liberalism that was to typify the most Radical and controversial Liberal government of all – that of 1906–10 – was fostered not in the Edwardian period, but in the two decades before when Radical, Progressive and collectivist influences gradually took control of the party caucuses, municipalities and expanding suburbia. The type of Liberal collectivism that emerged was one which often benefited the middle classes as much as the workers. Demands for public libraries, baths, parks and community facilities were as much the demands of wealthy suburbanites as the poor. Indeed in some cases, such as South Leicester, favourable rating clauses meant that many argued the wealthier suburbs were obtaining disproportionate benefit from increasing local public expenditure. Similarly demands for minimum wages obtained middle-class support, not just on humanitarian grounds, but because of fears that rural contractors could obtain council contracts by paying lower wages than urban entrepreneurs. In an era when problems of industrial relations and growing class tension increasingly dominated political discussion, Liberal Radicalism appeared to offer practical solutions that could act in the interest of both the trade unionist and the employer. Joseph Chamberlain's departure from Liberal ranks did not destroy the prospects for Radical Liberalism. Indeed in the decade after Chamberlain left the party Radicalism made great strides

[54] With the exception, of course, of a small number of Chamberlainite Radicals who left the party in 1886 as a consequence of the Home Rule crisis.

in both Manchester, which came to be seen as the spiritual home of New Liberalism, and Leicester, where it faced much stronger institutional barriers.

Despite the importance of regional and local factors in explaining the major political trends of the time, they do need to be placed in a wider national context. In particular, there is the puzzle of why an explicitly New Liberal agenda – clearly so influential in many urban Liberal associations in the 1890s – was not adopted until after the 1906 election by the Liberal leadership. Part of the answer lies in the general suspicion of the value of programmatic politics. Gladstone was notoriously sceptical about the value of programmatic politics, but he was flexible enough to accept the Newcastle Programme.[55] He was also prepared to allow Asquith to advocate a Liberal municipal programme in the early months of his fourth ministry. This was a move which actively encouraged many Liberal Associations, including Manchester and Leicester, to bring forward their own proposals.[56] Gladstone's fourth ministry also framed a programme to encourage municipalities to counter the problem of seasonal unemployment by bringing forward public works schemes. Rosebery, having established a reputation as a Progressive because of his work on the London County Council, seemed the obvious figure to develop these policies into a national Radical programme. Unfortunately differences over the party leadership and imperial policy in the wake of Gladstone's resignation meant national policy-making was crippled for almost a decade. Thus if there was one event that marked the end of the Victorian Liberal ascendancy, it was not the Home Rule crisis, but rather the resignation of Gladstone. Remarkably few contemporary commentators foresaw the problems that might develop. Some elements of the Irish community in Manchester were worried about Rosebery's position on Home Rule and feared it might lead to a split with the main body of the Liberal Party – although Rosebery's 'Edinburgh speech' in March 1894 went some way to allaying their fears.[57] Some Radicals feared that his position in the Lords was untenable and he would soon have to choose 'between the classes and the masses'.[58] In general, however, critics like Henry Labouchere, who derided the notion of a peer premier, attracted little support as Liberals sought to avoid the type of splits that their opponents were trying to encourage.[59]

Rosebery's great advantage was that he was very much a 'dark horse'. While moderate Liberals felt that his social background would ensure that he would not undertake 'irresponsible' campaigns against the peerage, Radicals like Leicester's J. Page Hopps could look to Rosebery's work on the LCC as an indication of what his 'sensible Socialism' could do for the country as a whole.[60] Yet because of the Gladstonian shadows which fell across his premiership and the disputed nature of his

[55] H.C.G. Matthew, *Gladstone 1875–1898* (Oxford, 1995), 320–24.

[56] Sometimes, of course, influenced by Fabian Socialists. M. Bevir, 'Fabianism, Permeation and Independent Labour', *Historical Journal*, 39 (1996), 179–96.

[57] See details of the St. Patrick's Day Demonstration in the Free Trade Hall, *MG*, 19 March 1894.

[58] See correspondence columns, *MG*, 13 March 1894.

[59] Leader, *MG*, 3 March, 1894

[60] *LDM*, 5 March 1894. Quoted from the *Westminster Gazette*.

leadership he was never able to develop his own distinctive programme. Moreover Rosebery's greatest skill, that of man management, could not be fully utilised while he occupied a seat in the Lords and his principal rival for the leadership led the House of Commons.[61] Liberals at grass-roots level clearly did not anticipate any great changes in the direction of the party. While accepting that Gladstone's premiership would one day come to a close, they looked to Rosebery as the natural successor, prepared by Gladstone to maintain the dynasty. Consequently there was little debate in the constituencies about Rosebery's succession or discussion about the problems of his position in the Lords.

Indeed there were two remarkable features of Gladstone's resignation that suggest individual party leaders were not as powerful in national political life as sometimes suggested. Firstly despite Gladstone's massive popularity in the party at large, his cabinet was able to force his resignation from office on a characteristically Gladstonian issue – his opposition to increased naval estimates. This would seem to suggest both that power at cabinet level remained highly centralised amongst Westminster elites and that even a leader with a massive popular following had but a tenuous hold on power. Gladstone had seemingly redefined the party in his own image, becoming a nineteenth-century icon in the process. He was the unchallenged leader of the party in the constituencies and in the National Liberal Federation. Yet he still relied on the cabinet as the primary source of his day-to-day authority. It was the loss of cabinet, not national support, which proved his downfall. Gladstone could never be quite the autocrat which opponents – and sometimes historians – tried to depict. By the late nineteenth century the Liberal Party had become an increasingly complex organism. Although Gladstone was able to transform the political landscape with great crusades on Bulgaria and Ireland, by the end of the 1880s real policy innovation was coming from elsewhere. The party's 'official' programme for his final ministry was the product of the National Liberal Federation, not the party leader or the Whips' Office.[62] Gladstone was an important component in the Liberal Party's electoral appeal, but was not the only component.[63] It is remarkable just how little the party and press at local level marked the passing of Gladstone's premiership. This may have been because the resignation had been expected – rumours had been circulating for up to a week before the official announcement – and because Gladstone's likely successor was already known. Even allowing for these circumstances, it is surprising that the passing of such a legend should receive less

---

61 *Economist*, 24 March 1894. For details of the leadership struggle see P. Stansky, *Ambitions and Strategies*: *The struggle for the leadership of the Liberal party in the 1890s* (Oxford, 1964).

62 For background on the growth of the National Liberal Federation see F. Herrick, 'The Origins of the National Liberal Federation', *Journal of Modern History*, 17 (1945), 116–29; B. McGill, 'Francis Schnadhorst and Liberal Party Organisation', *Journal of Modern History*, 34 (1962), 19–39; R. Watson, *The National Liberal Federation from its commencement to the General Election of 1906* (London, 1907).

63 P. Readman, 'The 1895 General Elections and political change in later Victorian Britain', *Historical Journal*, 42 (1999), 467–93.

press coverage than the resignation of a local MP – yet this was precisely the case in Leicester in March 1894. Local MP J.A. Picton announced his retirement from the Commons at the same time Gladstone resigned the party leadership. The *Leicester Daily Mercury*, the town's leading Liberal newspaper, gave more prominence to the resignation of Picton and his potential successor than they did to the resignation of Gladstone and the Liberal leadership question. The day after the resignations the paper led not with the end of the Gladstonian premiership, but with the retirement of Picton.[64] The Leicester Liberal Association's general meeting a week later made only passing reference to the party leadership question, while the selection of a new parliamentary candidate dominated the business.[65]

The nineteenth century was an era in which local events remained central to most citizens' political education and experiences. This is not to deny that national party leaders were important in giving political movements a sense of direction and unity.[66] However, it was the ideas that leaders represented, not the leaders themselves, that were of key importance. Gladstonian Radicals like Sir Henry Roscoe in Manchester were not thrown into despair by Gladstone's resignation because of the overwhelming confidence they had that the values he represented would endure.[67] In an era before radio and television, the local press, local party members and local politicians were the primary conduit for these ideas to the mass electorate. Thus the nature and structure of local politics remained of central importance for a party's success, especially in urban areas where party competition was more intense and contested local elections more numerous. Indeed in some respects the importance of local political parties continued to grow in the last two decades of the nineteenth century. Evidence from Manchester and Leicester suggests that as municipal activities grew in complexity and required new centralised forms of management, political parties increasingly took direct responsibility for municipal elections and for the management of municipal government. Parties and the political press could not be kept in a state of relative dormancy between parliamentary elections if they faced municipal by-elections and municipal controversies every few months. Consequently, the community activity of local political parties intensified and their role in urban government expanded. Such bodies often set their own priorities and initiated their own campaigns on either local concerns or national issues with a special local relevance. Indeed local campaigns could sometimes even overshadow the most important national issue – as Leicester's agitation on the vaccination question proved during the 1886 Home Rule crisis.

The underlying strength of local Liberal elites and party organisation can therefore be a key factor in explaining the survival and revival of the Liberal Party during the difficult decade after the resignation of Gladstone. The ideological outlook of

64 *LDM*, 4 March 1894.

65 *LDM*, 10 March 1894.

66 This phenomenon of 'hero-worship' was, of course, common to many European political and religious movements of the 'long nineteenth century'. E.F. Biagini, *Liberty, Retrenchment and Reform: Popular Liberalism in the Age of Gladstone, 1860–80* (Cambridge, 1991), 422.

67 *MG*, 1 March 1894.

local Liberal politics could vary quite markedly by area and the gradual transition to a Progressive or New Liberal agenda was uneven. Significantly, however, by 1895 the most 'moderate' or conservative element within local Liberal politics – the aldermanic municipal leadership – had apparently gone into terminal decline in both Leicester and Manchester. Even in those towns where left-wing influences were less pronounced the language of Progressivism was increasingly replacing that of fiscal retrenchment. Workers were promised shorter hours and minimum wages while middle-class suburbanites were offered the prospect of improved pavements and local public libraries. The new agenda was one that could seemingly appeal across classes and retain all but the most reactionary and revolutionary forces under the Liberal umbrella. The final decade of Gladstonian leadership did not see the party ossify or become a single-issue party. At local level there were signs that a quiet revolution was taking place and that Liberalism was being redefined to give it relevance for the coming century. The vitality and commitment of a generation of Liberals in the constituencies was able to overcome the period of destructive infighting at Westminster. Only a world war, with its accompanying social and political turmoil, could destroy that optimism and vitality.

Appendix One

Biographical Notes

Manchester

Ashton, Thomas G.
Cotton manufacturer and prominent figure in the Manchester Liberal Association and Manchester Liberal Union; served until 1885 as secretary of the Manchester Liberal Association; later became the treasurer of the Manchester Liberal Union and the chairman of the North West Manchester Liberal Association; Liberal MP for Hyde 1885–86; defeated as Liberal candidate for Hyde in 1886 and 1892; Liberal MP for Luton 1895 to 1911; elevated to the peerage as Lord Hyde of Ashton in 1911.

Armitage, Benjamin (Chomlea)
Major Congregationalist and Liberal party benefactor; president of Manchester Chamber of Commerce 1877–81; close friend of John Bright; Liberal MP for Salford and then Salford West from 1880–86; fought Salford West unsuccessfully as a Liberal candidate in 1886 and 1892; became strong advocate of arbitration to resolve labour disputes after the disastrous Manchester Gas Strike of 1889. [*Faces and Places*, 3, 129]

Arrandale, Matthew
Prominent United Methodist; general secretary of the United Machine Workers Association from 1885; president of the Manchester and Salford trades council; president of the Gorton sub-division Liberal Association; one of the first working-class magistrates in Manchester; defeated as Liberal candidate in Ardwick ward in 1891; elected as Liberal councillor for All Saints' ward in June 1895; strong advocate of Liberal Progressive Municipal Programme and eight-hour day. [*Faces and Place*s, 7, 145]

Birdsall, George
Prominent Liberal activist in Moss Side; leading critic of the Conservative and Anglican-dominated Moss Side local board; elected on to the new Moss Side District Council in 1894; pioneer of Progressive Liberal agenda in local politics.

Boyle, Daniel
Born in County Fermanagh; railway worker; secretary of the East Manchester Irish National League, vice-president of Catholic Registration Association, vice-president North-East Manchester Liberal Association, strong supporter of the Liberal

Progressive Municipal Programme, elected Liberal councillor for New Cross Ward in 1894; successful municipal career with Tramway's committee – which became known as 'Dan Boyle's railway' due to the number of Irishmen employed in tramway operations. [*Faces and Places*, 8, 113]

Brocklehurst, Frederick

Came to Manchester after John Trevor offered him the secretaryship of the Labour Church movement; 1894 elected member of the National Administrative Council of the ILP; unsuccessful ILP candidate in Bolton in 1895; elected for Harpurhey ward, Manchester in 1897, defeating the chairman of the corporation parks' committee who had earlier been instrumental in securing his imprisonment for lecturing in public parks; later defected to the Conservatives. [*Faces and Places*, 9, 209]

Butterworth, Walter

Glass manufacturer; council member of the Manchester Literary Club 1891; actively involved in the Ancoats brotherhood; committee member of the Manchester Reform Club and later a city councillor and chairman of the municipal art gallery committee; long-standing servant of the Manchester Liberal Union and from 1903 honorary secretary of the Manchester Liberal Federation. [*Faces and Places*, 15, 86]

Clay, George

Prominent Unitarian; elected as Liberal councillor for Oxford ward in 1882, but frequently in dispute with ward association; joined Liberal Unionists in 1886 but took little part in party activities; defeated Gladstonian opponent in 1891 and became alderman in 1893; Justice of the Peace; died December 1896. [*Faces and Places*, 8, 75]

Crosfield, John H.

Prominent United Methodist, total abstainer; active in the Liberation society; staunch Radical and advocate of increased labour representation, selected as official Liberal parliamentary candidate for Gorton, but persuaded to stand down after arbitration dispute found in favour of Liberal opponent Richard Peacock; Liberal councillor for Ardwick 1884–87; elected Liberal councillor for Openshaw in 1890 and immediately appointed alderman; influential Radical voice in municipal politics until his death in 1899. [*Faces and Places*, 3, 158]

Guthrie, Edwin

Prominent advocate of the Progressive Municipal programme and a close friend and ally of C.P. Scott; persuaded the Liberal Association to toughen its response to the ILP by bringing forward more Liberal working-class candidates; a key figure in Sir Henry Roscoe's South Manchester election campaigns.

Higginbottam, Lloyd

Head of a mechanical engineering firm; elected as an independent candidate to Gorton Local Board in 1888 and later became its chairman; elected as Liberal candidate for

St. Mark's, Gorton in 1891, and immediately appointed alderman; president of the Gorton Liberal Association; an advanced Liberal accepted by all wings of the party; his decision not to accept the Liberal nomination for Gorton on the retirement of William Mather contributed to the Gorton party's collapse.

Holland, William H.

Prominent Wesleyan and temperance advocate; owned cotton spinning business based at Miles Platting, one of largest employers in North-East Manchester; director of the Manchester Chamber of Commerce; president of the North-East Manchester Liberal Association 1885–89; unpopular with Radical grass-roots opinion in North-East Manchester; MP for Salford South 1892–95, MP for Rotherham 1899–1910. [*Faces and Places*, 3, 97]

Hopkinson, Alfred

Prominent Anglican; Prof. of Law at Owen's College from 1875; father veteran Liberal who had been mayor and served on corporation for 30 years; right-wing Liberal who was only reluctantly adopted as Liberal candidate for East Manchester in 1885; central figure in the formation of the Manchester Committee for the Maintenance of the Legislative Union and the Manchester Liberal Unionist Association; unsuccessfully contested South-West Manchester as Liberal candidate in 1892; largely withdrew from Manchester politics after moving to London in 1889. [*Faces and Places*, 4, 102]

Hopkinson, John

Prominent Congregationalist; partner in engineering firm and chairman of the Carnforth Iron Co.; councillor for St. Luke's ward 1861–72; alderman from 1872 to death in 1902; mayor 1882–83; veteran municipal servant whose reputation was somewhat sullied by the city council scandals of 1885–87; became a Liberal Unionist after 1886 but did not play a very prominent role in party politics.

Kelley, George D.

General secretary of the society of Lithographic Printers; secretary of Manchester and Salford Trades Council; strong Lib–Labber; president of the Labour Electoral Association; Liberal councillor for St. Clement's ward 1891–95; Labour MP for South-West Manchester 1906–10 (January). [*Faces and Places*, 2, 92]

King, John

Veteran municipal leader; Liberal councillor for Oxford 1856–67; alderman from 1867; mayor 1874–75; also served as chairman of the powerful finance committee in the early 1890s; joined the Liberal Unionists in 1886, attracted controversy for his role in the council scandals of the 1880s and trade union criticism for accepting the chairmanship of the Manchester Carriage and Tramways Company while retaining an important position on its regulatory authority – the city council. [*Faces and Places*, 2, 117]

Mather, William

Joint owner of the Salford ironworks; well known as a philanthropic, Radical employer; active in both the Salford Liberal Associations and the Manchester Liberal Union; journeyman parliamentarian; held the marginal South Salford parliamentary seat for the Liberals between 1885–86; MP for Gorton 1889–95; controversially supported ILP candidate Richard Pankhurst in Gorton at the 1895 general election; returned to Westminster as Liberal MP for Rossendale 1900–1904. [*Faces and Places*, 15, 334]

McCabe, David ('Dan')

President of the Michael Davitt Branch of the Irish National League; Vice-President of Catholic Registration Association; vice-president of the North Manchester Liberal Association; became one of first Irish Catholics to be elected to the city council when elected as a Liberal for St. Michael's ward in 1889;Justice of the Peace; well known for philanthropic work in Salford. [*Faces and Places*, 8, 55]

Pankhurst, Richard M.

Called to the Bar in 1867 and member of the Northern Circuit; husband of Emmeline Pankhurst; republican; controversially resigned from the Liberal Party in 1883 to stand, unsuccessfully, as an Independent Liberal candidate in the Manchester by-election of that year; founder member of the Manchester Radical Association, stood as Liberal–Labour candidate in Rotherhithe in 1885; on returning to Manchester joined the ILP and again stood unsuccessfully for parliament in 1895, this time as ILP candidate in Gorton; caused a sensation by persuading the sitting Gorton Liberal MP, William Mather to come out in support of his candidature. [*Faces and Places*, 4, 33]

Roscoe, Sir Henry E.

Prominent chemist and Radical politician; appointed first professor of chemistry at Owen's College in 1857; elected to the Royal Society in 1863 and served as vice-president of its council 1881–82 and 1888–90; influential campaigner for technical education and a member of Sir Bernhard Samuelson's Commission on Technical Instruction; MP for South Manchester 1885–95; served on several Royal Commissions, including that which led to the amended Alkali Acts of 1891 and 1892; in 1896 became vice-chancellor of London University. [E. Thorpe, *The Rt. Hon. Sir Henry Enfield Roscoe* (London, 1916)]

Royle, John

Prominent Wesleyan from Wilmslow; total abstainer; head of a boot and shoe manufacturing firm; served on Manchester Board of Guardians, right-wing Liberal regarded as the 'sternest of economists', returned unopposed as Liberal councillor for the central Collegiate Church ward in July 1894.

Scott, C.P.

Editor of the *Manchester Guardian*; passionate advocate of Home Rule and pioneer of the New Liberalism; fought North-East Manchester unsuccessfully as Liberal candidate in 1886, 1891 and 1892; later controversially stood down from North-East Manchester in favour of ILP candidate Leonard Hall; MP for Leigh, Lancashire from 1895–1906; continued to play an active part in Manchester Liberal politics serving as president of both the Manchester Liberal Unions and, from 1903, the Manchester Liberal Federation.

Smallman, Frederick

Formerly a railway clerk; became a specialist vegetarian retailer and restaurateur; passionate advocate of free education, independent Radical candidate in the 1888 Manchester School Board elections; Liberal councillor for St. John's ward 1889–92 and for Exchange ward 1894–96; an important member of the Radical and Progressive group on the council in the early 1890s. [*Faces and Places*, 4, 13]

Smith, Walton

Philanthropist and social reformer; Liberal councillor for New Cross ward 1868 to 1883; alderman from 1883; did much to promote a new Progressive municipal agenda in the 1880s after a series of embarrassing scandals undermined Liberal authority; chaired the unhealthy dwellings committee of the city council from 1886 and pioneered council housing in the city.

Southern, James W.

Prominent Congregationalist; timber merchant; prominent in movement to re-establish the National Reform Union, served for six years as Poor Law guardian on the Chorlton Board; councillor for St. Clement's ward 1877–83; councillor for St. Luke's from 1884 to 1897, when he was made an alderman; became a strong critic of council corruption in the 1880s and emerged as one of the Liberal party's most influential figures in the 1890s. [*Faces and Places*, 3, 9]

Thompson, Stephen C.

Brewer; key figure credited with much of the responsibility for the Conservative revival in East Manchester; much disliked by Liberal opponents – the *bête noir* of temperance reformers; introduced Balfour to Manchester politics and acted as his *de facto* agent; Conservative councillor for Ardwick 1879–91; alderman 1891–94; emerged as the leading critic of Liberal municipal administration but never recovered from his business failing – the reason for his political retirement; returned briefly as councillor for Arwick in 1897 until his death in 1899.

Biographical Notes

Leicester

Banton, George
Prominent trade unionist; chairman of the trades council and Independent Labour Party; formerly a Liberal sympathiser and a critic of socialism; member of the Westcotes Liberal ward committee and a supporter of H. Woolley's Liberal candidature as late as 1893; by 1894 he had joined the ILP and was an important ILP influence in the trades council; later developed a municipal career as a Labour representative for Wyggeston Ward; Labour MP for East Leicester 1918–24.

Barfoot, William
Proprietor of a large yarn-spinning business; veteran alderman who represented Castle ward on the town council after 1891; advocate of arbitration in trade disputes; a relatively rare example of a Liberal municipal leader who also played a role in the wider Liberal Party; president of the Liberal Club.

Burgess, Joseph
Journalist and ILP activist; correspondent for the *Manchester Courier*, sub-editor of the *Cotton Factory Times* and editor of the *Workman's Times*; member of the National Administrative Council of the ILP; a Liberal during his time in Yorkshire, he became an influential figure in socialist journalism; his unsuccessful ILP candidature in 1894 and 1895 did much to establish the credibility of the Leicester branch of the ILP; later an unsuccessful Labour candidate in Glasgow Camlachie (1906) and Montrose (1908 and 1910 (January) – the latter when he stood without the official endorsement of the NAC).[*Wyvern*, 12 July 1895]

Broadhurst, Henry
One of the country's leading Lib–Lab figures; 1872 president of the Labour Representation League; from 1875 secretary of the parliamentary committee of the TUC; MP for Stoke 1880–85; MP for Bordesley 1885–86; MP for Nottingham West 1886–92; defeated Liberal candidate in Great Grimsby; MP for Leicester 1894–1906; the decision of Leicester Liberals to invite Broadhurst to stand for parliament in the by-election of 1894 did much to slow the momentum of the local ILP. [H. Broadhurst, *Henry Broadhurst MP: the story of his life from a stonemason's bench to the Treasury bench told by himself* (London, 1901).]

Canner, Thomas
Prominent Conservative Party organiser in the mid-1880s; attracted controversy when charged with breaking the Corrupt Practices Act as a Conservative candidate for North St. Margaret's ward in 1885; committee chairman of the active but financially insecure Conservative Working-Men's Club which collapsed after the 1886 election.

Coppack, Charles
Journalist, political lecturer and registration organiser; agent for Harborough in 1886; although a little-known figure, his organisational work did much to establish Liberal pre-eminence in the county constituencies in 1885–86; between 1886–92 he worked on most of the major parliamentary by-elections in the country.

Cope, Thomas
Senior member of the local Conservative gentry; major landowner in West Leicestershire; called to the Bar in 1866; lord of the manors of Osbaston and Barlestone; chairman of the Midland Agricultural and Dairy Institute; chairman of Bosworth Conservative Association; Justice of the Peace; could do little to prevent growing Liberal strength in Bosworth parliamentary elections, but maintained the Conservatives' position in rural election campaigns; from 1885, vice-chairman of the county council, Bosworth Rural District Council and board of guardians.

Cort, Richard
Prominent Liberal trade unionist who departed from the party over industrial relations conflicts; formerly a member of the Belgrave ward Liberal executive; president of the Belgrave branch of the increasingly militant NUBSO; opposed Liberal nominee Samuel Hudson (shoe manufacturer).

De Lisle, Edwin
Prominent member of the Conservative North Leicestershire gentry; deputy lieutenant of Leicestershire, member of the Loughborough Board of Guardians; exploited Liberal divisions in Loughborough to revive the Conservative Party in the constituency; Conservative MP for Loughborough 1886–92.

Ellis, James
Senior member of the famous Ellis family with interests in landowning, quarrying and coalmining; chairman of the South Leicestershire Liberal Association and Leicester Liberal Association; very influential in the county's Liberal politics and regarded as being broadly sympathetic to 'advanced' Liberalism; MP for Bosworth 1885–92.

Faire, Samuel
Joint head of Faire Bros. and Co., boot and shoe manufacturers; Chamberlainite Liberal Unionist; president and chairman of the Leicester Liberal Unionist Association; active in local Liberal Unionism until merger of party with Conservatives; director of the Leicester Constitutional Club Co.; leading local philanthropist; High Sheriff for Leicestershire; knighted in 1905.

Faire, William Arthur
Prominent Anglican and Liberal Unionist; brother of Samuel; boot and shoe manufacturer; vice-president of the Church of England Temperance Society; served

on the executive committees of both the Leicester and Melton Liberal Unionist Associations.

Fielding Johnson, Thomas

Managing Director of Fielding and Johnson, the largest spinning firm in the town; one of the coterie of wealthy Liberal businessmen who left the Liberal party over Home Rule in 1886, although played little role in town politics; best known for his philanthropic work and as an educational benefactor; chairman of the Charity Organisation Society 1885–86; chairman of the Provident Dispensary 1890–95.

Gee, Harry S.

Leading Liberal Unionist businessman; chairman of Stead and Simpson's, boot manufacturers; chairman of Leicester Tramway Company; president of Leicester Chamber of Commerce; chairman of the Leicestershire Banking Company; frequently a speaker at political rallies, but did not seek high public office.

Hart, Israel

Influential figure in Liberal municipal politics between 1874–95; wholesale clothier; mayor of Leicester on four occasions; aspirant MP who was regularly passed over by the Leicester Liberal Association in favour of outside candidates; knighted in 1894 and returned to London a year later; defeated as Liberal candidate for Hythe in 1895 and 1899 and as Liberal candidate for Hackney Central in 1900.

Hawley, E.W. (Miss)

Pioneering female Liberal activist; leading figure in the Leicester branch of the Women's Liberal Association; first female president of the Leicester and District Teachers' Association.

Hazell, Walter

Partner in printing and publishing business; advocate of profit sharing; a surprising choice as the candidate to represent 'moderate' Liberal opinion at Westminster, he was much attacked for his industrial relations record by the ILP; in all three elections he contested he polled several thousand fewer votes than his Lib–Lab colleague, Henry Broadhurst; MP for Leicester 1894–1900.

Johnson Ferguson, J.E.

Wealthy Liberal patron and MP; controversial Radical figure who won a bitter selection contest to serve as Liberal MP for Loughborough 1885–86 and 1892–1900; frequently in conflict with his local Liberal Association, he eventually broke with the association following local Liberal attitudes to the Unionist Education Bill of 1896; defeated as Liberal parliamentary candidate for Burton in 1900.

Logan, John W.

Senior partner in firm of railway contractors, Logan and Hemmingway; won the marginal Harborough seat on the death of T.K. Tapling and subsequently made it a safe Liberal seat; a frequent and popular public speaker, he was an important figure in the Liberal Party's 1890s revival in South-East Leicestershire; served as MP for Harborough for two periods 1891–1904 and 1910–16.

Marris, S.A.

Congregationalist and freemason; director of the Coffee House Co.; member of the Knighton Sanitary Authority and Highway Board; controversial Liberal opponent of the extension of Leicester's town boundaries; elected for the Knighton and Oadby division in the first county council elections defeating the well-known Liberal Unionist and incorporationist, Ald. Thomas Wright. [*Wyvern*, 29 June 1894].

McArthur, Alexander

Son of a Wesleyan minister; former member of the legislative assembly of New South Wales; member of the first London School Board; very reluctant supporter of Home Rule; 'moderate' MP for Leicester until 1892. [*MFP*, 28 November 1885]

McLaren, Charles B.B.

Barrister with considerable commercial interests; called to the Bar 1874; Queen's Counsel 1897; business interests in coal, rail, steel, shipping and landowning; regarded as being on the Radical wing of the party; Liberal MP for Stafford 1880–86; MP for Bosworth 1892–1910.

Millican, William

Leading Conservative in the Leicester town council; Justice of the Peace; retired Lieutenant Colonel of the Volunteers; active in various organisational roles in the Conservative Party and a vice-president of the Conservative Club; active and articulate Conservative public speaker; unsuccessful, and somewhat reluctant, Conservative candidate in Leicester in 1885; died November 1889. [*LDM*, 4 November 1889]

Packe, Hussey

Member of the north Leicestershire gentry and a dissident Whig Liberal; unsuccessful Liberal candidate in North Leicestershire in 1874 and 1880; he was controversially rejected by the Radical Loughborough Liberal Association in 1885 for a more 'advanced' candidate and rejected offers to stand for the adjacent Melton constituency; rapidly became disaffected with the party and played very little role in local politics; stood unsuccessfully for the Conservatives in Loughborough in 1900.

Picton, J. Allanson

Former Congregationalist minister at Cheetham, Leicester and Hackney before being disowned by Congregationalists for his latitudinarian views; member of the first London School Board; controversially selected by the Leicester Liberal Association as their Radical parliamentary candidate in preference to Richard Chamberlain; reluctant supporter of Home Rule; MP for Leicester 1884–94.

Rolleston, John F.L.
President of the Leicester Conservative Association and a key mover in the formation of a permanent Conservative registration organisation in Leicester after 1885; chairman of Leicester Conservative Association from 1890; unsuccessful Conservative parliamentary candidate in Leicester 1894 and 1895; Conservative MP for Leicester 1900–1906 (defeated twice in 1906); Conservative MP for Hertford 1910 (January)–1916.

Sedgwick, George
Prominent Unitarian and Liberal trade unionist; participated in the formation of the National Union of Boot and Shoe Operatives in 1874 and served as its first agent; general secretary of the NUBSO until 1886, when resigned to become factory inspector; Liberal member of the school board 1879–86; member of the TUC parliamentary committee; Justice of the Peace 1886; first chairman of the Leicester Working-Men's Club.

Sloane, John
Prominent Irish Liberal councillor; represented West St. Mary's ward 1867–76; influential sanitary reformer and Radical; key figure in the organisation of municipal and parliamentary election campaigns until the mid-1880s. [*MFP*, 15 August 1891].

Tapling, T.K.
Head of a major London warehouse and carpeting firm, Tapling and Co., called to the Bar in 1881; nationally recognised stamp collector; unsuccessful Conservative candidate in Harborough 1885; MP for Harborough 1885–91; his premature death in 1891 at the age of just 35 was a major blow to the local Conservatives who did not win the Harborough seat again until after the First World War. [*MFP*, 18 April 1891]

Titley, Richard
Vicar of Barwell, in the Bosworth constituency; Justice of the Peace; rare example of an Anglican Churchman holding public office; influential Conservative figure in an otherwise Liberal-dominated constituency; Conservative member of the Leicestershire County Council for Barwell and from 1894 a Conservative member of Hinckley Rural District Council and Barwell Parish Council.

Wakerley, Arthur
Leading Leicester architect and developer; largely responsible for developing the new suburb of North Evington; formerly a Conservative, but elected to the borough council as a Liberal in 1886; chairman of the council's highways committee from 1895 and at the age of 35 made the borough's youngest ever mayor; twice the unsuccessful Liberal candidate in the Melton division in 1895 and 1906; served periods as president of the Liberal Association, the Temperance Union and the

Property Owner's Association. [J. Farquhar, *Arthur Wakerley 1862–1931* (Leicester, 1984).]

Whitehead, James

Representative of Leicester's 'moderate' Liberal opinion at Westminster; London alderman 1881–82; sheriff of London and Middlesex 1884–85; unsuccessful Liberal candidate in Westmorland, Appleby 1885 and 1886; negotiator in the Great London Dock strike of 1889; skilful manoeuvring from sympathisers in Leicester meant that he met with little opposition for the Leicester Liberal nomination; played little role in Leicester's local politics; MP for Leicester 1890–94.

Windley, Thomas

Co-founder and publisher of the *Midland Free Press*, the area's best known Radical journal; elected as a Liberal to the town council for North St. Margaret's Ward in 1872; chairman of the sanitary committee from 1876–1921; promoter of the controversial quarantine system for dealing with smallpox; twice mayor in 1900 and 1901.

Wood, Edward

Influential Baptist and patron of the Victoria Road Baptist Church; best known as a director of Freeman, Hardy, Willis, boot manufacturers; leading 'moderate' Liberal in the council chamber; mayor on four occasions – 1888, 1895, 1901, 1906.

Woolley, Harry H.

Prominent Liberal trade unionist; Treasurer of the NUBSO from 1885 and also served as secretary of the influential No.1 branch of that union; served as chairman of the trades council and the boot trade arbitration board.

Wright, Thomas

Controversial Liberal and then Liberal Unionist alderman; prime mover of proposals to extend the boundaries of the town and the principal architect of the 1891 extension measures; he was widely expected to be the Unionist candidate for Leicester at the 1892 general election and caused a minor sensation by declining at short notice; his return to the Liberal ranks was a major reason for the collapse of the Leicester Liberal Unionist Association; after the 1895 general election he went back to the Unionists.

Appendix Two

Parliamentary Election Results 1885–1895

[From F.W.S. Craig (ed.), *British Parliamentary Election Results, 1885–1918*, second edition (Aldershot, 1989), 136, 148–53, 317.]

Leicester (Two Seats)

Electors	Turnout	Candidate	Party	Vote	%
1885					
21,671	83.5	J.A. Picton	Lib	11,480	39.1
		A. McArthur	Lib	11,121	37.9
		W. Millican	Con	6,751	23.0
1886					
21,671	71.3	J.A. Picton	Lib	9,914	39.2
		A. McArthur	Lib	9,681	38.3
		R. Bickersteth	LU	5,686	22.5
1892					
		J.A. Picton	Lib	Unopposed	
		J. Whitehead	Lib	Unopposed	
1894	(29/8)				
23,125	77.2	H. Broadhurst	L–Lab	9,464	33.8
		W. Hazell	Lib	7,184	25.6
		J.F.L. Rolleston	Con	6,967	24.9
		J. Burgess	ILP	4,402	15.7
1895					
24,113	78.2	H. Broadhurst	L–Lab	9,792	33.6
		W. Hazell	Lib	7,753	26.5
		J.F.L. Rolleston	Con	7,654	26.2
		J. Burgess	ILP	4,009	13.7

Manchester East

Electors	Turnout	Candidate	Party	Vote	%
1885					
9,779	84.3	A.J. Balfour	Con	4,536	55.0
		A. Hopkinson	Lib	3,712	45.0
1886					
9,779	78.5	A.J. Balfour	Con	4,160	54.2
		J.H. Crosfield	Lib	3,516	45.8
1886 (11/8)					
		A.J. Balfour	Con	Unopposed	
1892					
11,418	86.7	A.J. Balfour	Con	5,147	52.0
		J.E.C. Munro	Lib	4,749	48.0
1895 (1/7)					
		A.J. Balfour	Con	Unopposed	
1895					
11,991	83.4	A.J. Balfour	Con	5,386	53.9
		J.E.C. Munro	Lib	4,610	46.1

Manchester North

Electors	Turnout	Candidate	Party	Vote	%
1885					
8,703	82.9	J.F. Hutton	Con	4,093	56.8
		C.E. Schwann	Lib	3,118	43.2
1886					
8,703	78.8	C.E. Schwann	Lib	3,476	50.7
		J.F. Hutton	Con	3,380	49.3
1892					
9,747	84.2	C.E. Schwann	Lib	4,258	51.9
		J.M. Yates	Con	3,953	48.1
1895					
10,179	80.5	C.E. Schwann	Lib	4,327	52.8
		A.H.A. Morton	Con	3,872	47.2

Manchester North-East

Electors	Turnout	Candidate	Party	Vote	%
1885					
8,579	84.3	J. Fergusson	Con	4,341	60.0
		R. Blennerhassett	Lib	2,893	40.0
1886					
8,579	82.0	J. Fergusson	Con	3,680	52.3
		C.P. Scott	Lib	3,353	47.7
1891	(8/10)				
9,288	85.8	J. Fergusson	Con	4,058	50.9
		C.P. Scott	Lib	3,908	49.1
1892					
9,449	88.6	J. Fergusson	Con	4,239	50.7
		C.P. Scott	Lib	4,129	49.3
1895					
9,893	83.2	J. Fergusson	Con	3,961	48.2
		E. Holt	Lib	3,720	45.2
		J. Johnson	ILP	546	6.6

Manchester North-West

Electors	Turnout	Candidate	Party	Vote	%
1885					
12,685	86.3	W. Houldsworth	Con	5,834	53.3
		J. Slagg	Lib	5,111	46.7
1886					
12,685	78.4	W. Houldsworth	Con	5,489	55.2
		H. Lee	Lib	4,453	44.8
1892					
		W. Houldsworth	Con	Unopposed	
1895					
11,741	72.6	W. Houldsworth	Con	4,997	58.6
		T.F. Byrne	Lib	3,526	41.4

Manchester South

Electors	Turnout	Candidate	Party	Vote	%
1885					
8,534	81.0	H.E. Roscoe	Lib	3,791	54.8
		P. Royle	Con	3,121	45.2
1886					
8,534	75.9	H.E. Roscoe	Lib	3,407	52.6
		T. Sowler	Con	3,072	47.4
1892					
10,228	81.2	H.E. Roscoe	Lib	4,245	51.1
		Viscount Emlyn	Con	4,064	48.9
1895					
10,945	80.7	Marq. of Lorne	LU	4,457	50.4
		H.E. Roscoe	Lib	4,379	49.6

Manchester South-West

Electors	Turnout	Candidate	Party	Vote	%
1885					
8,890	82.0	Lord F. Hamilton	Con	3,929	53.9
		J. Bright	Lib	3,362	46.1
1886					
8,890	79.1	J. Bright	Lib	3,570	50.8
		Lord F. Hamilton	Con	3,459	49.2
1892					
9,674	79.6	J. Bright	Lib	3,924	51.0
		A. Hopkinson	LU	3,776	49.0
1895					
9,496	78.9	W.J. Galloway	Con	3,994	53.3
		J.M. Astbury	Lib	3,496	46.7

Lancashire, Gorton

Electors	Turnout	Candidate	Party	Vote	%
1885					
10,334	84.7	R. Peacock	Lib	5,300	60.6
		D.I. Flattely	Con	3,452	39.4
1886					
10,334	84.4	R. Peacock	Lib	4,592	52.6
		Vis. Grey	Con	4,135	47.4
1889	(22/3)				
10,674	88.7	W. Mather	Lib	5,155	54.5
		E.F.G. Hatch	Con	4,309	45.5
1892					
11,782	87.3	W. Mather	Lib	5,255	51.1
		E.F.G. Hatch	Con	5,033	48.9
1895					
12,961	78.1	E.F.G. Hatch	Con	5,865	57.9
		R.M. Pankhurst	ILP	4,261	42.1

Summaries of Municipal Election Results

Manchester 1890–95 (Annual November Elections - Contested wards only)

Ward	Liberal		Con / Unionist		ILP	
	Wins	Seats	Wins	Seats	Wins	Seats
All Saints'	2	2	1	1	0	0
Ardwick	0	0	3	3	0	0
Blackley	1	2	1	2	0	0
Bradford	1	1	0	0	1	1
Cheetham	0	0	2	2	0	0
Collegiate	0	0	1	1	0	0
Crumpsall	1	1	1	1	0	0
Exchange	4	4	0	0	0	0
Harpurhey	2	2	3	3	0	0
Longsight	2	3	1	2	0	0
Medlock St	1	1	3	3	0	0
Miles Platting	1	1	2	2	0	0
New Cross*	4	6	0	2	0	0
Newton Heath	1	2	3	4	0	0
Openshaw	2	3	2	3	1	1
Oxford	0	0	2	2	0	0
Rusholme	2	2	1	1	0	0
St. Anne's	0	0	2	2	0	0
St. Clement's	3	3	2	2	0	0
St. George's	1	1	3	3	0	0
St. James's	0	0	0	0	0	0
St. John's	2	2	4	4	0	0
St. Luke's	2	2	1	1	0	0
St. Mark's	4	6	1	1	0	0
St. Michael's	5	5	1	1	0	0

Notes

* New Cross was a 'double ward' with two councillors retiring annually.

These figures relate to the annual round of municipal election each November. They include double vacancy contests where these were held on the same day as the annual November municipal elections but otherwise exclude all by-elections. In the case of multiple vacancy contests the party with the largest average vote per candidate is credited with 'winning' the ward election – even if another party has won one of the seats.

[Sources: *The Official Handbook of Manchester and Salford*, series (Manchester, 1891–96), *Leicester Daily Mercury, Leicester Daily Post*]

Leicester 1891–96 (Annual November Elections – Contested wards only)

Ward	Liberal		Con / Unionist		ILP	
	Wins	Seats	Wins	Seats	Wins	Seats
Abbey	2	4	1	1	0	0
Aylestone	5	1	1	1	0	0
Belgrave	3	4	2	3	0	0
Castle	3	5	1	1	0	0
Charnwood	3	5	3	3	0	0
De Montfort	0	0	2	4	0	0
Humberstone	2	4	0	0	0	0
Knighton	0	2	2	2	0	0
Latimer	3	5	0	0	0	0
Newton	2	4	0	0	0	0
St. Martin's	3	4	0	1	0	0
Spinney Hill	2	4	0	0	0	0
Westcotes	3	5	2	2	0	0
Wycliffe	4	6	0	0	0	0
Wyggeston	4	6	0	0	1	1

Notes

These figures relate to the annual round of municipal election each November. They include double vacancy contests where these were held on the same day as the annual November municipal elections but otherwise exclude all by-elections. In the case of multiple vacancy contests the party with the largest average vote per candidate is credited with 'winning' the ward election – even if another party has won one of the seats.

[Sources: *The Official Handbook of Manchester and Salford*, series (Manchester, 1891–96), *Leicester Daily Mercury, Leicester Daily Post*]

Appendix Three

Factions within the Liberal Group on the Manchester City Council 1885–1895

Progressive / Radical Group

Name	**Ward**	**Date First Elected**	**Status**
Abbot, T.C.	St. Clement's	1890	Cllr.
Birkbeck, W.	New Cross	1887	Cllr.
Brown, W.	St. Michael's	1870	Ald.1885
Butterworth, W.	Crumpsall	1890	Cllr.
Carhart, R.	St. George's	1891	Cllr.
Eggington, T.	St. Luke's	1892	Cllr
Fullerton, J.B.	New Cross	1887	Cllr.
Greenhow, J.H.	Oxford	1891	Cllr.
Hutt, J.	Bradford	1885	Cllr.
Kelley, G.D.	St. Clement's	1891	Cllr.
McCreesh, J.	St. Michael's	1891	Cllr.
Saxon, J.	Openshaw	1891	Cllr.
Smith, W.	New Cross	1868	Ald. 1883
Stanley, G.	Blackley	1890	Ald. 1890
Trevor, W.	Newton Heath	1890	Cllr.
Uttley, T.	Longsight	1890	Cllr.
Wainwright, W.H.	St. Mark's	1890	Cllr.
Well, J.H.	St. Michael's	1890	Cllr.

'Moderate' Group

Name	**Ward**	**Date First Elected**	**Status**
Brooks, J.	Collegiate	1885	Cllr.
Heywood, A.	Collegiate	1843	Ald. 1853
Higginbottom, L.	St. Mark's	1890	Ald. 1890
Plummer, H.	Rusholme	1892	Cllr.
Rawson, H.	Exchange*	1856	Ald. 1894
Rushworth, J.	Cheetham	1880	Ald. 1892
Thompson, J.	Ardwick	1865	Ald. 1879

Notes

* Rawson represented Cheetham as a councillor from March 1856 to March 1861 and from November 1862 to April 1865. He was first elected for Exchange Ward in 1884.

The above factions have been determined from study of voting records for ten key voting divisions at full council meetings between 1885 and 1895. They were the motions/amendments:

1. Proposing the abolition of the office of alderman (6 January 1886).
2. Proposing that all council members be directly elected (27 October 1886).
3. Supporting a committee report for the removal of 'Unhealthy Dwellings'(16 March 1887).
4. Refusing the granting of a theatrical licence to George Scott for the 'Palace of Varieties' (6 April 1892).
5. Amending council standing orders to prevent recommendations being brought before council which advocated salary increases of more than 10 per cent for officials earning more than three guineas a week (21 September 1892).
6. Allowing the Manchester and Salford Trades Council to hold meetings in the Town Hall (5 October 1892).
7. Suggesting further investigation of allegations against a senior police officer (1 March 1893).
8. Deferring consideration of pay rises to senior officials, except in exceptional circumstances (1 March 1893).
9. Moving the 'previous question' to halt discussion of a 48-hour week for corporation manual labourers (3 October 1894).
10. Instructing the pavings committee to introduce an eight-hour day for corporation workmen (25 September 1895).

Councillors and aldermen who voted on the Progressive/Radical side on a ratio of more than three to one have been classified as part of the Progressive/Radical group.

Councillors and aldermen who voted on the 'moderate' side on a ratio of more than three to one have been classified as part of the 'moderate' group.

To be eligible for consideration councillors and aldermen must have attended and voted in at least four of the divisions listed above. These calculations therefore largely neglect 'regular' non-attendees and those who served as councillors or aldermen for only very short periods.

These calculations exclude all Liberal Unionists as they were regarded as being in alliance with the Conservatives after 1892.

[Sources: *Manchester City News*, *Manchester Courier*, *Manchester Guardian* and the Manchester City Council *Proceedings*.]

Bibliography

All archival material in the bibliography is listed with the appropriate collection reference number where one is available. In a few instances there is no one catalogue number that covers all material consulted. In the case of the minutes of the Manchester Liberal Union for the 1890s, held at the Manchester Central Library, there is a small discrepancy between sub-numbers shown in the archival catalogue and the material itself – the numbers that appear on the material are listed here. In a very few cases the Manchester Central Library catalogue displays two reference numbers for printed material, one of which is obsolete. For clarity only the current archival reference numbers are provided here. The National Reform Union's bound pamphlet collection is anonymously catalogued as a 'political pamphlet collection' and although I was unable to confirm its origins, the nature of the material suggests that it has indeed come from the Manchester-based NRU. In more than 100 volumes, it represents a valuable and little-known asset for the late-nineteenth-century political historian.

Manuscript Sources

Manchester

George Birdsall Correspondence, Manchester Central Library, M158/1/1.

Robert Blatchford Correspondence, Manchester Central Library, MSF 920 5 B27.

John Bright Correspondence, Manchester Central Library, MISC 473.

Manchester Corporation Committee and Letter Books, Manchester Central Library, M9, M227.

Manchester Liberal Association Minute Books, Manchester Central Library, M283.

Manchester Liberal Union Minute Books, Manchester Central Library, M283.

Manchester Reform Club Minute Books, John Rylands University Library of Manchester.

Moss Side Letters, Manchester Central Library, M158/1.

Odds and Ends Magazine of the St. Paul's Literary Society, Vols XXXV (1889) XXXVI (1890) XL (1894), Manchester Central Library, M38/4/2/35–6, 40.

Parliamentary Election Expense Returns (Manchester), Manchester Central Library, MISC 268.

Rochdale Reform Association Minutes, Rochdale Record Office.

C.P. Scott Correspondence, John Rylands University Library of Manchester, *Guardian* archive boxes 118–30.

William Axon papers, Manchester Central Library, M158/2.

Withington Conservative Association Minutes, Manchester Central Library, M128/1/2.
Withington Conservative Club Minutes, Manchester Central Library, M128/1/1.

Leicester

Henry Broadhurst Papers, British Library of Economic and Political Science, Vol VI.
East St. Margaret's Ward Liberal Association Minute Book, Leicestershire Record Office, 11 D 57/5.
Harborough Liberal Association Minute Books, Leicestershire Record Office, DE 1637.
Leicester and Leicestershire Conservative Club Minute Books, Leicestershire Record Office, DE 1574.
Leicester Constitutional Club Minutes, Leicestershire Record Office, DE 1574.
Leicester Liberal Association Minute Book, Leicestershire Record Office, 11 D 57.
Leicester Liberal Club Board of Directors' Minute Book, Leicestershire Record Office 10 D 62/1–12.
Leicester Town Council Minutes, Leicestershire Record Office, CM 1/18–30, CM8.
Leicester Town Clerks' Letter Books, Leicestershire Record Office, 22/D/57/102.
Leicester Secular Society Minute Books, Leicestershire Record Office 10 D 68.
Liberal Association for Harborough and Bosworth Divisions Minute Books, Leicestershire Record Office, DE 1637.
Lubenham Conservative Club Minutes, Leicestershire Record Office, DE 4590/9–10.
South Wigston Conservative Club Minutes, Leicestershire Record Office, DE 562/1.

General/Other

Joseph Chamberlain Papers, Birmingham University Library.
Frances Johnson Collection, British Library of Economic and Political Science, FJ 1893–96.
ILP Minute Books and Archive, British Library of Economic and Political Science, M890/1 ILP 1/1.
National Liberal Club Archive, Bristol University Library, DM 668, DM 1134 (JN1129.L4.P2).

Archival Printed Sources

Manchester

George Birdsall Cuttings Book, Manchester Central Library, f379.4273 Bil.

City of Manchester, *Council Members from Incorporation* (annotated), Manchester Central Library, BR352.OL12 M99.

Manchester and District Liberal Unionist Association circular, 19 June 1891, Manchester Central Library, Local Studies Box 517.

Manchester and Salford Sanitary Association Annual Reports, Manchester Metropolitan University Library (Microfilm).

Manchester and Salford Trades Council Annual Reports, Manchester Central Library, 331.88 M30 LHN.

Manchester Cuttings Collection, Volume II, 1880–1892, Manchester Central Library, F942.7389 M119.

Manchester Chamber of Commerce Monthly Record, Manchester Central Library (Microfilm).

Manchester Domestic Mission Annual Reports, Manchester Metropolitan University Library (Microfilm).

Manchester Ratepayers' Association Annual Reports, Manchester Central Library, P3416/15.

Manchester Religious Pamphlet Collection, Manchester Central Library, LHB 44.

Moss Side Election Broadsides, Manchester Central Library, LB3.

Moss Side Urban District Council Broadsides, Manchester Central Library, LB7.

National Reform Union Pamphlet collection, Manchester Central Library, 306 N6.

C.P. Scott Cuttings Book, John Rylands University Library of Manchester, *Guardian* Archive Box 74.

C.P. Scott Cuttings (loose), John Rylands University Library of Manchester, *Guardian* Archive 136/1–7.

Slater's Manchester and Salford Directory (Manchester 1892), Manchester Central Library, 914 273 M2.

Leicester

Gould, F.J., *The History of Leicester Secular Society* (Leicester, 1900), Leicestershire Record Office, 10/D/68/17.

Leicester Burgess Roll 1891–92, Leicestershire Record Office, DE 3278/172 SRI.

Leicester Liberal Party Miscellaneous Papers, Leicestershire Record Office 10 D 64/1–6.

Leicester Secular Society Scrapbook, Leicestershire Record Office, 10/D/68/6.

Leicester Working-Men's Conservative Club *Rules*, Leicestershire Record Office, DG 24/755.

National Union of Boot and Shoe Operatives Monthly Reports, Leicestershire Record Office, DE 3989/40–45.

General/Other

National Liberal Federation pamphlets, John Rylands University Library of Manchester (Microfilm).

National Union pamphlets, John Rylands University Library of Manchester, (Microfilm).
Women's Suffrage collection pamphlets, Manchester Central Library (Microfilm).

Contemporary Publications (pre-1935)

Manchester

Axon, W.E.A., *Annals of Manchester* (Manchester, 1886).
Galloway, J.R., 'The Evidence of Statistics in Relation to our Social Conditions', *Transactions of the Manchester Statistical Society*, 18 December 1889, 1889–90, 25–50.
Balfour, A.J., *Chapters of Autobiography* (London, 1930).
Brocklehurst, F., *I was in Prison* (London, 1898).
Hall, F., *A Northern Pioneer: The Story of J.R. Lancashire* (London, 1927).
Haslam Mills, W., *The Manchester Reform Club 1871–1921* (Manchester, 1921).
Hertz, G.B., *The Manchester Politician, 1750–1912* (London, 1912).
Hopkinson, M. and Hopkinson, E., *John and Alice Hopkinson, 1824–1910* (London n.d).
Hopkinson, Sir A., *Penultima* (London, 1930).
Horsfall, T.C., 'The Government of Manchester', *Transactions of the Manchester Statistical Society*, 13 November 1895, 1895–96, 1–28.
Horsfall, T.C., *Ought Mayors and Chairmen of Committees of Town Councils be Appointed for Long Periods of Time and be paid Salaries to Enable Them to Give All Their Working Time to the Service of the Community?* (Manchester, 1903).
Lawson, R.G., *The City Council Seen From the Inside* (Manchester ,1904).
Leech, Sir B.T., *History of the Manchester Ship Canal* (Manchester, 1907).
Mather, L.E., *The Rt. Hon. Sir William Mather* (London, 1925).
Marcroft, A., *Landmarks of Local Liberalism* (Oldham, 1913).
Moss, F., *Fifty Years Public Work in Didsbury* (Manchester 1915).
Pankhurst, E., *My Own Story* (London, 1914).
Rooke, G., 'On the Report of the Royal Commission on the Aged Poor, 26th February 1895', *Transactions of the Manchester Statistical Society*, 11 December 1895, 1895–96, 29–55.
Roscoe, Sir H.E., *The Life and Experiences of Sir Henry E. Roscoe* (London, 1906).
Rowley, C., *Fifty Years of Work Without Wages* (London 1912).
Rowley, C., *Fifty Years of Ancoats: Loss and Gain* (Manchester, 1899).
Royle, D.K., *William Royle of Rusholme* (Manchester, 1924).
Royle, William, *Rusholme: Past and Present* (Manchester, 1905).
Scott, J., *Leaves from the Diary of a Citizens' Auditor* (Manchester, 1884).
The Official Handbook of Manchester and Salford, series, (Manchester, 1884–96).
Thorpe, E., *Sir Henry Enfield Roscoe*, (London, 1916).

Leicester

Biggs, J.T., *Sanitation Versus Vaccination* (London, 1912).
Broadhurst, H., *Henry Broadhurst MP: the story of his life from a stonemason's bench to the Treasury bench told by himself* (London, 1901).
Clarke Nuttal, G., *Guide to Leicester and Neighbourhood* (Leicester 1905).
Cooper, T., *Life of Thomas Cooper* (London, 1872).
Gould, F.J., *The History of the Leicester Secular Society* (Leicester, 1900).
Greening, E.O., *A Pioneer of Co-partnership* (Leicester, 1923).
Howes, C., *Leicester – its Civic and Social Life* (Leicester, 1927).
Knight, D.J. (ed.), *Thomas Harrold papers* (Leicester, 1990).
Lott, F.B., *The Centenary Book of the Leicester Literary and Philosophical Society* (Leicester, 1935).
Pike, W. and Scarfe, W., *Leicestershire and Rutland at the Opening of the Twentieth Century* (Brighton, 1902), reprint (Edinburgh, 1985).
Read, R., *Modern Leicester* (London, 1881).
Storey, J. *Historical Sketch of Some of the principal Works and Undertakings of the Council at the Borough of Leicester* (Leicester, 1895).
Wakerley, A., *North Evington, Leicester* (Leicester, 1913).

General/Other

Engels, F., *The Condition of the Working Class in England*, reprint (Chicago, 1984).
Hobhouse, *L.T., Democracy and Reaction* (London, 1904).
Hobson, J.A., *The Psychology of Jingoism* (London, 1901).
Rowntree, B.S., *Poverty: A Study of Town Life* (London, 1901).
Russell Smart, H., *Municipal Socialism* (Manchester, 1895).
Webb, S. and Webb, B., *English Local Government*, reprint (London, 1963).

Press and periodicals

Manchester

County Forum Gazette
Faces and Places
Gorton Reporter
Manchester City News
Manchester City Lantern and Free-Lance
Manchester Courier
Manchester Evening News
Manchester Evening Mail
Manchester Free Press and Northern Counties Advertiser

Manchester Guardian
Manchester Saturday Halfpenny
Manchester Weekly Post
Manchester Weekly Times
Manchester Examiner
Moss Side District News
Northern Advance
Pioneer
South Manchester Chronicle
South Manchester Gazette
Spy
The City Ledger
The Leader and General Advertiser
The People's Cause
Transactions of the Manchester Statistical Society

Leicester

Hinckley News
Hinckley Times
Leicester Advertiser
Leicester Chronicle
Leicester Daily Express
Leicester Daily Mercury
Leicester Daily Post
Leicester Journal
Midland Free Press
Pioneer
The Countryman
Weekly Herald
Wyvern

General/Other

Catholic Herald
Clarion
Commonweal
Cotton Factory Times
Economist
Fortnightly Review
Justice
Labour Prophet
Labour Leader
Methodist Recorder

Nineteenth Century
Pall Mall Gazette
The Liberal Magazine
Weekly Herald
Workman's Times
Westminster Gazette

Unpublished Theses

Manchester

Bather, L., 'A History of Manchester and Salford Trades Council', Unpublished PhD thesis, University of Manchester, 1956.

Farnie, D., 'The English Cotton Industry, 1850–1896', Unpublished MA thesis, University of Manchester, 1953.

Fielding, S., 'The Irish Catholics of Manchester and Salford: Aspects of their Religious and Political History, 1890–1939', Unpublished PhD thesis, University of Warwick, 1988.

Hill, J., 'Working Class Politics in Lancashire 1885–1906: A Regional Study in the Origins of the Labour Party', Unpublished PhD thesis, University of Keele, 1969.

Jones, B., 'Manchester Liberalism 1918–1929: the electoral, ideological and organisational experience of the Liberal Party in Manchester, with particular reference to the career of Ernest Simon', Unpublished PhD thesis, University of Manchester, 1997.

Lowe, W.J., 'The Irish in Lancashire, 1846–1871; a Social History', Unpublished PhD thesis, Trinity College, Dublin, 1975.

McGhie, S., 'Liberal Politics in Manchester, Oldham and Stoke-on-Trent, 1906–1922', Unpublished PhD thesis, Manchester Metropolitan University (forthcoming).

Rushton, P., 'Housing Conditions and the Family Economy in the Victorian Slum: a Study of a Manchester District (Ancoats), 1790–1871', Unpublished PhD thesis, University of Manchester, 1977.

Seuss Law, G., 'Manchester's Politics 1885–1906', Unpublished PhD thesis, University of Pennsylvania, 1975.

Smith, L., 'John Trevor and the Labour Church Movement,' Unpublished MA thesis, Huddersfield Polytechnic, 1985.

Taylor, A., 'Ernest Jones: his later career and the structure of Manchester politics, 1861–1869', Unpublished MA thesis, University of Birmingham, 1984.

Whitaker, P., 'The Growth of Liberal Organisation in Manchester from the Eighteen Sixties to 1903', Unpublished PhD thesis, University of Manchester, 1956.

Leicester

Abisror, A., 'Stoneygate – A Leicester Victorian Suburb 1891–1914', Unpublished MA thesis, University of Leicester, 1994.

Cox, D., 'The Rise of the Labour Party in Leicester', Unpublished MA thesis, University of Leicester, 1959.

Little, A., 'Chartism and Liberalism: Popular Politics in Leicestershire 1842–1874', Unpublished PhD thesis, University of Manchester, 1991.

Rimmington, G.T., 'The Historical Geography of the Engineering Industry in Leicester', Unpublished MA thesis, University of Leicester, 1959.

General/Other

Barrow, L., 'The Socialism of Robert Blatchford and the *Clarion* newspaper 1889–1918', Unpublished PhD thesis, University of London, 1975.

Meyer, S.H., 'Organised Religion and English Working Class Movements, 1850–1914', Unpublished PhD thesis, University of Manchester, 1961.

Summers, D.F., 'The Labour Church and Allied Movements in the Late Nineteenth and early Twentieth Centuries', Unpublished PhD thesis, University of Edinburgh, 1958.

Books

Manchester

Butler, R., *As They Saw Her…Emmeline Pankhurst* (London, 1970).

Davies, A. and Fielding, S. (eds), *Workers' Worlds; Cultures and Communities in Manchester and Salford* (Manchester, 1992).

Chorley, K., *Manchester Made Them* (London, 1950).

Clarke, P.F., *Lancashire and the New Liberalism* (Cambridge, 1971).

Farnie, D., *The Manchester Ship Canal and the Rise of the Port of Manchester* (Manchester, 1980).

Fowler, A. and Wyke, T. (eds), *The Barefoot Aristocrats* (Littleborough, 1987).

Frow, E. and Frow, R., *To Make That Future Now! A History of the Manchester and Salford Trades Council* (Manchester, 1976).

Hammond, J.L., *The Making of the Manchester Guardian* (Manchester, 1932).

Hewitt, M., *The Emergence of Stability in the Industrial City: Manchester 1832–1867* (Aldershot, 1996).

Howe, A.C., *The Cotton Masters* (Oxford, 1984).

Kelly, A., *Lydia Becker and the Cause* (Lancaster, 1992).

Kidd, A., *Manchester*, second edition (Keele, 1996).

Redford, A., *The History of Local Government in Manchester, Volume Three: The Last Half Century* (London, 1940).

Simon, S.D., *A Century of City Government* (Manchester, 1938).
Spiers, M., *Victoria Park, Manchester* (Manchester, 1976).
Stancliffe, F.S., *John Shaw's 1738–1938* (Manchester 1938).
Walton, J., *Lancashire: A Social History 1558–1939*, reprint (Manchester, 1994).
Williams, B., *The Making of Manchester Jewry* (Manchester, 1976).

Leicester

Baynton, H. and Pitches, G., *Desirable Locations – Leicester's Middle Class Suburbs* (Leicester, 1996).
Elliott, M., *Victorian Leicester* (London, 1979).
Ellis, I.C., *Records of Nineteenth Century Leicester* (Leicester, 1935).
Evans, R.H.(ed.), *The Victoria History of the County of Leicester*, IV (1958).
Farquhar, J., *Arthur Wakerley 1862–1931* (Leicester, 1984).
Fox, A., *A History of the National Union of Boot and Shoe Operatives 1874–1957* (Oxford, 1958).
Francis, H.J., *A History of Hinckley* (Hinckley, 1930).
Lancaster, B., *Radicalism, Co-operation and Socialism: Leicester working-class politics 1860–1906* (Leicester, 1987).
Nash, D. and Reeder, D. (eds), *Leicester in the Twentieth Century* (Stroud, 1993).
Patterson, A.T., *Radical Leicester* (Leicester, 1954).
Simmons, J., *Leicester Past and Present: Volume II The Modern City*, (London, 1974).

General/Other

Anderson, G., *Victorian Clerks* (Manchester, 1976).
Barker, M., *Gladstone and Radicalism: The Reconstruction of Liberal Policy in Britain, 1885–94* (Brighton 1975).
Blake, R., *The Conservative Party from Peel to Thatcher*, paperback edition (London, 1985).
Bebbington, D.W., *The Nonconformist Conscience: Chapel and Politics, 1870–1914* (London, 1892).
Biagini, E.F.(ed.), *Community and Citizenship: Liberals, Radicals and collective identities in the British isles, 1865–1931* (Cambridge 1996).
Biagini, E.F., *Liberty, Retrenchment and Reform: Popular Liberalism in the Age of Gladstone 1860–80* (Cambridge 1991).
Biagini, E.F. and Reid, A. (eds), *Currents of Radicalism; Popular Radicalism, organised labour and party politics in Britain, 1850–1914* (Cambridge, 1991).
Blake, R., *The Conservative Party From Peel to Thatcher*, paperback edition (London, 1985).
Cannadine, D., *Class in Britain* (London, 1998).
Cole, G.D.H., *British Working Class Politics, 1832–1914* (London, 1941).

Collins, N., *Politics and Elections in Nineteenth century Liverpool* (Aldershot, 1994).

Cooke, A.B. and Vincent, J., *The Governing Passion: Cabinet Government and Party Politics in Britain, 1885–1886* (Brighton, 1974).

Craig, F.W.S. (ed.), *British Parliamentary Election Results 1885–1918*, (Aldershot, 1989).

Crossick, G. (ed.), *The Lower Middle Class in Britain* (London, 1977).

Dangerfield, G., *The Strange Death of Liberal England* (London, 1936).

Denecke, D. and Shaw, G. (eds), *Urban Historical Geography – Recent Progress in Britain and Germany* (Cambridge, 1988).

Dennis, R., *English Industrial Cities in the Nineteenth Century – A Social Geography*, reprint (Cambridge, 1986).

Dyos, H.J., *Victorian Suburb: A Study in the Growth of Camberwell* (London, 1961).

Emy, H.V., *Liberals, Radicals and Social Politics, 1892–1914* (Cambridge 1973).

Everitt, A. (ed.), *Perspectives in English Urban History* (London, 1973).

Felman, D. and Stedman Jones, G. (eds), *Metropolis London* (London, 1989).

Feuchtwanger, E.J., *Gladstone*, second edition (London, 1989).

Forster, J., *Class Struggle and the Industrial Revolution: Early Industrial Capitalism in three English Towns* (London, 1974).

Fraser, D., *Urban Politics in Victorian England* (Leicester, 1976).

Fraser, P., *Joseph Chamberlain; Radicalism and Empire, 1868–1914* (London, 1966).

Freeden, M., *The New Liberalism: An Ideology of Social Reform* (Oxford, 1978).

Freeden, M., *Liberalism Divided: A Study in British Political Thought* (Oxford, 1986).

Garrard, J., *Democratisation in Britain* (Basingstoke, 2002).

Garrard, J., *Leadership and Power in Victorian Industrial towns, 1830–1880* (Manchester, 1983).

Garrard, J., Jary, D., Goldsmith, M. and Oldfield, A.(eds), *The Middle Class in Politics* (Farnborough, 1978).

Green, E.H.H., *The Crisis of Conservatism: the politics, economics and ideology of the Conservative Party, 1880–1914* (London, 1995).

Hamer, D.A., *Liberal Politics in the Age of Gladstone and Rosebery* (Oxford, 1972).

Hammond, J.L., *Gladstone and the Irish Nation* (London, 1938).

Harvie, C., *The Lights of Liberalism: University Liberals and the challenge of democracy, 1860–86* (London, 1976).

Harris, J., *William Beveridge – A Biography*, revised edition (Oxford, 1997).

Harris, R. and Larkham, P. (eds), *Changing Suburbs: Foundation, Form and Function* (London, 1999).

Hay, J.R., *The Origins of the Liberal Welfare Reforms* (London, 1975).

Hennock, E.P., *Fit and Proper Persons – Ideal and Reality in Nineteenth Century Urban Government* (London, 1973).

Hirst, F.W. and Redlich, J., *Local Government in England* (London, 1902), Volume II.

Howell, D., *British Workers and the Independent Labour Party 1888–1906* (Manchester, 1983).

Hurst, M., *Joseph Chamberlain and West Midlands Politics, 1885–1895* (Oxford 1962).

Hurst, M., *Joseph Chamberlain and Liberal Reunion* (London, 1967).

Jagger, P.J. (ed.), *Gladstone* (London, 1998).

James, D., Jowitt, T. and Laybourn, K., *The Centennial History of the Independent Labour Party* (London, 1993).

Jay, R., *Joseph Chamberlain: A Political Study* (Oxford, 1981).

Jenkins, T.A., *Gladstone, Whiggery and the Liberal Party, 1874–1886* (Oxford, 1988).

Jenkins, T.A., *The Liberal Ascendancy 1830–1886* (London, 1994).

Johnson, J. and Pooley, C. (eds), *The Structure of Nineteenth Century Cities* (London, 1982).

Jones, A., *The Politics of Reform 1884* (Cambridge, 1972).

Joyce, P., *Work, Society and Politics: The Culture of the Factory in Later Victorian Britain* (Brighton, 1980).

Joyce, P., *Visions of the People, Industrial England and the Question of Class, 1848–1914* (Cambridge, 1991).

Joyce, P., *Democratic Subjects: the self and the social in nineteenth-century England* (Cambridge, 1994).

Kinzer, B. (ed.), *The Gladstonian Turn of Mind: Essays presented to J.B. Conacher* (London, 1985).

Kirk, N., *The Growth of Working Class Reformism in Mid-Victorian Britain* (London, 1985).

Lawrence, J., *Speaking for the People; party, language and popular politics in England, 1867–1914* (Cambridge, 1998).

Lubenow, W.C., *Parliamentary Politics and the Home Rule Crisis* (Oxford, 1988).

Lyons, F.S.L., *Ireland Since the Famine* (London 1973).

MacBriar, A.M., *Fabian Socialism and English Politics, 1884–1918* (Cambridge 1962).

MacDougall, I. (ed.), *Essays in Scottish Labour History* (Edinburgh, 1978).

Marsh, P., *Joseph Chamberlain, Entrepeneur in Politics* (London, 1994).

Masterman, L., *C.F.G. Masterman*, second edition (London, 1968).

Matthew, H.C.G., *Gladstone 1809–1974*, paperback edition (Oxford, 1986).

Magnus, P., *Gladstone*, (London, 1954).

McKibbin, R., *The Ideologies of Class: social relations in Britain 1880–1950*, (Oxford, 1990).

Morley, J., *Life of Gladstone* (London, 1901).

Morris, A.J.A. (ed.), *Edwardian Radicalism 1900–1914* (London, 1974).

Morris, J., *Religious and Urban Change: Croydon 1840–1914* (Woodbridge, 1992).

Morris, R. and Rodger, R. (eds), *The Victorian City: A Reader in British Urban History 1820–1914* (Harlow, 1993).

Munson, J., *The Nonconformists* (London, 1991).

Olsen, D., *The Growth of Victorian London* (London, 1976), 210.

Ostrogorski, M., *Democracy and the Organisation of Political Parties*, two volumes (London, 1902).

Parry, J., *Democracy and Religion: Gladstone and the Liberal Party, 1867–1875* (Cambridge, 1986).

Parry, J., *The Rise and Fall of Liberal Government in Victorian Britain* (Yale, 1993).

Pelling, H., *Origins of the Labour Party, 1880–1900*, second edition (Oxford, 1965).

Pelling, H., *The Social Geography of British Elections, 1885–1910* (London, 1967).

Perkin, H., *The Origins of Modern English Society 1780–1880*, reprint (London, 1971).

Pugh, M., *The Tories and the People* (Oxford, 1985).

Saint, A. (ed.), *London Suburbs* (London, 1999).

Savage, M., *The Dynamics of Working Class politics: the labour movement in Preston 1880–1940* (Cambridge, 1987).

Searle, G.R., *The Liberal Party Triumph and Disintegration, 1986–1929* (Basingstoke, 1992).

Shannon, R., *Gladstone and the Bulgarian Agitation 1876* (Brighton, 1975).

Silverstone, R. (ed.), *Visions of Suburbia* (London, 1997),

Skidelsky, R., *Politicians and the Slump* (London, 1967).

Southgate, D., *The Passing of the Whigs 1832–1886* (London, 1962).

Stansky, P., *Ambitions and Strategies: The Struggle for the Leadership of the Liberal Party in the 1890s* (Oxford, 1964).

Stedman-Jones, G., *Languages of Class* (Cambridge, 1983).

Steele, E.D., *Palmerston and Liberalism, 1855–1865* (Cambridge, 1991).

Tanner, D., *Political Change and the Labour Party, 1900–1918* (Cambridge, 1990).

Thompson, E.P., *The Making of the English Working Class*, 1980 edition reprinted (London, 1991).

Thompson, F.M.L. (ed.), The Rise of Suburbia (Leicester, 1982).

Thompson, P., *Socialists, Liberals and Labour – The Struggle for London 1885–1914* (London, 1967).

Thorns, D., *Suburbia* (London, 1972).

Waller, P.J., *Town, City and Nation: England 1850–1914* (Oxford, 1983).

Waters, C., *British Socialists and the Politics of Popular Culture, 1884–1914* (Manchester, 1990).

Williams, W.E., *The Rise of Gladstone to the Leadership of the Liberal Party 1859–1868* (Cambridge, 1934).

Vernon, J., *Politics and the People: a study in English political culture, c.1815–1867* (Cambridge 1993).

Zebel, S.H., *Balfour: A Political Biography* (Cambridge, 1973).

Articles

Manchester

Clarke, P.F., 'The end of Laissez Faire and the Politics of Cotton', *Historical Journal*, 15 (1972), 493–512.

Garrard, J., 'The Salford Gas Scandal of 1887', *Manchester Region History Review*, 2 (1988–89), 12–20.

Greenall, R., 'Popular Conservatism in Salford', 1868–86, *Northern History*, 9 (1974), 123–38.

Hill, J., 'Manchester and Salford Politics and the Early Development of the Independent Labour Party', *International Review of Social History*, 26 (1981), 171–201.

Read, D., 'Truth in News, Reuters and the Manchester Guardian, 1858–1964', *Northern History*, 31 (1995), 281–97.

Reid, N., 'Manchester and Salford ILP', *North West Labour History Society Bulletin*, 5, 25–31.

Shepherd, J., 'James Bryce and the Recruitment of Working Class Magistrates In Lancashire', *Bulletin of the Institute of Historical Research*, 51 (1979), 155–69.

Leicester

Cox, D. 'The Labour Party in Leicester: A Study in Branch Development', *International Review of Social History*, 6 (1966), 197–211.

Evans, R.H., 'The Biggs Family of Leicester', *Transactions of the Leicester Archaeological and Historical Society*, XLVIII (1972–73).

General/Other

Bailey, V., 'In Darkest England and the Way Out: the Salvation Army, social reform and the Labour Movement, 1885–1910', *International Review of Social History*, 29 (1984), 133–71.

Bebbington, D.W., 'Nonconformity and Electoral Sociology 1867–1918', *Historical Journal*, 27 (1984), 633–56.

Berger, S., 'The decline of Liberalism and the rise of Labour: the regional approach', *Parliamentary History*, 12 (1993), 84–92.

Bernstein, G., 'Liberalism and the Progressive Alliance in the Constituencies 1900–1914: Three Case studies', *Historical Journal*, 26 (1983), 617–40.

Bevir, M., 'Fabianism, Permeation and Independent Labour', *Historical Journal*, 39 (1996), 179–96.

Blewett, N., 'The franchise in the United Kingdom', 1885–1918, *Past and Present*, 32 (1965), 27–56.

Brown, C., 'Did urbanisation secularise Britain?', *Urban History Yearbook* (1988).

Cannadine, D., 'Residential differentiation in nineteenth century towns: from shapes in the ground to shapes in society', in J. Johnson and C. Pooley, (eds), *The Structure of Nineteenth Century Cities* (London, 1982), 235–51.

Cannandine, D., 'Victorian cities: how different?', *Social History,* 2 (1977), 457–87.

Davis, J. and Tanner, D., 'The Borough Franchise after 1867', *Historical Research,* 69 (1996), 306–27.

Dawson, M., 'Liberalism in Devon and Cornwall, 1910–31: "The Old-Time Religion"', *Historical Journal*, 38 (1995), 425–37.

Doyle, B., 'Urban Liberalism and the "Lost Generation": Politics and Middle Class Culture in Norwich 1900–1935', *Historical Journal*, 38 (1995), 617–34.

Dunbabin, J., 'Some Implications of the 1885 British shift towards Single-Member Constituencies: A Note', *English Historical Review*, 89–100.

Durbach, N., 'Class, Gender and the Conscientious Objector to Vaccination 1898–1907', *Journal of British Studies*, 42 (2002), 58–83.

Glaser, J.F., 'English Nonconformity and the Decline of Liberalism', *American Historical Review*, 63 (1957–8), 352–63.

Hennock, E.P., 'Finance and Politics in Urban Local Government in England, 1835–1900', *Historical Journal*, 4 (1963), 212–25.

Hennock, E.P., 'The Measurement of Urban Poverty: From the Metropolis to the Nation, 1880–1920', *Economic History Review*, 40 (1987), 208–27.

Howard, C., 'Joseph Chamberlain and the "Unauthorized Programme"', *English Historical Review*, 65 (1950), 477–91.

Howarth, J., 'The Liberal Revival in Northamptonshire, 1880–1895: A Case study in Late Nineteenth Century Election', *Historical Journal*, 11 (1969), 78–118.

Howe, J., 'Liberals, Lib–Labs and Independent Labour in North Gloucestershire, 1890–1914', *Midland History*, 11 (1986), 117–37.

Howkins, A., 'Edwardian Liberalism and industrial unrest: a class view of the decline of Liberalism', *History Workshop Journal*, 4 (1977), 143–61.

Jeffrey, T., 'The suburban nation: politics and class in Lewisham', ,in D. Felman. and G. Stedman Jones, (eds), *Metropolis London* (London, 1989), 189–216.

Joyce, P., 'The Factory Politics of Lancashire in the Later Nineteenth Century', *Historical Journal*, 18 (1975), 525–53.

Joyce, P., 'The Return of History: Postmodernism and the Politics of Academic History in Britain', *Past and Present*, 158 (1998), 207–35.

Kirk, N., 'In Defence of Class: A critique of recent revisionist writings upon the nineteenth-century English working class', *International Review of Social History*, 32 (1987), 2–47.

Lambert, R., 'A Victorian National Health Service: State Vaccination 1855–71', *Historical Journal* 5 (1962), 1–18.

Lawrence, J., 'Popular Radicalism and the Socialist Revival in Britain', *Journal of British Studies*, 31 (1992), 163–86.

Lawrence, J., 'Class and gender in the making of urban Toryism, 1880–1914', *English Historical Review*, 108 (1993), 629–52.

Laybourn, K. and Reynolds, J., 'The Emergence of the Independent Labour Party in Bradford', *International Review of Social History*, 20 (1975), 313–46.

Lloyd, T., 'Libs–Labs and "unforgivable electoral generosity"', *Bulletin of the Institute of Historical Research*, 48 (1975) 255–9.

Mayfield, D. and Thorne, S., 'Social History and its Discontents: Gareth Stedman Jones and the Politics of Language', *Social History*, 17 (1992), 165–88.

Matthew, H., McKibbin, R. and Kay, J.A., 'The Franchise Factor and the Rise of the Labour Party', *English Historical Review*, 91 (1976) 723–52.

McKibbin, R., 'Why was there no Marxism in Great Britain?', *English Historical Review*, 99 (1984), 297–331.

Miele, C., 'From aristocratic idea to middle-class idyll: 1690–1840', in A. Saint, (ed.), *London Suburbs* (London, 1999), 31–60.

Millward, R. and Sheard, S., 'The Urban Fiscal Problem, 1870–1914: government expenditure and finance in England and Wales', *Economic History Review*, 48 (1995), 501–35.

Pennybacker, S., '"The millennium by return of post": reconsidering London Progressivism 1889–1907',; in D. Felman and G. Stedman Jones (eds), *Metropolis London* (London, 1989), 129–62.

Powell, D., 'The Liberal Ministries and Labour, 1892–1895', *History*, 68 (1983), 408–26.

Powell, D., 'The New Liberalism and the Rise of Labour, 1886–1906', *Historical Journal*, 29 (1986), 369–93.

Quinault, R.E., 'Lord Randolph Churchill and Tory Democracy, 1880–1885', *Historical Journal*, 22 (1979), 141–65.

Readman, P., 'The 1895 General Election and Political Change in Late Victorian Britain', *Historical Journal*, 42, (1999) 467–93.

Roberts, A.W., 'Leeds Liberalism and Late Victorian Politics,' *Northern History*, 5 (1970), 131–56.

Savage, M., 'The Rise of the Labour Party in local perspective', *Journal of Regional and Local Studies*, 10 (1990), 1–16.

Steinburg, M., '"A Way of Struggle": Reformations and affirmations of E.P. Thompson's class analysis in the light of postmodern theories of language', *British Journal of Sociology*, 48 (1997), 471–92.

Tanner, D., 'Elections, Statistics and the Rise of the Labour Party, 1906–1931', *Historical Journal*, 34 (1991), 893–908.

Thompson, J., 'After the Fall: Class and Political Language in Britain, 1780–1900', *Historical Journal*, 39 (1996), 785–806.

Thompson, T., 'Liberals, Radical and Labour in London 1880–1900', *Past and Present*, 27 (1964), 73–101.

Vernon, J., 'Who's afraid of the linguistic turn? The politics of social history and its discontents', *Social History*, 19 (1994), 81–97.

Winstanley, M., 'Oldham Radicalism and the Origins of Popular Liberalism, 1830–1852', *Historical Journal*, 36 (1993), 619–43.

Weiler, P., 'The New Liberalism of L.T. Hobhouse', *Victorian Studies*, 16 (1972), 135–61.

Index

agriculture 18, 60-66, 73, 99, 197, 200, 251
All Saints (Leicester) 147
All Saints (Manchester) 101, 171, 174-6, 178
allotments 205, 209
Amalgamated Society of Engineers 31
Amalgamated Society of Joiners 31
Amalgamation (of outdistricts) 140, 179-83, 196-9, 273
anarchism 222, 239
Ancoats 87, 127, 139, 214, 221
Anglican *see* Church of England
Anti-Compulsory Vaccination League 55-6, 72, 100-104, 119 *see also* vaccination
Ardwick 19, 42, 46, 141, 143, 224, 267
aristocracy 3, 6-7, 15, 270
Armitage, Benjamin 94-5
Ashby 61-3, 67
Ashton, Thomas 50
Asquith, Herbert 12, 124, 276
Axon, William 137, 183-6
Aylestone 60, 62, 100, 195, 198-200, 203-7, 242

Balfour, Arthur 19, 46, 95, 126, 141, 265
Banton, George 240, 242, 244, 248
Baptist churches 173, 182, 192, 272 *see also* Nonconformity
Barfoot, William 109, 149, 157
Bazley, Thomas 37, 90, 128, 137
Belgrave 60-64, 70, 191-2, 195-6, 198-200, 203-5, 207, 241-2
Birdsall, George 177, 180, 182, 186
Birmingham 12, 16, 18, 26, 32, 36, 54, 57, 82, 97-8, 99, 120, 151, 264, 266
'Birmingham Model' 36, 54, 57, 108, 120, 147
Bishop of Salford 81
Blatchford, Robert 218-220, 223, 229
Blennerhasset, R. P. 44-6, 52
'Boot and shoe' 18, 54, 105, 148, 203, 237, 239, 240, 243, 251, 253, 256, 258, 267, 274
Bosworth (constituency) 60, 62-9, 71
Bradford Conference 1888, 88
brewing interest 18, 95, 126, 138, 141, 267
Bright, Jacob 26, 28. 30, 32, 37, 39-41, 44, 46, 52, 93, 94, 179, 222, 232
Bright, John 16, 26, 35, 77, 83, 89, 94, 263
Bright, Ursula 222
Broadhurst, Henry 237, 243-8, 252, 257-8, 274
Brocklehurst, Frederick 219-20, 246
Burgess, Thomas 245-8, 251-3, 257-8
Burnley 46-7, 52, 87
Butterworth, Walter 143
by-elections, municipal
- Abbey, 1895, 254
- All Saints 1895, 176
- and inter-party relations 114-5.
- Castle 1893, 251
- Knighton, 118
- New Cross 1894, 22
- party involvement, significance of 278
- Salford, 216
- Westcotes 1892, 155
- Wyggeston 1894, 250

by-elections, parliamentary
- Burnley 1887, 46, 87
- Gorton 1889, 81
- Harborough 1891, 111
- influence of success in 140
- Leicester 1856, 53
- Leicester 1894, 164-5, 244-9, 252, 258
- Manchester 1876, 26
- Manchester 1883, 19, 26-34, 36, 46, 51, 77, 128
- North East Manchester 1891, 81, 94, 216, 221, 223

Canner, Thomas 58, 113, 117
Carlton Club 59
caucus 31, 33-4, 41, 43, 48, 51, 59, 84, 96,

119, 177, 217, 243, 275
Chamberlain, Joseph 10, 12, 16, 20 35, 52, 57-8, 86-8, 99, 108, 118, 120, 263-5, 275
Chamberlain, Richard 56-8, 99, 107, 243
Chamberlainite 49, 106-7, 109
charities 68, 127, 162 *see also* philanthropy
Chartist legacy 15-7, 26, 42, 53-4, 88, 147-8, 238
Chesters Thompson, Stephen 18-9, 95, 126, 128, 130-1, 134-41, 149, 214, 267
Church of England / Established church 6, 46, 49, 54, 60, 66, 68-9, 89, 105-6, 182, 184, 186, 193, 272, 281
citizens' auditor 126-30, 134, 233
citizenship 6, 8
City Ledger 135
Clarion 218, 220, 229
Clepham, E. 55, 57, 63, 109
Cobden, Richard 31,
collectivism 12-3, 124-5, 209, 225, 252-3, 255, 258, 263-4, 269, 271-2, 275, *see also* local government
Congregational churches 172-3, 192, 257 *see also* Nonconformity
Cope, Thomas 60
corruption 12, 61, 90, 126-35, 179, 184
Cort, Richard 241, 243, 251-2
cotton 15-6, 18, 170, 213, 267, 269
cotton famine 267
Crosfield, John 37, 47-52, 134, 140, 144, 268

Dangerfield, George 5
Davitt, Michael 31, 244
demonstrations 14, 17, 65, 103-5, 108, 127, 222, 226-7,
Disestablishment 46, 49, 68-9, 90, 105-7, 116, 176-7, 186, 258

education 14, 60, 79, 81, 148, 154-5, 171, 174, 179, 181-2, 184, 186, 192-3, 205, 217, 224, 247-8, 256, 278
eight hour day 144, 176, 225
election expenses 30
electricity 132
Ellis, James 66, 68, 71, 197, 203, 205-6, 249
employers 66-7, 108, 124, 164-5, 203, 221, 228, 240, 246, 251-3, 258, 266, 275
ethnic 8, 14, 18, 214, 220, 271
Evington 60, 191, 193, 195, 197-8, 200, 202, 207,

Fabian Society 216, 230, 238, 276
Faire, Samuel 109, 117, 119, 148, 192
Fallowfield 171, 173
Fielding Johnson, Thomas 105, 107-8, 148, 193
franchise 3, 4, 7, 11, 15, 25, 28, 35, 47-8, 53, 59, 61-2, 66-7, 110, 112, 125, 183, 193, 256, 267
free trade 3-4, 15-6, 73, 148, 269
Free Trade Hall 83, 86, 89, 177, 276
Free Speech Hall 68

gas 13, 90, 132-3, 144, 153, 155, 165, 179, 181, 201, 208-9, 215, 226, 264
'gas and water socialism' 264
Gladstone, William Ewart 3, 4, 7-12, 16, 20-1, 25, 28, 29 , 31, 34, 48, 54, 70, 77, 83, 86, 90, 97, 99, 102, 105-6, 113-4, 120, 169, 175, 264, 266,
  attitude to Newcastle programme 276
  attitude to trade unions 258
  home rule 263
  political legacy 276-8
  resignation 177, 225, 234, 242, 276
Gladstone Club and Institute (Leicester) 110
Gladstone Club (Rochdale Road, Manchester) 221
Gladstone Working-Men's Liberal Club (Charles Street, Leicester) 242
Gladstone-MacDonald pact 259
Glass, Percy 29, 31, 37-8, 83
Gorton 47-52, 81, 140, 144, 214, 226-7, 231-4, 266, 268
Goschenite 49
guardians of the poor 100-101, 123, 250, 254-6
Guthrie, Edwin 16, 43, 172, 179, 182, 185-6, 224-5, 234,

Hall, Leonard 215, 218-20, 222-3, 226, 228-232, 235
Hardie, Keir 228-232, 242, 246-7, 258
Harborough (constituency) 62, 65, 66-9, 71, 103, 110-1, 196
Harpurhey 125, 143, 220, 224

Hartington, Lord 7, 10, 35, 86, 94, 120, 263, 265
'Hartingtonian' / Hartingtonite 49, 77, 84, 114
Hazell, Walter 164, 245-6, 252, 258
Hinckley 60, 62-3, 65, 67
Holyoake, George 56, 61, 69
home rule
  Chamberlain 20
  class politics 7-8, 169, 175-6, 214, 269
  Gladstone 4-5, 10, 25, 83, 86, 169
  'Hawarden Kite' 83
  Independent Labour Party, 223, 226, 274
  Leicester 99-120, 148, 246, 252, 278
  Manchester 44-6, 51-2, 77-98, 126, 131, 235
  municipal politics 126, 131, 148
  Nonconformists 6, 14
  provinces 16, 263-6
Hopkinson, Alfred 45-7, 52, 86, 89, 93-4, 175
Horsfall, T.C. 129, 137
hosiery, 18, 60, 62, 237, 240, 252, 254-5, 267
Houldsworth, William 44, 46
House of Commons 10, 29, 35, 64, 115, 160, 277-8
House of Lords 35-6, 38, 42, 45, 49, 51, 59, 61, 106-7, 176-7, 264-6, 276-7
housing 12, 16-7, 123-4, 137-40, 172-3, 176, 191-2, 202, 205, 208, 225, 256 *see also* Royal Commission on the Housing of the Working Classes 1885
hustings 149

Independent Labour Party 13, 19-21, 52, 54, 124, 143, 144-6, 150, 166, 176, 185, 213-4, 219-259, 265, 268, 274-5.
imperialism 50, 70, 169
Irish Catholic 18, 71, 80
Irish community
  electorate 18, 31, 41, 77, 80-6, 99, 140, 173-4, 214, 221-6, 268-9, 276
  relations with labour bodies 226, 242, 244, 268, 274
Irish Nationalism 10, 14, 18, 31, 44-5, 77, 80-6, 102, 104, 117, 175, 221-6, *see also* home rule

Jewish community 18, 214,
John Shaw's Club 15
Johnson Ferguson, J.E. 68, 72, 103-4

Kelley, George 98,144, 185, 217, 227
Knighton 105-6, 110-1, 117-119, 190-2, 195-200, 203-7

Labour Church 173, 213, 218-220, 224, 257
Labour Electoral Association 216-7, 219, 224
Labour Leader 228-9, 242
Labour Party 5, 7, 9, 13, 143, 237-8, 258 *see also* Independent Labour Party
Landlords 137-8, 180, 181
land speculation 194, 197
land values 208, 252
Lee, Joseph
Leicester Conservative Club 54, 58-9, 60, 102, 108-9, 112-3
Leicester Conservative Registration Association 113
Leicester Constitutional Club 112, 119
Leicester Daily Mercury 55, 101, 155, 244, 247, 278
Leicester Liberal Association 59, 62, 63, 70, 73, 109, 114, 116, 149, 153-4, 165, 204, 239, 268, 274, 278
Leicester Liberal Club 54, 69-70, 117, 149
Leicester School Board 68, 154-5, 196-7, 239, 250
Leicester Working-Men's Conservative Club 61
Leigh 68, 223
Lever, Ellis 133
Liberal Party
  Leicester *see* Leicester Liberal Club
  Manchester *see* Manchester Liberal Association, Manchester Liberal Club, Manchester Liberal Union
  national party 3-21
  provincial party *see* entry for town or locality
  ward associations *see* entry for district
Liberal Unionists
  defections to 47, 52, 72, 77-80, 82, 89-91, 103, 105-7, 110, 118-9, 171

local government 130-2, 136, 139, 141-2, 145, 152, 158-9, 163, 192, 205, 214
Manchester Reform Club 85, 94-6
organisation 82-9, 97, 105, 112, 116-9, 266 *see also* Manchester Liberal Unionist Associaton
relations with the Conservatives 86-7, 90-4, 97, 107-8, 112-4, 116-9, 175-7
support in urban Britain 266, 269
Liberal Reunion 10, 84, 87, 89, 95, 109, 113, 120
Liverpool 18, 80, 139, 174, 269, 272
Lloyd George, David 9
local government 123-166
aldermanic authority 128-146, 150, 158-9
collectivism 15, 123-4, 128-166
committee system 132-3
mayoralty 17, 53, 64, 70, 90, 115, 116, 118, 129, 134, 137, 159, 161-2, 240, 244
partisanship 12, 123-166, 273
redistribution 62, 139-40
reform 101, 179-187, 263, 265
scrutiny 19, 126-135, 151-8
town clerk 139, 197, 200
Local Government Board 12, 100, 129, 179-80, 194, 255
local option 59
local boards of health 49, 60, 62-4, 176, 178-186, 193-5, 198-200, 241, 272
Logan, John W 68, 111
London 11-13, 15, 34, 38, 58-9, 71, 106-7, 116, 124, 128, 162-3, 170, 190, 203-4, 214, 219, 229, 238, 264, 269-70, 273, 276
London and Southern Counties Labour League, 238
Longsight, 140-2, 174-6, 178, 185, 231
Loughborough (constituency) 60-1, 65, 68, 72, 103
Lorne, Marquis of 176-7

magistrates 67, 71, 100, 141, 239
Manchester and Salford Sanitary Association 137-40
Manchester City News 135, 144, 230
Manchester Domestic Mission 137
Manchester Examiner 29, 32, 89
Manchester Guardian 32, 80, 93-4, 172, 181, 223,
Manchester Junior Reform Club 27
Manchester Liberal Association 25-7, 32, 34, 38-40, 42, 77, 79, 144
Manchester Liberal Club 80
Manchester Liberal Union 79, 82-4, 140, 142, 145, 172, 175-6, 226, 231, 234-5, 268, 273
Manchester Liberal Unionist Association 86-9,
Manchester Palace of Varieties 14, 141
Manchester Radical Association 26, 34-8, 275
Manchester Ratepayers' Association 125, 128, 134
Manchester Reform Club 27-8, 77-9, 85, 93-6, 228
'Manchester School' 15, 16, 77, 94
Manchester School Board 152, 179, 217-8, 223
Manchester Ship Canal 13, 213
Manchester Statistical Society 123, 129, 138
Manchester Weekly Post 84
market 18, 127
Market Bosworth 60, 63
Market Harborough 62
Marris, S.A. 196, 199
Marxism 5-8, 265
Mather, William, 89, 215-6, 232
May Day 227
Mawdsley, James 18, 213
McArthur, Alexander 55, 64, 102-5, 109, 115, 119
McCabe, Daniel 81, 226
McLaren, Charles 56
Melton (constituency) 60, 63-4, 66, 68-9, 71-2, 119
Merchant Shipping Bill 35
Methodist churches 173, 182, 192 *see also* Nonconformity
meritocracy 3, 174, 185-6, 206
Midland Free Press 17, 55, 70, 155, 239
military 14, 67
Millican, William 71, 194
mining 47, 61-2, 227
minority clause 29
Moss Side 79, 171, 173-4, 177-85, 272

Moss Side Liberal Club 177, 179-80, 183-5

National Liberal Federation 4, 10, 20, 66, 116, 225, 264, 277
National Reform Union 79, 87, 223
National Union of Boot and Shoe Operatives 54, 148, 239, 239, 242-3, 246, 251, 254, 258
National Union of Gas Workers and General Labourers 215
National Union of Shop Assistants 216, 221
New Cross 28, 42-3, 78-9, 81, 90-1, 128, 220, 224, 226
'new Radicalism' 25
newspapers 17, 65, 70, 85, 112, 135, 155, 172, 218, 229, 234, 253, 256
Nonconformity 6, 8-9, 14-8, 45,47-8, 53-4, 60, 68, 70,-71, 73, 100, 103, 155, 162, 169-170, 173, 176-7, 179, 182-4, 186-7, 189, 192, 193, 201, 205, 217, 224, 237, 244, 257-8, 269-72, *see also* Baptists churches, Congregational churches, Methodist churches, Unitarian churches
Norbury Williams, Stephen 37, 43, 128

Openshaw 47, 50, 140, 226, 231
Openshaw Reform Club 47
Owen's College 45, 174 *see also* Victoria University

Packe, Hussey 72, 148
Paget, Thomas T. 53, 71, 103, 110-1
Pankhurst, Richard 26-34, 38, 41, 43, 50-2, 128, 174, 216, 223, 226, 230-233, 275
Parnell, Charles S. 31, 81
patron 36, 38, 39, 43, 48, 110, 151, 162, 171, 179, 186, 221
Payne, George 34, 38, 51, 128
Peacock, Richard 47-51, 266
pensions 138, 222
Peterloo 15, 87-8,
philanthropy 31, 48, 105, 137, 148, 189, 218 *see also* charities
Picton, J. Allanson 55-59, 64, 69-71, 73, 103-5, 108-9, 189, 242, 248, 278
Police 90, 102, 108-9, 141
Pomona Gardens 35, 45, 77
Progressive 11-13, 126, 134, 137, 142-4, 213-235, 272, 274, 279
  Alliance 11, 234-5
  London, 12, 265, 269-70, 276
  Municipal Programme 98, 124, 144-5, 150-51, 165-6, 172, 176, 205, 209, 213-235, 253-5, 255, 265, 272, 274
  origins 124, 144, 146, 169-170
  'slates' 178-186
Primrose League 18, 85, 103, 112
Prince, L.D. 40-41, 43-4, 52, 223, 233-4
property 17, 102, 104-5, 137-9, 144, 156, 165, 169, 172-86, 193, 197, 199-200, 202-3, 225
public health 13, 16, 123, 170, 205, 208
public libraries 17, 123, 125, 155, 170, 179-181, 184, 186, 190, 192, 198, 200, 205, 207, 209, 272, 275, 279

quarrying 62

railways 47-8, 105, 178, 185, 191-2, 213-4, 226-7, 266
rates 13, 19, 126, 132, 153-5, 165-6, 178, 180, 184-5, 194-201, 207, 250, 256
redistribution 25, 30, 37, 39, 53, 59-63, 70, 79, 204, 268, 274
Reform Act 1832, 7
Reform Bill 1866, 4
Reform (Franchise) Bill 1884, 28, 35, 47, 268
religious equality 3
religion 4, 8, 14, 17, 54, 87, 162, 169, 173, 181-4, 186, 192, 217-8, 224 257, 267, 269, 271-2, 278 *see also* Church of England, Baptists churches, Congregational churches, Irish Catholic, Methodist churches, Nonconformity, Unitarian churches
retrenchment 31, 205, 208, 279
Roby, H.J. 34, 37-8, 83, 95, 216
Rochdale 83, 89
Rolleston, John F. L. 112, 117, 149, 202, 204
Roscoe, Sir Henry 39, 45-6, 52, 97, 171, 173, 174-8, 182, 186, 278
Rosebery, Lord 12, 20, 264, 276-7
Rowley, Charles 31, 44, 127, 140, 221
Royal Commission on the Housing of the

Working Classes 1885, 137 *see also* housing
Royal Commission on the Aged Poor 1895, 123
Royal Statistical Society 124
Rusholme 79, 91, 142-3, 171, 173-6
Rylands, Peter 46, 87

Salford 18, 80, 81, 90, 91, 94, 98, 132-3, 137, 143, 145, 170, 173, 185, 214, 216, 220, 224, 227-9
Salisbury, Lord 118
sanitation 123, 124, 136-140, 172, 176, 193-5, 196, 199-205, 208, 209, 225
sanitary reform 42, 124, 136-140, 144, 195, 198, 199-205, 225
Schnadhorst, Francis 56, 222, 225, 246, 277
Schwann, Charles 39, 45-6, 52, 83, 179
Scott, C.P. 12, 16, 21, 27, 32, 42, 81, 89, 94-5, 145, 171, 177, 185, 214, 216-8, 221-6, 226, 230-4, 274
Scott, George 141
Scott, Joseph 127-8, 134
secular movement 53, 56, 69, 238, 271
'shopocracy' 21, 185
Simpson Gee, Harry 68, 105-6, 109, 197, 244
Slagg, John 26, 28-30, 37, 39, 44, 46, 50, 52, 171
slum 124, 136, 138, 144, 170, 172, 178, 184, 225
Smith, Walton 42, 124, 134, 136-9
Smith, Thomas 54, 157, 203-4, 239
Social Democratic Federation 13, 216, 219, 224, 240, 242
Socialism 9, 13, 19, 49, 144, 164, 213. 215-220, 224, 226-7, 231-3, 237-42, 244-7, 253-4, 257, 259, 265, 274, 276
Socialist League 13, 215, 238
Southern, James 124, 128, 132, 143, 224
Stoneygate 57, 106, 156, 189-93, 271
strikes 116, 215, 240, 252,
suburbs, 43, 60, 63-4, 79, 91-2, 125, 147, 156, 168-209, 242, 263, 269-7
  electoral over-representation 202-3
  heterogeneity 7, 173-4, 263
  London 13-4, 170, 190, 270
middle class 116, 119, 143, 169-70, 172, 189-90, 196, 201
  industrial 47, 69, 140, 143-4, 146, 191, 203, 266
  'mixed' 37, 173-4, 187, 191, 202
  villages 62, 198

Tapling, T. K 111
Taylor, J.E. 81
Taylor, Peter 53-5, 58-9, 107
temperance 17, 88, 141-2, 176, 193, 246, 248
tenant 127, 129, 137, 180-1, 197
Thirlmere 123, 125-6
Titley, Richard 60
town clerk 139, 197, 200
town hall 64, 81, 135, 147, 218, 274
town's meeting 125
trade union 14, 16, 25, 56, 59, 148, 161-5, 172, 213-8, 226-8, 237-252, 255-6, 258, 274-5 *see also* Amalgamated Society of Engineers, Amalgamated Society of Joiners, National Union of Boot and Shoe Operatives, National Union of Gas Workers and General Labourers, National Union of Shop Assistants
trades council 56-8, 77, 98, 144, 156, 164, 176, 206, 216-9, 227, 237-50, 254-6, 257 tramways 144, 162, 170, 172, 215, 225
Trevor, John 173, 218-9, 256

'Unauthorised Programme' 99, 263-5
unemployment 9, 12, 144, 172, 249, 255-6, 276
Unitarian churches 48, 173, 218, 267 *see also* Nonconformity

vaccination 17, 55-6, 72, 100-104, 119, 196, 266, 278 *see also* Anti-Compulsory Vaccination League
Victoria Hotel 129-30, 132, 134-5, 137
Victoria University 45, 171, 174 *see also* Owen's College
'villa Toryism' 170 *see also* suburbs

wages 144, 162, 164, 166, 185, 215, 252, 255, 274-5, 279
Wakerley, Arthur, 17, 111, 156, 162-3, 191,

197, 199, 206
ward boundaries 118, 147, 149, 202, 204
Whitehead, James 116-7, 244
Women's Suffrage Society 28
women 28, 216
Woolley, Harry 164, 242
Workman's Times 245
working men's clubs 58, 61, 65, 110-111, 242
Wright, Thomas (of Leicester) 107, 115, 118-9, 152, 156, 158-9, 163, 194, 196, 199-200, 244

For Product Safety Concerns and Information please contact our EU representative GPSR@taylorandfrancis.com
Taylor & Francis Verlag GmbH, Kaufingerstraße 24, 80331 München, Germany

www.ingramcontent.com/pod-product-compliance
Lightning Source LLC
Chambersburg PA
CBHW070554270326
41926CB00013B/2306